1 AND 2 THESSALONIANS

1 and 2 Thessalonians

A Socio-Rhetorical Commentary

Ben Witherington III

WILLIAM B. EERDMANS PUBLISHING COMPANY
GRAND RAPIDS, MICHIGAN / CAMBRIDGE, U.K.

Wm. B. Eerdmans Publishing Co.
2140 Oak Industrial Drive N.E., Grand Rapids, Michigan 49505 /
P.O. Box 163, Cambridge CB3 9PU U.K.

Printed in the United States of America

11 10 09 08 07 06   7 6 5 4 3 2 1

Library of Congress Cataloging-in-Publication Data

Witherington, Ben, 1951-
    1 and 2 Thessalonians: a socio-rhetorical commentary / Ben Witherington III.
        p.   cm.
    Includes bibliographical references and indexes.
    ISBN-10: 0-8028-2836-1 / ISBN-13: 978-0-8028-2836-1 (pbk.: alk. paper)
    1. Bible. N.T. Thessalonians — Socio-rhetorical criticism.   I. Title.

    BS2725.52.W58 2006
    227′.8107 — dc22
                                                                2006028680

www.eerdmans.com

I would like to give a special thanks to Sam Eerdmans and indeed the whole Eerdmans family and all those who work at Eerdmans, especially John Simpson, who have been my editors and friends over many years now. It is refreshing to work with publishers who have a vision and sense of mission to try new things, publish innovative material, and help move the scholarly and indeed the pastoral discourse along to new insights and levels. To all of you I say "well done, good and faithful servants." It is an honor to work with you. Thank you for believing in me, and in this series of socio-rhetorical commentaries. It is turning out well.

Pentecost 2006

Contents

Preface

Since I first began down the road of writing socio-rhetorical commentaries on the New Testament in the early 1990s a great deal of water has gone under the bridge, to say the least, especially in the study of the rhetorical side of the equation. If a measure of the impact of a line of approach is shown both by its growth in practitioners and its growth in detractors, then rhetorical criticism has clearly already left a crater the size of the famous one in Arizona. We now even have handbooks on rhetorical criticism of the New Testament.[1]

Yet lest we think that this is just another fad of New Testament interpretation that will come and go, rhetorical analysis of Paul's letters based on the realization that Paul used Greco-Roman rhetoric has been going on since the Greek Church Fathers began writing commentaries and sermons on Paul's compositions (e.g., John Chrysostom), continued through the Middle Ages, was practiced in the Renaissance and by the Reformers (including Calvin, Luther, and especially Melanchthon), was practiced by the Jesuit order from the rise of the order through to the present, and has been practiced after the rise of modern historical criticism in Europe, North America, South Africa, Australia, and a variety of other places.[2] This then is not a new discipline but rather one of the first forms of analysis of the Greek New Testament of any sort.

Why then did most NT scholars abandon the art of rhetorical criticism about a third of the way into the twentieth century? The problem, at least in Europe and in North America, came when major universities in the early twentieth century stopped *requiring* the study of the Greek and Latin classics, and stopped *requiring* courses in rhetoric. The practice of comparing the insights

---

1. See C. J. Classen, *Rhetorical Criticism of the New Testament* (Leiden: Brill, 2002).
2. See the review of this matter in Classen, pp. 1-28.

from these disciplines to New Testament studies fell largely into disuse because of this change in required curriculum and also because of the rise of modern source, form, and redaction criticism. A few still used rhetorical criticism as a tool for studying the Bible between 1930 and 1970, but it was not until George Kennedy and Hans Dieter Betz and to a lesser degree William Wuellner sparked the revival of rhetorical criticism of the New Testament in the 1970s that we began again to have a good deal of serious scholarly work done in this field. We are now beginning to reap the full benefits of some thirty-plus years of concentrated work in this area.

One of the interesting issues that has arisen in the recent revival of the art is of course what sort of rhetorical approach one should take to something like Paul's letters. Should we follow the guidelines of the new rhetoric or should we stick with classical rhetoric of the Hellenistic and Roman periods?[3] For my part, and despite much interesting work being done using the "new" rhetoric, I see such exercises as largely falling under the heading of hermeneutics (or new uses of the NT text), rather than actual attempts at exegesis, by which I mean attempts to analyze the original form and get at the intended meaning of and in a given ancient text in its original *Sitz im Leben*.

I say this not least because Paul is quite innocent of the new rhetoric that has arisen in the modern era and would without doubt be surprised at the uses his texts have been put to in recent days.[4] It is however a proper historical question to ask if Paul used the Greco-Roman rhetoric of his own day in his letters, and a large number, if not the majority, of scholars now recognize that he certainly did, although predictably they differ as to *how* he used the ancient "art of persuasion."

One of the things that has become increasingly clear to me in the process of doing socio-rhetorical commentaries on the New Testament is that modern form and literary-critical approaches appear less and less satisfactory as tools for making sense of even the structure of texts, never mind the intent, meaning, and strategy of the texts. In a recent essay Charles Wanamaker rightly complains that formal analysis in the past has been overly formalistic and atomistic (dealing with too small amount of material) or has stretched categories past the breaking point in unhelpful ways. To call 1 Thess. 1.2–3.10 a "thanksgiving pe-

---

3. The standard reference work is H. Lausberg's two mammoth volumes originally published in 1960 and now available in English as *Handbook of Literary Rhetoric: A Foundation for Literary Study* (Leiden: Brill, 1998). See also the equally huge volume edited by S. E. Porter, which is rather inaptly titled *Classical Rhetoric in the Hellenistic Period 330 B.C.–A.D. 400* (Leiden: Brill, 1997). The title is inapt since at least half of the period specified is not Hellenistic but rather Roman, or Greco-Roman if one prefers.

4. Consider for example the innovative essay by J. D. Hester, "A Fantasy Theme Analysis of 1 Thessalonians," in S. E. Porter and D. L. Stamps, eds., *Rhetorical Criticism and the Bible* (Sheffield: Sheffield Academic, 2002), pp. 504-25.

riod" is not really to characterize properly either the form or the vast majority of the content of that material. Nor does it help us much to get at the intent or meaning of the text. It is especially notable that form-critical analysis of the letter does not really help us discern what is going on in the central portion of the document, the "body-middle" as it is sometimes called. As Wanamaker concludes, while both epistolary and rhetorical analyses are important for studying Paul's letters, when they are wed "it is a marriage of unequal partners. Rhetorical analysis, both of the ancient and the modern varieties, takes us far closer to the issues that really matter: meaning and significance, intention and strategy."[5] I agree, and I also agree that epistolary analysis for the most part only really helps us with the beginnings and endings of Paul's letters.

Long ago Helmut Koester rightly warned "when 1 Thessalonians was composed, no species or genre of the Christian letter existed, nor was there a pattern for the incorporation of particular sub-genres and forms, nor had the literary vocabulary and terminology for this type of writing been established." He goes on to stress that we do not have extant private letters with substantial thanksgiving sections or moral or eschatological discourses. He explicitly denies what Abraham Malherbe, Stanley Stowers, and others try to suggest, namely that we have extant parenetic letters representing a developed genre before or during Paul's time which share the features of 1 Thessalonians.[6] On the whole, I think his critique is historically correct. Letter writing was just becoming an art in Paul's time, and the problem of anachronism is a real one when it comes to comparing Paul's letters with later Christian and Greco-Roman letters. Parenesis was not, or not yet, a letter genre in its own right in the middle of the first century A.D. What Koester did not realize is that we need to examine 1 Thessalonians primarily as a discourse rather than as a literary artifact. It is certainly not "sui generis" when it comes to rhetorical form.

In turning to 1 and 2 Thessalonians I am turning to some of the earliest, if not the earliest, letters of Paul and indeed some of the earliest documents in the New Testament. Thus, we may hope to learn from these documents whether Paul even from the outset of his letter-writing career chose to structure his letters according to both epistolary and rhetorical conventions or if he only followed the former at this stage of his career. We must bear in mind however in

---

5. C. Wanamaker, "Epistolary Analysis: Is a Synthesis Possible?" in *The Thessalonians Debate: Methodological Discord or Methodological Synthesis?* ed. Karl P. Donfried and Johannes Beutler (Grand Rapids: Eerdmans, 2000), pp. 255-86, here p. 286. One should also compare the careful conclusions of D. F. Watson, "The Integration of Epistolary and Rhetorical Analysis of Philippians," in *The Rhetorical Analysis of Scripture: Essays from the 1995 London Conference,* ed. S. E. Porter and T. H. Olbricht (Sheffield: JSOT, 1997), pp. 398-426.

6. H. Koester, "1 Thessalonians — Experiment in Christian Writing," in F. F. Church and T. George, eds., *Continuity and Discontinuity in Church History: Essays presented to G. H. Williams* (Leiden: Brill, 1979), pp. 33-44.

approaching these two letters that Paul had already been apostle to the Gentiles for a very long time indeed and wrote these letters after or in the middle of his second missionary journey.[7]

These letters do not reflect Paul in the nascent stages of his thinking about a variety of matters, nor in the nascent stages of his ministry. We would do better, then, not to speak of the Paul of these letters as "the early Paul," but we can speak of these as some of the earlier extant Pauline letters.[8] As such they provide us with an important window on the early social formation of the Christian movement in its Pauline form in Greco-Roman settings. Indeed they reveal something to us of the birth of the Christian movement as it began to have an existence apart from early Judaism.[9]

I will say at this juncture that the socio-rhetorical approach to the New Testament has born considerable fruit already, helping us to recover an understanding of many things which we would have otherwise been oblivious to if we had continued to examine the New Testament documents and especially the Pauline documents using just form criticism, epistolary categories, and other forms of literary criticism. I do not see epistolary analysis of Paul's letters as in any way necessarily at odds with rhetorical analysis, indeed I think the two approaches are complementary.

What I would insist on, however, is that Paul's letters are in the main meant to be heard, not read, written as they are in and for oral settings and an environment where perhaps only 10% of the audience could read or write. I would insist that these Pauline documents are indeed surrogates for oral speech, surrogates for what Paul would have said if he were with the recipients. Thus, apart from their epistolary framework, these documents are basically transcripts of speeches. R. F. Collins puts it this way: "His letter was, in the circumstances of his absence from the Thessalonians, the way in which his oral communication was in fact communicated to them. It was 'written' by someone

---

7. On the issue of the evidence of Acts and Pauline chronology see my *The Paul Quest* (Downers Grove: InterVarsity, 1998), pp. 304-31.

8. See A. Malherbe, *The Letters to the Thessalonians* (New York: Doubleday, 2000), p. 13. In my view, the earliest of Paul's extant letters is Galatians. See my *Grace in Galatia*, (Grand Rapids: Eerdmans, 1998).

9. By this I mean that the parting of the ways is already in progress and in evidence as early as the earliest written New Testament documents, which is to say well before the fall of Jerusalem around A.D. 70. Doubtless the separation happened at differing rates and in differing ways in different places and was especially slow to come to completion in the Holy Land itself, where there remained a large concentration of Jewish Christians even well after the fall of Jerusalem (see the Introduction to my *The Gospel of Matthew* [Macon: Smyth and Helwys, 2006]). But in the Diaspora these letters, written in the early 50s, already bear witness to separation from the synagogue, as indeed does Paul's letter to the Galatians written in A.D. 49 or early A.D. 50.

who was speaking. It was read to a gathering of Thessalonians who heard it. It was in fact an oral communication from speaker to hearer. . . . His letter was a means for long distance oral communication." Collins adds: "Paul's letter to the Thessalonians gives ample evidence that the apostle's manner of composing his letter was analogous to the way in which Hellenistic rhetors composed their speeches. The vocabulary, style, and postscript of the letter indicate that Paul 'wrote' it as a speech-act."[10] Failure to attend to the oral and aural dimensions of Paul's letters is a very significant failure indeed, missing much of the nuance in Paul's way of arguing and persuading. Epistolary analysis is not sufficient for these sorts of things.[11]

There are good reasons for insisting on these things. Cicero (106-43 B.C.) was the earliest writer we know of to reflect on the character of letter writing, and he refers to letter writing as a speech act.[12] Demetrius and pseudo-Libanus speak of letter writing as something to be done in the same manner as a dialogue or written conversation "for a letter is like the other half of a dialogue" (Demetrius, *De elocutione* 223). Even after Paul's day when there had been a long history of letter writing in Greek and Latin, Philostratus of Libanius (third century A.D.) stressed that letters should be characterized by the kind of language one would use in a public speech, with attention to eloquence and the oral dimensions of communication *(De epistulis).* As Collins suggests, when one begins to attend to the oral dimensions of Paul's letters it becomes clear that they are meant to be heard.[13]

Even more important, failure to recognize the species of rhetoric Paul is using and such crucial matters as where the thesis statement or final summary of the speech is leads to all sorts of misinterpretations of these documents. In short, rhetorical criticism of Paul's letters is essential, not optional, for understanding them. Furthermore, rhetorical criticism is not just about nor should it be limited to micro-rhetoric (e.g., the use of rhetorical questions). Paul has structured his discourses according to the rhetorical conventions of his day, and

---

10. R. F. Collins, "'I Command That This Letter Be Read': Writing as a Manner of Speaking," in Donfried and Beutler, eds., *The Thessalonians Debate,* pp. 319-39, here pp. 332, 338.

11. This is a point which some seem oblivious to. For example, efforts have been made to characterize the material in 1 Thess. 1.2–3.13 or a large portion of this section as a thanksgiving period. This is simply false. Only 1 Thess. 1.2-3 is actually like an epistolary thanksgiving or health prayer, an element which tended to be brief and formulaic in Greco-Roman letters. The rest of that entire section of 1 Thessalonians reads like a rhetorical *narratio,* a narration of past events relevant to the discourse in this document. This is a case where the rhetorical division of the document makes far better sense than the attempt to impose epistolary categories on it.

12. See the discussion by Collins, "I Command That This Letter Be Read," p. 338.

13. Collins, "I Command That This Letter Be Read," p. 323.

attention to this helps us to understand what to give weight to, what is dramatic hyperbole, what is sarcasm, what is polemic, and so on. It also helps us to analyze the problems or exigencies he may have been addressing, whether he was indirectly dealing with opponents, and how much (or better how little) mirror-reading is permissible when dealing with Paul's acts of persuasion.

The rhetorical situation Paul is dealing with in these Thessalonian letters is both familiar and also, as we shall see, delicate, since the Christians in Thessalonike are under pressure and even apparently enduring some persecution. Paul is taking a pastoral role here in a direct way, because these are his converts, and he has addressed them before. Unlike the rhetorical situation when Paul wrote to a group of Christians in Rome whom by and large he had not converted, and indeed most of whom he had never met and who were living in a place he had yet to visit,[14] here Paul can be more direct, intimate, and personal. I would suggest that we have here the continuation of the conversation Paul has been having with the Thessalonians in person (which is why he is able to say things like "we already instructed you . . ." or "we have no need to write . . ."), and as such it should be seen as either second or third order discourse — discourse with those previously addressed, and perhaps even with intimates and friends.[15] Paul is not pulling his punches or withholding his true thoughts or feelings here. These things need to be borne in mind as we begin to work through these letters.

Finally, it needs to be remembered that Paul is not only dealing with one of his first congregations here. He is dealing with Christians who do not live in a Roman colony city, unlike the social situation in Philippi or in Corinth, places where their leader would or should have more clout and respect than he apparently did in Thessalonike. It will be necessary to consider and explore what the social situation in this city must have been like both during and after Paul's visit there for any Christian when their leader would not necessarily have been seen as having an honorable place in the *cursus honorum* in that city.

One gets the sense that Paul and his converts were swimming upstream in that setting, and in some ways the environment of pressure and persecution seems more like that which John of Patmos addressed in the 90s when he wrote to Christians in seven cities in the province of Asia, than like what we find in Galatia or Rome when Paul wrote to Christians in those places.[16] The problems of marginalization in the larger culture, and the formation of leadership structures for a sect need to be considered. As Abraham Smith has stressed: "Both

---

14. See B. W. Witherington and D. Hyatt, *The Epistle to the Romans* (Grand Rapids: Eerdmans, 2004).

15. On this distinction see B. W. Witherington and D. Hyatt, *The Epistles to Philemon, Colossians, and Ephesians* (Grand Rapids: Eerdmans, forthcoming).

16. See my *Revelation* (Cambridge: Cambridge University Press, 2002).

1 and 2 Thessalonians are powerful witnesses to the early church's struggles with the suffering of its members. The Thessalonian letters make it clear that separation from leaders, alienation from former friends, and perennial threats of persecution and even death were not solely the concerns of the fledgling communities behind the Synoptic Gospels . . . , the virtually introverted Johannine believers, and the persecuted minority group addressed by John's apocalypse."[17] These are just some of the socio-rhetorical issues that need to be borne in mind and sorted out in this commentary.

Malherbe, in a revealing comment in his recent important commentary on 1 and 2 Thessalonians, says: "Paul's two letters to the Thessalonians . . . have fascinated me because they open windows onto newly founded Christian communities as no other documents do. They reveal the challenges recent converts faced and how Paul, aware of their problems, acted pastorally in writing to them. . . . I hope that this commentary will contribute to a greater awareness that Paul was as much concerned with the moral, emotional, and spiritual nurture of his converts as he was with their theological development."[18] I can only say "amen" to these sentiments and likewise hope this socio-rhetorical commentary will contribute to the same sort of enlightenment about Paul the pastor as well.

---

17. A. Smith, "The First Letter to the Thessalonians," in *The New Interpreter's Bible*, vol. XI, ed. L. E. Keck (Nashville: Abingdon, 2000), p. 673.

18. Malherbe, *The Letters*, p. xi.

Abbreviations

AusBR	*Australian Biblical Review*
BAGD	W. Bauer, W. F. Arndt, F. W. Gingrich, and F. W. Danker, *Greek English Lexicon of the New Testament and Other Early Christian Literature,* 2nd ed. (Chicago: University of Chicago Press, 1979)
BEvT	Beiträge zur evangelischen Theologie
Bib	*Biblica*
BZ	*Biblische Zeitschrift*
CBQ	*Catholic Biblical Quarterly*
CIG	*Corpus inscriptionum graecarum*
CIJ	*Corpus inscriptionum judaicarum*
CIL	*Corpus inscriptionum latinarum*
CTM	*Currents in Theology and Mission*
ET	*Expository Times*
ETSMS	Evangelical Theological Society Monograph Series
FS	Festschrift
HTR	*Harvard Theological Review*
ICC	International Critical Commentary
IG	*Inscriptiones graecae*
Inst. Or.	Quintilian, *Institutio Oratio*
Int	*Interpretation*
JBL	*Journal of Biblical Literature*
JSNT	*Journal for the Study of the New Testament*
JSNTS	*Journal for the Study of the New Testament* Supplements
JTSA	*Journal of Theology for Southern Africa*
LW	Luther's Works
MT	Masoretic Text

Neot	*Neotestamentica*
New Docs	*New Documents Illustrating Early Christianity* (North Ryde: Macquarie University/Grand Rapids: Eerdmans, 1976-97)
NICNT	New International Commentary on the New Testament
NovT	*Novum Testamentum*
NTS	*New Testament Studies*
RB	*Revue Biblique*
RelStud	*Religious Studies*
SBL	Society of Biblical Literature
SBLDS	Society of Biblical Literature Dissertation Series
SBLSP	*Society of Biblical Literature Seminar Papers*
ST	*Studia Theologica*
TGl	*Theologie und Glaube*
ThH	Théologie historique
TQ	*Theologische Quartalschrift*
TynBul	*Tyndale Bulletin*
WW	*Word and World*
WUNT	Wissenschaftliche Untersuchungen zum Neuen Testament
ZNW	*Zeitschrift für die Neutestamentliche Wissenschaft*
ZTK	*Zeitschrift für Theologie und Kirche*

Bibliography

Commentaries

We are well blessed with commentaries on 1 and/or 2 Thessalonians, but apart from Wanamaker's very few show even a nodding acquaintance with Greco-Roman rhetoric, though a few more interact with matters of social history and social context. We may look forward to the better integration of the two subjects when K. P. Donfried publishes his commentary in due course. The more helpful commentaries now available include:

Beale, G., *1 and 2 Thessalonians* (Downers Grove: InterVarsity, 2003).

Best, E., *A Commentary on the First and Second Epistles to the Thessalonians* (London: Black, 1972).

Bruce, F. F., *1 and 2 Thessalonians* (Waco: Word, 1982).

Malherbe, A., *The Letters to the Thessalonians* (New York: Doubleday, 2000) is at present the current standard technical commentary. There are now a whole series of helpful critical reviews of this commentary from the fall of 2004 at the SBL website under the RBL Newsletter by M. M. Mitchell, E. Krentz, C. Wanamaker, J. Lambrecht, and others.

Marshall, I. H., *1 and 2 Thessalonians* (Grand Rapids: Eerdmans, 1983).

Morris, L., *The First and Second Epistles to the Thessalonians* (Grand Rapids: Eerdmans, 1991).

Richard, E. J., *First and Second Thessalonians* (Collegeville: Liturgical, 1995).

Rigaux, B., *Les Épitres aux Thessaloniciens* (Paris: Gabalda, 1956) is one of the great classics and one of the most comprehensive studies of these letters in the modern era.

Masson, C., *Les Deux Epitres de Saint Paul aux Thessaloniciens* (Neuchatel: Delachaux et Niestle, 1957) is another helpful French study.

Wanamaker, C., *Commentary on 1 and 2 Thessalonians* (Grand Rapids: Eerdmans, 1990) is one of the first historically oriented socio-rhetorical commentaries on these letters. It remains very helpful.

Williams, D., *1 and 2 Thessalonians* (Peabody: Hendrickson, 1992).

Smith, A., "The First Letter to the Thessalonians," "The Second Letter to the Thessalonians," in *The New Interpreter's Bible,* vol. XI, ed. L. E. Keck (Nashville: Abingdon, 2000), pp. 673-772. Both are all too brief but helpful and cognizant of Greco-Roman rhetoric.

Lightfoot, J. B., *Notes on the Epistles of St. Paul* (Winona Lake: Alpha, reprint). The same comment can be made here.

The study which led scholars to think of 2 Thessalonians as post-Pauline was W. Wrede, *Die Echtheit des zweiten Thessalonicherbriefs* (Leipzig: Hinrichs, 1903), who amazingly dated 2 Thessalonians to the second century despite its citation in early second-century sources such as Polycarp. Commentators who follow Wrede include:

Menken, M. J. J., *2 Thessalonians* (London: Routledge, 1994), along with Smith (listed above) one of the more helpful of this group.

Trilling, W., *Untersuchungen zum zweiten Thessalonicherbrief* (Leipzig: St. Benno, 1972).

———. *Der zweite Brief an die Thessalonicher* (Neukirchen: Neukirchener, 1980).

See also C. H. Giblin, "2 Thessalonians 2 Re-Read as Pseudepigraphal: A Revised Reaffirmation of *The Threat to Faith,*" in R. F. Collins, ed., *The Thessalonian Correspondence* (Leuven: Leuven University Press, 2000), pp. 459-69, and the literature cited there.

B. Witherington, *Grace in Galatia* (Grand Rapids: Eerdmans, 1998) is of relevance for analyzing the early Pauline period, as are Witherington and D. Hyatt, *The Epistle to the Romans* (Grand Rapids: Eerdmans, 2004); Witherington, *The Acts of the Apostles* (Grand Rapids: Eerdmans, 1998); Witherington, *Friendship and Finances in Philippi* (Harrisburg: Trinity, 1994); and Witherington, *Revelation* (Cambridge: Cambridge University Press, 2003).

Gorday, P., *Ancient Christian Commentary in Scripture,* vol. IX (Downers Grove: InterVarsity, 2000) is the relevant volume dealing with the Thessalonian correspondence in this wonderful series that give us a feel for how the Fathers read the various books of the Bible.

Seminal Monographs and Essay Collections

The study of the Thessalonian correspondence has been something of a growth industry in the last several decades, especially as scholars have tried to understand the earliest phase of early Christianity. Some of the more helpful works include the following.

Of those volumes that deal with religion, politics, and social context two of the more helpful are both edited by R. A. Horsley, *Paul and Empire: Religion and Power in Roman Imperial Society* (Harrisburg: Trinity, 1997). See especially in that volume

Donfried, K. P., "The Imperial Cults of Thessalonica and Political Conflict in 1 Thessalonians," pp. 215-23.
Koester, H., "Imperial Ideology and Paul's Eschatology in 1 Thessalonians," pp. 158-66.

From Horsley's second volume *Paul and Politics: Ekklesia, Israel, Imperium, Interpretation* (Harrisburg: Trinity, 2000), see especially

Wright, N. T., "Paul's Gospel and Caesar's Empire," pp. 160-83.
Segal, A., "Some Aspects of Conversion and Identity Formation in the Christian Community of Paul's Time," pp. 184-90, responding to Wright.

The best general introduction for this study is a collection of essays edited by J. P. Sampley, *Paul in the Greco-Roman World* (Harrisburg: Trinity, 2003). There are many excellent essays in this volume but three deserve special mention:

Forbes, C., "Paul and Rhetorical Comparsion," pp. 134-71.
Sampley, J. P., "Paul and Frank Speech," pp. 293-318.
Watson, D. F., "Paul and Boasting," pp. 77-100.

One particular scholar, K. P. Donfried, has spent much of his career dealing with Paul and the Thessalonian correspondence. There is now a very helpful collection of career-spanning essays:

Donfried, K. P., *Paul, Thessalonica, and Early Christianity* (Grand Rapids: Eerdmans, 2002).

The volume edited by R. F. Collins entitled *The Thessalonian Correspondence* (Leuven: Leuven University Press, 2000) includes the following helpful studies:

Broer, I., "'Der Ganze Zorn ist schon uber sie gekommen.' Bermerkungen zur Interpolationshypothese und zur Interpretation von 1 Thess 2.14-16," pp. 137-59.

Carras, G. P., "Jewish Ethics and Gentile Converts: Remarks on 1 Thes 4,3-8," pp. 306-15.

Danker, F., and R. Jewett, "Jesus as the Apocalyptic Benefactor in Second Thessalonians," pp. 486-98.

Delobel, J., "The Fate of the Dead according to 1 Thes 4 and 1 Cor 15," pp. 340-47.

Donfried, K. P., "1 Thessalonians, Acts, and the Early Paul," pp. 3-26.

Getty, M. A., "The Imitation of Paul in the Letters to the Thessalonians," pp. 272-83.

Gillman, F. M., "Jason of Thessalonica (Acts 17,5-9)," pp. 39-49.

Gillman, J., "Paul's *Eisodos*: The Proclaimed and the Proclaimer (1 Thes 2,8)," pp. 62-70.

Hartman, L., "The Eschatology of 2 Thessalonians as Included in a Communication," pp. 470-85.

Holland, G., "'A Letter Supposedly from Us': A Contribution to the Discussion about the Authorship of 2 Thessalonians," pp. 394-402.

Holtz, T., "The Judgment on the Jews and the Salvation of all Israel 1 Thes 2,15-16 and Rom 11,25-26," pp. 284-94.

Koester, H., "From Paul's Eschatology to the Apocalyptic Schemata of 2 Thessalonians," pp. 441-54.

Marshall, I. H., "Election and Calling to Salvation in 1 and 2 Thessalonians," pp. 259-76.

Mencken, M. J. J., "The Structure of 2 Thessalonians," pp. 373-82.

Schmidt, D., "The Syntactical Style of 2 Thessalonians: How Pauline Is It?" pp. 383-93.

Tuckett, C. M., "Synoptic Tradition in 1 Thessalonians?" pp. 160-82.

Vanhoye, A., "La Composition de 1 Thessaloniciens," pp. 73-86.

The collection of essays edited by K. P. Donfried and J. Beutler entitled *The Thessalonians Debate* (Grand Rapids: Eerdmans, 2000) came from SNTS seminars held from 1995 to 1998. This volume, as its title suggests, concentrates more specifically on some of the debatable issues in these letters such as 1 Thess. 2.13-16. All the articles dealing with rhetoric are listed in the section on that topic below. Some of the other helpful articles in this volume are:

Donfried, K. P., "The Scope and Nature of the Debate: An Introduction and Some Questions," pp. 3-27.

Holtz, T., "On the Background of 1 Thessalonians 2.1-12," pp. 69-80, with response by J. S. Vos, pp. 81-88.

Lambrecht, J., "Thanksgivings in 1 Thessalonians 1–3," pp. 135-62.

————, "A Structural Analysis of 1 Thessalonians 4–5," pp. 163-78.

Merk, O., "1 Thessalonians 2.1-12: An Exegetical-Theological Study," pp. 89-113, with response by J. A. D. Weima, pp. 114-31.

Schoon-Janssen, J., "On the Use of Elements of Ancient Epistolography in 1 Thessalonians," pp. 179-93.

Sociological and Social History Studies

Of a general nature but very helpful on the development of early Christianity is E. Schnabel, *Early Christian Mission,* vol. 2: *Paul and the Early Church* (Downers Grove: InterVarsity, 2004), pp. 1160-68 on Thessalonike. Though dated, the essays of J. B. Lightfoot, *Biblical Essays* (reprint, Grand Rapids: Baker, 1979) are still helpful, not least because Lightfoot is attuned to Paul's use of rhetoric.

For a general orientation to the world Paul operated in see M. Goodman, *The Roman World 44 B.C.–A.D. 180* (London: Routledge, 1997). For the study of Macedonia and its history see R. Malcolm Errington, *A History of Macedonia* (Berkeley: University of California Press, 1990). Even more comprehensive is M. B. Sakellariou, *Macedonia: 4000 Years of Greek History and Civilization* (Athens: Ekdotike Athenon S.A, 1983). A brief but helpful study is D. W. J. Gill, "Macedonia," in *Acts in Its First Century Settings,* vol. 2: *Graeco-Roman Setting* (Grand Rapids: Eerdmans, 1994), pp. 402-9. R. Riesner, *Paul's Early Period* (Grand Rapids: Eerdmans, 1998), is helpful for integrating such material into an understanding of Paul's early ministry. Broader still is Witherington, *New Testament History* (Grand Rapids: Baker, 2001). A very influential article which helped set the social history discussion of Thessalonians in motion is E. A. Judge, "The Decrees of Caesar at Thessalonica," *RTR* 30 (1971): 1-7. One should also see Judge's recent article "Latin Names around a Counter-Cultural Paul," in *The Bible and the Business of Life: Essays in Honour of Robert J. Banks's Sixty-Fifth Birthday,* ed. S. C. Holt (Adelaide: ATF, 2004), pp. 68-84.

Several doctoral dissertations and special studies have been turned into monographs of relevance to the study of the Thessalonian correspondence:

Ascough, R. S., *Paul's Macedonian Associations* (Tübingen: Mohr, 2003).

Bauckham, R., *The Fate of the Dead* (Leiden: Brill, 1998).

de Vos, C. S., *Church and Community Conflicts: The Relationships of the Thessalonian, Corinthian, and Philippian Churches with their Wider Civic Communities* (Atlanta: Scholars, 1997).

Garnsey, P., *Famine and Food Supply in the Graeco-Roman World: Responses to Risk and Crisis* (Cambridge: Cambridge University Press, 1988).

Guthrie, W. K. C., *The Greeks and Their Gods* (London: Hodder and Stoughton, 1950).

Hock, R., *The Social Context of Paul's Ministry: Tentmaking and Apostleship* (Philadelphia: Fortress, 1980).

Hopkins, K., *Death and Renewal* (Cambridge: Cambridge University Press, 1983).

Kreitzer, L., *Striking Images* (Sheffield: Sheffield Academic, 1996).

MacMullen, R., *Paganism in the Roman Empire* (New Haven: Yale University Press, 1981).

Malherbe, A., *Paul and the Popular Philosophers* (Minneapolis: Fortress, 1989).

————, *Paul and the Thessalonians* (Philadelphia: Fortress, 1987).

Nicholl, C. R., *From Hope to Despair in Thessalonica: Situating 1 and 2 Thessalonians* (Cambridge: Cambridge University Press, 2004).

Oglivie, R. M., *The Romans and Their Gods in the Age of Augustus* (London: Chatto and Windus, 1969).

Pfitzner, V. C., *Paul and the Agon Motif: Traditional Athletic Imagery in the Pauline Literature* (Leiden: Brill, 1967).

Still, T. D., *Conflict at Thessalonica: A Pauline Church and Its Neighbours* (Sheffield: Sheffield Academic, 1999).

Tachau, P., *"Einst" und "Jetzt" im Neuen Testament* (Göttingen: Vandenhoeck und Ruprecht, 1972).

Wengst, K., *Pax Romana and the Peace of Jesus Christ* (Philadelphia: Fortress, 1987).

Winter, B. W., *Philo and Paul among the Sophists* (2nd ed.; Grand Rapids: Eerdmans, 2002) and especially his *Seek the Welfare of the City: Christians as Benefactors and Citizens* (Grand Rapids: Eerdmans, 1994).

The *New Documents Illustrating Early Christianity* series emanating from MacQuarrie University continues to be enormously helpful in understanding the social milieu of early Christianity, and thankfully Eerdmans has taken up the publication of the series. The editor of the more recent volumes is S. Llewelyn. The editor when the series began in 1981 and through the 1980s was G. H. R. Horseley.

On the process of ancient letter writing see E. R. Richards, *Paul and First Century Letter Writing* (Downers Grove: InterVarsity, 2004), pp. 163-70. One should also compare B. W. Witherington, *The Paul Quest* (Downers Grove: InterVarsity, 1998), pp. 100ff.; H. Gamble, *Books and Readers in the Early Church* (New Haven: Yale University Press, 1995); J. Murphy' O Connor, *Paul the Letter Writer* (Collegeville: Liturgical, 1995); and E. R. Richards's other book, *The Secretary in the Letters of Paul* (Tübingen: Mohr, 1991). There is also a helpful discussion in *New Docs* 7, pp. 48-57.

The important study of T. L. Wilder, *Pseudonymity, the New Testament, and Deception* (Lanham: University Press of America, 2004), exposes the facile

assumptions about pseudonymous epistles and their literary and moral accept-
ability in the first century A.D. See also R. J. Bauckham, "Pseudo-Apostolic Letters," *JBL* 197 (1988): 469-94; and R. F. Collins, *Letters That Paul Did Not Write*
(Wilmington: Glazier, 1988).

Theological Studies

Two recent studies help provide overviews of the theological issues in 1 and
2 Thessalonians. One is the especially helpful study of K. P. Donfried, in
Donfried and I. H. Marshall, *The Theology of the Shorter Paulines* (Cambridge:
Cambridge University Press, 1993), pp. 3-113. We may also note the volume edited by J. M. Bassler, *Pauline Theology*, vol. I: *Thessalonians, Philippians,
Galatians, Philemon* (Minneapolis: Fortress, 1991) which offers essays from the
SBL Pauline Theology Seminar sessions. This seminar sometimes operated
with the flawed assumption that the individual letters have distinctive or discrete theologies, and there was accordingly far too much of an attempt to iso-
late what Paul says in one or another letter from what he says in the rest of his
correspondence. Nonetheless, we may point especially to the following essays:

Bassler, J. M., "Peace in All Ways: Theology in the Thessalonian Letters. A Re-
    sponse to R. Jewett, E. Krentz, and E. Richard," pp. 71-85.
Jewett, R., "A Matrix of Grace: The Theology of 2 Thessalonians," pp. 63-70.
Krentz, E., "'Through a Lens': Theology and Fidelity in 2 Thessalonians," pp. 53-
    62.
Richard, E. J., "Early Pauline Thought: An Analysis of 1 Thessalonians," pp. 39-52.

A helpful older theological monograph of direct relevance to the study of these
letters is that by I. H. Marshall, *Kept by the Power of God: A Study of Perseverance
and Falling Away* (Minneapolis: Bethany Fellowship, 1969), which should be
compared to J. Gundry Volf, *Perseverance and Falling Away in Paul's Thought*
(Tübingen: Mohr, 1990).

On Pauline ethics in general see J. Barclay, *Obeying the Truth* (Edinburgh:
Clark, 1991). On the issue of Pauline sexual ethics see also D. B. Martin, *The Corinthian Body* (New Haven: Yale University Press, 1999).

On the prophetic critique of Jewish leaders see O. H. Steck, *Israel und das
gewaltsame Geschick der Propheten* (Neukirchen: Neukirchener, 1967).

Rhetorical Resources

We now have several introductory guides to rhetoric and the Bible or the NT.
C. J. Classen, *Rhetorical Criticism of the New Testament* (Leiden: Brill, 2002) is
helpful and succinct. The volume edited by S. E. Porter and D. L. Stamps, *Rhetorical Criticism and the Bible* (Sheffield: Sheffield Academic, 2002) has some
interesting essays as well, including K. K. Yeo, "The Rhetoric of Election and
Calling Language in 1 Thessalonians," pp. 526-47. The essay by J. D. Hester, "A
Fantasy Theme Analysis of 1 Thessalonians," pp. 504-5 is interesting, but not an
example of analyzing the NT through Greco-Roman rhetoric. One could also
consult several of the chapters in my *The Paul Quest*, or more briefly one could
read G. A. Kennedy, "The Genres of Rhetoric," in *Handbook of Classical Rhetoric
in the Hellenistic Period 330 B.C.–A.D. 400*, ed. S. E. Porter (Leiden: Brill, 1997),
pp. 43-50. One of the most helpful monographs which shows how rhetorical
analysis of an epideictic sort helps in the analysis of several of Paul's letters is
R. R. Jeal, *Integrating Theology and Ethics in Ephesians* (Lewiston: Mellen,
2000).

Methodological issues are still in a state of flux in rhetorical study of the
NT, as can be discerned when one reads C. Wanamaker, "Epistolary Analysis: Is
a Synthesis Possible?" in *The Thessalonians Debate*, pp. 255-86. One should also
compare the careful conclusions of D. F. Watson, "The Integration of Epistolary
and Rhetorical Analysis of Philippians," in *The Rhetorical Analysis of Scripture:
Essays from the 1995 London Conference*, ed. S. E. Porter and T. H. Olbricht
(Sheffield: JSOT, 1997), pp. 398-426.

On the epistolary side of things H. Koester, "1 Thessalonians — Experiment in Christian Writing," in F. F. Church and T. George, eds., *Continuity and
Discontinuity in Church History: Essays presented to G. H. Williams* (Leiden:
Brill, 1979), pp. 33-44 is helpful. For an epistolary analysis see G. P. Wiles, *Paul's
Intercessory Prayers* (Cambridge: Cambridge University Press, 1974). See also
S. Stowers, *Letter Writing in Greco-Roman Antiquity* (Philadelphia: Westminster, 1986), and C. J. Bjerklund, *Parakalo. Form, Funktion und Sinn der parakalo-
Satze in den paulinischen Briefen* (Oslo: Universitetforlaget, 1967).

We now also have in English some standard resources as well, for example, H. Lausberg, *Handbook of Literary Rhetoric: A Foundation for Literary Study*
(Leiden: Brill, 1998) and the equally huge volume edited by S. E. Porter which is
rather inaptly titled *Classical Rhetoric in the Hellenistic Period 330 B.C.–A.D. 400*
(Leiden: Brill, 1997), since the first four centuries of the Christian era are not
part of the Hellenistic era.

Two monographs have set the tone of the discussion of rhetoric in 1 and
2 Thessalonians, the ground-breaking volume by R. Jewett, *The Thessalonian
Correspondence: Pauline Rhetoric and Millenarian Piety* (Philadelphia: Fortress,
1986), and F. W. Hughes, *Early Christian Rhetoric and 2 Thessalonians* (Shef-

field: Sheffield Academic, 1986). All too brief but helpful is M. M. Mitchell, "1 and 2 Thessalonians," in *The Cambridge Companion to St. Paul* (Cambridge: Cambridge University Press, 2003), pp. 51-63. B. C. Johanson, *To All the Brethren: A Text-Linguistic and Rhetorical Approach to 1 Thessalonians* (Stockholm: Almqvist and Wiksell, 1987) is more a text-linguistic study than a rhetorical study, if one has Greco-Roman rhetoric in view. G. Lyons, *Pauline Autobiography* (Atlanta: Scholars, 1985) is helpful, as he is rhetorically adept and understands how narrative works in a rhetorical piece. See also N. Petersen, *Rediscovering Paul* (Philadelphia: Fortresss, 1985) on narrative. The following articles and monographs dealing with rhetoric are also helpful in the study of 1 and 2 Thessalonians:[1]

1 Thessalonians

Burgess, T. C., *Epideictic Literature* (Chicago: University of Chicago Press, 1902).
Chapa, J., "Consolatory Patterns? 1 Thes 4,13.18. 5,11," in Collins, ed., *The Thessalonian Correspondence,* pp. 220-28.
————, "Is First Thessalonians a Letter of Consolation?" *NTS* 40 (1994): 150-60.
Chase, J. R., "The Classical Conception of Epideictic," *Quarterly Journal of Speech* 47 (1961): 293-300.
Collins, R. F., *The Birth of the New Testament: The Origin and Development of the First Christian Generation* (New York: Crossroad, 1993), especially pp. 132-39.
————, "'I Command That This Letter Be Read': Writing as a Manner of Speaking," in Donfried and Beutler, eds., *The Thessalonians Debate,* pp. 319-39.
Coppens, J., "Miscellanées bibliques LXXX. Une diatribe antijuive dans 1 Thess. II,13-16," *ETL* 51 (1975): 90-95.
Cornelius, E., "Die funksie van die 'danksegging(s)' in 1 Tessalonisense," *HTS* 49 (1993): 57-84.
DeSilva, David, "'Worthy of His Kingdom': Honor Discourse and Social Engineering in 1 Thessalonians," *JSNT* 64 (1996): 49-76.
Donfried, K. P., "The Epistolary and Rhetorical Context of 1 Thessalonians 2:1-12," in Donfried and Beutler, eds., *The Thessalonians Debate,* pp. 31-60.
Fantham, E., "Imitation and Decline: Rhetorical Theory and Practice in the First Century after Christ," *Classical Philology* 73 (1978): 1-16, 102-16.
Focant, C., "Les Fils du Jour (1 Thes 5,5)," in Collins, ed., *The Thessalonian Correspondence,* pp. 348-55.
Hester, James D., "The Invention of 1 Thessalonians: A Proposal," in *Rhetoric,*

1. Thanks to my long-time friend Duane Watson for help with this bibliography.

Scripture and Theology: Essays from the 1994 Pretoria Conference, ed. Stanley E. Porter and Thomas H. Olbricht (JSNTSup 131; Sheffield: Sheffield Academic, 1996), pp. 251-79.

Holtz, T., "On the Background of 1 Thessalonians 2:1-12," in Donfried and Beutler, eds., *The Thessalonians Debate,* pp. 69-80.

Hoppe, R., "Der erste Thessalonicherbrief und die antike Rhetorik. Eine Problemeskizze." *BZ* 41 (1997): 229-37.

———, "The Epistolary and Rhetorical Context of 1 Thessalonians 2:1-12: A Response to Karl P. Donfried," in Donfied and Beutler, eds., *The Thessalonians Debate,* pp. 61-68.

Hughes, F. W., "The Rhetoric of 1 Thessalonians," in Collins, ed., *The Thessalonian Correspondence,* pp. 94-116.

———, "The Rhetoric of Letters," in Donfried and Beutler, eds., *The Thessalonians Debate,* pp. 194-240.

———, "The Social Situations Implied by Rhetoric," in Donfried and Beutler, eds., *The Thessalonians Debate,* pp. 241-54.

Johanson, B. C., *To All the Brethren: A Text-Linguistic and Rhetorical Approach to 1 Thessalonians* (Stockholm: Almqvist and Wiksell, 1987).

Kieffer, R., "L'eschatologie en 1 Thessaloniciens dans une perspective rhétorique," in Collins, ed., *The Thessalonian Correspondence,* pp. 206-19.

Kloppenborg, J. S., "ΦΙΛΑΔΕΛΦΙΑ, ΘΕΟΔΙΔΑΚΤΟΣ and the Dioscuri: Rhetorical Engagement in 1 Thessalonians 4.9-12," *NTS* 39 (1993): 265-89.

Krentz, E., "1 Thessalonians: Rhetorical Flourishes and Formal Constraints," in Donfried and Beutler, eds., *The Thessalonians Debate,* pp. 287-318.

Lyons, G., *Pauline Autobiography: Toward a New Understanding* (Atlanta: Scholars, 1985).

Malherbe, A. J., "Exhortation in First Thessalonians," *NovT* 25 (1983): 238-56.

———. "'Gentle as a Nurse': The Cynic Background to 1 Thess ii," *NovT* 12 (1970): 203-17.

Merk, O., "1 Thessalonians 2:1-12: An Exegetical-Theological Study," in Donfried and Beutler, eds., *The Thessalonians Debate,* pp. 89-113.

Olbricht, T. H., "An Aristotelian Rhetorical Analysis of I Thessalonians," in *Greeks, Romans, and Christians: Essays in Honor of Abraham J. Malherbe,* ed. D. Balch et al. (Minneapolis: Fortress, 1990), pp. 216-36.

Palmer, D. W., "Thanksgiving, Self-Defence, and Exhortation in 1 Thessalonians 1–3," *Colloquium* 14 (1981): 23-31.

Rosenfield, L., "The Practical Celebration of Epideictic," in *A Synoptic History of Classical Rhetoric,* ed. J. J. Murphy (Davis: Hermagoras, 1983), pp. 131-55.

Schlueter, C. J., "1 Thessalonians 2.14-16: Polemical Hyperbole" (Ph.D. dissertation, McMaster University, 1992).

Schoon-Janssen, J., "On the Use of Elements of Ancient Epistolography in

1 Thessalonians," in Donfried and Beutler, eds., *The Thessalonians Debate,* pp. 179-93.

————, *Umstrittene "Apologien" in den Paulusbriefen. Studien zur rhetorischen Situation des 1.Thessalonicherbriefes, des Galaterbriefes und des Philipperbriefes* (Göttingen: Vandenhoeck und Ruprecht, 1991).

Selby, Gary S., "'Blameless at His Coming': The Discursive Construction of Eschatological Reality in 1 Thessalonians," *Rhetorica* 17 (1999): 385-410.

Smith, A., *Comfort One Another: Reconstructing the Rhetoric and Audience of 1 Thessalonians.* Louisville: Westminster John Knox, 1995.

————, "The Social and Ethical Implications of the Pauline Rhetoric in 1 Thessalonians" (Ph.D. dissertation, Vanderbilt University, 1990).

Sumney, J. L., "The Bearing of a Pauline Rhetorical Pattern on the Integrity of 2 Thessalonians," *ZNW* 81 (1990): 192-204.

Vanhoye, A., "La Composition de 1 Thessaloniciens," in Collins, ed., *The Thessalonian Correspondence,* pp. 73-86.

Vos, J. S., "On the Background of 1 Thessalonians 2:1-12: A Response to Traugott Holtz," in Donfried and Beutler, eds., *The Thessalonians Debate,* pp. 81-88.

Walton, S., "Paul in Acts and Epistles: The Miletus Speech and 1 Thessalonians as a Test Case" (Ph.D. dissertation, University of Sheffield, 1997).

————, "What Has Aristotle to Do with Paul? Rhetorical Criticism and 1 Thessalonians," *Tyndale Bulletin* 46 (1995): 229-50.

Wanamaker, C. A., "Epistolary vs. Rhetorical Analysis: Is a Synthesis Possible?" in Donfried and Beutler, eds., *The Thessalonians Debate,* pp. 255-86.

Watson, D. F., "Paul's Appropriation of Apocalyptic Discourse: The Rhetorical Strategy of 1 Thessalonians," in G. Carey and L. G. Bloomquist, eds., *Vision and Persuasion: Rhetorical Dimensions of Apocalyptic Discourse* (St. Louis: Chalice, 1999), pp. 61-80.

Weima, J. A. D., "The Function of 1 Thessalonians 2:1-12 and the Use of Rhetorical Criticism: A Response to Otto Merk," in Donfried and Beutler, eds., *The Thessalonians Debate,* pp. 114-31.

Wick, P., "Ist I Thess 2,13-16 antijüdisch?" *TZ* 50 (1994): 9-23.

Winter, B. W., "The Entries and Ethics of Orators and Paul (1 Thessalonians 2:1-12)," *Tyndale Bulletin* 44 (1993): 55-74.

————, "Is Paul among the Sophists?" *Reformed Theological Review* 53 (1994): 28-38.

Wuellner, Wilhelm, "The Argumentative Structure of 1 Thessalonians as a Paradoxical Encomium," in Collins, ed., *The Thessalonian Correspondence,* pp. 117-36.

————, "Greek Rhetoric and Pauline Argumentation," in *Early Christian Literature and the Classical Intellectual Tradition,* ed. W. R. Schoedel and R. L. Wilken (Paris: Beauchesne, 1979), pp. 177-88.

2 Thessalonians

Holland, G. S., *The Tradition That You Received from Us: 2 Thessalonians in the Pauline Tradition* (Tübingen: Mohr, 1988).

Hughes, F. W., *Early Christian Rhetoric and 2 Thessalonians* (JSNTSup 30; Sheffield: Sheffield Academic, 1989).

————, "The Social World of 2 Thessalonians," *Listening* 31 (1996): 105-16, especially pp. 107-11.

Menken, M. J. J., *2 Thessalonians* (New Testament Readings; New York: Routledge, 1994), especially pp. 20-26.

Sumney, J. L. "The Bearing of a Pauline Rhetorical Pattern on the Integrity of 2 Thessalonians," *ZNW* 81 (1990): 192-204.

Articles of General Interest on 1 and 2 Thessalonians

Aus, R. D., "The Liturgical Background of the Necessity and Propriety of Giving Thanks according to 2 Thess. 1.3," *JBL* 92 (1973): 432-38.

————, "The Relevance of Isaiah 66.7 to Revelation 12 and 2 Thessalonians 1," *ZNW* 67 (1976): 252-68.

Bammel, E., "Preparation for the Perils of the Last Days: 1 Thessalonians 3.3," in *Suffering and Martyrdom in the New Testament: Studies Presented to G. M. Styler by the Cambridge New Testament Seminar,* ed. W. Horbury and B. McNeil (Cambridge: Cambridge University Press, 1981), pp. 91-100.

Bassler, J. M., "The Enigmatic Sign: 2 Thessalonians 1.5," *CBQ* 46 (1984): 496-510.

Betz, O., "Der Katechon," *NTS* 9 (1962-63): 276-91.

Cohen, S., "Was Timothy Jewish?" *JBL* 105 (1986): 251-68.

Hooker, M. D., "Interchange in Christ," *JTS* n.s. 22 (1971): 349-61.

————, "Interchange and Atonement," *BJRL* 60 (1977-78): 462-81.

Howard, T., "The Literary Unity of 1 Thessalonians 4.13–5.11," *Grace Theological Journal* 9 (1988): 163-90.

Hughes, F. W., "The Social World of 2 Thessalonians," *Listening* 31.2 (1996): 105-16.

Jensen, J., "Does *Porneia* Mean Fornication? A Critique of Bruce Malina," *NovT* 20 (1978): 161-84.

Jewett, R., "The Form and Function of the Homiletic Benediction," *Anglican Theological Review* 51 (1969): 18-34.

————, "The Agitators and the Galatian Congregation," *NTS* 17 (1970-71): 198-212.

Klassen, W., "The Sacred Kiss in the New Testament," *NTS* 39 (1993): 122-35.

Krentz, E., "Thessalonians, First and Second Epistles to the," *ABD* 6, pp. 515-22.

————, "Traditions Held Fast: Theology and Fidelity in 2 Thessalonians," in Collins, ed., *The Thessalonian Correspondence,* pp. 505-15.

Malherbe, A., "Gentle as a Nurse: The Cynic Background to 1 Thess. 2," *NovT* (1970): 203-17.

Malina, B., "Does *Porneia* mean Fornication?" *NovT* 14 (1972): 10-17.

Manson, T. W., "St. Paul in Greece: The Letters to the Thessalonians," *BJRL* 35 (1952-53): 428-47.

Mitchell, M. M., "Concerning *peri de* in 1 Corinthians," *NovT* 31 (1989): 229-56.

Otzen, P., "'Gute Hoffnung' bei Paulus," *ZNW* 49 (1958): 283-85.

Rigaux, B., "Tradition et redaction dans 1 Th. v.1-10," *NTS* 21 (1974-75): 318-40.

Roetzel, C., "1 Thess. 5.12-28: A Case Study," in *Society of Biblical Literature Annual Papers,* ed. L. McGaughy (Chico: Scholars, 1972), pp. 370-75.

Russell, R., "The Idle in 2 Thess. 3.6-12: An Eschatological or a Social Problem?" *NTS* 34 (1988): 105-19.

Schmidt, D., "1 Thess. 2.13-16. Linguistic Evidence for an Interpolation," *JBL* 102 (1983): 269-79.

Wenham, D., "Paul and the Synoptic Apocalypse," in *Gospel Perspectives: Studies of History and Tradition in the Four Gospels,* vol. 2, ed. R. T. France and D. Wenham (Sheffield: JSOT, 1981), pp. 345-75.

Witherington, B., "The Influence of Galatians on Hebrews," *NTS* 37 (1991): 146-52.

————, "Not So Idle Thoughts about *Eidolathuton,*" *Tyndale Bulletin* 44 (1993): 237-54.

Introduction

The "Metropolis" of Macedonia and Its History

The city of Thessalonike had a long and colorful history before Paul arrived there in A.D. 50 or 51 in the midst of his so-called second missionary journey, recorded in Acts 15.40–18.23.[1] As part of the Roman Empire the city of course fell under Roman rule, but that rule was indirect by the time Paul came; that is, the city was part of a senatorial province. It was not a Roman colony city, founded or transformed into a retirement center for Roman soldiers and other Roman officials. Its form of government, its language of jurisprudence, and its cultural ethos were different than in a Roman colony,[2] although with the rise of the emperor cult in Thessalonike, there was a constant reminder of who the overlords were.[3] Never-

---

1. I say "so-called" because Paul stayed a long period of time, at least a year and a half, in Corinth during this journey. It is from Corinth, not the home base in Antioch, that Paul wrote one if not both of the Thessalonian letters. On references to this city in the NT see Acts 17.1-13; Phil. 4.16; 2 Tim. 4.10. See B. Witherington, *The Paul Quest* (Downers Grove: InterVarsity, 1998), pp. 318-19.

2. E. Schnabel, *Early Christian Mission 2: Paul and the Early Church* (Downers Grove: InterVarsity, 2004), pp. 1162-63 rightly stresses: "Despite the presence of Romans in the provincial government, which had its seat in Thessalonike . . . among the merchants and traders, the city was thoroughly Greek, organized according to Greek patterns with a council *(boule . . .)*, assembly of the citizens *(demos . . .)* and magistrates *(politarchai . . .)*, and minting (bronze) coins with Greek legends."

3. As C. Wanamaker, *Commentary on 1 and 2 Thessalonians* (Grand Rapids: Eerdmans, 1990), p. 3 notes this meant that the law of Rome did not replace local legal institutions. Thessalonike did not have to absorb large numbers of retired soldiers, which left "the local ruling elite in control of the city with its traditional institutions intact."

1

theless, the fact that only 2% of the inscriptions found in the city are in Latin is telling. Even in the Roman period this remained largely a Greek city.

The civilization of mainland Greece and Macedonia had a continuous social, political, and literary history from at least the eighth century B.C. While in Greece culture was based on the city-state model, in Thessaly and Macedonia things were a bit different. There were kings, beginning with Philip, then Alexander, and then Alexander's general Cassander, then others. Cassander combined the old city of Therme with twenty-six minor settlements to form the city Thessalonike in 316-315 B.C. The city, built with a Hippodamian layout with insulae measuring 102 by 58.5 meters, was named after Alexander's step-sister Thessaloniki, the last surviving member of his family and Cassander's wife.[4]

The city's location was excellent, at the head of the Thermaic Gulf,[5] which provided one of the best harbors in the Aegean Sea. The city was also on a major trade route running north to south and so was of military as well as commercial importance. "It was the key to the whole of Macedonia."[6] It is not a surprise that the poet Antipater in the first century B.C. called the city "the mother of all Macedonia" (*Anthologia Palatina* 4.428). Cicero was impressed enough by his time in Thessalonike to say that the city's inhabitants were "lying in the lap of the Roman Empire" (*De Provinciis Consularibus* 2).

The antipathy between Macedonians and Greeks was such that in 197 B.C. the Achaean league welcomed Roman offers to liberate Greece from Macedonian rule. But Greece realized too late that the Hellenistic kings like Cassander had been far less prone to interfere in the local affairs of Greek city-states than the Romans would be. When resistance grew Rome came with all its might and crushed it, a military operation that concluded with the sack and destruction of Corinth in 146 B.C.[7] Macedonia had already fallen as an independent kingdom after the battle of Pydna when King Perseus was defeated and the region quietly received Rome as its new patron in 168 B.C. The Roman general Aemilius Paullus designated Thessalonike the capital of one of the four regions of Macedonia in 168,[8] and then it became the capital of the unified senatorial province

---

4. See now Schnabel, *Early Christian Mission* 2, p. 1160.

5. Pliny, *Natural History* 4.10.17 describes it as in the middle of the bend of the Thermaic Gulf. Xerxes chose its natural harbor as the place to station his fleet (Herodotus 7.121). Livy mentions its busy dockyards (44.10).

6. J. B. Lightfoot, *Biblical Essays* (Grand Rapids: Baker, reprint), p. 254.

7. See M. Goodman, *The Roman World 44 B.C.–A.D. 180* (London: Routledge, 1997), pp. 229-30.

8. Aemilius Paulus offered a good piece of rhetoric in saying that the Thessalonians should remain free to demonstrate that Rome did not enslave people (Livy 45.30.2). All the while the report in Rome was that some 300,000,000 sesterces were extracted from the province (Pliny, *Natural History* 33.17). "Freedom" did not come cheaply. See D. W. J. Gill, "Mace-

in 146 B.C.. The province was named after the city and also included Epirus and parts of Illyricum.[9]

Greece suffered for its resistance to Rome more than Macedonia did. In Macedonia, the "tradition of subservience to powerful monarchs . . . had instilled the habit of obedience, or, at least, the avoidance of open opposition."[10] One of the clearest proofs of Roman favor in the region is that in 130 B.C. the Romans built the Via Egnatia, a major highway connecting its cities, including Philippi and Thessalonike, with Dyrrachium on the Adriatic Sea.[11] The road was constructed by and named after one Cnaeus Egnatius, as the inscription on the milestone about six miles outside Thessalonike shows, which also tells that it was about 267 miles from Thessalonike to Dyrrachium.[12] Almost directly across the sea from Dyrrachium was Brundisium and the Via Appia, the main road from the east into Rome. Thessalonike was thereby linked directly with Rome, and this aided the growing prosperity of the city.[13]

The citizens of Thessalonike deliberately cultivated and solicited the benefaction of Rome.[14] Pompey in flight from Rome resided there with his entourage in 49-48 B.C., and many of the knights and senators who fled with him joined him there, making the city a second Rome, with the consecration of a site for the authoritative convening of the "true" Senate.[15] And again when the tide turned against Brutus and Cassius, the city supported Antony and Octavian. This paid off handsomely when first Antony in 42 B.C. and then Octavian (having become the first emperor) granted the city the status of a "free city" (Pliny the Elder, *Natural History* 4.36), which gave it an independent form of government (involving five or six politarchs holding annually chosen

---

donia," in *Acts in its First Century Settings* 2: *Graeco-Roman Setting,* ed. D. W. J. Gill and C. Gempf (Grand Rapids: Eerdmans, 1994), p. 402.

9. There was a rebellion in the region in about 148 B.C. which was crushed and led to the deportation of the entire Macedonian aristocracy (including civic and military leaders). See H. Hendrix, "Thessalonica," in *ABD* 6, pp. 523-27, here p. 524.

10. Goodman, *The Roman World,* p. 232.

11. Polybius (34.12.9) and Cicero (*De Provinciis Consularibus* 4) know of an earlier military road from Illyricum to Byzantium. The Romans apparently built over it and/or improved parts of it. See R. Riesner, *Paul's Early Period* (Grand Rapids: Eerdmans, 1998), p. 339.

12. See Strabo 7.7.4; cf. Gill, "Macedonia," p. 409. The road went east from Thessalonike about the same distance as it went west. On his second visit to Macedonia Paul apparently traveled the length of the road from Thessalonike to the Adriatic (cf. Acts 20.2; Rom. 15.19).

13. See R. Malcolm Errington, *A History of Macedonia* (Berkeley: University of California Press, 1990), pp. 132-34.

14. It is interesting that the famous orator Cicero spent six months in exile there in 58 B.C., writing some eighteen letters during that time without once really describing the city or his environs in general.

15. Hendrix, "Thessalonica," p. 524.

magistracies)[16] and thus allowed it to cultivate local patrons as well as those in Rome.

The town council (*dēmos*) collaborated with the politarchs, who convened town council meetings to keep the peace and make major decisions. We learn of some of the functions of this body in Greek culture from inscriptions. We have one honorific decree in which a *dēmos* (in this case on Samos in the fourth century B.C.) votes to honor two persons "upon hearing the *euaggelia* ('good news')."[17] The status of a free city also meant that Thessalonike could mint its own coins and even imperial coins. The city was promised freedom from military occupation and granted various tax concessions.[18] During the war among the rulers of Rome, which had reached into the area (e.g., Philippi), Thessalonike had lent its support to the Second Triumvirate and in particular to Octavian, who turned out the winner in the struggles against Antony and Cleopatra.

The war had raged from 44 B.C. to 31 B.C., culminating in the battle at Actium when Antony and Cleopatra were decisively defeated. Once this struggle was over Thessalonike "entered into a period of unparalleled peace and generally improving economic circumstances as commercial activity underwent considerable development."[19] The geographer Strabo was to call the city the "metropolis" of all Macedonia (*Geography* 7, fragment 21), not least because within its walls it had a population of perhaps as much as 65,000 to 80,000. Those living just outside the walls brought that number to about 100,000.[20] This was a city that in many ways suited Paul's urban strategy for spreading faith in Jesus.[21] It was a city full of artisans, manual laborers, sailors, and orators. We have an inscription from the first century A.D. mentioning associations of Roman merchants and sea merchants (IG X.2.1.32-33). We have further inscriptions indicating a guild of purple dyers (also in Philippi; see Acts 16), blacksmiths, and other dyers (IG X.2.1.291, 391, 758). Paul, practicing his trade,

---

16. The evidence of Acts 17.6 that there were politarchs in this city has been confirmed by an inscription on the Vardar Gate now found in the British Museum. There is also supplementary inscriptional evidence about politarchs even from Berea. See *New Docs* 2, pp. 104-5.

17. *New Docs* 3, p. 13.

18. There was a sense in which Thessalonike was a free-standing city and not part of the "commonwealth of Macedonia" in that it was given special privileges and exempted from some taxes, unlike the rest of the province. This was a way of recognizing or bestowing a special honor rating on this city and so securing its loyalty to Rome.

19. Wanamaker, *1 and 2 Thessalonians*, p. 4.

20. Lucian's estimate of the population from slightly after Paul's time is about the same (*Asinus* 46.2).

21. Much later in Christian history, before the foundation of Constantinople, Thessalonike nearly became the capital of the Christian world. See Lightfoot, *Biblical Essays*, p. 255 and notes.

would have fit in well here. But Thessalonike was not an educational or philosophical center like Athens.[22]

The Thessalonians erected a statue of Augustus with the upraised right hand of a hero and a temple to Augustus as well (IG X.2.31-32), both of which Paul surely saw during his visit. "The statue has been dated to the reign of Gaius ('Caligula') or Claudius, and it is one of the few objects recovered at the city which can be dated with certainty to the time of Paul's visit. It is perhaps in the context of so effusive an outpouring of honors for Augustus that one should understand Paul's condemnation of those who promote 'peace and security' (1 Thess. 5.3 — a Julio-Claudian program of *pax et securitas?*)."[23] Even more interestingly, all the Macedonians chose to honor Augustus by declaring that they were inaugurating an "Augustan era," an era of unprecedented cooperation and commercial exchange between Macedonians and Romans.[24] Already, during the lifetime of Augustus there were priests of the imperial cult there,[25] and the presence of the cult is shown by coins minted there which have the deified Julius Caesar on one side and Augustus as "divi filius" on the other (IG X 2.1 31).[26] We know of a Caesareum already built in the time of Augustus which had a sanctuary (*naos* — IG X.2.1.31)

What is sometimes overlooked is that the emperor cult was syncretized with the local worship of the Cabiri, the mystic deities of Samothrace (a cult patronized by Philip and Alexander), and so here the emperor was deified as *Kabeiros,* as the coins show.[27] Kabeiros is described as "the ancestral and most holy of all gods" in an inscription (IG X.2.1 199). He is depicted as a youthful

---

22. The presence of orators and the absence of philosophical schools here should have been taken into account by A. Malherbe in *The Letters to the Thessalonians* (New York: Doubleday, 2000). For Paul to write to a largely non-elite congregation in Thessalonike as if he were offering a symposium for moral philosophers would have been singularly inappropriate. The audience knew orators and rhetoric, but their knowledge of moral philosophy cannot have been as extensive. That required "secondary" education. Cicero mentions no philosophers' schools or real institutions of "higher learning" in the city. It was a commercial, cultic, and political center. We do however have evidence that the rhetorician Lucian stayed here in the second century (see Schnabel, *Early Christian Mission* 2, p. 1161). The poets Antipatros and Philippos lived here in the first century A.D., but this probably says more for its aesthetic and scenic qualities than for its academic offerings.

23. Hendrix, "Thessalonica," p. 524.

24. See M. B. Sakellariou, *Macedonia: 4000 Years of Greek History and Civilization* (Athens: Ekdotike Athenon, 1983), pp. 195-96.

25. Hendrix, "Thessalonica," p. 524: "From this period also dates the establishment of a 'priest and agonothete of the Imperator Augustus son of god' and a priest of Roma and Roman benefactors. A group of 'Roman benefactors' received honors at Thessalonica from at least 95 B.C.E."

26. See Riesner, *Paul's Early Period,* p. 339.

27. See Lightfoot, *Biblical Essays,* pp. 257-58.

figure holding a blacksmith's hammer in his left hand and wearing a short chiton. According to legend, after he was decapitated by his two brothers his head was wrapped in purple cloth and buried at the foot of Mt. Olympus.[28] By combining the worship of the Kabeiros with that of the emperor, Thessalonike had clearly made the emperor their own personal deity. The cult of the emperor was also linked with the worship of Roma and the "Roman benefactors." Inscriptions mention the *agōnothetēs*, the organizer of the games (IG X 2.1 31, 133).[29]

Macedonians had by and large adopted and assimilated Greek culture and language as their own, but not the democratic city-state model of government. Greek religion and, later, the imperial cult, were welcomed. Along with indigenous cults like that of Cabirus, Greek cults like that of Dionysius, foreign cults like that of Isis and Serapis,[30] and the Roman imperial cult, there were Jews and then Christians in the city.[31] It was religiously a pluralistic environment, to say the least.[32] The cult of Dionysius may be alluded to in Paul's warning against getting drunk at night (1 Thess. 5.5-8).[33] That one of the districts of the city was named after this god shows the importance of his cult.

During the reign of Tiberius the imperial tax burden became excessive and the provinces of Achaea and of Macedonia filed grievances with the emperor. It did them no good. Angered, Tiberius made Macedonia an imperial province and recalled its governor in A.D. 15 (Tacitus, *Annales* 1.76). This decision was reversed by Claudius in A.D. 44 so that Macedonia was again a senatorial province and Thessalonike became once more the provincial capital.[34] Other favors came the way of the city, which was allowed to celebrate both Olympic and Pythian games (CIG I, 1068), a considerable source of revenue for the city. We will notice as we work particularly through the eschatological material in 1 Thessalonians 4–5 and 2 Thessalonians 2 that Paul is transferring political language previously applied to the emperor to Jesus (and others). As far as Paul is concerned, the only God who ever walked the earth was Jesus, not the emperor, and he wishes to make this clear. The other

---

28. See Schnabel, *Early Christian Mission* 2, p. 1164.

29. Schnabel, p. 1165.

30. Hendrix, "Thessalonica," p. 525.

31. See the discussion in K. P. Donfried, *Paul, Thessalonica, and Early Christianity* (Grand Rapid: Eerdmans, 2002).

32. See C. Steven de Vos, *Church and Community Conflicts: The Relationships of the Thessalonian, Corinthian, and Philippian Churches with their Wider Civic Communities* (Atlanta: Scholars, 1997).

33. Riesner, *Paul's Early Period*, p. 333.

34. Claudius was in some respects a traditional Roman and believed that the Senate should have viable functions and authority.

pagan cults do not receive this same degree of indirect critique or response, as we will see.[35]

It was risky to use such familiar language. In Acts 17 Paul and his coworkers get into trouble with the politarchs of Thessalonike, being accused of defying the decrees of Caesar and saying there is another king named Jesus (17.6-7). What decrees of Caesar? In all likelihood E. A. Judge is right that what is being referred to is an oath of loyalty to Caesar and Rome administered by the politarchs. An example of such an oath that was administered in Paphlagonia reads

> I swear . . . that I will support Caesar Augustus, his children and descendants throughout my life in word, deed and thought . . . that in whatsoever concerns them I will spare neither body nor soul nor life nor children . . . that whenever I see or hear of anything being said, planned or done against them I will report it . . . and whomsoever they regard as enemies I will attack and pursue with arms and the sword by land and by sea. . . .[36]

The cost of "freedom" and the Pax Romana in one's city was unswerving loyalty to the emperor. Caught up in the patronage/benefaction and reciprocity network between Rome and its major cities of the empire, Thessalonike had to take seriously troublemakers like Paul proclaiming another absolute Lord.[37] Paul seems to have fallen afoul of the city officials for both the rhetoric he used in proclaiming Jesus and the content of his presentation. Fortunately for him, even if he was banned from Thessalonike by one politarch or another, the banishment was only valid while that person remained in office.

The social situation Paul faced in Thessalonike was also complicated by the status of Jews in the empire after the expulsion of Jews from Rome in A.D. 49. While we have not yet found an inscription older than the second century A.D. Thessalonian synagogue inscription (CIJ 693), there is little reason to doubt the claim made in Acts 17 that in the middle of the first century Jews had a meeting place in Thessalonike for Sabbath services and other meetings. The inscription dedicates the place to the Most High God, possibly with the addi-

---

35. See pp. 139-42 below and cf. H. Koester, "From Paul's Eschatology to the Apocalyptic Schemata of 2 Thessalonians," in *The Thessalonian Correspondence*, ed. Raymond F. Collins (Leuven: University of Leuven Press, 1990), pp. 441-58, here p. 446. This same essay can be found in *Paul and Empire: Religion and Power in Roman Imperial Eschatology*, ed. R. A. Horsley (Harrisburg: Trinity, 1997), pp. 158-66. One of the more interesting features of 1 Thessalonians is its similarity in some respects to the Areopagus address in Acts 17. Both of these Pauline speeches reflect a certain knowledge of pagan philosophy, and do not exhibit the OT echoes we find in various other Pauline letters.

36. E. A. Judge, "The Decrees of Caesar at Thessalonica," *RTR* 30 (1971): 1-7, here p. 6.

37. See the discussion in Witherington, *New Testament History* (Grand Rapids: Baker, 2001), p. 263.

tion of the name Yahweh in transliteration (CIJ 693D).[38] Even more important
is the inscription found on a sarcophagus that refers to Jews named Jacob and
Anna and to synagogues (plural).[39] This suggests a thriving Jewish populace in
this city in the second or third century and requires that there was a Jewish
presence in the city in the previous century.

But when had Jews first come to Thessalonike, and why? Josephus (*Apion*
1.200-204) tells us that Jewish mercenaries served in the army of Alexander the
Great. We also know that during the Hasmonean period there was a great deal
of traffic between Judea and Greece, with many Jews heading west to Greece
(1 Macc. 12.2-7; 15.22-23; 2 Macc. 5.9; Josephus, *Antiquities* 12.225; 14.149-55). We
have an inscription about Jews in Athens dating to the second century B.C. (IG
II.2.12609). A letter of Herod Agrippa to Caligula mentions Macedonia as one
place where Jews already lived in some numbers (Philo, *Legatio ad Gaium*
281).[40] We may take it then as a secure conclusion, even if one leaves Acts 17 out
of account, that there were a good number of Jews in Thessalonike when Paul
arrived, perhaps even some exiles from Rome. Equally interesting is the presence of a Samaritan community in Thessalonike attested by a bilingual inscription in Samaritan and Greek (CIJ 693A). The danger for monotheists in this environment, be they Jewish, Samaritan, or Christian, was the constant cultural
pressure in the direction of syncretism, especially because other eastern cults,
such as those from Egypt, were quite readily being blended with some of the local deity celebrations.[41]

If Paul indeed came and preached in the synagogue in Thessalonike proclaiming that the Thessalonians needed to turn from idols, worship the one
true God, and recognize his only Son Jesus (1 Thess. 1.9),[42] we can understand
why some Jews would immediately be alarmed. Already in a compromised situation because of the very recent expulsion of Jews from Rome, Jews in

---

38. See the discussion in I. Levinskaya, *The Book of Acts in its First Century Setting* 5:
Diaspora Setting (Grand Rapids: Eerdmans, 1996), p. 155.

39. Levinskaya, p. 155.

40. See Riesner, *Paul's Early Period*, p. 344 for an assessment of this data.

41. Though there is little mention of Thessalonike in post-first century A.D. literature,
Melito in his *Apology*, written in the middle of the second century, mentions that the Emperor Antoninus Pius had written to the people of the city telling them to take no new actions against the Christians there (see Eusebius, *Hist. Eccles.* 4.26). Tertullian in the early third
century mentions the churches in Thessalonike and Philippi as places where the apostles' letters are still read in the original language (*De Praescriptione Haereticorum* 36). Aristarchus is
listed by Bede as an early minister, and Gaius as an early bishop by Origen. See Lightfoot, *Biblical Essays*, p. 268.

42. A message which Paul saw as his attempt to implement the decree of James recorded in Acts 15, which expected Gentiles to stay away from pagan temples and the idolatry
and immorality believed to transpire there.

Thessalonike knew they had to show the utmost loyalty to the emperor lest they too be suspected of sedition. If they had, unawares, allowed Paul to preach his message in their synagogue, they themselves could be accused of being trouble-makers or disloyal to the ethos of the city. This explains both the enormous re-action of Jews recounted in Acts 17.6 and the equally polemical response and outburst by Paul in 1 Thess. 2.14-16.

Thessalonike depended on the goodwill and patronage of the emperor. It could not allow major disturbances created by minorities, especially those involving a *superstitio* which had created disturbances elsewhere in the em-pire (see Acts 17.6a). Claudius had already acted against squabbles in the syn-agogue about Jesus in Rome. There was no reason Jews in Thessalonike might not feel the wrath of the emperor as well if they were caught disturbing the Pax Romana.[43]

So to avoid official investigation, interference, and reprisals the Jewish leaders of the synagogue acted quickly. Jason and some other Christians had to post some sort of bond or surety, perhaps offering a promise of no more trou-ble, and were released by the politarchs, but they wisely sent Paul and Silas away under cover of night, lest the Jewish officials or the politarchs find them still in the city. We will say more about this. Suffice it to say here that the social situa-tion was difficult for the Thessalonian Christians, who were opposed by both pagans and Jews and were even persecuted, it would appear. Into this situation Paul had to write these early letters.

Authorship, Date, and Occasion of the Letters

The authorship of 1 Thessalonians is not in dispute. There is near universal consensus that Paul wrote this letter and that it predates most if not all of his other letters. But should we conclude that it or 2 Thessalonians had multiple authors in view of their frequent use of "we" and their listing of Paul, Silas, and Timothy as authors in the epistolary prescript?[44]

---

43. Indeed, as early as A.D. 41 Claudius wrote to Jews in Alexandria telling them to stop fomenting trouble and he called them a plague throughout the empire. The anti-Semitism of Romans in general, including especially the emperors, needs to be kept in view in evaluating the social situation. See B. Witherington, *The Acts of the Apostles* (Grand Rapids: Eerdmans, 1998), pp. 539-44.

44. In 1 Thessalonians the frequency of "we" as opposed to "I" is 96.7% and in 2 Thessalonians it is 93.9%. Compare this to only 8.7% in Philippians. See S. R. Llewelyn, "Letters in the Early Church," in *New Docs* 7, pp. 53-54. This phenomenon needs to be ex-plained. I would suggest it has something to do with the fact that the founding of the church in Thessalonike was a team effort, and, though Paul is doing the speaking, he is speaking for

While it is possible that Timothy or Silas may have been the scribe for either or both of these documents, there are telltale signs that Paul dictated them. For example, in 1 Thess. 5.27 Paul uses a first person singular verb in directing the audience to read the letter.[45] The even clearer remark in 2 Thess. 3.17 refers to Paul's individual and recognizable signature. As E. Krentz points out about 1 Thessalonians, "Though the letter is written in the first person plural throughout, Paul's viewpoint is consistently preeminent (cf. 2.1-11: the character of the initial preaching and manual labor; 2.18: Paul's [personal] desire to visit; 3.1: Paul alone in Athens). There is nothing to suggest that either Silvanus or Timothy participated in the writing," or at least the dictating, of this letter.[46] The same can be said for 2 Thessalonians, assuming for the moment its Pauline origin. What perhaps can be said is that Paul believes that what he is saying also speaks for Silas and Timothy and that he wants his audience to know that he is not alone in his concern for and exhortations of his converts.

The dating of these letters is somewhat disputed, though in a fairly narrow range. Some would date 1 Thessalonians as early as A.D. 49, others somewhere in the range of 50 to 52.[47] I think that Paul wrote this letter from Corinth before he left to head east, which in all likelihood means sometime in A.D. 51, but will say more about the occasion of the letter after discussing 2 Thessalonians.

The authorship of 2 Thessalonians and accordingly its date and occasion are very much in dispute. Perhaps more than any other factor it is the perceived difference in eschatology between 1 Thessalonians 4–5 and 2 Thessalonians 2 that has led some commentators to conclude that 2 Thessalonians must be pseudonymous and perhaps written well after the death of Paul.[48] But a sudden

---

the leadership team, even though he is its head and spokesperson, the one, for instance, who sends Timothy back to Thessalonike.

45. See R. F. Collins, "'I Command That This Letter Be Read': Writing as a Manner of Speaking," in K. P. Donfried and J. Beutler, eds., *The Thessalonians Debate* (Grand Rapids: Eerdmans, 2000), pp. 331-32.

46. E. Krentz, "Thessalonians, First and Second Epistles to the," *ABD* 6, p. 515.

47. We even have the speculation of K. P. Donfried, "1 Thessalonians, Acts and the Early Paul," in R. F. Collins, ed., *The Thessalonian Correspondence* (Leuven: Leuven University Press, 2000), pp. 3-26 that 1 Thessalonians is from the early 40s! This is based on an argument from silence (when Paul says in Gal. 1.21 that he went to Syria and Cilicia after visiting Jerusalem this really means he went in that direction and kept going all the way to Thessalonike and on to Corinth!) and on a dating of Claudius's edict of expulsion to A.D. 41. Clearly, A.D. 49 is more likely. See Witherington, *Acts of the Apostles,* pp. 539-44.

48. See for example M. J. J. Menken, *2 Thessalonians* (London: Routledge, 1994), who dates the letter somewhere from 80 to even into the second century, despite Polycarp's citation of it as a letter by Paul in about 110! Cf. Mencken, *2 Thessalonians: Facing the End with Sobriety* (London: Routledge, 1994). Other writers who identify 2 Thessalonians as post-Pauline include C. Masson, *Les Deux Epitres de Saint Paul aux Thessaloniciens* (Neuchatel: Delachaux et Niestle, 1957); R. F. Collins, *Letters That Paul Did Not Write* (Wilmington: Glazier, 1988).

second coming of Christ (1 Thess. 5.1-11) and signs of his coming (2 Thess. 2.3-12) are juxtaposed in Mark 13:14-37. Furthermore, 2 Thessalonians does not provide a list of events expected to precede the parousia so as to enable the reader to say when Christ will come. It provides, rather, a proof that the day of the Lord had not occurred even though some at Thessalonike apparently thought it had (2.2).[49]

There are also serious problems with the other usual arguments against Pauline authorship of 2 Thessalonians. For one thing, the evidence for the existence of Christian epistolary pseudepigrapha in the first century is slender if not completely lacking,[50] unless the *Epistle of Barnabas* is such a document.[51] Furthermore, there is clear evidence that there was concern in the first-century Greco-Roman world about literary forgeries, which may explain why Paul emphasizes the signing of his documents.[52] Especially problematic for those wanting to see 2 Thessalonians as post-Pauline is its situation-specific character. As K. P. Donfried, T. Still, and A. Malherbe have all pointed out, it is "difficult to imagine a setting where a letter specifically addressed to the Thessalonians by Paul would be relevant and convincing to a non-Thessalonian church some thirty or more years after the Apostle's death."[53]

W. Wrede's argument had the most influence in convincing scholars that because 2 Thessalonians seems to be patterned on 1 Thessalonians it must be a later imitation of the genuine Pauline letter.[54] The following parallels suggested to Wrede that parts of 2 Thessalonians were derivative and based on 1 Thessalonians:

1 Thess. 1.6-8	2 Thess. 1.4
1 Thess. 2.12-13	2 Thess. 2.13-14
1 Thess. 3.11	2 Thess. 2.16
1 Thess. 4.1	2 Thess. 3.1

49. So Wanamaker, *1 and 2 Thessalonians*, p. 18.

50. I am of course leaving out of account for the moment canonical texts, as one must first demonstrate there were such early Christian letters in general before one begins considering the possibility that there may be some in the canon that fit this genre of document.

51. I am referring here to letters that arise from and are addressed to a specific *Sitz im Leben*, as 2 Thessalonians certainly is.

52. See now the study of T. L. Wilder, *Pseudonymity, the New Testament, and Deception* (Lanham: University Press of America, 2004).

53. Donfried, *Paul, Thessalonica, and Early Christianity*, p. 66; T. D. Still, *Conflict at Thessalonica: A Pauline Church and its Neighbours* (Sheffield: Sheffield Academic, 1999), p. 58; Malherbe, *The Letters*, p. 373.

54. W. Wrede, *Die Echtheit des zweiten Thessalonicherbriefs* (Leipzig: Hinrichs, 1903), pp. 95-96. He dates 2 Thessalonians to 100-10. Wanamaker, *1 and 2 Thessalonians*, pp. 17-28 provides a useful survey of the arguments put forth for the non-Pauline character of 2 Thessalonians.

1 Thess. 4.1-2   2 Thess. 3.6-7
1 Thess. 4.10-12   2 Thess. 3.10-12
1 Thess. 5.23   2 Thess. 3.16[55]

The parallels are not all equally convincing, but they do show that some parallels of phrasing and ideas occur in these two documents in generally the same order, though it hardly looks like 2 Thessalonians reflects direct literary dependence on 1 Thessalonians.[56] This suggests, as does the identical addressors, that these documents were composed in reasonably close proximity to each other in time, while the same ideas and phraseology were on Paul's mind.

The parallels suggest that 1 Thessalonians was probably written earlier than 2 Thessalonians since, especially in the eschatological passages, the material in 2 Thessalonians looks like a further clarification of what has been said on the subject. In fact, the conclusion of the eschatological argument in 2 Thessalonians 2 refers to holding fast to the teaching passed on previously, *including that passed on by letter* (v. 15). This is most naturally taken as a reference to the eschatological teaching in 1 Thessalonians.[57]

The major problems with an argument for 2 Thessalonians being post-Pauline include the destruction of the Temple in Jerusalem in A.D. 70. It is hard to get around the fact that 2 Thess. 2.4 is talking about *the* Temple of the true God, the biblical God, the one in Jerusalem. A forger or even an imitator surely would have avoided a form of prediction of the Temple's demise that did not match up more clearly with the historical actualities, for Titus did not exactly

55. Not all scholars will evaluate this data in the same way. E. Krentz, "Thessalonians, First and Second Epistles to the," pp. 519-22 stresses the difference in tone, small differences in style and vocabulary, and perceived differences in theology, leading to the conclusion of pseudonymity. What he does not really take into account is the differing rhetorical character of the two Thessalonian letters and the differing social situations being addressed. The second letter must deal with present persecution and the equally real befuddlement about eschatology, perhaps in part based on a misunderstanding of what Paul said in 1 Thessalonians 4–5. The second letter is certainly not intended to be a letter of consolation or encouragement, but rather a deliberative argument trying to get the Thessalonian Christians to change some of their beliefs and behavior.

56. It is instructive for instance to compare the situation with Colossians and Ephesians, where a good case can be made for literary dependence of the latter on the former, especially near the end of both documents. There is no long sequence of words or sentences in 2 Thessalonians that exactly replicate 1 Thessalonians.

57. One can also note 2 Thess. 3.17, which refers to "all my letters." This certainly presupposes letters Paul had written in the past. Unless this is pure hyperbole it also suggests more than one letter that Paul has written previously, which may provide a small piece of further support for the contention that Galatians is Paul's earliest extant letter. I would submit that Gal. 6.11 is one of the things Paul is thinking back to when he speaks about his autograph in 2 Thess. 3.17.

play out the script suggested in 2 Thess. 2.3-4.[58] If an imitator or forger wanted verisimilitude, he would surely have either omitted discussing this matter or would have discussed it in more precise terms with the benefit of hindsight.

2 Thess. 2.2 warns against purported Pauline letters, and the authenticating signature in 3.17 matches up with what Paul says in Gal. 6.11 is his practice, namely to conclude a letter in his own hand. It would take a cheeky forger to warn *against* forging in the midst of his copying of a genuine Pauline letter while at the same time protesting vigorously at the end of the document that this was from the hand of Paul.[59] In other words, there are serious moral problems raised by 2 Thessalonians if it is a pseudepigraph. There would surely be the clear intent to deceive the audience while at the same time trying to form or shape them morally in a Pauline manner. These two rhetorical aims are not compatible.

While there were certainly pseudepigraphal letters in antiquity,[60] unlike some other genres (e.g., early Jewish apocalyptic works often attributed to one patriarch or another) it was not a *regular* part of the literary conventions for the letter genre to have a falsely attributed author. The vast majority of ancient letters, Jewish, Greco-Roman, or Christian, were not pseudonymous. Furthermore, as T. L. Wilder has shown, the early church did not see pseudepigraphy as a harmless literary technique. By and large "early Christians had scruples regarding literary property and documents which purported to be the works of others."[61] Indeed, in the second century and afterward Christians went to some lengths to make clear the apostolic character or the link with apostles that various first-century Christian documents had. Furthermore, the vast majority of ancient letters were ad hoc documents, situation-specific, and thus not of the generic sort that would readily suit a variety of audiences in a variety of times and circumstances. 2 Thessalonians is such a situation-specific document, which in itself makes it hard for one to make the case for the pseudonymity of this letter.

---

58. See B. Rigaux, *Les Épitres aux Thessaloniciens* (Paris: Gabalda, 1956), p. 145.

59. It is also hardly plausible that a forger would base his Pauline copy on a document he himself saw as pseudonymous. It is thus not convincing to refer what is said in 2 Thess. 2.2 to 1 Thessalonians. It must instead refer to some hypothetical forgery. See C. R. Nicholl, *From Hope to Despair in Thessalonica: Situating 1 and 2 Thessalonians* (Cambridge: Cambridge University Press, 2004), p. 10.

60. On which see R. J. Bauckham, "Pseudo-Apostolic Letters," *JBL* 197 (1988): 469-94. As Bauckham points out, for a letter of this sort to pass muster, it had to address plausibly both an apparent original audience and the later real audience in terms that both would have found helpful and cogent, which is no small task. For this reason, such letters tended to be general or generic, not ad hoc or specific, lest the veil of pseudonymity slip from the face of the forger.

61. Wilder, *Pseudonymity*, p. 246.

Then, too, as Nicholl points out, this letter needs to have been written early enough in the second half of the first century that it could be included in the collection of Pauline letters and be cited as Pauline by Polycarp (ca. 107-17) already in his *Philippians* 11.3-4 (citing 2 Thess. 1.4 and 3.15). Furthermore, if it was written pseudonymously when some of Paul's converts still lived in Thessalonike, they would surely have known it was not by Paul, as he was dead. There is, in short, a major problem of date and/or provenance of the letter if it is not by Paul, and, as we shall see in the commentary itself, the exegesis of the letter itself supports the contention that this letter is from Paul's hand.[62]

The issue of the integrity of this letter is also a contributing factor in the discussion of pseudonymity. Generally speaking those who think we have multiple letters in 2 Thessalonians think it has been put together by a post-Pauline author or editor. J. L. Sumney has noted how 2 Thess. 1.3-12 and 2.13–3.5 are parallel in various ways and meet the criteria for being called the deliberate use of a rhetorical pattern (in this case an A B A pattern). More to the point, this is a pattern that Paul also uses elsewhere in 1 Corinthians and 1 Thessalonians. There is a difference in perspective between the parallel passages that are nested within the two prayer sections in 2 Thessalonians. We might add that the second section builds on the first as well. This argument supports both the case for the integrity of 2 Thessalonians and also its authenticity.[63]

Wanamaker argues that 2 Thessalonians is the earlier of the two letters. He first notes the classic form of the argument of the priority of 2 Thessalonians offered by T. W. Manson: (1) the persecution which seems to be happening in the present in 2 Thess. 1.4-7 appears to be a thing of the past in 1 Thess. 2.14; (2) the problem of disorder seems to be a new development in 2 Thess. 3.11-15 but is already a known problem in 1 Thess. 4.10-12; (3) the Pauline signature as a mark of all his genuine letters in 2 Thess. 3.17 is pointless unless 2 Thessalonians is the first of these letters; (4) the remark in 1 Thess. 5.1 that the readers do not need to be told about the timing of the end is especially apt if they have already heard 2 Thess. 2.1-12; and (5) the expression "now concerning" in 1 Thess. 4.9, 13, and 5.1 seems to be a formula used to introduce answers to questions raised earlier by the recipients, 4.9-13 responding to a question raised because of 2 Thess. 3.6-15 and both passages responding to anxieties created by 2 Thess. 2.1-12 about the fate of those who have died before the

---

62. It is not a surprise that F. W. Hughes abandons altogether trying to date 2 Thessalonians since he wants to see it as post-Pauline, and with the abandoning of date he cannot really provide a proper provenance for the letter as a pseudepigraph. See his "The Social World of 2 Thessalonians," *Listening* 31.2 (1996): 105-16.

63. J. L. Sumney, "The Bearing of a Pauline Rhetorical Pattern on the Integrity of 2 Thessalonians," *ZNW* 81 (1990): 192-204. See especially the charts on p. 194 for 1 Corinthians and 1 Thessalonians and then the parallels listed on pp. 203-4 from the two passages in 2 Thessalonians.

parousia.[64] Some of these arguments have a certain plausibility to them *if* one assumes that 2 Thessalonians reflects the initial intense situation, including persecution, and 1 Thessalonians a later less volatile situation. But, as R. Jewett points out, things might well have become more unstable after the writing of 1 Thessalonians, and indeed there may have been more than one juncture at which the Thessalonian Christians were persecuted.[65] In fact, it is likely that both things transpired as the situation continued to be unstable.

The *peri de* or "now concerning" formula in itself only indicates a familiar or standing topic. Unless the words "the things you wrote" are added, as in 1 Cor. 7.1, it does not signal something that the audience has raised. The argument about the signature is also not a strong one. In 2 Thessalonians there is clearly a concern about pseudonymous writings apparently purporting to come from Paul (see 2 Thess. 2.2), which leads to the stress on the signature later in this letter. 2.15 surely is most naturally taken as an indicator that this letter is a second letter. The aorist of *edidachthete* in that verse likely goes with *di' epistolēs hēmōn,* which surely indicates that the letter referred to was written in the past and hence is likely to be our 1 Thessalonians. The argument of Wanamaker that the verb here is an epistolary aorist or a perfective passive is surely special pleading.[66]

One can just as well argue that 1 Thess. 5.27 is not a remark that presupposes the autograph in 2 Thessalonians. It presupposes rather that there is more than one house church in Thessalonike, so all the brothers and sisters needed to have the opportunity to hear this document. Manson's other arguments are answered by the supposition that some topics addressed in both letters were first raised when Paul was present and teaching for some months in Thessalonike. In other words, it is not that 1 Thessalonians presupposes what we hear in 2 Thessalonians but that at least some of the things dealt with in a more detailed or specific way in 2 Thessalonians were already initially discussed when Paul was with his converts or in 1 Thessalonians. The issue of eschatology which links these two letters also links them with the situation Paul will have initially confronted in Thessalonike, namely the prevalence of imperial eschatology and the need for critique of it.[67]

Wanamaker argues that Paul wrote 2 Thessalonians while he was in Athens, after he had left Thessalonike and Beroea but before he went to Corinth.

---

64. T. W. Manson, "St. Paul in Greece: The Letters to the Thessalonians," *BJRL* 35 (1952-53): 428-47.

65. See R. Jewett, *The Thessalonian Correspondence* (Philadelphia: Fortress, 1986), pp. 24-25.

66. Cf. Wanamaker, *1 and 2 Thessalonians,* pp. 40-41 and contrast both Jewett, *Thessalonian Correspondence,* pp. 26-30, and Nicholl, *From Hope to Despair,* pp. 9-10.

67. On which see pp. 139-43 below.

He maintains that Timothy delivered this letter (see 1 Thess. 3.1-5), which was partly prompted by Paul's assumption that the Christians in Thessalonike were currently enduring persecution. This is a possible argument, but it overlooks two important points. First, neither Acts 17 nor 1 Thess. 3.1-5 mentions Timothy carrying a letter with him when he went from Athens to Thessalonike. Rather what is mentioned is that Paul's anxiety was such that he needed reassurance that the Thessalonians were holding fast to the faith, and so he sends Timothy personally to strength the converts there. Paul reminds them of what he said when he was with them about the inevitability of persecution.

Second, as R. Jewett points out, 1 Thessalonians does not mention an earlier letter to the Thessalonians, but it does mention in its *narratio* other events that occurred between Paul's time in Thessalonike and the writing of the letter. Rhetorically it would be singularly inept to fail to mention the important letter we know as 2 Thessalonians if it were one of these events Paul reminds his readers of. It would be "unnatural in an epistolary situation to refer to distant phases of a relationship without taking into account the intervening phases that alter the relationship or add critical new information."[68] Wanamaker in the end falls back on the rather weak argument that 1 Thess. 3.1-5 reflects some of the same issues and topics reflected in 2 Thessalonians. This is of course true, but it need mean no more than that these were ongoing issues and problems that needed to be addressed more than once. Persecution, once it begins, seldom involves only one attack if both parties continue to live in close proximity to each other and issues remain unresolved and indeed apparently intractable. Some of these issues can be seen in a clearer light once we consider the rhetoric and rhetorical situation of 1 and 2 Thessalonians and then look closer at the social context of these letters.

The Epistolary and Rhetorical Situation of the Thessalonian Correspondence

Interpreting as Rhetoric Rather Than as Epistle

Among the substantial literary and rhetorical issues to deal with when trying to assess 1 and 2 Thessalonians is the degree to which we allow epistolary conventions to dictate how we read these documents, which were meant to be read aloud to the audience in Thessalonike. It is no surprise that in a text-oriented era such as our own many are inclined to treat these documents as primarily something written, as letters, rather than as something meant to be spoken,

---

68. See Jewett, *Thessalonian Correspondence*, pp. 29-30.

namely a discourse. This is a mistake, not because there are no epistolary features to these documents (of course there are, at the beginning and end of each of them). It is rather a mistake of emphasis, for the majority of this material was not meant to be read as ancient business or personal letters were often read or as essays or moral treatises were read.[69] Paul is a pastor speaking from his heart in these letters in a cogent, compelling, and rhetorically effective way. He is writing in such a way that the content of the document can be orally delivered in a house church worship setting. The failure to consider the social and religious context in which the Thessalonians would have heard this material is a significant one.

Perhaps the clearest example of the weaknesses that arise when one chooses to study Pauline documents merely according to certain epistolary considerations while ignoring or dismissing rhetorical considerations is shown in the otherwise fine and important commentary by A. Malherbe.[70] The first problem in terms of categorization is Malherbe's attempt to see 1 and 2 Thessalonians (especially the former) as parenetic letters. This is especially odd when one hears arguments about 1 Thessalonians 1–3 being a long thanksgiving period or a triple thanksgiving section and parenesis proper does not begin until chs. 4–5, or until ch. 2 in 2 Thessalonians. These letters clearly contain parenesis or moral exhortations, but they also include much other material. Indeed the majority of the material in 1 Thessalonians is *not* parenesis. Nor does the parenetic content in these documents define the form of the documents themselves.

M. Mitchell in her telling but appreciative critique of Malherbe's commentary makes the following points: (1) It would appear that what prompted Malherbe's approach is his analysis of a particular passage in Dio Chrysostom where that popular philosopher, with tongue firmly in cheek, sets out to convince his audience of the differences between sophistic rhetors and himself (see

---

69. This is the sort of misstep we find in the essay of J. Schoon-Jansen, "On the Use of Elements of Ancient Epistolography in 1 Thessalonians," in *The Thessalonians Debate*, pp. 179-93. For example, while recognizing the use of epideictic rhetoric in 1 Thessalonians he still tries to see the overarching framework in terms of ancient "friendship" letters, despite the lack of such terms in the letter (on which see pp. 159-61 below). He analyzes the material on the basis of Demetrius of Phaleron, *Peri Epimeneias*. This document, however, dates to the third century A.D. and is pseudonymous. There is no certainty that there were detailed conventions for writing friendship letters in the first century B.C. or, if there were, that these conventions would have been known widely enough to have affected Paul's writing. If there were such conventions, why does Cicero not seem to know them and why do the letters of Seneca hardly reflect such knowledge?

70. There are now six interesting reviews of Malherbe's commentary to be found at the SBL website as part of the Review of Biblical Literature for Sept. 2004. We will refer to them by author name and pages as they exist in each review.

Oratio 32.11-12). But in fact, as Mitchell points out, Dio's *Oration to the Alexandrians* is indeed a rhetorical speech following both deliberative and epideictic conventions. He is not really contrasting rhetoric in general with substantive philosophical or moral teaching. I would add that Dio is overtly distinguishing his own discourse from sophistic rhetoric. By contrast he is offering serious and substantial rhetoric.[71] He is not trying to replace rhetoric with moral philosophizing. Whatever philosophizing or moral exhorting he will do, he will do it in rhetorical form. Malherbe finds resonances in 1 Thess. 2.1-9 with the philosophical traditions of exhortation represented by Dio, but what he fails to note is that Dio only serves up such material within a rhetorical form and with a rhetorical sensibility about how he will say things and how he may best persuade his audience. To miss the tongue-in-cheek critique of sophistic rhetoric by a rhetorician is to miss something crucial. (2) As Mitchell shows, Malherbe makes a category mistake from a form-critical point of view. "For him parenesis stands as a counter-thesis to other proposals about the genre and purpose of these letters as either apocalyptic, rhetorical (epideictic, deliberative, or forensic argumentation), consolatory or didactic. Malherbe presents parenesis as a designation superior to any of these other options."[72] Indeed, he even tries to subsume consolatory traditions under the heading of exhortation/parenesis all the while discounting rhetoric and downplaying the apocalyptic dimensions of 2 Thessalonians 2. (3) Malherbe seeks to use the Church Fathers, chiefly John Chrysostom, to show that it was realized early on that Paul was writing pastoral documents, which is of course true but does not in any way (formally or in terms of content) distinguish these letters from Paul's other letters, nor does it rule out the use of rhetoric or apocalyptic or anything else.

The term "pastoral" describes the spiritual ethos or orientation of a document, not its genre or form. All of Paul's letters have a pastoral dimension to them, and all of them entail parenesis as well. This does not help us settle the issue of the form of his argumentations and acts of persuasion. (4) Mitchell shows how slippery is Malherbe's use of the term "parenesis" itself, including his use of the Greek term as found in the Church Fathers. Sometimes he sees it as a style of presentation, but then also maintains that it is also an epistolary type, and in addition a description of content in the document.[73] Can the term really be aptly used in all these ways? What is especially telling is that when Malherbe lists the features of a parenetic style (the call to imitate someone, antitheses, the reminder of the qualities of virtuous people, advice given to a son

---

71. On which point see B. W. Winter, *Are Paul and Philo among the Sophists?* (Cambridge: Cambridge University Press, 1996). See Mitchell's critique, p. 2.

72. Mitchell, p. 3 of review.

73. Mitchell, p. 4.

by a father) he provides us with a list of things that can just as easily be said to characterize deliberative rhetoric (call to imitation, advice, comparison, antithesis) or epideictic rhetoric (reminder of the virtues of someone). In other words, these features of form and content are not specific to parenesis. They are also found in rhetorical as well as non-rhetorical documents. (5) Mitchell shows that Theodoret uses "parenesis" of advice or exhortation and as such to refer only to a specific part of 1 Thessalonians: 4.1–5.12.[74] In other words he uses the term of content, not style or the form of the whole letter. Malherbe has no support from the Fathers for his use of the term for something other than some of the content of the document. (6) Mitchell demonstrates that the Fathers do not place Paul's letters within a tradition of consolatory letters even while they recognize that Paul offers consolation in various places in his letters, including in the Thessalonian correspondence.[75] (7) The attempt to minimize the eschatological and apocalyptic material in 1 Thess. 4.13–5.11 and 2 Thess. 2.1-12 by suggesting that they are not apocalyptic but rather pastoral in function sets up a false dichotomy. They are apocalyptic in substance, but the material is used for a pastoral end or aim.[76] "But Chrysostom and Theodoret saw these sections as pastoral *precisely because they were so vividly* apocalyptic."[77] The end result of this extensive critique is that Malherbe's commentary is a muddle when it comes to the form of the material, has not demonstrated that either 1 or 2 Thessalonians is a parenetic letter as a whole, misreads what the Fathers say about such matters, and neglects the fact that Church Fathers such as Theodoret and Chrysostom were perfectly clear about the rhetorical character of these Pauline letters and realized that recognizing their rhetorical character was crucial to understanding them.

C. Wanamaker points out that Malherbe's commentary gives far less space to 2 Thessalonians than to 1 Thessalonians, perhaps because Malherbe finds far fewer connections to the moral philosophers in 2 Thessalonians, citing fewer than thirty parallels there, compared to nearly a thousand in 1 Thessalonians.[78] This strongly suggests that it is really only 1 Thessalonians that bears comparison with the tradition of moral philosophy and "pastoral" counsel of the era.

But what all the reviewers rightly go on to add is that Malherbe has shown that in these letters Paul uses to a remarkable degree terms and phrases which had resonances with pagan religious and moral vocabulary. This is the great contribution of Malherbe's study. It shows how these letters would be

74. Mitchell, pp. 6-7.
75. Mitchell, pp. 8-9.
76. Mitchell, p. 10.
77. Mitchell, p. 10.
78. Wanamaker, p. 2 of critique.

words on target for the largely Gentile audience in Thessalonike. Malherbe also realizes that Paul uses the moral philosophical language of his day in his own way, recontextualizing the material so that it illuminates his gospel and his pastoral message. Paul is not merely bandying about certain buzzwords or phrases to impress his pagan converts.[79] The detailed attention to exegetical particulars also makes Malherbe's commentary a very valuable study.

If, then, Malherbe's proposal about the genre of these documents must be rejected, what should we say about them? There has been now, for the last twenty or so years, a detailed discussion about the rhetorical character of these documents and it has born considerable fruit. At the outset it must be stressed that epistolary categories are really not adequate to explain much of what we find in these documents, as the methodological debate attests. For one thing, as we have already pointed out in critique of Malherbe, while these documents certainly include parenesis (advice/exhortation), that characterizes only a minority of the material in the documents. For another thing, the attempt to subsume 1 Thessalonians 1–3 under the heading of a thanksgiving period or a triple period simply does not account for the actual content we find in those chapters. To be sure, 1.2-3 speaks of always thanking God (and two verses is about the normal length of wish prayers in ancient Greco-Roman letters), and 2.13 adds one sentence of something else Paul is thankful for, as does 3.9,[80] which leads to a concluding benediction or prayer wish in 3.11-13. Thus one can say that prayer language frames this entire section (chs. 2–3 and 3.11-13). But the vast majority of material in these chapters is not devoted to prayer or even rehearsing things for God in a prayer or even a prayer report. In fact, I would say that only in 3.11-13 is God directly prayed to or invoked. The rest of the material in even these few verses is a report of what Paul always does or has prayed.

Rather what we have in 1 Thess. 1.4–3.10 is a narrative in chronological order of a series of events presented in a personal and pastoral way.[81] This narrative serves as a reminder of the pertinent facts that the Thessalonians need to reflect on. In other words in terms of form, we have here a proper rhetorical *narratio,* as we shall see further in the commentary itself.

Apart from the opening and closing greetings, including the greeting

79. See the review by J. Lambrecht, p. 2.
80. One must be cautious here, because what 1 Thess. 3.9 does is to tell the Thessalonians what Paul now can be thankful to God for, and 1.2-3 and 2.13 again speak to the human audience telling them what Paul is thankful for. These are not in fact words directed to God. Only in 1 Thess. 3.11-13 are God and his activity actually invoked directly.
81. This in fact has been recognized for a long time by those who studied Paul's letters with a knowledge of Greco-Roman rhetoric. A good example from the nineteenth century is J. B. Lightfoot. In his commentary on 1 Thessalonians he calls 1 Thess. 1.2–3.11 the *narratio* or narrative portion of the letter. See his *Notes on the Epistles of St. Paul* (Winona Lake: Alpha, reprint), pp. 5, 8.

with a holy kiss (1 Thess. 1.1; 5.26; 2 Thess. 1.1-2), the reference to the wish prayer (1 Thess. 1.2-3; 2 Thess. 1.3-4), the charge to have the letter read aloud to all the brothers (1 Thess. 5.27), and the reference to the autograph with closing greeting (2 Thess. 3.17), there is little evidence of the use of regular epistolary conventions in these documents. Equally important, when epistolary forms are used, as in the wish prayer (or even more in the invocation or benedictions) they are modified in a thoroughly Christian manner. Paul makes the formal epistolary conventions his own, serving his pastoral purposes. The overwhelming majority of the content of these documents does not submit to epistolary analysis because it does not in the main reflect those highly stylized and formal conventions. Rather these documents to a far greater degree reflect rhetorical conventions.

It will be argued in this commentary that we have two different sorts of rhetoric in 1 Thessalonians and 2 Thessalonians. The former is an example of epideictic rhetoric, while the latter is clearly an example of deliberative rhetoric. This to a very significant degree accounts for the differences between these two documents.

The Genre and Purposes of 1 Thessalonians

In the Greek setting, epideictic rhetoric was by its nature the rhetoric of display and demonstration, the rhetoric of praise and blame. It was also especially appropriate for a document that was intended to be a part of and to inculcate worship. G. A. Kennedy puts it this way: "Epideictic is perhaps best regarded as including any discourse, oral or written, that does not aim at a specific action or decision but seeks to enhance knowledge, understanding, or belief, often through praise or blame, whether of persons, things, or values. It is thus an important feature of cultural or group cohesion. Most religious preaching . . . can be viewed as epideictic."[82]

It is clear enough that one of the major rhetorical aims of 1 Thessalonians is to remind the audience of much that they already know, and then in chs. 4–5 to enhance that knowledge and understanding (see 1.4; 2.1, 9, 10; 4.1, 13; 5.1). The pedagogical tone of the letter and its deep warm emotion is precisely what we would expect in a piece of epideictic oratory meant to help people remember, understand, and learn. This letter reflects no evidence of "opponents" in the traditional Pauline sense, nor of a divided congregation, nor of any attempt to get the audience to change policy or orientation (which requires deliberative rhetoric). This is a progress-oriented letter of encouragement, not a problem-

---

82. G. A. Kennedy, "The Genres of Rhetoric," in *Handbook of Classical Rhetoric in the Hellenistic Period 330 B.C.–A.D. 400*, ed. S. E. Porter (Leiden: Brill, 1997), pp. 43-50, here p. 45.

solving letter, unlike 1 Corinthians or 2 Thessalonians. The peroration in
1 Thess. 5.16-22 stresses that the recipients need to continue to persevere in
things they are already doing — holding on to the good they have already
grasped and avoiding the evil.

L. Rosenfield reminds us that epideictic rhetoric celebrates what is already true or exists, and attempts to inculcate an attitude of awe, respect, even
wonder in the listener in regard to these realities. Effusive language is in part the
tool used to inculcate this attitude of awe or even reverence in the listener.
Epideictic is the language of someone bearing witness to a reality or truth, and
the audience is those who are meant to take it to heart and commit to memory
what they have heard (as Parmenides fragment 6 says quite clearly). Again this
is precisely what we find in 1 Thessalonians, where the call to commit to memory and to learn from what is remembered is very clear. This sort of rhetoric, if
done well, creates in the audience "a beholding wonder, an overwhelming sense
of exultation that sweeps over us when we catch a glimmer of excellence abid-
ing in a familiar object or event. This jubilation is on the order of an admiring
gratitude. . . . And it is this re-creation of aesthetic revelation that the Greek orator sought to achieve through *em-phasis,* a sharing with the community of his
wonder-at-invisibles, an act of testimony that took precedent over simple persuasion."[83]

Epideictic rhetoric is primarily about testimony and appreciation, not
primarily about argumentation and proofs. But the audience is not just to appreciate. They are being reminded of what is true — what they already do or
ought to know. They are being urged to embrace these truths or virtues.
Epideictic rhetoric triggers remembrance of fundamental things. While in the
Roman setting this sort of rhetoric could have a practical function (for example
as an encomium at a funeral),[84] in the Greek setting it was far more often used
for the purpose of offering a panegyric to a god or a hero of the past or some
great virtue or the like (see Quintilian, *Inst. Or.* 3.7.3).

As Quintilian reminds us, epideictic rhetoric is not the rhetoric that seeks
to deal with an issue or a problem. The arguments in an epideictic piece may
bear a semblance of a proof, but since displaying and expositing one's subject is
the function of this rhetoric, it is not noted for syllogistic logic or disproving a
point. "The proper function of panegyric is to amplify and embellish its

---

83. L. Rosenfield, "The Practical Celebration of Epideictic," in *Synoptic History of Classical Rhetoric,* ed. J. J. Murphy (Davis: Hermagoras, 1983), pp. 131-55, here p. 138.

84. In fact, in a Roman setting epideictic rhetoric was primarily and sometimes almost
exclusively, used for encomia or funeral oratory. See Kennedy, *The Art of Rhetoric,* pp. 21-23.
This is perhaps why Paul does not really use epideictic rhetoric when he is addressing the
Christians in Rome. See B. Witherington and D. Hyatt, *The Epistle to the Romans* (Grand
Rapids: Eerdmans, 2004), pp. 1ff.

themes" (*Inst. Or.* 3.7.6). Amplification and embellishment usually took the form of hyperbole (use of "all" or "always" words as in 1 Thess. 5.16-22), as well as the use of a good deal of repetition for emphasis. In general, epideictic rhetoric is highly emotional and meant to inspire the audience to appreciate something or someone, or at the other end of the spectrum, despise something or someone. Epideictic rhetoric seeks to charm or to cast odium.

Aristotle says that one of the first aims of such rhetoric is to excite admiration of someone or something (*Rhet.* 3.2.5). Paul pulls out the stops in 1 Thessalonians trying to strengthen the emotional bonds with his audience, to reassure them they are on the right track, to remind them of how gentle he was with them while he was present, and so forth. All this is quite apropos in epideictic rhetoric. It needs to also be borne in mind that in epideictic oratory (especially in its funerary form), it was common to speak about the state and location of the deceased, which is precisely what we find in 1 Thess. 4.13-18. Reassuring words about the deceased indeed was almost de rigueur for such oratory.

Quintilian reminds us that the same form of ornamentation will not suit the three different species of rhetoric (*Inst. Or.* 8.3.11-12). Listen to his description of the aim of epideictic rhetoric:

> For the oratory of display aims solely at delighting the audience, and therefore develops all the resources of eloquence and deploys all its ornament, since it seeks not to steal its way into the mind nor to wrest the victory from its opponent, but aims solely at honor and glory. Consequently the orator, like the hawker who displays his wares, will set forth before his audience for their inspection, no, almost for their handling, all his most attractive reflections, all the brilliance that language and the charm that figures can supply, together with all the magnificence of metaphor and the elaborate art of composition that is at his disposal.

In general what one would expect from epideictic rhetoric is more use of metaphor, use of more elaborate, euphonious, elegant, or attractive words, and arrangements of words to "sound" better. Epideictic rhetoric does not have its setting in debate, discussion, dialogue, or diatribe. It is unlike forensic and deliberative rhetoric in this respect. It is found in monologues, speeches, lectures, or sermons offered to an audience without expectation of direct response. It is more like an official pronouncement or a letter of comfort and encouragement meant to be received, believed, appreciated, and appropriated, but not to be responded to in the form of correspondence or debate.

Since there are not really formal proofs in an epideictic piece of oratory, there is not really a requirement to offer a thesis to be "proved." Nevertheless, in the *exordium* it was appropriate to offer a preview of coming attractions — including a remark about what the hearers will be reminded of. We see this in

1 Thess. 1.3 with the announcement of remembrance — remembrance before God leads to rehearsal of what is remembered, and then the hearers remember and embrace their past, their heritage, and their values.

This applies to the whole document but is particularly at work in the long *narratio* in chs. 1–3. From a rhetorical point of view, a *narratio* is a statement of pertinent facts relevant to the discourse (Quintilian, *Inst. Or.* 4.2.31; Aristotle *Rhet.* 3.16.1-11). Here we have a reminder of the story thus far about Paul's relationship with the Thessalonians.[85] The particular sort of *narratio* we are dealing with seeks to win the belief of the audience or reaffirm what they already know to be true about themselves (see *Rhetorica ad Herennium* 1.8.12). Quintilian stresses that "praise in general terms may be awarded to noble sayings and deeds. . . . I do not agree that panegyric concerns only questions regarding what is honorable" (*Inst. Or.* 3.7.28).[86]

Throughout this discourse the audience is being asked to learn or remember, not to change their conduct. Exhortations toward the end of the epideictic discourse were appropriate and to be expected and amounted to reminding, informing, or praising certain kinds of behavior, not asking for a change in belief or behavior. Epideictic oratory tended to focus on the core values of a society or some subset of a society and sought to affirm, reaffirm, or even inculcate such values (see Aristotle, *Rhetoric* 2.18.1391b.17). It was surely a form of rhetoric heard frequently in Thessalonike, in view of the occasions for panegyric not only in connection with cultic "ovations" to one god or another (including the emperor), but also due in festivals celebrating the city and in the games.

With the rise of the empire and the demise of any sort of real democracy (except in the micro-assemblies of small groups that were not official political bodies, such as church meetings), epideictic oratory became an increasingly important feature of the culture, especially with the increase in Olympic style games and the spread of the emperor cult. It is thus a form of rhetoric which would be very familiar to both Paul and his converts in Thessalonike.

Rhetorical analysis of 1 Thessalonians in the last twenty-five or so years has led most scholars to the conclusion that 1 Thessalonians is a fairly clear example of epideictic rhetoric (though a few have opted for deliberative rhetoric).[87] Several features of the letter which lead to this conclusion can be mentioned. First, Paul praises or thanks God for the Thessalonians' virtues right at

---

85. On the then–now motif used regularly in the NT see P. Tachau, *"Einst" und "Jetzt" im Neuen Testament* (Göttingen: Vandenhoeck und Ruprecht, 1972).

86. Notice how very easily the epideictic showpiece on love in 1 Corinthians 13 leads immediately into the imperative in 14.1 ("follow the way of love . . .").

87. See, e.g., F. W. Hughes, "The Rhetoric of 1 Thessalonians," in *The Thessalonian Correspondence*, pp. 94-116, here p. 97, and especially the overview of rhetorical analyses in S. Walton, "What Has Aristotle to Do with Paul? Rhetorical Cricitism and 1 Thessalonians," *Tyndale Bulletin* 46 (1995): 229-50.

the outset of the document. Their work produced by faith, their labor prompted by love, and their persistence/endurance inspired by hope are already put forward in 1.3. Paul returns to this familiar triad of faith, hope, and love in speaking again about Christian virtue in 1 Corinthians 13.[88] Second, note the effusiveness and hyperbole in the opening and elsewhere in this document. Paul uses the words "all," "always," and "everywhere" (e.g., 1.8 and especially the *peroratio* in 5.16-22). Third, notice the ongoing stress on anamnesis, on remembering. The Thessalonians are even reminded how they imitated Paul and became models for others in their faith and faithfulness. The call to imitation or modeling would be a deliberative move, but the reminder about it is clearly epideictic, appealing to a virtue already demonstrated.

Here is where we note that the often troublesome 1 Thess. 2.14-16 is simply another example in the *narratio* of how the Thessalonians have exhibited honorable mimesis, in this case imitating the suffering Jewish Christians in Judea, while "the Jews" are to be blamed for their conduct. This is a textbook example of an epideictic contrast between praiseworthy and blameworthy behavior.[89] When one sees the rhetorical function of that material, which is certainly vehement but is not a broadside against all Jews, and when one realizes that outbursts of strong emotion are normal in an epideictic oration, especially where human suffering and loss are involved, one realizes that there is no need for an interpolation theory at all. This document in some ways sounds like the impassioned heart cry of a worrying parent, who is suffering the loss of contact with children (2.17) and is suffering even more because the children are or have been suffering. Pathos, the appeal to the deeper emotions, is common throughout an epideictic speech, whereas it is more confined to the *peroratio* in a deliberative speech.

A *narratio* is meant to state those facts which have generated the discourse. They make clear to a certain extent the rhetorical situation or exigency that prompted the discourse. In forensic rhetoric the *narratio* would of course focus on the "facts" from the past relevant to the legal case, and in deliberative rhetoric there might be mention of facts which constitute the problem and have prompted writing or speaking. But in epideictic rhetoric the *narratio* serves to reaffirm and remind the audience of what they already know to be true about themselves (see *Rhetorica ad Herennium* 1.8.12). There is to be a distinct account of facts, persons, times, and places related in a positive way (Quintilian, *Inst. Or.* 4.2.36), and there is a stress on conveying the mental attitudes and motives of the one who is speaking or writing (cf. Aristotle, *Rhet.* 3.16.10; Quintilian, *Inst. Or.* 4.2.52). Cicero says that this sort or form of *narratio*

---

88. On which see B. Witherington, *Conflict and Community in Corinth* (Grand Rapids: Eerdmans, 1995), pp. 264-73. Notice as well how at the end of the *narratio* Paul reemphasizes that two of these virtues were confirmed by Timothy's visit (3.6-7).

89. See rightly Hughes, "Rhetoric of 1 Thessalonians," p. 102.

"should possess great vivacity, resulting from fluctuations of fortune, contrast of characters, severity, gentleness, hope, fear, suspicion, desire . . . pity, sudden change of fortune, unexpected disaster, sudden pleasure, a happy ending to the story" (*De Inventione* 1.27).

Even a casual reading of 1 Thess. 1.4–3.10 shows that Paul has produced a *narratio* which embodies many of these traits and emotions. "It thus seems no accident that Paul narrates at length in honorific and affective language the changes of fortune he experienced (2:17-18), his gentleness (2:7-8), the early disaster in Philippi (2:2), and not least his pleasure at Timothy's news of the Thessalonians' continued faithfulness and love (3:6-7)."[90] The intent of the *exordium*, which here, as in some of Paul's other letters (e.g., 1 Corinthians) overlaps with the epistolary wish prayer/thanksgiving, was to establish rapport with the audience so that they would be well-disposed to hear the rest; indeed it was intended as a *captatio benevolentiae* — intended to capture the goodwill of the audience. Paul does this by praising and giving thanks for the Thessalonians' work, perseverance, and triadic virtues.

There is no trace of Pauline opponents in this letter, in the sense of Christian rivals, but there is a deep concern about pressure and persecution, both past and in the future from outsiders, apparently mainly from Jews initially, but from Gentiles once Paul has left. Yet when Paul writes 1 Thessalonians, these things seem in the main to be in the past. What prompted in part the writing of 2 Thessalonians was persecution again rearing its ugly head and problems of faith and praxis arising as a result. 1 Thessalonians was written in a lull between such causes of suffering, a lull for which Paul is thankful, being even more grateful that his converts have weathered the storm. This letter serves to further bond Paul to his converts, as misery has helped created company or *koinonia*.

In this *narratio*, which takes up almost half of the discourse, Paul engages in inoffensive self-praise as well as praise of the Thessalonians.[91] He portrays

---

90. Hughes, "Rhetoric of 1 Thessalonians," p. 99. I agree with his critique of B. C. Johanson, *To All the Brethren: A Text-Linguistic and Rhetorical Approach to 1 Thessalonians* (Stockholm: Almqvist and Wiksell, 1987), pp. 159-60 that we cannot see all of 1 Thess. 1.2–3.13 as having the qualities of both an *exordium* and a *narratio*. There did however need to be a smooth transition from the former to the latter, and since we have such a transition already in 1.3-5, we have a general allusion to the past, which Paul will go on to recount. The *exordium* was to serve as a general introduction to establish rapport with the audience, with the *narratio* getting down to specific facts that were relevant and that prompted the discourse. This is what we find in 1 Thessalonians.

91. This was an appropriate part of epideictic rhetoric and of that general cultural ethos, however uncomfortable some moderns may be about those who toot their own horns. See Hughes, "Rhetoric of 1 Thessalonians," pp. 101-2. On the conventions of inoffensive self-praise see Witherington, *Conflict and Community in Corinth*, pp. 432-37. On this convention one should especially consider Plutarch's famous treatise *On Inoffensive Self Praise*.

himself as hard-working, faithful, and showing parental concern and compassion, while the Thessalonians are portrayed as faithful under pressure and persecution — all things which call for praise. "Thus the function of the *narratio* is to recount the events in Paul's and the Thessalonians' common past that showed there had been good reason for the Thessalonians to have 'full assurance' (1:5) when their apostle founded the church by means of *logos*, 'power', and the Holy Spirit."[92] The *narratio* is brought to a close with one of the standing topics of such epideictic speeches — praise for standing firm (the theme is repeated in 5.8), something Paul turns into a full-blown *peroratio* in that much later piece of Pauline rhetoric in Eph. 6.10-18.

Honorific prayers are a very normal part of epideictic rhetoric, not least in funeral oratory, and one form they take is an appeal to the deity to act in some way to strengthen the audience, especially if they are suffering loss or suffering in some other way. This is precisely what we find in 1 Thess. 3.11-13. Just as the opening thanksgiving prayer gave a preview of what is to come in the *narratio*, so in 3.11-13 we have a preview of topics that will be addressed in the *exhortatio*, which is in 4.1–5.15. Epideictic rhetoric does not really require a "thesis" statement or proposition to be "proved," and we do not have one in this letter unless one identifies 3.11-13 as one. In my view this is not necessary since the prayer signals what is to come. "Increase in love" (3.12) presages the discussion in 4.9-12, "establish your hearts blameless" (3.13) presages the first exhortation/reminder in 4.1-8, and "at the coming of our Lord" previews the third exhortation/reminder in 4.13-18.[93] The prayer then serves as a transition to the beginning of the exhortations, which will continue in two more parts (5.1-11 and 5.12-15).

Exhortations in several parts were not uncommon at the end of epideictic pieces of rhetoric, even including funeral oratory. For example, Plato, *Menexenus* 246B-249E has at the end of the speech an exhortation to children to be virtuous, an exhortation against too much grieving, and an exhortation to the city itself. Such general instructions coupled with wishes and wish prayers were the very sum and substance of epideictic rhetoric, which often had a moralizing tone or intent.

Besides funeral rhetoric, one of the main sorts of epideictic speeches was the consolatory speech (*paramythetikos*). Menander points out quite clearly that such speeches could deal with the preferability of the next life to this one and the current blessed state of the dead (also in funeral oratory) and he advises that this sort of rhetoric, whether funerary or consolatory, should involve and end with prayer. 1 Thessalonians fits all these guidelines quite nicely.[94]

---

92. Hughes, "Rhetoric of 1 Thessalonians," pp. 101-2.

93. See Hughes, "Rhetoric of 1 Thessalonians," p. 105.

94. A majority of those scholars who have evaluated the rhetoric of 1 Thessalonians closely have concluded that we have epideictic rhetoric here. Besides Hughes, we may also

The epistolary and rhetorical structure of 1 Thessalonians can be outlined as follows:

Epistolary Prescript and Greeting — 1.1
Thanksgiving Report/*Exordium* — 1.2-3
Narratio — 1.4–3.10
Concluding and Prospective Wish Prayer *(Transitus)* — 3.11-13
Exhortatio — 4.1–5.15   (1) Holy Living — 4.1-8
                          (2) Holy Loving — 4.9-13
                          (3) Saints Asleep, the King Returns — 4.13-18
                          (4) "Ready for a Thief in the Night" — 5.1-11
                          (5) Honor the Workers, Live Peacefully with
                              Others — 5.12-15
Peroratio — 5.16-21
Concluding Wish Prayer — 5.23-24
Closing Greetings and Charges — 5.25-27
Benediction — 5.28[95]

What is immediately noticeable here is that we are dealing not so much with arguments as pastoral remarks by one who loves his new converts and is anxious about them since they are under fire. The pastoral tone and spiritual character

---

note W. Wuellner, "The Argumentative Structure of 1 Thessalonians as Paradoxical Encomium," in *The Thessalonian Correspondence*, pp. 117-36; R. Jewett, *The Thessalonian Correspondence*, pp. 71-78; Johanson, *To All the Brethren*, pp. 52-54; D. Patte, *Paul's Faith and the Power of the Gospel* (Philadelphia: Fortress, 1983), pp. 126-29; G. Lyons, *Pauline Autobiography* (Atlanta: Scholars, 1985), pp. 219-21, and among those who have written full-scale commentaries on 1 and 2 Thessalonians, Wanamaker, *1 and 2 Thessalonians*, pp. 47-48. Wullener tries to be even more specific by identifying the document as a paradoxical encomium on suffering with joy and waiting for the Lord while already experiencing spiritual fullness, taking 1.6 as the central axiom or thought of the discourse. I myself am not convinced by the idea that Paul is taking the approach here known as *insinuatio*. This discourse is nothing if not frank and direct. Paul is not playing his cards close to the vest or withholding anything until later. And suffering is not the main theme of the discourse, even though it is an important one. Also unconvincing is Wuellner's attempt to argue that 5.23-28 is the *peroratio*. Vv. 25-28 have an epistolary character and function and vv. 23-24 is a closing prayer.

95. A. Smith, "The First Letter to the Thessalonians," in *The New Interpreter's Bible*, vol. XI, ed. L. E. Keck (Nashville: Abingdon, 2000), p. 686 goes for a simpler analysis, identifying 1.1-5 as the *exordium* (but this fails to distinguish the epistolary prescript), 1.6–5.22 as the *probatio*, and 5.23-28 as the *peroratio* (but that ignores the closing epistolary elements). Unlike Jewett, Smith does not properly recognize the epideictic character of Paul's address here, and that affects how he views the rhetorical structure. See Hughes, "Rhetoric of 1 Thessalonians," pp. 109-16 for a very extensive rhetorical outline of 1 Thessalonians which differs a bit from our own in some of the divisions.

of the material is clear. This is no philosophical discourse or lecture. Nor is Paul trying to establish his authority (the term "apostle" appears nowhere in this letter). Not only do we have prayer reports and a wish prayer, we have benedictions as well, all of which is perfectly appropriate if this material is treated as a part of an act of worship (not a funeral service, but a regular act of worship) in which the heart and soul of this document serves as the discourse or sermon or homily for that worship service. While all of Paul's letters are pastoral in character, not all of them are homilies; many of them really are acts of persuasion involving arguments — for example, 2 Thessalonians.[96]

The Rhetorical Setting and Structure of 2 Thessalonians

For a variety of reasons, 2 Thessalonians has received less attention than 1 Thessalonians. This is unfortunate since it takes some of the themes of 1 Thessalonians and develops them further, and sometimes in new directions. This is not a rhetorical move that is without parallel in the Pauline corpus for we find the same sort of phenomenon in an even more evident way in Colossians and Ephesians.

It is unfortunate however that the discussion of the "problem" of the parallels between 1 and 2 Thessalonians has not usually taken into account Greco-Roman rhetorical conventions, because they can indeed illuminate the discussion. The proper question to be asked would be: what does a rhetorician do when his discourse is not fully understood or its implications not fully taken and applied? The answer is: give another discourse based on the first one, amplifying what has been said before but dealing with whatever problems which may have arisen from the first discourse and also in the interim since it was delivered.

In other words, the relationship between 2 Thessalonians and 1 Thessalonians would be that 2 Thessalonians is a deliberative discourse and therefore has a different tone and rhetorical species than the first letter, but based on the first and dealing with some of the same topics. This sort of rhetorical and situational development more than adequately accounts for both some of the literary similarities between the two discourses and also their differences. The two letters address two stages in a developing situation.[97] We will say more on this shortly.

---

96. See Malherbe, *The Letters*. His instincts are right that there was something different going on in 1 Thessalonians compared to say 1 Corinthians or Romans, Galatians, Philippians, or even 2 Thessalonians. But there are some interesting similarities between what we find in Ephesians, which is a circular homily, and this document, which is a homily written to a particular congregation.

97. See now especially Nicholl, *From Hope to Despair*.

From the rhetorical point of view one needs to remind oneself that this is an ongoing conversation, and while Paul may have been somewhat reticent to say all he was sensing needed to be said in 1 Thessalonians, in 2 Thessalonians, when it comes to trouble spots he is definitely less inhibited. This is not necessarily because the situation has deteriorated noticeably since the writing of 1 Thessalonians. It is probably primarily because Paul is beyond the opening salvo and is now able, having established rapport with the audience and reestablished contact through the first letter, to move on to second order moral discourse, attempting to make some corrections in the belief and behavior of the audience.

We must envision, I think, a fair period of time after Paul left Thessalonike, went to Berea, went to Athens, then to Corinth, heard back about his converts being under duress, and then wrote 1 Thessalonians (surely not before spring A.D. 51 if the Jerusalem council was in A.D. 50). Further time would have had to go by as well between the writing of 1 Thessalonians, its effect on the congregation (allowing time for them to get confused about the timing of the second coming issue and to have endured another round of social pressure and suffering), time for Paul to hear back about these things, and finally time for him to write 2 Thessalonians. The rhetoric we find in these two documents requires time for the social situation to have developed some since Paul left town and between the writing of the two letters.[98] It is not certain that Paul wrote 2 Thessalonians from Corinth. He could have sent it from Ephesus (see Acts 18.19-20), but Corinth is more probable. All this probably places 1 Thessalonians in late A.D. 51 or early A.D. 52 and 2 Thessalonians a bit later.[99]

2 Thessalonians is just as much punctuated with the language of prayer as 1 Thessalonians (1.3: thanksgiving, 11: prayer; 2.13: thanksgiving; 3.1-2: prayer). In this regard the worship character of the document is very much like the longer 1 Thessalonians. But unlike 1 Thessalonians things that require correction in both belief and behavior are attended to in 2 Thessalonians. Some of the recipients have misunderstood Christ's return and the events that will precede it, and some have been idle. The rhetorical exigency which leads to the writing of this second letter is clearly these problems, along with the continuing suffering the converts are enduring.

In his detailed study of the rhetoric of 2 Thessalonians F. W. Hughes demonstrates with some care that deliberative topics and ways of framing the acts of persuasion in this letter are operative here.[100] More helpful on the actual rhetorical arrangement and structure of the material is Wanamaker, who rightly

---

98. Though see pp. 183-85 below.

99. See pp. 35-36 below.

100. F. W. Hughes, *Early Christian Rhetoric and 2 Thessalonians* (Sheffield: Sheffield Academic, 1989), pp. 51-74, especially pp. 68-73.

recognizes that we must distinguish the epistolary prescript in 1.1-2 from the *exordium* that follows it, just as the epistolary postscript in 3.16-18 must be distinguished from the rhetorical material that precedes it.[101] The arrangement of the material between these epistolary brackets is determined by rhetorical rules about invention and arrangement.

Wanamaker, following Hughes and Jewett, sees 2 Thess. 2.1-2 as the *partitio*, the division of the *propositio* into two parts. They see no *narratio* in this discourse, which was in fact not required in a deliberative discourse. They also see an *exhortatio* on work in ch. 3. Some of this is helpful and correct, but some of it is not on target. For example I would suggest that 3.1-5 is an exhortation to pray and 3.6-12 an exhortation to stay away from busybodies and to work.

Few scholars have adequately appreciated what a difference rhetorical analysis makes in dealing with the difficulties of 2 Thessalonians, especially when one recognizes the rhetorical species of this document — which is deliberative.[102] Here we do indeed have the rhetoric of advice and consent, the rhetoric that deals with what is coming in the future, the rhetoric which seeks a change of belief and practice in the audience. The epistolary and rhetorical structure of 2 Thessalonians may be outlined as follows:

Epistolary Prescript — 1.1-2
Exordium/thanksgiving prayer — 1.3-10 — The Destiny of the Sacred
    Sufferers and the Terrible Tormentors
Propositio — 1.11-12 — Persuasion by a Praying Proposition
Refutatio — Argument One: Prelude to the Parousia — 2.1-12
Thanksgiving/Firm Living — 2.13-15
Transitus — Another Wish Prayer — 2.16-17
Final Request — 3.1-5
Probatio — Argument Two/*Exhortatio* — Working Hypothesis —
    3.6-12
Peroratio — On Shunning and Shaming without Excommunicating —
    3.13-15
Wish Prayer/Benediction — 3.16
Epistolary Closing/Autograph — 3.17
Closing Wish Prayer/Benediction — 3.18.[103]

---

101. See Wanamaker, *1 and 2 Thessalonians*, pp. 213-14, 291-93.

102. Donfried begins to grasp this in his essays, but still has offered the thesis that 2 Thessalonians was written by Timothy to explain some of the differences with 1 Thessalonians. See Donfried, *Paul, Thessalonica, and Early Christianity*, pp. 49-67.

103. One may compare the rhetorical analysis in Hughes, *Early Christian Rhetoric and 2 Thessalonians*, pp. 68-73, which is more detailed than this analysis. We are however agreed

As an example of how detailed rhetorical analysis helps explain some of the mysteries of Pauline discourse, consider the *exordium*/thanksgiving prayer (1.3-10). It was not an epistolary convention at all to give a "preview of coming attractions" in the opening prescript of a letter or in the opening health wish or prayer. Yet Paul clearly does use this portion of his discourses quite regularly to foreshadow what is yet to come. We may see this clearly also in 1 Corinthians 1, another deliberative piece of oratory.[104] Paul does this because he is mainly following rhetorical rather than epistolary conventions in these letters. An *exordium* serves the purpose of making the audience well disposed to what will follow by building rapport, but it also clearly serves the purpose of introducing or hinting about one of the subjects on which the rhetor will discourse (*Inst. Or.* 4.1.1). Quintilian says that one does not introduce all one's topics in the *exordium,* only "the points which seem most likely to serve our purpose." Only these "should be selected for introduction in the *exordium*" (*Inst. Or.* 4.1.23).

But Paul does not mention the problem of the idle in the *exordium* in 2 Thessalonians. This was a sore point or a sticking point apparently, and so Paul defers dealing with it until later in the discourse, after he has won over the audience on other points (namely, eschatology). This sort of modus operandi is called *insinuatio* and Paul also uses it in Romans, deferring dealing with the sticky issue of Jews and their future until chs. 9–11, and in Philemon.[105]

In 2 Thessalonians the *exordium* deals only with matters eschatological and the peroration only with the issue of idleness. This lack of overlap between the beginning and end of the discourse supports the contention that the problem of idleness should not be connected with or seen as a subset of the eschato-

---

that this letter reflects deliberative rhetoric. Strangely, the problem with Hughes's analysis of the authorship issue (concluding that it is post-Pauline) is that it does not properly take the rhetorical situation into account. For him the difference in eschatology is what really argues for differing authors in 1 and 2 Thessalonians. But 2 Thessalonians 2 is a response to the wrong sort of imminentism, not a comment on the same issues as 1 Thessalonians 4 or on the second coming in the same way or using the same rhetorical approach as 1 Thessalonians 5. The attempt to compare 2 Thessalonians with Colossians and Ephesians as both deutero-Pauline is a weakness as well since these letters are quite different from 2 Thessalonians. Finally, as Nicholl points out, Hughes simply misanalyzes the eschatological remarks in 2 Thessalonians 1–2. For example Nicholl (*From Hope to Despair,* p. 156, n. 37) stresses that "Hughes . . . could hardly be further from the point when he claims that 2 Thessalonians 1 is a warning, consisting of two options for readers: either believe Paul's witness and so be among the elect, or be among those who do not know God/do not obey the gospel and so suffer eternal destruction. Verses 6 and 8-9, which refer to a negative fate at the parousia, relate to unbelievers alone, whilst verses 7a and 10 which refer to a positive destiny at the parousia, concern believers alone. There is a sustained contrast between the destiny of believers and that of unbelievers throughout the chapter."

104. See Witherington, *Conflict and Community in Corinth,* pp. 82-93.
105. On which see Witherington and Hyatt, *The Letter to the Romans,* pp. 40-46.

logical problem. "2 Thessalonians is an intentionally worked-out document of deliberative rhetoric with a clear goal: to refute those who say 'whether by spirit or *logos* or a letter as from us, that the Day of the Lord has already come'. Additionally, the author has as a goal the correction of certain behavior . . . the behavior of people who evidently do not work for their living. . . ."[106]

One thing that most clearly distinguishes 2 Thessalonians from 1 Thessalonians is the latter's lack of a *narratio*, a rehearsal of pertinent facts. This was certainly not required or expected in deliberative rhetoric as it would be in forensic rhetoric and to a lesser extent in epideictic rhetoric. By further contrast, we do have a *propositio* in 2 Thessalonians, unlike in 1 Thessalonians, which also attests to the fact that these two discourses represent differing species of rhetoric. Deliberative rhetoric was all about proposing policy changes, affecting both belief and especially behavior, in terms of what was expedient or harmful, advantageous or not, honorable or shameful. Paul here, like rhetors before him, is urging his audience to believe and behave honorably and suggesting that this is expedient so that they may be honored and deemed worthy when Christ returns. As Hughes says, the appeal to what is honorable and advantageous is quintessentially a deliberative appeal,[107] and this discourse in 2 Thessalonians is of that ilk.[108] Thus like an ambassador for a great king, Paul sends his letter as Christ's emissary urging a change in the course of belief and behavior in Thessalonike. The first letter had largely been laudatory, this one must be more of an act of persuasion and exhortation.

Even children were trained in deliberative oratory. Quintilian suggests that children write down the scripts or narratives that they will use in deliberative oratory and then says "written narratives should be composed with the utmost care. It is useful at first, when a child has just begun to speak, to make him repeat what he has heard with a view to improving his powers of speech; . . . thereby strengthening the memory" (*Inst. Or.* 2.4.15). Repetition and recapitulation, sometimes in the pattern of repeating a theme with variations, was not only of the essence of rhetorical training of the young, but was also seen as a good rhetorical tool to reinforce concerns for an audience. Paul is using this kind of technique in 2 Thessalonians. Quintilian goes on to say about repetition: "What pleasure can an orator hope to produce, or what impression even of the most moderate learning, unless he knows how to fix one point in the minds of the audience by repetition, and another by dwelling on it, how to digress from and return to his theme. . . . It is qualities such as these that give life and vigor to oratory" (*Inst. Or.* 9.2.4).

---

106. Hughes, *Early Christian Rhetoric and 2 Thessalonians*, pp. 73-74.
107. See Hughes, "The Rhetoric of the Letters," in *The Thessalonians Debate*, pp. 234-35.
108. See the lengthy demonstration of the rhetorical species of this document in Hughes, *Early Christian Rhetoric and 2 Thessalonians*, pp. 51-74.

Quintilian goes on to stress that deliberative oratory, as Cicero had previously averred, could be about questions of expediency, but "I should prefer Cicero's view that this kind of oratory is primarily concerned with what is honorable" (*Inst. Or.* 3.8.1). It will be noted that both in the *exordium* and in the *propositio* the theme of honorable behavior that results in being counted worthy by God and in Jesus being glorified in his followers is stressed (2 Thess. 1.5, 11). Under the heading of what is honorable, Quintilian includes "right, justice, piety, equity, and mercy" (*Inst. Or.* 3.8.26), themes that will crop up in 2 Thessalonians. He adds that "religion, too, has its place in the discussion" (*Inst. Or.* 3.8.29), including persuasion about a change in beliefs and behaviors.

Quintilian also stresses that sometimes the advantageous course of action will seem better or more profitable to the audience than the honorable one, and so one will have to stress what is honorable. Paul deals with his converts on the issue of working and not relying on others (i.e., in terms of patronage) with an awareness of this proper rhetorical approach. He shows why working rather than clientage is ultimately a more honorable and advantageous course for the Christian. He also heeds the advice that sometimes the most effective way to persuade someone to do or believe something is by "pointing out the appalling consequences that will follow the opposite policy" (*Inst. Or.* 3.8.39). We will have some of that in 2 Thessalonians as well, particularly in the *exordium* and first argument.

It has been frequently noted that there is more stress in 2 Thessalonians than in 1 Thessalonians on the authority of the speaker (though the prescript in 2 Thessalonians does not trot out Paul's apostolic credentials). There is a good rhetorical reason for this. While there is no crisis over Paul's authority in Thessalonike, 2 Thessalonians, unlike 1 Thessalonians, is deliberative rhetoric and so we should expect some appeal to authority, however brief. Quintilian stresses "what really carries greatest weight in deliberative speeches is the authority of the speaker. For he who will have all persons trust his judgment as to what is expedient and honorable should both possess genuine wisdom and excellence of character" (*Inst. Or.* 3.8.12-13). In other words, if scholars had been aware of the rhetorical conventions Paul was following they would not have made the mistake of suggesting that the appeal to authority in 2 Thessalonians must reflect a post-Pauline author or situation or that there was some crisis over Pauline authority in Thessalonike.

As mentioned above, there was probably not a large interval between the writing of these two documents, for the rhetoric of the first letter is still fresh in Paul's mind, and is assumed to still be fresh in the audience's mind. Whereas in 1 Thessalonians 5 Paul has assumed and argued that he did not need to tell the audience about times and seasons with regard to the day of the Lord, in 2 Thessalonians Paul realizes that he does need to speak of this matter because apparently some were saying that the day of the Lord had already transpired. Such talk had a certain plausibility because Paul had spoken of the possible imminence of the "thief in the night" and of the indeterminacy of the timing. Paul refutes the idea by pointing out events that must transpire before the day of the Lord. The Thessalonians did not need further reassurance about deceased Christians' status in Christ,[109] but they did need further instructions about what would precede the parousia, as a way of staving off some form of over-realized eschatology. Clearly the eschatological teaching has gone from the more vague reassurances about the coming of the thief in the night to a more specific treatment of the precursory events.

In 1 Thess. 2.9; 4.11; and 5.14 the subject of the idle was raised, indirectly by mentioning his own working and the need for Christians to work with their hands and more directly in his final exhortation to warn those who were out of line, which included the idle. But in 2 Thess. 3.6-13 things are taken a step further rhetorically. Now Paul advises shunning idle believers and reminds the audience of the rule he gave while he was present with them ("let those who will not work not eat"). He gives a direct command as their apostle: they are to "settle down and earn the bread they eat." Furthermore, the non-idle are to take note of those who do not follow the advice given in this discourse (3.12-14) and shun and so shame them, warning them as fellow believers.

Either the work situation has deteriorated since the writing of 1 Thessalonians or more likely Paul is now more bold in his way of dealing with it. I am suggesting the latter reading of the situation because Paul tells us that he *already* noticed the problem while he was present and offered the dictum *then* that non-workers should not be fed. The development between 1 and 2 Thessalonians had more to do with what Paul thought was rhetorically appropriate in epideictic and deliberative rhetoric, with the latter also reflecting second order moral discourse. The problem had existed when Paul was present and when he wrote 1 Thessalonians, and now in 2 Thessalonians he must be direct in dealing with it. Again, nowhere in either 1 or 2 Thessalonians does Paul directly connect the work issue with the eschatological issue or suggest that the latter is the cause of the former.

On the whole then it seems likely that 2 Thessalonians was written not very long after 1 Thessalonians as a follow-up discourse, sorting out some things that were troubling and upsetting the *koinonia* of the community, a community which is still suffering and fragile and small and can hardly afford internal divisions over beliefs or social problems. 2 Thessalonians may also have been written from Corinth, but perhaps from Ephesus,[110] in the latter part of A.D. 52 or in 53.[111] Cumanus was exiled after his bloody tyranny in Judea in 52.

---

109. See pp. 126-30 below.

110. See pp. 9-11 above.

111. We may perhaps speak of a terminus ad quem in A.D. 54, when the young Nero came to the throne. Before 54 there was more pressure on Jews and others to avoid proselytiz-

If that had occurred by the time Paul wrote, Paul would have had no problem conceiving of a pagan ruler invading the inner sanctum of the Temple in Jerusalem, as he does in 2 Thessalonians 2. After all, Cumanus had killed many Passover pilgrims at the beginning of his reign. What could be next?

The Social Situation of Paul and His Converts in Thessalonike

There is something to be learned about both Paul's and his converts' social situation in Thessalonike from examining both Acts 17 and these Pauline letters. I have shown elsewhere the reasons to think that Acts 17 is historically substantive, not least because its author was a sometime companion of Paul.[112] We will consider Acts 17 first to tease out the social setting of our letters.

By the time Paul arrived in Thessalonike that city was well and truly enmeshed in the emperor's social network of patronage, benefaction, and reciprocity, the end result of which was that local officials would not take kindly to someone questioning the loyalty oath sworn to the emperor, even indirectly. The Acts account reports that here as elsewhere Paul sought out the Jewish presence, looking for the synagogue. What we are not told is that Paul went immediately to the synagogue.

It is likely that Paul took some time to first establish himself in the city, practicing his trade of working with his hands, which presumably involved leather-working or tent-making. 1 Thess. 2.9 suggests that Paul was not alone in practicing his trade. He may have worked in the house of a fellow Jew with the same trade (Jason, Acts 17.6), or he may have set up shop in the agora. In this way Paul could avoid burdening whatever converts he made in Thessalonike with having to support him or being beholden to some patron in the city.

It would appear that Jason was the first contact and convert in the city and his home the place where Paul was thought or known to reside. We can expand what can be said about Jason if we equate him with the Jason referred to in Rom. 16.21, who is in Corinth with Paul. The main reason for connecting the two is that in the same verse a man named Sosipater is mentioned, and in Acts 20.4 we hear of a Sopater (the shortened form of the same name) from Beroea

---

ing for Jewish forms of religion in the wake of the debacle in 49 in Rome. This pressure may have fueled the persecution of the Christians in Thessalonike, who would have been regarded as threatening the viability of the Jewish community there and indeed threatening the Pax Romana, hence the pagan official's treatment of Paul and his coworkers. See the judicious assessment of the whole issue of the authenticity of 2 Thessalonians in Jewett, *The Thessalonian Correspondence*, pp. 3-18.

112. On this see Witherington, *Acts of the Apostles*, pp. 503-11.

who is accompanying Paul. So these two Christians may have traveled to Corinth, having been enlisted as two of Paul's coworkers from Macedonia. We also learn from Rom. 16.21 that Jason is definitely a Jew.[113] As we shall see, it would appear that he must have been reasonably well off since he was capable of housing the church, apparently hosting Paul, and also posting bond after the disturbance in Thessalonike. What this story also suggests is that he was a known leader of the local Christians and so was held responsible for their behavior. He was housing those who had "turned the world upside down" (Acts 17.6), in other words those who were politically subversive.

The Thessalonian Christians suffered at the hands of fellow Gentile Macedonians. The root of *symphyletai* in 1 Thess. 2.14 means "tribe" (see Gal. 2.15).[114] To refer more broadly to fellow townspersons of whatever ethnicity Paul could have used *sympolites* (cf. Eph. 2.19).[115] This agrees with the apparent contrast in 1 Thess. 2:14 between "the Jews" and "your own countrymen." That verse with 2.2b shows that both Paul and his converts suffered repeatedly at the hands of non-Christians.[116] It cannot be ruled out that the "fellow countrymen" included some Jews along with the Gentile majority, but 2.14 probably refers not to the initial (Jewish) outburst against Paul and Silas which drove them from town but to subsequent pressure or persecution of the fledgling Christians left behind in Thessalonike. Thus Paul does not include himself or his leadership team within the group mentioned as attacked by the "fellow countrymen."[117]

The business side of Paul's social life would have put him in contact with both Jews and Gentiles, although observant Jews would often avoid leather-workers since they were viewed as unclean due to contact with dead animals' hides. There were guilds of leather-workers throughout the Greco-Roman world. For example, we have an inscription from the first century A.D. from Phrygia which speaks of the honors bestowed by "the most venerable guild of leather-workers" (IGRR 907). At Termessus in Pisidia a guild of leather-workers erected a statue to their benefactor (I Pisidia 93). In Lydia an association of leather-workers set up an honorary inscription at a member's tomb (SEG XXIX

---

113. See F. M. Gillman, "Jason of Thessalonica," in *The Thessalonian Correspondence*, pp. 39-49.

114. See Still, *Conflict at Thessalonica*, p. 221.

115. This suggests that the vast majority of converts in Thessalonike were Gentiles.

116. I quite agree with Still, *Conflict at Thessalonica*, p. 128 against Malherbe that Paul is not merely referring to inner psychological conflict or anxiety, though that is not excluded. No, this is about real non-Christian opposition to Paul's work there. See Wanamaker, *1 and 2 Thessalonians*, p. 93. On Paul and the *agōn* motif see V. C. Pfitzner, *Paul and the Agon Motif: Traditional Athletic Imagery in the Pauline Literature* (Leiden: Brill, 1967). The imagery is of course of actual physical distress or strain.

117. See the discussion in Gillman, "Jason of Thessalonica," pp. 44-45.

1183). It would appear that Paul learned his trade from his family, which he regularly practiced to support himself in new venues (cf. Acts 18.3), and it is very
plausible that his family had been given Roman citizenship because of their
contributions to the Roman cause, namely making tents and leather goods for
the Roman army in Cilicia.[118] Jews, unlike some high-status Gentiles (cf. Plutarch, *Pericles* 2.1), did not have a problem with manual labor, but it may have
been a hard sell for Paul to convince some of his higher-status Gentile converts
to work with their hands.[119]

We may envision then Paul coming to Thessalonike, setting up shop or
setting up in someone's shop, perhaps Jason's.[120] As he says in 1 Thess. 2.9, he
worked night and day in the shop.[121] He may have done this for some time before he spoke in the synagogue there. The invitation to speak in the synagogue
would not have come soon after he arrived in town or without someone in the

118. See Witherington, *The Paul Quest*, pp. 128-29. There were the same inducements in
Thessalonike as in Corinth to practice the trade there. It was a big cosmopolitan seaport
town, a commercial center, and a place where games were held. In short people needed temporary shelters (tents) there from time to time, as well as leather goods (sandals, wine con-
tainers, etc.). 1 Thessalonians 2 when compared to 1 Corinthians 9 suggests that Paul practiced his trade regularly in these sorts of cities, not least because he wanted to avoid slipping
into the role of a client of some wealthy patron.

119. On this entire matter see the discussion in Witherington, *Conflict and Community
in Corinth*, pp. 208-9. R. Hock, *The Social Context of Paul's Ministry: Tentmaking and Apostleship* (Philadelphia: Fortress, 1980), p. 36 points out that high-status Gentiles (including officials) were likely to stigmatize artisans as uneducated, like slaves, or of low social significance.
Artisans were not accorded status or invited to dinners at posh villas. This is true enough, but
the local guild of leather-workers, which Paul may have joined, would not have seen their
profession as ignoble, and some of its members would have been quite well-to-do. "Money"
talked in antiquity as today, and social drawbacks could be overcome as one climbed up the
social ladder through commercial success. Seaport towns like Thessalonike depended on
commerce and trade. The ultra-wealthy could afford to look down their noses at artisans and
merchants and say things such as that plying a trade left one with no time to develop virtue
and build one's social network of friends and clients and that bending over to sew was de-
meaning, even women's work (see R. S. Ascough, *Paul's Macedonian Associations* [Tübingen:
Mohr, 2003], p. 172). But there were many who did not feel that way about it in the Greco-
Roman world, and it may be doubted that the majority of Paul's converts felt that way, especially Jews and mercantile Gentiles. But some of Paul's converts may have been higher-status
Gentiles or clients of such people and were "idle," probably seeing such manual work as beneath them. Paul's exhortations on work reflect such a scenario (see pp. 122-24 below). His
references to idleness need not suggest that the Thessalonian Christians were all manual
workers (against Ascough), though doubtless a few were.

120. See the discussion in A. Malherbe, *Paul and the Thessalonians* (Philadelphia: Fortress, 1987), pp. 12-17.

121. On this whole matter of Paul's manual labor and its significance see Hock, *The Social Context of Paul's Ministry*, pp. 20-21.

synagogue becoming convinced that Paul could ably and appropriately address the audience on a Sabbath.[122] Paul ending up staying in Thessalonike long enough to establish a congregation there, longer than the few weeks that seem to be pictured in Acts 17, which apparently tells of the beginning and then the concluding three weeks of Paul's time in the city.[123] Here we may be helped by the study of R. S. Ascough, who notes that Paul uses language that comes from the universe of discourse of guilds and associations. It is not impossible that Paul proselytized within an association of leather workers as well as going to the synagogue, though he does not directly refer to associations being an issue in these letters. There is perhaps some possibility that the "idle" were those who refused to participate in an association and had been ostracized, but the explanation involving patrons and clients makes better sense.[124]

Acts 17.2 indicates that Paul was allowed to speak in the synagogue for three consecutive Sabbaths. This may suggest a certain amount of receptivity to at least some of what he was saying, not least because he was expounding the Hebrew Scriptures in the process. His message is said to have involved three main themes: the Messiah must suffer and rise, as the proper interpretation of the Scriptures suggests; Jesus did in fact die and rise again, as Paul and various eyewitnesses can attest; and therefore this Jesus that Paul proclaims must be the Messiah. Some Jews were converted (v. 4), as were a great many "devout Greeks," including some prominent women (vv. 4, 12). We may presume that these "Greeks" were synagogue adherents or at least occasional synagogue attenders.

This outcome provoked jealousy among some of the Jewish leaders (v. 5). Jews were already in a somewhat precarious or even marginalized position after various proclamations and actions of Claudius since A.D. 41. They could hardly afford to lose what local support they had among local Gentiles, especially among the social elite, whether men or women. Someone decided that drastic action against Paul was necessary, and they stirred up the "agora men," presumably the unemployed and often disgruntled day laborers that hung around the agora hoping for work.[125] Paul and Silas were hunted for to bring them before the town council, but only Jason and some other new believers could be found

---

122. Acts 17.1-5 does not tell us how soon after coming to town Paul spoke in the synagogue, nor does it really hint or suggest that it was nearly immediately upon arrival. Such invitations to speak were not normally offered to strangers out of the blue. Luke's account is in any case a brief summary of what happened, not a blow-by-blow description.

123. Lightfoot, *Biblical Essays*, p. 259 concludes from the success of Paul with the Gentiles, from his reference to a period of time of working night and day in the city, and from the notices given in Phil. 4.16 that Paul must have spent some months in Thessalonike.

124. Ascough, *Paul's Macedonian Associations*, pp. 162-90. This use of association language might also tell us something about not only Paul's social level but also that of the majority of his converts as well. On patrons and clients see pp. 43-44 below.

125. See Witherington, *Acts*, pp. 506-7. These may well have been Jews.

and were taken to the politarchs, who had the jurisdiction to deal with the situation with some dispatch. Paul and Silas were accused of upsetting the stability of the city and acting contrary to the emperor's decrees.[126] Either allegation could get Paul and Silas thrown in jail or out of town, and there was real plausibility to the latter charge. Paul was telling his listeners to turn from idols (1 Thess. 1.9), which would presumably include the statue of the emperor.

If this is what was alleged about Paul, he was unrepentant, for in 1 Thessalonians 4 and 2 Thessalonians 2 he continues to claim that things often said of the emperor are actually true only of Jesus. E. A. Judge has plausibly suggested that the decrees that Paul might have been accused of infringing, besides those prohibiting seditious language, were prohibitions against predicting a change of rulers or a coming new one. Tiberius had already issued such an edict earlier in the century forbidding such prophetic remarks (see Dio Chrysostom 57.15.8).[127]

Paul was a dangerous person to have around since the benefactions of the emperor might cease and the city might be censured if it harbored enemies of Rome. Rebellions had come from this city before and reprisals had been taken against it.[128] The politarchs not surprisingly took this matter very seriously and in effect banished Paul and Silas (a ruling which would expire within the year). This may well be what Paul is alluding to when he says that Satan hindered or blocked his return to the city (1 Thess. 2.18).

Timothy is not mentioned in the Acts account, and so presumably there was no ban on his returning.[129] Jason had to provide a guarantee (involving a cash security) of the good behavior of himself and his friends, and this in part meant that Paul and Silas would leave town quietly. It is no surprise then that Paul's letters would advise his converts to live quietly and mind their own business. It may be wondered whether he really wanted to go to off-the-beaten-track Beroea, but that is indeed where he went next, some fifty miles south and west of Thessalonica on a lesser road.

Both 1 and 2 Thessalonians are interesting documents for many reasons, but one is that they have little of the realia that we find in most of Paul's other letters. There are no real personal greetings, no mentions of the collection for Jerusalem, no references to the particulars of future travel plans, no rehearsal of or reliance on apostolic status. Perhaps in all these regards they reflect the fact that

126. See pp. 5-7 above.
127. See Judge, "The Decrees of Caesar at Thessalonica," who is followed by K. P. Donfried, "The Cults at Thessalonica," now found in *Paul, Thessalonica, and Early Christianity,* pp. 21-48.
128. See pp. 2-3 above.
129. It might also be suggested that he had not gone to Thessalonike with Paul on the first visit.

Paul's mission work in that region was in its nascent stages. But they do tell us a few things about Paul's social situation and his modus operandi and about the social situation in Thessalonike (e.g., there is some sort of leadership structure in the church, but it appears to be very primitive and nondescript: 1 Thess. 5.12).

Acts 17 suggests that there were some people of means and reasonably high social status among the first converts. This would certainly include Jason, who presumably hosted the church. Jewett is surely right that both the textual and the practical and archaeological evidence suggests that "it is essential to assume the presence of a few patrons whose houses were large enough to serve as centers for house churches."[130] Christians had to meet somewhere, and in homes, especially if the synagogue had expelled them, was the likely venue.

Aristarchus of Thessalonike is among Paul's traveling companions in Acts 19.29; 20.4; 27.2. Those listed in 20.4 apparently accompanied Paul to Jerusalem with the collection for the church there and so were perhaps persons of some social status and able to take time off and finance their own travel. This is probably the same Aristarchus that is in Rome with Paul in Col. 4.10 and Phlm. 24, where he is called a coworker of Paul. It is possible that he is also the Aristarchus (son of another Aristarchus) in a list of Macedonian politarchs. If so, he was a high-status person indeed. Perhaps he was married to one of the "leading women" in Paul's first group of converts mentioned in Acts 17.[131]

Part of the fabric and ethos of 1 and 2 Thessalonians is the theme of suffering, which is revealing about the social situation of both Paul and his converts in this city. Among other things it indicates that they were not of such high status that the residents of the city, even the minority Jewish residents, saw them as untouchable.[132] Almost at the outset of 1 Thessalonians (1.6) we are told that the converts there received the Word in much *thlipsis*. Despite Malherbe's suggestions to the contrary, this is unlikely to mean merely anxiety or mental stress.[133] In view of 1 Thess. 2.14-15, we must take this term in its normal sense of "suffering," which can include physical suffering, even persecution. It is true that *thlipsis* can refer at times to economic suffering or hardship, but

130. Jewett, *Thessalonian Correspondence,* p. 120.

131. See B. Winter, *Seek the Welfare of the City: Christians as Benefactors and Citizens* (Grand Rapids: Eerdmans, 1994), pp. 46-47.

132. In such a highly stratified society, those of lower social status almost never could afford to take someone of higher status to court, or in this case to the politarchs. One who was shamed in such an agonistic situation would become persona non grata and could not do business or be a client, among other things. The enmity conventions would come into play against one who failed in accusations against a high-status person. For example, in Corinth (Acts 18) Gallio refused to act on the complaints of the Jews, probably because Paul was a Roman citizen in a Roman colony city. The rules were different in Thessalonike, and the Jews were able to get some action taken against Paul, which, as 1 Thess. 2.14-16 shows, he was very angry about.

133. See Malherbe, *Paul and the Thessalonians,* pp. 46-48.

even in 2 Cor. 8.1-5, 13, where it is connected to extreme poverty, it is not a synonym for poverty but an accompanying condition of poverty. The context in
1 Thessalonians 2 points toward physical suffering. 3.3-4 refers to "these afflic-
tions/sufferings" (plural) which prompt the sending of Timothy.[134] This surely
does not mean mental anxieties or impoverishments but rather a series of epi-
sodes of suffering probably caused by persecution. V. 4 is quite specific: Paul
warned even while present that persecution would happen.

    1 Thess. 3.7 speaks of Paul's own distress and suffering/persecutions that
he was enduring as well, presumably at Corinth. This was nothing new. He had
suffered considerably in Philippi shortly before coming to Thessalonike, but his
Philippian converts had remained loyal and had sent him support at least once
while he was in Thessalonike (Phil. 4.16).

    2 Thess. 1.4 indicates there are still trials and suffering going on among
the Christians in Thessalonike. We now have a detailed and convincing study by
T. Still that the language of affliction in 1 and 2 Thessalonians "is best construed
as external opposition which Paul and the Thessalonian Christians experienced
at the hands of unbelievers." Still also adds that the opposition was at least initially instigated by Jews, and it was this which led to Paul being driven from the
city.[135] Still also suggests that after Paul left the abuse of Christians likely came
from the Gentile converts' fellow Gentiles "over their conversion to Pauline
Christianity and the resocialization process that this 'turning' entailed. Paul responded to the conflict in Thessalonica with apocalyptically laced and polemi-
cally charged rhetoric which may be described as pastoral towards insiders and
less than charitable towards outsiders."[136] The converts in Thessalonike were
being pressured to conform to social codes and norms of various sorts, not the
least of which was conformity to the patterns of support for the emperor's patronage through honoring him cultically. The Jewish Christians in Thessalonike may have perhaps been used to a minority status and would not have

---

134. Examining 1 Thess. 3.1-5 closely, two things come to light. First, Paul was surely
not in Athens when he wrote these remarks. Otherwise he would have said "to be left alone
here" rather than "to be left alone in Athens" (Donfried, *Paul, Thessalonica, and Early Christianity*, p. 212). Second, "we" in 1 Thess. 3.1-5 may in part be rhetorical in view of v. 5's "I could
stand it no longer." Was Timothy ever in Athens? Luke's account does not say so, so Donfried
(pp. 213-14) suggests that Paul may have sent Timothy from Berea back to Thessalonike or
sent him a message from Athens to Berea to go back (but Donfried thinks this less likely because it suggests that Paul had new information). If it is either of these it is more natural to
take the text to mean the latter, since Paul has also said that he agreed (with whom — Silas?)
to remain in Athens. It is Paul's anxiety about the volatile situation and his converts, not new
information, which causes him to send Timothy back, who may have been in either Athens
or Berea when the request for him to go back was issued.

    135. Still, *Conflict at Thessalonica*, pp. 287-88.
    136. Still, *Conflict at Thessalonica*, p. 288.

been forced to participate in these civic duties, but since the majority, perhaps the large majority, of Paul's converts in Thessalonike seem to have been Gentiles (some synagogue adherents, some not), social pressure may have been considerable on Gentile Christians to conform, and they may have suffered in a variety of ways, including physically and economically.

We see in 1 Corinthians 8–10 what could happen. In Corinth, some Gentile Christians were still going to social dinners in pagan temples, making contacts, building social networks, concluding financial arrangements, and drumming up business. Suddenly, Paul tells them not to do so anymore, that it is not a non-religious or neutral act to go there. I would suggest that the language about turning from idols to the living God in 1 Thessalonians 1 is not just theological rhetoric, but had a social and practical component along the lines of what we find in 1 Corinthians 8–10. This would entail not only not dining in pagan temples but also not participating in pagan religious festivals (presumably including the Olympic style games).[137] Suddenly, such Gentiles in Thessalonike who made such a commitment would become personae non grata with relatives, neighbors, and business partners. They would lose some of their social network and business relationships and might cease to be the clients of important city patrons and become idle. Paul's advice to them is clear: "work with your own hands, live quietly, and don't draw attention to yourselves."

Paul's stress on his working and on the need for all Christians to work (1 Thess. 2.9; 4.11; 5.14; 2 Thess. 3.6-13) and his not wanting to be a burden (1 Thess. 2.9) could be construed as suggesting that the Thessalonians were not as a whole well off.[138] Furthermore, Paul himself was trying to avoid the entangling alliances of a patron-client relationship by providing for himself and not putting himself into an unequal power relationship where he was at someone else's beck and call.[139] He wanted the gospel offered freely without charge and without it appearing that he was some hired teacher or after-dinner speaker who would say anything to get paid and make a living.

He wants Christians in Thessalonike to avoid becoming clients as well and thereby becoming idle and busybodies. While some of those he is critiquing in 1 Thess. 4.11 and 2 Thess. 3.11 may have been the "agora men," the idle day laborers, it is more likely that he was thinking of those who were idle because they were supported by some patron. Paul counters this by urging one

---

137. In other words, I think Paul was already enforcing the decree of James found in Acts 15 when he came to Thessalonike, the essence of which was: Stay away from pagan temples and the activities that go on there. See B. Witherington, "Not So Idle Thoughts about *Eidolothuton*," *Tyndale Bulletin* 44 (1993): 237-54.

138. Ascough, *Paul's Macedonian Associations*, p. 166.

139. Accepting support from a distant patron was another matter, since it did not entangle Paul in a local situation where he was an in-house teacher or the like. In other words, it did not encumber but instead enabled his freedom in ministry at the remote location.

and all to "do the good," which refers to giving benefactions to others. But of course one must have earned some income to be able to be such a benefactor, which in turn normally requires work.[140] More speculative but very possible is the suggestion that Paul's call for quietism is related to the idea that a client would be a sort of lobbyist, meddler, busybody for his patron since he does not need to work to provide for himself (cf. Epictetus 3.22.97). B. Winter concludes, "he is forbidding the life of a client for members of the Christian community."[141] While this is just a good conjecture, it makes better sense than the suggestion that some Christians in Thessalonike were idle out of belief that the parousia would happen at any moment and that there was consequently no point to work. This reads too much into 1 Thess. 1.10.

Juvenal (*Satires* 5.2.80; 5.110-13, 142-45) ridicules the sycophant client who is happy to be dependent on his patron, singing the patron's praises in public and private and dining at his table, while otherwise living the life of the idle. While Paul had a right to be paid for his gospel work (2 Thess. 3.8-9) he refused that right lest someone see him as a paid client. He set an example for all his converts to follow.[142] "Paul's purpose was to wean such persons away from the welfare syndrome."[143] This would also be a cautionary word to people like Jason and perhaps others who were of higher status not to encourage idleness by enlisting Christian clients.

---

140. On this entire matter see B. W. Winter, *Seek the Welfare of the City: Christians as Benefactors and Citizens* (Grand Rapids: Eerdmans, 1994), pp. 41-60.

141. Winter, *Seek the Welfare,* p. 51.

142. This was a different matter than receiving support from a Christian congregation in another town (see Phil. 4.15). Paul calls that a matter of "giving and receiving," which is to say an exchange between equals, a reciprocity, which is a whole different social convention than patronage and clientage. What is envisioned is missionary support that Paul received from the Philippians. See B. Witherington, *Friendship and Finances in Philippi* (Harrisburg: Trinity, 1994), pp. 123-24.

143. Winter, *Seek the Welfare,* p. 53.

COMMENTARY ON
1 THESSALONIANS

Epistolary Prescript — 1.1

Paul and Silvanus and Timothy to the assembly of Thessalonians in God the Father and the Lord Jesus Christ, grace and peace.[1]

Paul has taken the standard epistolary prescript and its three elements (addressor, addressee, greeting) and modified it. Except in Romans, Paul normally names or mentions others as co-senders or endorsers of the document that is being sent, but only here and in 2 Thess. 1.1 do we have three senders. As we have already noted, both Thessalonian letters are characterized by frequent use of "we" referring to the senders.[2] This probably does not mean that these documents are the product of a committee, but it is possible that Silas or Timothy helped in their composition. By naming all three Paul makes clear that he does not stand or speak alone in what he says in these documents. He speaks for a ministry team, which adds to the rhetorical force and authority of what is said.[3] To reject what is said is not just to reject Paul's word.

---

1. Faced with such a short and perfunctory prescript, some scribes expanded it to include words from 2 Thess. 1.2, either "from God the Father and the Lord Jesus Christ" (D, various western Witnesses including numerous minuscules) or "from God our Father and the Lord Jesus Christ" (ℵ, A, I, and numerous others). Yet we have witnesses of both the Alexandrian and Western text types that have the shorter reading (B, G, 1739, numerous others) and as Metzger, *TC*, p. 629 says, there is no good reason why these additions would have been omitted if they were original.

2. See pp. 9-11 above.

3. J. B. Lightfoot, *Notes on the Epistles of St. Paul* (Winona Lake: Alpha, reprint), p. 5 rightly puts it this way: "Silvanus and Timotheus . . . stood very much in the same position as St. Paul with respect to the claim which they had on the obedience of their Thessalonian converts: and thus the Apostle throughout uses the plural 'we beseech.' . . ."

It is notable that Paul does not mention his apostolic status, which was not an issue in these letters. Clearly the situation is not what it was in some of Paul's other churches and Paul does not feel the need to defend his status or role with the converts. He does not seem to think that there is resistance to his authority or word in this particular congregation, internal divisions over him and his gospel, or any real interpersonal issues between himself and his converts. All opposition comes from outside the congregation in Thessalonike.

Paulos, which in Greek means something like "short," was presumably chosen by Paul because of its closeness in sound to his Hebrew name Saul.[4] The name Paul occurs some 158 times in the NT, 128 of them in Acts.[5] Silvanus is the Latinized form of Silas, which in turn is the Aramaic form of the Hebrew Saul, so the two men had the same name. Silvanus was sent to Antioch with the Decree of James (Acts 15.22, 32), and it is probable that he continued to travel with Paul on this second missionary journey as Acts depicts it (Acts 15.40–16.40). Acts 16.37-39 indicates that he, like Paul, was a Roman citizen (which may explain the Latin name Silvanus even though he is a Jew). As such he could continue to represent the concerns of the Decree, namely that Gentile converts should avoid pagan idolatry and immorality and in particular stay out of pagan temples, where such things were known to transpire. The concern was in part that such activities would be a horrific witness to Jews by those who were part of the Christian assembly and would make things difficult for Jewish Christians and their witness in the synagogue whether in the Holy Land or in the Diaspora.

Silvanus was apparently Paul's primary aide in Philippi and Thessalonike (Acts 16.19, 25, 29; 17.4), even though Timothy joined the missionary tour in southern Galatia (16.1-3). We do not know what happened to Timothy when Paul and Silas went to Thessalonike, as neither Acts nor these letters tell us. Later Paul sent Timothy to Thessalonike from Athens (1 Thess. 3.2) to check on how his fledgling converts were weathering the storm there. Then Timothy and Silvanus rejoined Paul in Corinth (Acts 18.5) and participated with Paul in the spreading of the gospel in Corinth (2 Cor. 1.19).

Timothy, according to Acts 16.1-3, was a young man who had a Jewish mother and a Greek father in Lystra, where Paul found him. 2 Tim. 1.5 and 3.15 indicate he had been raised learning the OT Scriptures, having both a mother Eunice and grandmother Lois who had sincere faith.[6] 1 Cor. 4.15-17 indicates

---

4. He would not have chosen *Saulos* for the very good reason that that Greek word used as a name would be the butt of many jokes — it means to walk like a prostitute.

5. See E. Richard, *First and Second Thessalonians* (Collegeville: Liturgical, 1995), p. 37.

6. This might mean Jewish faith or Christian faith, apparently the latter. This would mean that Paul had converted these women in Lystra and then later Timothy as well, perhaps on one of Paul's subsequent trips through the town. Paul passed through twice on his first missionary journey, and then again on the second journey (Acts 16.3) at which point he picked up Timothy.

that Paul in the end was the one who converted Timothy, and 2 Tim. 1.6 makes clear he received "the gift of God" through Paul's laying on of hands. Some have made a great deal of Acts 16.3 because it says that Paul circumcised Timothy. It must be remembered, however, that Timothy's devout mother and grand-mother were Jews, so this was not inappropriate.[7] Paul may have seen this as making Timothy more useful in Jewish settings; he could be the Jew to the Jew and the Gentile to the Gentile just like Paul (1 Corinthians 9). It is clear from references like Phil. 2.22 and from the letters written to Timothy that Paul saw and treated Timothy as his special spiritual child and as one of his most reliable and steadfast partners in ministry. He includes Timothy in epistolary prescripts not only here but also in 2 Cor. 1.1; Phil. 1.1; Phlm. 1 (cf. Col. 1.1). Clearly he was an important figure in early Christianity about whom we wish we knew much more.

What is especially interesting about this prescript is that Paul does not re-fer to a Christian assembly in a particular place as in almost all his later letters, but rather to a people, "the assembly of Thessalonian people" (see the similar phrasing in Col. 4.16: "the assembly of the Laodiceans"). *Ekklēsia* was not a technical religious term, though we often translate it "church."[8] For an audi-ence overwhelmingly composed of Macedonian Gentiles "the assembly of Thessalonians" would have conjured up the old Greek democratic assemblies, which were called *ekklēsiae*. In common usage, *ekklēsia* was the coming together of the *dēmos*, not the group of people thus assembled.[9] Thus the term refers, of course, not to a building but to the active gathering together of believers for worship and fellowship. One might translate it here "the gathered assembly of Thessalonians in God." This reminds us once more that this letter was to be read out when the gathered assembly met for worship. It is addressed to the

---

7. The argument that Paul viewed Timothy as a Gentile and circumcised him anyway makes no sense of Acts let alone of what Paul says his views are on the matter in his letters, but see S. Cohen, "Was Timothy Jewish?" *JBL* 105 (1986): 251-68.

8. As F. F. Bruce, *1 and 2 Thessalonians* (Waco: Word, 1982), p. 7 puts it: "The noun *ekklesia* 'church, assembly' would not have any sacral association in the minds of recent con-verts from paganism." It is true enough that the term is readily found in the LXX as the trans-lation equivalent of Hebrew *qahal*, which also means assembly (e.g., Deuteronomy 23), but what is especially telling here is that Paul never assumes any knowledge of the Greek OT in the Thessalonian letters. He neither quotes nor directly alludes to it, presumably because his audience is almost all Gentiles who do not know the Scriptures. This means, I think, that we may conclude that Paul uses this terminology because of the resonance it would have with his Greek converts, many of whom did not know the OT at all. He uses it as a term that conjures up the old Greek *ekklēsiae* where rhetoric was the mode of discourse.

9. "Chez les Grecs, l'*ekklesia* rassemblement du *demos* la réunion, au sens actif, de l'assemblee, non pas le corps assemble." B. Rigaux, *Les Épîtres aux Thessaloniciens* (Paris: Gabalda, 1956), p. 348.

body at corporate worship and was not meant primarily for private reading like a personal letter might be.[10] The term was perhaps also deliberately chosen by Paul to distinguish this assembly from the *synagōgos* (cf. James 2.2).[11]

The use of *ekklēsia* is not of incidental significance, especially since Paul will address this audience in a rhetorical way, just as was done in civic assemblies, most frequently in deliberative form. The implication is that the audience must be treated with respect as free persons who must listen to the persuasion offered by Paul and respond appropriately. If he gives an epideictic speech, they are to listen, learn, remember, praise, be thankful, and further cultivate the faith and virtues praised. If he gives a deliberative speech, as in 2 Thessalonians, they are to listen to the arguments and see if they are persuaded to change their belief and behavior.[12] Either way, Paul is not offering up the rhetoric of empire and iron-fisted dictators laying down the law. He is inculcating freedom, decision-making, and nurture in the faith (cf. Gal. 5.1), respecting his converts as persons of sacred worth who are capable of making good informed decisions, by the grace of God.

Paul believed this not least because this assembly was "in God the Father and the Lord Jesus Christ."[13] "With this phrase Paul specifies that the *ekklēsia* of the Thessalonians is of a distinct character, which he defines in Christian and not OT terms."[14] The assembly of Christians meets in the presence of the Father and the Lord, neither of whom are the emperor, even though the emperor went by such titles (e.g., "Father of the fatherland," "Lord," "Savior"). This is reminiscent of the OT notion of God convoking an assembly of Israel in the desert.[15] D. Williams says this phrase expressed "the idea that the church was at rest in God. In the world it had no rest. It was a persecuted church."[16] It is worth pondering whether this idea was fresh in Paul's mind because in Acts 17.28 he speaks of God "in whom we live and move and have our being."[17]

---

10. Of course private letters were read aloud at home in this era, but not before a collection of friends and neighbors. Paul's letters, even Philemon and only excepting the Pastorals, are not private letters though they are deeply personal. They are letters for the church to hear and heed as a group.

11. It is no surprise that James, writing from Jerusalem, would use that term for the assembly of Christians. It appears that Paul however was the first to use *ekklesia* of the Christian assembly, and it reflects his vision of how to relate to Gentiles, using language that already has resonance for them.

12. On 2 Thessalonians as deliberative rhetoric see pp. 29-31 above.

13. See the similar phrase in the papyrus letter below, pp. 54-55.

14. A. Malherbe, *The Letters to the Thessalonians* (New York: Doubleday, 2000), p. 99.

15. See Rigaux, *Les Épîtres*, p. 348.

16. D. Williams, *1 and 2 Thessalonians* (Peabody: Hendrickson, 1992), p. 22.

17. On the Pauline character of the Areopagus address, though it is rendered to some degree in Lukan diction, see B. Witherington III, *The Acts of the Apostles: A Socio-Rhetorical*

God is named as "Father" in the prescripts of all of Paul's letters. Paul may be intimating that far more important decisions of eternal significance are being made in this "assembly" compared to those made in the *dēmos* in Thessalonike. The counter-cultural rhetoric in this letter starts right at the beginning. And it is not the emperor who really comes bringing grace and peace, or benefaction and pacification. It is the Father and the Lord. While this prescript makes evident Paul's high christology (the church is just as much "in" the Lord Jesus as in God the Father), the one in 2 Thess. 1.1 will spell out where grace and peace come from.

The greeting itself is short, but it reflects a modification of both the traditional Greek and traditional Jewish greetings, notably with the Greek form of greeting first (*chairein* seems to be related to *charis*), followed by the Greek equivalent of "shalom" *(eirēnē)*, presumably because Paul's converts are mainly Gentiles and he is their particular apostle. What is interesting is that Paul uses a noun form of these words, whereas pagan salutations were verbal ("hail," "be well").[18] In 2 Macc. 1.1 we find *chairein* coupled with *eirēnē* (cf. *2 Baruch* 78.2), so it would appear that Paul is modifying earlier Hellenized Jewish forms of greeting.[19] "Peace" here does not primarily refer to an inner state, but rather to the wholeness and connectedness that comes from being at peace with God, which is to say in right relationship with God.[20] There is probably a liturgical overtone to this greeting since the letter was to be read out in a worship meeting when the assembly gathered in a home.[21] Worship in the presence of God is the context in which these things are to be contemplated.

Commentary (Grand Rapids: Eerdmans, 1998), pp. 511-29. Much depends on whether one thinks Luke had firsthand information from Paul on what was said on that occasion. I think he did. But see E. Best, *A Commentary on the First and Second Epistles to the Thessalonians* (London: Black, 1972), p. 62.

18. See Malherbe, *The Letters*, p. 100.

19. Richard, *First and Second Thessalonians*, p. 39.

20. Best, *First and Second Thessalonians*, p. 64.

21. C. Wanamaker, *Commentary on 1 and 2 Thessalonians* (Grand Rapids: Eerdmans, 1990), p. 71.

The *Exordium* — 1.2-3 —
A Preview of Coming Attractions

The function of an *exordium* was to establish the ethos of the speaker and establish rapport with the audience. It was also to hint at themes that were to follow and signal the character of the rhetoric. As Chrysostom realized (*Homilies* on 1 Thess. 1.1) the Thessalonians are being praised here indirectly as God is being thanked for their virtues including their perseverance.[1] One may expect the rhetoric of praise and blame to follow. What was to be gathered from this *exordium* about Paul was how much he cared for his converts and prayed for them. The *exordium* flows naturally into the *narratio* which is why some have had difficulty in discerning where one stops and the other starts.[2] Paul already begins to "tell the story" in vv. 4-5, and those verses could be seen as the conclusion of a Greek sentence which began in v. 2. Nevertheless, it is perfectly appropriate to put a full stop at the end of v. 3, which is to be preferred in this case, and make a fresh start where the *narratio* actually begins, at v. 4 (so NIV, NJB, NLT, NRSV).

An *exordium* was to be just a succinct introduction to the discourse, and the ones in 1 and 2 Thessalonians certainly meet that criterion. The rhetorical

---

1. It is an interesting exercise simply to work through the *Homilies* of Chrysostom on Paul's letters since the Greek of Paul was still a living language for Chrysostom, and rhetoric was still a tool of proclamation. For Chrysostom there was no doubt that Paul was a master rhetorician. That Paul refers to the Thessalonians being praised for their great faith and hard work at the outset of his homily shows what sort of rhetoric he saw being offered in this letter.

2. See the comment in J. B. Lightfoot, *Notes on the Epistles of St. Paul* (Winona Lake: Alpha, reprint), p. 9: Paul "overlays one proposition with another, the second just emerging beyond the first, and arising out of association with it, but not always standing in a clear relationship [i.e., in distinction from] to it."

function was to make the audience attentive and favorably disposed to the speaker and ready to receive instruction from him (*Inst. Or.* 4.1.5). In epideictic rhetoric one would expect that some of the highlights of things to be praised or blamed in what follows would be enumerated here, and we are not disappointed, for this is the case in vv. 2-3.

There are striking similarities with another Pauline piece of epideictic rhetoric, namely Ephesians: "The combined *exordium/narratio* begins at [Ephesian] 1:3 with language of worship (1:3-14) followed by thanksgiving for, and petition on behalf of the recipients (1:15-19) and a doxology (3:20-21). Embedded within this praise and petition is a statement of facts or *narratio* that gives some specific perspectives. . . ."[3] We find much the same in 1 Thessalonians with 3.11-13 serving the same function as Eph. 3.20-21, rounding off the *narratio* in a worshipful way. It was perfectly acceptable to combine the *exordium* and the *narratio* or run them together back to back as *Rhet. ad Alex.* 1438b.15-28 and 1442b.28-32 make quite clear. This is especially the case in epideictic rhetoric, where the flow of the discourse is continuous since the rhetorician is not offering individual proofs or arguments for some specific thesis.

What is sometimes missed about the *exordium* is that this introduction to the discourse was addressed to the judge (*Inst. Or.* 4 prologue 3). The thanksgiving to God the Father and the Lord Jesus Christ is a most appropriate proem to a rhetorical speech, including an epideictic one, if God and Jesus are viewed as the judges, especially if one of them is viewed as coming to pass judgment on human beings (see 1 Thess. 4.16–5.11 and 2 Thess. 2.1-12). Paul's *exordium* then meets the rhetorical requirements admirably for what ought to be introduced at the outset.

There is inevitably in epideictic rhetoric a great deal of repetition because its "proper function . . . is to amplify and embellish its themes" (*Inst. Or.* 3.7.6). Paul will follow carefully the rules for praising God as well as for praising humans, with his converts and even himself and his coworkers coming in for praise in 1 Thessalonians. There will be much thanks, prayer (and blessing, benediction, and doxology), remembering, and reiteration on themes of "your works/labors" and the constancy of the future hope.

Quintilian, in enunciating appropriate topics to discuss in the midst of the praise of a human being, says that "reference to omens or prophecies foretelling their future greatness" (*Inst. Or.* 3.7.11) are important and appropriate. It can readily be seen how 1 Thessalonians 4–5 will provide us with that sort of material in this epideictic speech. The praise of virtues is of course high on the list of things that this sort of speech should include: "it is well to divide our praises, dealing separately with the various virtues — fortitude, justice, self-

---

3. R. R. Jeal, *Integrating Theology and Ethics in Ephesians* (Lewiston: Mellen, 2000), pp. 73-74.

control and the rest of them and to assign to each virtue the deeds performed under its influence" (*Inst. Or.* 3.7.15). This we will find throughout 1 Thessalonians in the *exordium,* the *narratio,* the *exhortatio,* and the *peroratio.* Quintilian adds that mentioning deeds or works that surpass expectation and hope is especially appropriate, especially what is done self-sacrificially for others (*Inst. Or.* 3.7.16).

It is interesting, from a Greco-Roman point of view, what Quintilian says about appropriate denunciations or blaming. He speaks of denouncing "a race which is a curse to others, as for example the founder of the Jewish superstition" (*Inst. Or.* 3.7.21). There is very little clear denunciation or blaming in 1 Thessalonians, but 2.15-16 certainly falls into that category. An epideictic speech was expected to include both praise and blame. While Paul is no anti-Semite and 1 Thess. 2.15-16 should not be seen as an anti-Semitic tirade, as it simply repeats an OT-style critique of Jewish leaders who oppose prophetic figures, it is likely that these words would have been heard by a largely Gentile audience against the backdrop that Quintilian mentions. Romans especially were noted for their anti-Semitism, including emperors. Paul is not speaking into a vacuum of "no opinion" or an ethos of "welcoming diversity" when he makes such complaints.

We are always giving thanks to God concerning all of you, making remembrance in our prayers continually, remembering your works of faith and the labor of love and the constancy of hope[4] *in our Lord Jesus Christ in the presence of our God and Father.*[5]

When one compares the prescript to this section of the document it is immediately apparent how both are rounded off with a reference to God the Father and the Lord Jesus, only here the order of mentioning them in v. 3 is the reverse of what we find in v. 1. The prayer or health wish commonly followed the initial greeting in a first-century letter, but sometimes it would be left out, even in an anxious letter. Consider the following letter of about normal length from just after our period:

> Sentis to Proklos her brother, greetings *(chairein)*
>   You did well, brother, giving the two *colophonia* to Anchoubis, and write to me about the cost, and I will send it to you immediately. I did not send meat to you, brother, lest I bid you farewell! Finally I ask you sir, respect me

---

4. E. J. Richard, *First and Second Thessalonians* (Collegeville: Liturgical, 1995), p. 46 offers the translation "the dynamism of your faith, the dedication of your love, the constancy of your hope," but this places too much emphasis on the virtues and not enough on the activities that result from them, which is where the emphasis lies in the Greek.

5. There are no real textual issues in this section of the letter.

and come with the Ethiopian. Let us rejoice, Farewell. So do not do otherwise, but if you love me come . . . and let us rejoice.[6]

Here we see the convention of saying something positive at the outset ("you did well"). This was as necessary in plain letters as in rhetorical speeches to establish feelings of receptiveness to what may follow, making the recipient favorably disposed, especially if a request was coming.

This letter also shows how perfunctory and brief such letters were in antiquity, which simply punctuates how long Paul's letters are, but sometimes letters could have more intellectually challenging content, and indeed sometimes they could even be deemed to come from God or a god. We have a remarkable partial inscription from the first century A.D. from the Sarapeion in Thessalonike which reads as follows:

> . . . to come into the shrine, it appeared that in his sleep Sarapis was standing beside him and instructing him, upon arrival at Opous to report to Eurynomos the son of Timasitheos that he should receive 'him' [i.e., the god] and his sister Isis; and to give to Eurynomos the letter which was under his pillow. Waking up he [the supplicant/worshipper] was amazed at his vision and perplexed about what he should do because of the political hostility which he had towards Eurynomos. But falling asleep again he had the same dream, and when he awoke he discovered the letter under his pillow, just as was indicated to him. When he returned home he returned the letter to Eurynomos and reported the god's instructions. Eurynomos took the letter and after hearing what Xenainetos [the worshipper] said he was perplexed . . . because of the political hostility between them. . . . But when he read the letter and saw that its contents were consistent with what had been said beforehand by Xenainetos, he accepted Sarapis and Isis. After he provided hospitality for the gods in the house of Sosinike, she received them among her household gods and performed sacrifices for some time. After her death, Eunosta the grand-daughter of Sosibos transmitted the [cult] and administered the mysteries of the gods among those who also were non-participants in the rites.[7]

This displays a social context in which discussions of important religious matters by letter, indeed even by letter seen as a divine revelation, were accepted and familiar. Here it is appropriate to add that not only did the Thessalonians believe in divine communications from heaven via dream, vision, letter, or other means, so also did Paul. It is also apropos to mention that the Thessalonians would have been quite receptive to the idea that they might be visited by a di-

---

6. P. Florida 17, *New Docs* 1, p. 58, my translation.

7. Translation and commentary in *New Docs* 1, pp. 30-32.

vine being, a matter of no small relevance when Paul begins talking about the parousia of Jesus later in 1 Thessalonians.

References to health wishes and even prayer and worship were also not uncommon in ancient letters. For example in a letter from the first or second century we read the following:

> Herm[es] . . . [to his patron], Greetings *(chairein)*
> and that you may always remain in good health in your whole body for long years to come, since your good genius allowed us to greet you with respect and salute you. For as you also make mention of us on each occasion by letter, so I here make an act of worship [*proskynēma*] for you in the presence of the lords Dioskouroi and in the presence of the lord Sarapis and I pray for your safe-keeping during your entire life and for the health of your children and of all your household. Farewell in everything, I beg my patron and nurturer. Greet all yours, men and women. All the gods here, male and female greet you. Farewell. Thoth 16th.[8]

This is of course a letter from a client to a patron and so its deferential and even worshipful tone is not unexpected. It is striking, however, that Paul's tone in 1 Thessalonians is equally worshipful and respectful even though Paul writes as a religious and social superior (or at least an equal) to his converts. The line in this letter about making an act of worship in the presence of the deities supports the translation we have suggested above, "in God and Christ." This letter also makes clear how common it was to write about praying for someone in antiquity, and we also note the health-wish and prayer combination at the beginning and middle of this letter.

In v. 2 Paul speaks of always giving thanks to God for all his Thessalonian converts, and then he speaks of "making remembrance in our prayers continually."[9] One is left with the impression of regular, persistent, and insistent prayer on behalf of the Thessalonian converts. The theme of remembrance is important in epideictic rhetoric — remembering key persons, remembering one's heritage, remembering what one has been taught, remembering one's virtues.

The verb *eucharistoumen*, "thank," was used in rhetoric from an earlier

---

8. The reverse side of the papyrus reads "to Sarapeion the lord." CPR 19, *New Docs* 1, pp. 56-57.

9. On the analysis of the so-called thanksgiving periods in this letter and elsewhere in Paul see J. Lambrecht, "Thanksgivings in 1 Thes 1-3," in R. F. Collins, ed., *The Thessalonian Correspondence* (Leuven: Leuven University Press, 2000), pp. 183-205. While Lambrecht is aware of rhetorical analysis of this letter, he chooses largely to ignore it or to critique Jewett ineffectively. He also makes the mistake of conglomerating thanksgiving reports with wish-prayers and the like. That Paul thanks God regularly and in a reasonably similar form in various letters is no surprise. But thanksgiving is not a formal category but a description of content.

era, including Demonsthenes' famous *De Corona* speech (*De Corona* 92).[10] The original sense of the verb was "do a good turn to," "return a favor," and "be grateful." Later, from the time of Polybius on, it was used to express gratitude/thanks.

To "make remembrance" (cf. Rom. 1.9; Eph. 1.16; Phlm. 4) has the same sense as our modern phrase "remember me to so and so." Paul always uses the phrase to refer to prayer. He is bringing the Thessalonians up with God and giving thanks or praise to God for them, particularly that they exhibit Christian virtues under pressure and persecution.[11] "Make remembrance" is the main verb on which the following participles, "remembering" and "knowing," seem to be dependent.[12] V. 3 will express the grounds for the thanksgiving — what Paul knows about his converts.

We can see the use of the rhetorical device of alliteration here on the *p* sound: *pantote peri pantōn hymōn mneian poioumenoi epi tōn proseuchōn hēmōn,* "always for you all, remembering you in our prayers." Paul thus gives "a rhetorically impressive beginning in the oral reading of these letters (see also 5.16-22)."[13] He depicts himself as a virtuous man of constant and earnest prayer. "*Pantote* suggests that thanksgiving for the Thessalonians was an ongoing part of Paul's prayer life, and it is this that differentiates the apostle's assertion concerning the giving of thanks for the Thessalonians from a mere rhetorical device written in a pro forma way at the beginning of a letter, as in many of the Hellenistic letters from the period."[14]

"Continually" (*adialeiptos*) could go with what precedes (modifying "making remembrance") or with what follows ("remembering") but in either case here, as in 5.17, it is applied to prayer. This is of course a bit of rhetorical hyperbole, but it does mean repeatedly, regularly, on an ongoing basis. It "must refer to continual rather than continuous prayer and is a forceful indication of how much Paul lived in an atmosphere of communion with God."[15]

---

10. See Lightfoot, *Notes*, p. 9.

11. It is true we could translate this phrase as simply "to make mention," but since this document is all about reminding and remembering (see v. 3) the former translation is more likely.

12. However it is certainly possible to take "knowing" with what follows as well.

13. A. Malherbe, *The Letters to the Thessalonians* (New York: Doubleday, 2000), p. 107. What Malherbe fails to note is that 1 Thess. 5.16-22 is the peroration, and it was especially in the exordium and the peroration that one strove for eloquence that would inspire and move the audience. The deeper emotions especially would be appealed to in the peroration and rhetorical figures, alliteration, rhyme, and the like were especially concentrated in these parts of a discourse, all the more so in an epideictic one.

14. C. Wanamaker, *Commentary on 1 and 2 Thessalonians* (Grand Rapids: Eerdmans, 1990), p. 74.

15. I. H. Marshall, *1 and 2 Thessalonians* (Grand Rapids: Eerdmans, 1983), p. 51.

Proseuchon is a general word for prayer, but tended to be used of petitionary prayer, as here.[16] Giving thanks thus comes first and then petitions are mentioned next when the topic is prayer. Prayer should be about adoration and giving before it is about asking. Chrysostom stresses that the emphasis here is placed on the fact that God is the one chiefly responsible for the Thessalonian Christians' virtues and growing in grace: "For to give thanks to God for them is the act of one testifying to how they have advanced in the faith, . . . as though God himself had accomplished everything. Paul also teaches them moderation in their self-estimate, all but saying that all their growth is from the power of God" *(Homilies on 1 Thessalonians* 1).

V. 3 provides the grounds for both thanksgiving to God and praise of the Thessalonians: they must and have exercised the Christian virtues God has graced or blessed them with. The three phrases naming what is remembered could be taken as involving either objective or subjective genitives. For example, Marshall and Wanamaker take these phrases to refer to the work that results from faith, the labor that results from love, and the steadfastness that comes from hope, taking the second noun in each phrase as subjective genitive.[17] This is surely correct. Paul does not speak of a work that produces faith or a labor that produces love. For those who think that Paul simply opposes works to faith the first of these phrases must remain an eternal puzzle. In fact, in Galatians Paul only opposes a certain kind of works to faith, namely works of the Law. In that same letter he goes on to exhort Christians to all sorts of deeds and works under the rubric of "the Law of Christ." In short, Luther misread or over-read the contrast in Galatians, as this verse shows.[18]

These three phrases thus refer to three character traits or qualities or virtues (faith, love, and hope) which produce action. Work, labor, and perseverance come from these virtues.[19] While faith, love, and hope are not uniquely Christian virtues, they are certainly stressed more than in Greco-Roman literature, especially faith and love. This specific triad of virtues is found nowhere before Paul's letters, so he may have originated it to indicate the core Christian traits (1 Cor. 13.13; in the same order in Col. 1.4-5).[20] Paul is surely referring to

---

16. B. Rigaux, *Les Épitres aux Thessaloniciens* (Paris: Gabalda, 1956), p. 360.

17. Marshall, *1 and 2 Thessalonians,* p. 51.

18. B. Witherington, *Grace in Galatia* (Grand Rapids: Eerdmans, 1998), pp. 30-50 and see rightly Wanamaker, *1 and 2 Thessalonians,* p. 75.

19. These same three nouns, "work," "labor," and "perseverance," are found in the same order in Rev. 2.2.

20. See Malherbe, *The Letters,* p. 109. Greco-Roman writers might well emphasize other virtues more — justice, self-control, clemency, and other civic virtues. This triad was to inspire later Christians to wax eloquent — cf. Ignatius, *Polycarp* 6; *Ephesians* 14; Polycarp, *Philippians* 3. R. L. Wilken, in his recent masterful study *The Spirit of Early Christian Thought* (New Haven: Yale University Press, 2003) points out just how much some of the cardinal

deeds that these Christians did for their fellow Thessalonians, perhaps for their fellow Christians in Thessalonike, as 4.10 suggests, perhaps also for other Christians, as 2 Cor. 8.1-5 may suggest. The emphasis here is on work for good reason.[21] Paul knows and must deal with the idleness of some in due course. Thus he will stress the Thessalonians' and his own hard work before he gets to an exhortation like 1 Thess. 5.14.

It is clearly not a mere generality when Paul speaks of the constancy or perseverance the Thessalonians exhibited, a constancy born out of hope. They have experienced serious opposition (2.14) and in fact would again (see 2 Thessalonians). Nevertheless their hope for the future has led to their perseverance. It is not an accident that Paul emphases this virtue in the context of pressure and persecution and suffering (see the connection in Rom. 5.3).[22] Here Paul already alludes to the discussion of the nature of the future hope which will come in chs. 4–5. "Perhaps 'hope' has the emphatic position at the end of the triad because of the eschatological note of the whole letter."[23]

The hope is grounded in the Lord Jesus. It is not an abstract quality but a personal living hope involving a living relationship with an individual who can and will come and vindicate the Thessalonian Christians. The final phrase, "before God and our Father" could be taken with the preceding participle "remembering" at the beginning of v. 3 or with the immediately preceding phrase, " in our Lord Jesus Christ." 3.9 may suggest the former,[24] but the parallel between the end of the prescript in v. 1 and the end of v. 3 supports the latter more strongly. "Before God" is thus a visual reminder that Christ is in the very presence of God and is not just some human mediator figure but the divine Son who dwells in glory before and with the divine Father. 2.19 and 3.13 (cf. 2 Cor. 5.10) fill out the picture Paul has in mind nicely:[25] Christ is currently already dwelling in glory, before the throne and presence of God the Father. A day will come when Christians will appear before them both.

Christian virtues made the Christian movement stand out from the ethical flavor of the larger culture.

21. Malherbe, *The Letters*, p. 108 is right that the emphasis here is on the actions not on the virtues or qualities that produce them, with the actions placed in the emphatic position in each phrase.

22. Rigaux, *Les Épitres*, p. 366.

23. F. F. Bruce, *1 and 2 Thessalonians* (Waco: Word, 1982), p. 12.

24. See Wanamaker, *1 and 2 Thessalonians*, p. 76.

25. See Lightfoot, *Notes*, p. 12.

The *Narratio* — The Story Thus Far — 1.4–3.10

A *narratio* in a piece of epideictic rhetoric reviewed the facts which were deemed praiseworthy or blameworthy. Paul, as he did when he was with the Thessalonians, continues to take a gentle approach, concentrating on what is praiseworthy and mentioning only blameworthy actions of outsiders who have persecuted or caused the suffering of Paul or Paul's audience. The *narratio* could be included in or be added to the *exordium,* or it could stand alone as a separate section (*Rhet. ad Alex.* 1438b.15-28; 1442b.28-32). *Rhetorica ad Herennium* 1.8.12 refers to three types of *narratios,* the second being one used to win or confirm belief in the audience, incriminate one's adversary, or effect a transition to the topics to be discussed. Actually our lengthy *narratio* in 1 Thessalonians manages to serve all three of these functions.

We will discuss at the appropriate juncture whether 2.14-16 or some part of that passage should be seen as a *digressio* placing blame on opponents in an otherwise laudatory *narratio*.[1] Quintilian says that a narration in an epideictic piece of rhetoric that involves the praise of human beings is normally to be done in chronological order: "Praise awarded to character is always just. . . . It has sometimes proved the more effective course to trace a person's life and deeds in due chronological order" (*Inst. Or.* 3.7.15), which basically seems to be what we have in 1 Thess. 1.4–3.10 except for 2.15-16. It is indeed character and the deeds that reflect character, not physical attributes, social standing, good heredity, wealth, or other standard topics of praise that Paul will focus on here.

---

1. The other major piece of epideictic rhetoric we have from Paul may have a *digressio* (Eph. 3.2-13). See R. R. Jeal, *Integrating Theology and Ethics in Ephesians* (Lewiston: Mellen, 2000), p. 130, and see my forthcoming commentary on Philemon, Colossians, and Ephesians.

You know, brothers and sisters being loved by God, your election, because our gospel did not come unto you in word only but also in power and in the Holy Spirit and [in] much conviction, just as you know the kind of persons we were among you for your sake. And you became imitators of us and of the Lord, welcoming the word in much affliction/suffering with the joy of the Holy Spirit, with the result that you became a type/model for all the believers of Macedonia and in Achaea. For from you the word of the Lord has been caused to resound, not only in Macedonia and Achaea, but in all places your faith which you have toward God has spread, with the result that we do not have need to speak of it. For they themselves report concerning us what sort of reception upon entrance we received from you, and how you turned to God from the idols, to serve the living and real God and to wait for his Son from heaven, whom he raised from the dead ones, Jesus, the one rescuing us from the coming wrath.

For you yourselves know, brothers and sisters, that our entrance among you was not fruitless/in vain, but previously suffering and being insulted, just as you know, in Philippi, we chose freely/boldly in our God to speak to you the good news of God, being strongly contested/opposed [or "in much agony"]. For our appeal was not out of deceit nor from uncleanness [motives] nor in guile/subterfuge, but, just as we have been approved by God to be entrusted with the gospel, thus we speak, not as trying to please humans but to God the one who tests our hearts. For never once did we speak in a word of flattery, just as you know, nor on the motive of greed, as God is a witness, nor seeking glory from human beings, neither from you nor from others, having the power to impose our "weight"/authority as apostles of Christ, but rather as gentle[2] in your midst. As if a nursing mother cherishing her own child, thus longing for you we were determined to share with you not only the good news of God but also our very selves because you became very dear to us.

For remember, brothers and sisters, the labor of ours and the toil, night and day working in order not to be a burden to any of you, we preached to you the good

---

2. For the most part, this *narratio* does not have many textual issues, but in v. 7 we have good manuscripts that support the reading *nēpioi* ("children" — 𝔭65, ℵ, B, C*, D*, G, and many others) and other good manuscripts which support the reading *ēpioi* ("gentle" — A, K, P, and numerous minuscles). The problem with the reading *ēpioi* is that it is not found in any of the earlier Paulines and only at 2 Tim. 2.24 in the later ones. The problem with *nēpioi* is that Paul nowhere else applies it to himself, always to his converts. This latter reading has better external attestation, even though it would mean that once more Paul was mixing his metaphors (first he is the child, then he is the nursing mother). But "gentle" is appropriate at this juncture (contrast v. 6, where arrogance is eschewed) and it is a common enough Greek word. See Metzger, *TC*, pp. 629-30. A consideration that goes beyond the mere textual and contextual data is the fact that ancient nurses were expected to be gentle, not irascible, as ancient remarks show (Soranus, *Peri Gynaikeion* 32; Aulus Gellius, *Attic Nights* 12.1.21; see *New Docs* 2, pp. 7-8 for a nursing contract). For a general discussion see Malherbe, *Paul and the Popular Philosophers* (Minneapolis: Fortress, 1989), pp. 35-48, here p. 43 and note 53.

news of God. *You are our witnesses and God, how devoutly and righteously and blamelessly we behaved to those who believed, just as you know how each one of you as a father his own child encouraging you and consoling and imploring in order that you might walk worthy of God who is calling[3] you into his dominion and glory.*

And because of this also we give thanks to God continually because, receiving the word heard from us, you received not a word of a human being but just as it truly is — a word of God, who also is at work/active in you who believe. For you, brothers and sisters, became imitators/copies of the assembly of God, the one in Judea in Christ Jesus, because you suffered the same things and you from your own fellow countrymen just as also they from the Jews, who even executed the Lord Jesus and the prophets[4] and drove us out and did not please God and were hostile to all persons, hindered us from speaking to the nations in order that they might be saved, unto the filling up of their sins at all times, but the wrath came/has come on them to the full/unto completion/at last.

But we, brothers and sisters, having been orphaned from you for the time being, to the face not the heart, more than ever we are eager to see your faces with much longing. Because we wished to come to you, I myself Paul, and once and twice, and Satan blocked us. For what is our hope or joy or crown of boasting — is it not even you — in the presence of our Lord Jesus in his parousia? For you are our glory and joy.

So no longer being able to bear it we resolved, having been left in Athens alone, and we sent Timothy, our brother and coworker of God[5] in the good news of Christ, for the strengthening of you and encouraging of your faith, so that no one would be disturbed in these afflictions. For you know that we were set/placed for this. Because of this also I myself sent, no longer being able to endure, in order to know of your faith, whether perhaps the tempter had tempted you and our labor was for nothing/in vain.

But now Timothy has come to us from you and bringing good news to us of your faith and love and that you have remembered us always good, having a longing to see us just as also we you, because of this, we have been consoled, brothers

---

3. The present tense "calling" is to be preferred over the aorist "called" as the entering of the dominion is yet in the future in Paul's letters, and the context favors the present tense as well. The present tense reading has strong and varied support from B, D, F, G, H, K, L, P, and most of the minuscules. See Metzger, *TC,* p. 630.

4. This reading is clearly preferable to *idious prophetas,* which is the basis of the Textus Receptus rendering (and is found in a variety of secondary witnesses). The reading in the text has widespread (from many text types) and early support. See Metzger, *TC,* p. 630.

5. Some scribes found "coworker of God" too bold and so omitted "of God" (B, 1962). Others appear to have changed *synergos* to *diakonos.* Even though the latter has good support (א, A, P, and many others) it does not explain the origins of the reading "coworker of God," so the more difficult reading should be accepted. See Metzger, *TC,* p. 631.

and sisters, about you through all our distress and suffering, through your faith so that now we live if you yourselves stand firm in the Lord. For how are we able to give in exchange some thanks to God concerning you upon all the joy in which we rejoice because of you in the presence of our God, night and day most earnestly praying in order to see your faces and mend/make complete what is lacking of your faith?

Some general characteristics of this narration are worth mentioning. First, of course, is its highly emotive character, one of the more emotionally charged sections in the whole Pauline corpus. This is in no way surprising in a piece of epideictic rhetoric of this sort, but Paul's emotional expressions here are not pro forma or anything other than absolutely genuine and sincere. He does not need to generate pathos here: it is an inherent part of the story. He has chosen the appropriate rhetorical genre to express himself in this fashion. It would be expected that he would use some of the more grandiose terms and the "all" word (had their example and testimony really rung out to *all* Macedonia and Achaea, much less "everywhere"?), and it would be understood that this involved a certain amount of deliberate dramatic hyperbole. Such was the nature of ancient praise and blame conventions.

Another impression left by this section of the discourse is how often reference is made to work, suffering, consoling, encouraging, and the word of the Lord (sometimes called the good news, even the good news of God). Although we do have some reference to theological topics like election and the parousia they do not dominate the landscape of this part of the discourse. The focus is on the present and on the day-to-day trials and tribulations and other sorts of experiences of Paul and his converts. Once again, that present time focus is what one expects in epideictic rhetoric. The past or future are only brought up in so far as it may help the situation in the present, in this case the situation involving the Thessalonians' suffering. Notice as well the stress on "knowing" and "remembering" as opposed to new teaching. Indeed these words about knowing and remembering begin paragraphs or sentences at 1.4; 2.1, 9, 11; and 3.3. Paul is not trying to change belief and behavior in this discourse. He is simply reaffirming, reminding, and amplifying what the Thessalonian Christians should already know and believe. They are to continue to progress in the right direction, and any fresh insights or teachings are built on what they should already know. This is not a problem-solving discourse. It is oriented to progress, but sometimes progress under pressure amounts to simply standing firm or holding one's ground (3.8).

In terms of the style and form of this section, we find the usual long "periods" or sentences one associates with epideictic praise (e.g., 1.6-10; 2.5-8; 3.6-8). In 2.14-16 there is a sudden effort at creating a series of end rhymes with the *on* sound, as if this section is intended for maximum aural impact.

The story begins according to v. 4 in the heart and mind of God. Paul reminds his audience of "your election" and that they are loved by God (cf. 2 Thess. 2.13). As Lightfoot rightly stresses, *eklogē* is not used in the NT of election to "final salvation."[6] It refers rather to conversion here as the next line makes clear. The Thessalonians must be loved by God because, when Paul preached in Thessalonike, his preaching did not come to them in word only, but rather in power and in the Holy Spirit and with much conviction. This was surely the work of God and showed God's heart, that God desired them to be saved.

Paul's favorite terminology in addressing his audience directly as members of the Christian community is *adelphoi*. Though "brother" was occasionally used in early Judaism to express group membership or group identity (cf. Deut. 15.3, 12 to Josephus, *Ant.* 10.201 and Philo, *Spec. Leg.* 2.79-80), its use is rare in that context and incredibly frequent in the Pauline letters. It would appear that this usage actually goes back to Jesus (Mark 3.31-35), who uses kinship terms of spiritual relationships, including sister, mother, and father as well. Paul also occasionally speaks of himself as the father or even the mother of his converts, and once even refers to Jesus as the older brother of Christians (Rom. 8.29). As Wanamaker says, this logically made the Christians brothers and sisters as well (see 2 Cor. 6.18).[7] We must be wary of labeling these relationships examples of fictive kinship, because at least in Paul's mind there really was a spiritual relationship between all members of the body of Christ (e.g., 1 Cor. 12.13).

The Pauline documents which have the highest proportion of the terminology of calling and election are not Romans and Ephesians but 1 and 2 Thessalonians, where we find some eight instances (election in 1 Thess. 1.4; 5.9; 2 Thess. 2.13; calling in 1 Thess. 2.12; 4.7; 5.23-24; 2 Thess. 1.11; 2.14). Relevant on the same subject are the warnings about apostasy (1 Thess. 3.5) and the reassurance of God guarding the church (1 Thess. 5.23; 2 Thess. 2.3) and of God's faithfulness (1 Thess. 5.24; 2 Thess. 3.3). Thus the language of election is one thing that binds these two letters together and distinguishes them from other Pauline documents. 2 Corinthians, for instance, does not have this sort of language.

But what is the rhetorical intent and force of this language? It is clear enough that it is used to reassure and comfort the faithful in Thessalonike in a time of trial. But is it also intended to suggest that God had unilaterally chosen individual Thessalonians and that therefore these individuals were destined to persevere unto final salvation, come what may? That seems a very strange conclusion considering Paul's worry that his work in Thessalonike might have been in vain and his exhortations to perseverance. This deserves closer scrutiny.

6. J. B. Lightfoot, *Notes on the Epistles of St. Paul* (Winona Lake: Alpha, reprint), p. 12.
7. C. Wanamaker, *Commentary on 1 and 2 Thessalonians* (Grand Rapids: Eerdmans, 1990), p. 77.

A Closer Look: Election, Persecution, and Perseverance in 1 and 2 Thessalonians

The language of election and being beloved by God is not uncommon in the Pauline corpus. For example, the connection between God's love and election which we see in 1 Thess. 1.4 we also find in 2 Thess. 2.13; Rom. 9.11-13; and Col. 3.12. Paul applies to the Christian assembly election language which was used of Israel (e.g., Deut. 32.15; 33.12; Isa. 44.2). He applies election statements originally made only of Jews (Hos. 2.25) to Jews and Gentiles united in Christ (Rom. 9.28).[8]

Election for Paul is corporate. It was in ethnic Israel and is now "in Christ."[9] Paul carries over concepts of corporate election from early Judaism into his theologizing about the Christian assembly. But his use of texts like Hos. 2.25 does not mean that he operates with a replacement theology, as if God has reneged on his promises to Jews, but it does mean that those promises are now and in the future to be fulfilled through and by the Lord Jesus. The church has not replaced Israel, but Jews like Paul who believe in Jesus are viewed as the true Israel, the true descendants of Abraham, and those Gentiles who join them have become part of the people of God, grafted into the true olive tree.[10] Paul's is a fulfillment rather than replacement theology.

From Paul's viewpoint "election" does not guarantee the final salvation of individual Christian converts any more than it guaranteed the final salvation of individual Israelites in the past. Just as apostasy was and could be committed by individual Israelites, whom God then broke off from the people of God, at least temporarily (see Rom. 11.11-24), so there was also the same danger for individual Christians, hence all the warnings about falling away in 1 and 2 Thessalonians.

In his detailed discussion of the use of *eklektos* in the LXX and in Paul's letters (cf. 2 Thess. 2.13, 16; Rom. 8.33; Col. 3.12), I. H. Marshall rightly asks whether the term refers simply to an action of God, perhaps a pre-mundane action ("the people upon whom God has set his choice"), or to "the people upon whom God has set his choice and who have responded to the call."[11] His answer is that an "examination of the usage in the OT and in Judaism shows that the phrase 'the elect' is used of those who *have* become members of God's people and never of individuals *before* they have become members of God's people."[12]

This is correct, and we may add that apart from its occasional application to Israel's king (cf. later the application to Jesus), the language of election in the OT is applied corporately to a people, not to an individual. "Elect" *(bahir)* is normally used in the plural and so collectively of Israel. And, lest we think that being elect guarantees salvation texts like 2 Kgs. 23.27 tell of God rejecting Jerusalem after having chosen it.

---

8. I. H. Marshall, *1 and 2 Thessalonians* (Grand Rapids: Eerdmans, 1983), p. 262.

9. See the discussion in B. Witherington and D. Hyatt, *The Letters to Philemon, Colossians, Ephesians* (Grand Rapids: Eerdmans, 2006), ad loc.

10. See the discussion of Romans 9–11 in Witherington and Hyatt, *Romans*, pp. 246-49.

11. See Marshall, *1 and 2 Thessalonians*, p. 263.

12. Marshall, *1 and 2 Thessalonians*, p. 263, emphasis added.

Other texts speak of God choosing and anointing persons for specific historical purposes (e.g., Cyrus in Isa. 45.1), but these are not soteriological texts. This is the general context in which one must view the references to election in 1 and 2 Thessalonians.

In 1 Thess. 3.5 Paul speaks of his fear that he may have been laboring in vain due to the dangers of loss of faith facing the Thessalonian church because of their many tribulations. J. Gundry Volf[13] argues that while this *sounds* like a genuine worry that his converts might fall away or commit apostasy, what Paul was worried about was himself, his legacy, his own potential unfaithfulness to his calling, and whether in the end his own ministry was rooted in God's saving power.[14] "Paul thus feared being robbed of his 'hope and joy or crown of boasting . . . before our Lord Jesus at his coming' if his converts fell in persecution. . . . Paul is thus uncertain whether or not some of his converts will be numbered among the saved at the day of Christ."[15] In her view, Paul also worried that perhaps some had actually falsely professed faith in the first place.

It would be hard to say how many things are wrong with this sort of argument. In the first place, Paul has no uncertainty at all about whether God's power was active among the Thessalonians and converted them when Paul preached to them. He is in fact emphatic about this: the word came to them with power and in the Holy Spirit and with full conviction (1:5). He does not say that it came to just some of them in this way. There is no shred of evidence in these letters that Paul worried that some had falsely made a profession of faith, and psychologically and socially it is hard to imagine someone doing so in a social environment of pressure and persecution *not* to convert to this new "Jewish superstition."

In the second place, as Marshall says, this explanation

> fails to do justice to the fact that Paul's remarks are undoubtedly motivated by genuine concern for the welfare of his readers and not by personal concern for his own reputation at the parousia. Moreover, the language used shows that the purpose of sending Timothy to them was not to see whether they were truly converted, but rather to encourage converts to stand firm in the midst of persecution and to see what was the state of their faith. Paul's language deals with standing firm despite tribulation (3:3, 8) and repairing any weaknesses in their faith (3:10), not with the question of whether the readers actually possess faith.[16]

The worry and anxiety and pastoral concern of Paul in 1 Thessalonians about the spiritual danger his converts are truly in is hard to discredit or pass off as mere rhetorical flourish, much less to suggest it was really worry about himself.

---

13. I. H. Marshall, "Election and Calling to Salvation in 1 and 2 Thessalonians," in R. F. Collins, ed., *The Thessalonian Correspondence* (Leuven: Leuven University Press, 2000), pp. 259-76 and J. Gundry Volf, *Perseverance and Falling Away in Paul's Thought* (Tübingen: Mohr, 1990).

14. Gundry Volf, pp. 267-71.

15. Gundry Volf, pp. 271, 273-74.

16. Marshall, "Election and Calling," p. 261.

In 1 Thess. 1.4 "Paul's claim to knowledge of their election is related to his knowledge of their conversion."[17] "He wants to say both that the choice of God to save them was expressed in the fact that the Gospel came to them in power and that their response of faith shows that they now belong to the 'elect.'"[18] Paul says that not only he but also the Thessalonians can "know" that the Thessalonians are God's chosen. There is nothing here about an invisible elect among the mass of church-goers. This "knowing" comes from recognition of the positive response to the gospel received with joy and of changed lives, turning from idols to the living God. Indeed the chosen are all too visible and are enduring persecution because of it. What Paul certainly does not say, or want to say, is that the Thessalonians have believed because God chose them and caused them to believe.

In 1 Thess. 5.9 — "For God did not purpose/appoint/arrange things for/assign us to suffer wrath but rather to receive salvation through our Lord Jesus" — the "us" is those who are already Christians. This text is thus closely parallel to Rom. 8.28-30.[19] It has to do with the final destiny of human beings who are either lost or saved. The same antithesis may be found in Rom. 5.9-10. The verb *tithēmi* here in the middle with the preposition *eis* means "purpose for/unto" or "appoint for/unto." We may compare for example the same language in Acts 13.47, quoting the LXX of Isa. 49.6, where we hear of a people appointed to be a light to the Gentiles. Of course some Israelites failed to fulfill the destiny or purpose which God intended for the people, but not because they were not chosen or purposed by God for such a task or end. If we compare John 15.16 we see that the language of purposing and electing or choosing are used as virtual synonyms. What can be said about purposing can also be said about electing or choosing.

Gundry Volf argues on the basis of 1 Thess. 5.9 that Paul means that God has purposed for individual persons to receive final salvation and that this divine purpose will infallibly be brought to conclusion and completion. She stresses that the use of "receive" here indicates the actual reception of something, which she takes to mean pure passivity, not allowing for any positive effort toward the goal or purposed end by the recipient.[20] "Paul's statement that 'God has not destined us to wrath' relativizes human action."[21] Gundry-Volf also writes that "God's appointment to salvation does not make human obedience superfluous."[22] But if it is not superfluous or incidental to the outcome, then surely it is essential to the outcome. That final salvation is a gift to be received when Christ returns does not in any way relativize the importance of believers here and now persevering in the faith so that they might "be in that number when the saints go marching in." Nothing in 1 or 2 Thessalonians suggests otherwise, and indeed much suggests that persevering is something that Christians must actively

---

17. Marshall, "Election and Calling," p. 265.
18. Marshall, "Election and Calling," p. 265.
19. See on this text Witherington and Hyatt, *Romans*, pp. 227-31.
20. Gundry Volf, *Perseverance and Falling Away*, pp. 20-27.
21. Gundry Volf, *Perseverance and Falling Away*, p. 24.
22. Gundry Volf, *Perseverance and Falling Away*, p. 21.

purpose and engage in, for it is possible for them to fall or commit apostasy. This is why in the very same context in 1 Thess. 5.11 Paul warns the Thessalonians to be alert and watchful lest they be caught napping or even stumble in the dark.

1 Thess. 5.9 may also be compared to 2 Pet. 3.9, which says that God does not desire that any should perish but that all should come to repentance. God's desires are one thing, the outcome is another. Similarly God's purpose, design, or intent for Israel to be a light to the nations was one thing. Whether individual Israelites fulfilled that purpose was not merely up to God. It also required willing human participation. Acts 13.47 should especially be seen as parallel to 1 Thess. 5:9 when it comes to the force of the language about God's purposes or appointments.[23]

Since the Greek verb translated "appoint" in 1 Thess. 5.9 is applied to those who are heading for wrath as well as to those being saved, it may be asked whether Gundry Volf really wants to argue that God infallibly and inevitably appointed some for wrath from before the foundation of the world, come what may and do what they will. The answer is apparently no, that she does not want to argue that case. But then whatever "appoint" means for the lost is also what it means for the saved in this text, and in neither case is unilateral predestination apart from human response or willing participation in view.

There is in addition to the language of election the language of calling. What does it mean when Paul talks about being called or God calling a person? The issue here is whether calling means "effectual calling," whether calling is an action of God that includes and indeed prompts and necessarily assures the response of the one called. 1 Thess. 2.12 is a good example of how Paul can use this language: "calling" is not retrospective but prospective. It refers to the invitation or calling given to believers to enter the eschatological dominion in the future. In 4.7 Paul refers to the call that comes at conversion to change one's pattern of life or behavior. God is the one who calls, and he calls us not to uncleanness but in holiness. This way of putting it, in the midst of parenesis and exhortations of various sorts, makes clear that Paul thinks that unclean behavior is certainly possible but goes against one's calling, against the lifestyle one has been called to live. This text makes it clear that the ethical response to the call is an ongoing matter and that the potential of going against one's calling is also an ongoing possibility.[24]

In 1 Thess. 5.24 calling is something God does in the present ("the one who calls you"). This usage is very common in Paul's letters (Rom. 4.17; 9.11; Gal. 1.6, 15; 5.8; 1 Thess. 2.12; 2 Tim. 1.9). Paul promises that God, for his part, will be faithful and (taking this with the prayer in v. 23) is capable of entirely sanctifying a person and keeping him or her blameless "at/in the coming of the Lord Jesus." This is apparently what God will do at the eschaton because it involves the body as well as the human spirit, the resurrection, when the believer will be glorified and transformed into the likeness of Christ (see 1 Corinthians 15). In other words, Paul's prayer is that his converts will

---

23. See Marshall, "Election and Calling," pp. 266-68.
24. Marshall, "Election and Calling," p. 269.

be in the right condition when Christ comes to judge the world. This then would be similar to the eschatological statement in 2.12. This is not, in short, about the "perseverance of the saints" before and leading up to the return of Christ but about the condition of the believer at the time of the parousia. Had Paul wanted to speak of perseverance, he could have used the preposition *eis* and spoken of being kept blameless "unto/for," or the preposition *achri* and spoken of "until the coming. . . ." But he uses neither here.

Gundry Volf takes 5:23-24 to mean that since God will be faithful to the end "he will complete the salvation begun in their calling."[25] This conclusion misses the point that Paul is talking about God's direct action on behalf of the believer at the eschaton. Then God will raise the believer and present him or her pure and blameless and with a glorified body before Jesus at the judgment (see 2 Cor. 5.10). And there is the further problem that when Paul does talk about holiness and progressive sanctification during this lifetime he includes remarks like we find in 1 Thess. 4.3-5, where human actions are involved, not solely divine actions, and we have exhortations such as we find at 5.22 to hold on to the good and avoid evil. Confirmation that we are right in our eschatological interpretation of 5.23 can be found in 3.13, which refers to the ongoing process of God strengthening hearts so that believers will be blameless, not now but when Jesus returns with the holy ones. Obviously there is a relationship between progressive sanctification and final glorification, but the former involves both the strengthening and purifying work of God and also the correct responsive behavior of believers, whereas what happens at the eschaton is purely a matter of divine action. It will be too late to change one's behavior at that juncture.

Marshall sees in some of the similar texts in 2 Thessalonians (2 Thess. 1.11-12; 2.13-14) a parenetic character or implication to Paul's prayers, in two ways. First, praying that disciples will behave in a certain way is a good indirect way of urging or persuading them that they need to behave that way, and Marshall goes on to rightly point out the parenetic context of these prayers. Second, he also points out that these Pauline intercessory prayers have in them an element of doubt: Paul feels that he needs to pray for these things because it is not absolutely certain that his converts will persevere in the faith. Prayer is a vehicle which helps them to persevere by galvanizing both them and the Almighty to that good end.[26]

Here Gundry Volf takes the phrase "from the beginning" in 2 Thess. 2.13 to mean "from the beginning of time."[27] This is possible but it is based on a doubtful textual reading *(ap' archēs)*. *Aparchē* ("firstfruits") is well supported by B, F, P, and many other good witnesses and may well be original. Indeed it is the preferred reading of Metzger and the UBS textual committee[28] because (1) elsewhere, when Paul

---

25. Gundry Volf, *Perseverance and Falling Away,* p. 83, see pp. 81-83.

26. Marshall, "Election and Calling," pp. 272-73. On the parenetic context and content of various of these intercessory prayers see G. P. Wiles, *Paul's Intercessory Prayers* (Cambridge: Cambridge University Press, 1974).

27. Gundry Volf, *Perseverance and Falling Away,* pp. 13-19.

28. See Metzger, *TC,* pp. 636-37.

wants to say "from the beginning of creation/time/all eternity," he uses the phrase *pro/ apo tōn aiōniōn* (cf. 1 Cor. 2.7 and Col. 1.26); (2) except in Phil. 4.15 Paul uses *archē* to mean "power" (in the plural, "the powers"); (3) Paul regularly uses *aparchē* (e.g., 1 Corinthians 15 and some six other occurrences); and (4) elsewhere we know of examples where copyists changed *aparchē* to *ap' archēs* (see the textual apparatus for Rev. 14.4 and Rom. 16.5). It makes perfectly good sense to translate 2 Thess. 2:13 "God chose you (as) firstfruits to be saved through the sanctifying work of the Spirit. . . ." The Thessalonian Christians are saved both through their belief in the truth and through the sanctifying work of the Spirit, not just through the action of the Spirit. V. 14 then speaks of what happened at their conversion: they were called, chosen, and sanctified and they believed "through our Gospel" so at the eschaton they might share in the glory of the Lord Jesus. The emphasis is on the divine action, to be sure, but the human response of belief/faith/trust is also spoken of.

2 Thess. 3.3 gives a pastoral assurance that God will protect these converts under pressure from the Evil One. As Marshall says, this probably means that the Evil One's attacks, though real, will be in vain. As such this is close to the assurance Paul offers in 1 Cor. 10.13.[29] Gundry Volf takes this to mean that God will not allow the believer to fail the final test of perseverance, even though he allows small stumblings and acts of disobedience along the way.[30] The problem with this exegesis is that Paul is talking about protection from an external source of trial, tribulation, and temptation, not about a believer wrestling internally with the possibility of committing apostasy. The text is about protection, not a guarantee of human perseverance come what may. In Rom. 8.38-39 we again have a similar promise: no external force will separate the believer from the love of God. But not included in the list of such forces is the believer himself or herself. That text does not suggest that it is impossible for a called and chosen believing person to commit apostasy, and neither does 2 Thess. 3.3.[31]

What this discussion has shown is that Paul's reasoning on these matters is eschatological to the core. He speaks pastorally about what God has already accomplished through Paul's proclamation of the gospel in Thessalonike, is doing now with his calling still echoing in the ears of the believer, and will do when he raises the dead believers at the eschaton. Protology is not addressed in these discussions. In other words, the discussion of calling and election and perseverance comports with the *narratio* in 1 Thessalonians, which begins with the Thessalonians' conversion and moves forward relentlessly to the return of Christ. The *narratio* thus prepares admirably for what will be said in chs. 4–5 about the parousia and the state of the dead in Christ.

In v. 5 Paul explains why he gives thanks: because the gospel came to the Thessalonians and had its salvific effect on them. Paul calls the gospel message

29. Marshall, "Election and Calling," p. 274.
30. Gundry Volf, *Perseverance and Falling Away,* p. 81 and see pp. 76-78.
31. See Witherington and Hyatt, *Romans,* pp. 234-35.

both a "word" *(logos)*[32] and a piece of "good news" *(euangelion)*. The latter term occurs sixty some times in Paul's letters and is indeed Paul's favorite way of referring to the message he proclaims. It probably came to Paul from the Jerusalem Christian community, who in turn picked it up from Jesus, who was drawing on texts such as Isa. 52.7 and 61.1-2 (see Luke 4.18). *Euangelion* already had, then, religious resonances in regard to salvation, return from exile, reversal of fortunes, and the like. For Paul at least, it is not just a synonym for "word" or "message" but actually describes the content of the message, that it is good news. Paul seems to mean by *euangelion* the oral telling of the story of Jesus as the story of God's salvation breaking into human history. Paul does not, of course, use it to refer to a written document, since there were as yet no written Gospels.

But it is surely more than just fortuitous that *euangelion* was also in use in Roman imperial propaganda. The famous Priene inscription (9 B.C.) from near Ephesus reads as follows:

> . . . and since the Caesar through his appearance *(epiphanein)* has exceeded the hopes of all former good messages *(euangelia)*, surpassing not only the benefactors who came before him, but also leaving no hope that anyone in the future would surpass him, and since for the world the birthday of the god was the beginning of his good messages. . . .

The emperor's birth is thus associated with "good tidings." But the inscription focuses not just on his birth, which is but the beginning of the good messages, but also on the emperor's ongoing benefactions. The Thessalonians would probably have heard Paul's use of *euangelion* as referring to some blessing or benefaction from a deity, and they would not have been wrong in this conclusion from Paul's viewpoint. It may be that Paul uses such terminology frequently because it is part of his countercultural agenda to oppose the imperial rhetoric with the story of the Lord Jesus.[33] Notice also the term *plērophoria*, which with its verbal cognate appears some seven times in Paul's letters and only three times elsewhere in the NT (Luke 1.1; Heb. 6.11; 10.22). Though it can have the sense of "fulfillment," it also can mean "assurance" or "conviction," which is surely the sense here.[34]

---

32. There seem to be some echoes here of Jesus' parable of the sower (Mark 4). B. Rigaux, *Les Épitres aux Thessaloniciens* (Paris: Gabalda, 1956), pp. 380-81 points to the phrases "receive the word" and "with joy."

33. See the essays in *Paul and Empire,* ed. R. A. Horsley (Harrisburg: Trinity, 1997), particularly the essay by H. Koester and K. P. Donfried.

34. Lightfoot, *Notes,* p. 13 seems to think he is referring to the conviction Paul and other proclaimers had in conveying the word rather than how it was received or its effect. I disagree. The end of v. 5 parallels the end of v. 6 and so "in full conviction" parallels "with

V. 5b reminds Paul's audience of his manner of life among them. He stresses that it was for their sake. He will return to this theme at 2.9 and 3.11. This verse leads quite naturally into the next, v. 6, which mentions how the Thessalonians had become imitators of Paul and Jesus. There is no exhortation to become imitators, just a reminder that they have already done so. Calls to imitation were the provenance of deliberative rhetoric, but calls to remember the values one has already embraced belong to epideictic rhetoric.[35] Paul stresses that they have followed his example and that of the Christ and that this has plunged them into a hostile situation which led to persecution and suffering.[36] This was not something to be ashamed of but rather something to be proud of. The issue here though is not just similar suffering but also joy in the midst of suffering, a theme also found in early Jewish sources and elsewhere in Paul (2 Macc. 7.30; 4 *Maccabees* 10.20; 2 Cor. 6.10; 7.4-5; 8.2).[37] The "degree in which the believer is allowed to participate in the sufferings of his Lord, should be the measure of his joy."[38]

Malherbe's view that *thilipsis* here refers merely to mental distress or cognitive dissonance caused by receiving the gospel is inadequate in view of 1 Thess. 3.3 and 2 Thess. 1.4 and the fact that Paul says that this "suffering" paralleled that of Jesus and Paul. We have no evidence that Jesus suffered such internal distress on receiving the word. Furthermore, as Wanamaker points out, how could the Thessalonians be exemplars to those in Achaia and Macedonia if there was not more than anguish of heart involved here?[39] Smith is likely right that Paul has an eschatological view of these sufferings, namely that they are the sort of sufferings that were predicted for believers in the end times.[40] There is also a sort of subtle coaxing in v. 7, for if the Thessalonians have become models of grace under pressure and persecution for those in

---

joy." In both cases it is the work of the Spirit in the person that produces conviction and joy, even in the midst of suffering. See F. F. Bruce, *1 and 2 Thessalonians* (Waco: Word, 1982), p. 14.

35. This "Post-It note" reminder approach suggests that the recipients are "already substantially living and acting in the right way." So S. Stowers, *Letter Writing in Greco-Roman Antiquity* (Philadelphia: Westminster, 1986), p. 103.

36. Of course Wanamaker, *1 and 2 Thessalonians*, p. 80 is right that this is a not so subtle piece of indirect parenesis as well, encouraging them to keep on imitating and persevering as well.

37. See Marshall, *1 and 2 Thessalonians*, pp. 54-55. Cf. Heb. 12.2; Luke 6.22-23.

38. Lightfoot, *Notes*, p. 14.

39. Contrast Wanamaker, *1 and 2 Thessalonians*, p. 81, and especially E. Best, *A Commentary on the First and Second Epistles to the Thessalonians* (London: Black, 1972), p. 79, to A. Malherbe, *The Letters to the Thessalonians* (New York: Doubleday, 2000), p. 115. Internal distress is not ruled out, rather it is included and entailed with physical suffering.

40. A. Smith, "The First Letter to the Thessalonians," in *The New Interpreter's Bible*, vol. XI, ed. L. E. Keck (Nashville: Abingdon, 2000), p. 695. He compares texts like Dan. 12.1; Matt. 24.9-14; Mark 13.19, 24.

Achaia and Macedonia, then of course they are being encouraged to keep it up, bearing in mind that they are being watched. Paul uses here the Roman provincial designations. While these areas had been one region up until A.D. 44 under Roman rule, Claudius had separated them into two administrative provinces.

V. 8 makes this even clearer and more striking. "From you" is placed in the emphatic first position. *Exechetai* is a strong verb meaning something like "resound" or "roar like thunder."[41] Chrysostom even says that it can refer to the dramatic and loud sound of a trumpet.[42] The word of the Lord has sounded forth dramatically from the Thessalonians to all places.[43] Paul may be excused for a bit of dramatic hyperbole here, which is customary in epideictic rhetoric, and perhaps he is envisioning the fact that these converts live on the main north-south and east-west road (the Via Egnatia), so news traveled readily from their city throughout the region (cf. similarly Col. 1.6). But are we to think here of the Thessalonians or Paul and other traveling Christians having spread the word of the Lord?[44] It may involve all of these, but in this case particularly the latter, since Paul says he had no need to make such a report about them, though he did so anyway (2 Thess. 1.4), using the rhetorical trope of saying what he claims he has no need to say.

Vv. 9 and 10 belong together and conclude this part of the *narratio*. Paul will go on in 2.1-12 to say more about his entrance and reception in Thessalonike. *Eisodos* can in fact mean either "entrance"/"visit" in the active sense or "welcome" in the passive sense, and it may be that Paul uses it in both ways in rapid succession, passively here then actively in 2.1.[45] As J. Gillman rightly stresses, Paul is reminding the audience of his ethos while he was with them: he was warmly received and was seen as a person of integrity, one who embodied the message he proclaimed.[46]

Paul appears to be using a traditional formula here for conversion, perhaps taken from early missionary preaching, referring to it as a "turning around" or about-face (see especially Acts 14.15 and Gal. 4.9; 2 Cor. 3.16; cf. Acts 3.19; 9.35; 11.21; as a possible source Isa. 6.9-10 and Jer. 10.10). What the

41. See Lightfoot, *Notes,* p. 15.

42. Marshall, *1 and 2 Thessalonians,* p. 56.

43. Though the Greek phrase *en panti topō* can refer to places of worship (cf. John 11.48; Josephus, *Antiquities* 14.235), there is no indication that this is the meaning in our text, especially since Paul surely is not suggesting that the word had been taken to all the synagogues in the region and that there were no Christian purpose-built buildings yet.

44. The phrase "Word of the Lord" is found only here and in 2 Thess. 3.1 in Paul, but is common in Acts (8.25; 12.34; 13.44; and passim).

45. See Malherbe, *The Letters,* p. 118.

46. See J. Gillman, "Paul's *EISODOS*: The Proclaimer and the Proclaimed (1 Thes 2,8)," in *The Thessalonian Correspondence,* pp. 62-70.

Thessalonians have turned from is idols, and what they are turning to is the living and real God (cf. Heb. 9.14).[47]

In the LXX *eidōlon* seems to refer not only to the carved image of a deity but to the deity itself as well. These are phony (as opposed to "real") and dead (as opposed to "living") gods. By this Paul does not mean that the idols represent nothing. In 1 Cor. 8.4-6 he speaks of the many gods and lords, and in 1 Corinthians 10 he explains that those who worship idols are in fact worshiping demons. He does not see pagan religion as having no connection with the spiritual realm but as connected with the dark side and the evil beings of that realm. "Idol" is of course not a term that Gentiles used of their own gods, but is rather taken from the Jewish polemic against such false deities.

Here alone in Paul's letters does he speak of the "living" God (cf. John 1.9; 7.28; 15.1; 17.3; Exod. 34.6; Ps. 86.15; Isa. 65.16).[48] These verses make it quite plain that the overwhelming majority of the audience in Thessalonike must have been Gentiles (so also 2.14).[49]

V. 10 is a continuation of the previous verse and indicates the posture Christians should assume in light of the eschatological situation: they are to wait, and not just for anything which might come, but await *(anamenein)* the return of Christ. Paul does not use this verb elsewhere in reference to the parousia, but we find the same thought in 1 Cor. 1.7 and Phil. 3.20. The Thessalonians have already been taught some things about the return of Christ, but clearly not everything they need to know, as chs. 4 and 5 will show. Lightfoot points out that the leitmotiv of this document is "live a holy life that you may be prepared to meet your Lord," and one could actually say that that is the subtext of 2 Thessalonians as well.[50] The plural "heavens" reflects the Hebrew *shamayim*, but it appears clear from 2 Cor. 12.2 that Paul believed there are layers or levels in heaven. This is the only place in 1 or 2 Thessalonians where Jesus is called "the Son of God."

This verse alludes to the story within the story, namely the saving narrative about Jesus which is the basis of Paul's and the Thessalonians' stories of response to that story.[51]

> The basic plot, encapsulated in 4:14 and 1:10 is quite simple. Jesus died, God raised him from the dead, and at some future time Jesus will rescue those

---

47. Here we have an instance, of which many could be cited, in which the author of Hebrews reflects a knowledge of earlier Pauline letters, including Galatians, 1 Thessalonians, and 1 Corinthians. On this phenomenon see B. Witherington, "The Influence of Galatians on Hebrews," *NTS* 37 (1991): 146-52.

48. Best, *First and Second Thessalonians*, pp. 82-83.

49. Bruce, *1 and 2 Thessalonians*, p. 18.

50. Lightfoot, *Notes*, p. 16.

51. See M. Mitchell, "1 and 2 Thessalonians," in *The Cambridge Companion to St. Paul*, ed. J. D. G. Dunn (Cambridge: Cambridge University Press, 2003), pp. 51-63, here p. 52.

who believe in him from "the coming wrath" at his "parousia" or advent (2:19; 3:13; 4:15; 5:9, 23), a projected event described in the language of an imperial visit to the provincial city. The gospel story Paul offered the Thessalonian pagans is an updated version of Jewish apocalyptic narratives known to us from a range of extant writings both Biblical (such as Daniel 7 and 12) and apocryphal (4 Ezra, 1 Enoch, 2 Baruch, Dead Sea Scrolls), which forecast a dramatic divine intervention in human history to exact final judgment on the good and the evil. Paul's is an essentially post-messianic version of the apocalyptic tale (i.e. the Messiah has already come).[52]

Paul does not view the coming wrath as an impersonal force or an inevitable power programmed into human history. He sees it as an eschatological event that enters human history from outside and manifests the righteousness of God, who will come to judge the earth.[53] We will find the theme of divine wrath in both present and future in 2.16 and 5.9-10. There is in Paul's thinking an already-and-not-yet character to wrath just as there is to salvation, not least because he assumes that the eschatological age has already begun with the death and resurrection of Jesus. In the Gentile world the anger or wrath of a god required propitiation through sacrifice, and some Greek and Roman writers felt that such wrath, especially if it was capricious, was unworthy of a deity (cf. Euripides, *Bacchanals* 1348; Cicero, *De Officiis* 3.102). Closer to Paul's view is that found in the Jewish portion of the *Sibylline Oracles,* where Gentiles "are warned of God's firmly determined eschatological anger (3.545-72) because of, among other vices, their idolatry (5.75-89; 12.110-12). They are to seek the Deliverer (*rhyster*) from wrath (3.561), repent and seek God's forgiveness (4.158-70)."[54] Clearly Paul's view of this matter is Jewish in character, but when he uses the word "wrath" of God it does not refer to an irrational outburst of passion by God or a fit of temper. "Rather if God is holy, pure and righteous, then his wrath represents a just reaction to the wickedness of those who spoil and destroy the perfect society which it was his intention to create. God's wrath is always directed against evil and is not arbitrary and unprincipled."[55] Rom. 1.18; 2.5, 8; 3.5-6; 5.9 show that this was not an uncommon theme in Paul's letters and that he could refer to both present and future aspects or manifestations of God's wrath. As Wanamaker suggests, it is not only the hope of salvation but the fear of wrath which helps keep the converts on task and continuing to maintain and retain various essential Christian virtues, beliefs, and behaviors.[56]

52. Mitchell, pp. 52-53.
53. Best, *First and Second Thessalonians*, p. 85.
54. Malherbe, *The Letters*, p. 122.
55. Marshall, *1 and 2 Thessalonians*, p. 59.
56. Wanamaker, *1 and 2 Thessalonians*, p. 88.

Paul does not often, as he does here, refer to Christ as the "Deliverer," but we find the term in Rom. 11.26, which draws on the LXX rendering of Isa. 59.20, where the participle is used as a divine title.[57] As is appropriate at this point in the discourse, Paul is foreshadowing themes he will develop more fully in 1 Thess. 5.9-10. It is the Christ story which changed the story of Paul and the Thessalonians, and Christ's further intervention in person rather than just by word will bring their stories to the proper conclusion.

The social situation of the Thessalonians could not have been easy. They were no longer pagans and had not become part of a recognized or "legitimate" religion like Judaism. They were betwixt and between. As such, they were undergoing considerable persecution and pressure from their compatriots.[58] "To disassociate oneself from the worship of family and community deities would entail a serious disruption in one's relationships with family, friends, fellow club members, business associates and civic authorities. . . ."[59] Paul's sudden departure from Thessalonike could not have helped the situation, since it left the new converts in a vulnerable position. Though the essence of pagan religion was ritual, processions, and ceremony, Paul seems not to have left them with much liturgy for them to identify as religious behavior. There were no Christian temples, priests, or sacrifices, there is little in 1 and 2 Thessalonians to suggest that Paul had stressed the importance of celebrating the Lord's Supper, and baptism was a one-time rite. The social situation in Thessalonike was apparently tenuous at best, like that in Galatia.[60] The Thessalonians' considerable sense of social dislocation is the reason Paul encourages, supports, and praises them here.

In the next section of the narration, as in ch. 1, Paul will speak first and primarily about the preachers (2.1-12) and then about the converts (2.13-17) by way of reminder.[61] Having reminded them about their conversion and its nature Paul proceeds to say in 2.1 that this of course means that they know his visit with them was not in vain or an "empty" trip.[62] *Kenē* refers to the character of

---

57. See Bruce, *1 and 2 Thessalonians*, p. 20.

58. On which see below, pp. 186-90.

59. J. Barclay, *Obeying the Truth* (Edinburgh: Clark 1991), p. 58.

60. See B. Witherington, *Grace in Galatia* (Grand Rapids: Eerdmans, 1998), pp. 361-62. The difference is of course that in Galatia there were Christian agitators lobbying for the converts to become more Jewish in their religious behavior, whereas here the problem was more one of persecution.

61. Lightfoot, *Notes*, p. 18.

62. The *gar* which begins this verse makes clear that it is linked with what went before and in fact explains more elaborately some of the things suggested in ch. 1 (cf. 1.9 to 2.1, where we have the same phrase about the visit). In other words, we are still in the *narratio* and this is hardly where the narration began, against Wanamaker, *1 and 2 Thessalonians*, p. 91. Wanamaker is however certainly correct that providing positive and negative examples was com-

the missionaries' discourse, saying that it was not empty and vacuous (cf. Eph. 5.6; Col. 2.8), which is just another way of saying what was said in 1.5, only in a negative way.[63] The rhetorical handbooks spoke of rhetors who spoke merely to display their eloquence. Such speech was called "empty" (see *Inst. Or.* 12.16-17, 73-74; cf. *Rhet. ad Alex.* 1440b13).[64] The perfect tense of *gegonen* indicates that what was done on that first visit continued to have an ongoing effect.[65]

V. 2 speaks of Paul's problems in both Philippi and Thessalonike. Here he likely alludes to the episode recounted in Acts 16.19-40. In Philippi Paul suffered and was insulted. The term *hybristhentes* implies something important about Paul's sense of *dignitas*, that Paul saw himself as a person of considerable social status and should not have been treated as he was in Philippi.[66] This comports with the suggestion that Paul was a Roman citizen and expected better treatment, especially in a Roman colony city like Philippi.[67] His Thessalonian converts were told about how he was treated in Philippi ("as you know"). Undaunted, Paul and his coworkers went on to boldly and freely proclaim[68] the good news in Thessalonike, despite much opposition there as well. God, not circumstances, emboldened Paul to speak.[69] The term *agōn* refers to a contest and was usually used of athletic contests, but in this case it refers to the proclamation being hotly contested (see Acts 17.5-9).[70] The gospel here is called the gospel of God: there is a theocentric character to the gospel, especially as it is referred to in this document (see vv. 8-9; cf. Rom. 1.1; 15.16; 2 Cor. 11.7). It was, after all, God who raised Jesus from the dead (1.10) and set in motion the proclamation of the good news about his Son. God is mentioned some nine times in this section of the document.[71]

---

mon in rhetorical pieces and that there is no reason to see 2.14-16 as somehow out of place or an insertion. Praise is alternated with blame in epideictic rhetoric and this is what we find here. See pp. 84-87 below.

63. Bruce, *1 and 2 Thessalonians*, p. 24.

64. See Malherbe, *The Letters*, pp. 135-36.

65. See Best, *First and Second Thessalonians*, p. 91.

66. For example, as Lightfoot, *Notes*, p. 19 points out, "it was the essence of *hybris* that it could not be done to slaves." Cf. Aristotle, *Rhetoric* 2.2, 24.

67. Marshall, *1 and 2 Thessalonians*, p. 63.

68. In democratic Greece *parrhēsia* meant "freedom of speech." Paul treats his converts and congregations as persons and places where free speech is appropriate and in order.

69. Wanamaker, *1 and 2 Thessalonians*, pp. 92-93. This distinguishes Paul from Cynic and Stoic philosophers whose boldness was grounded in self. See rightly, Smith, "1 Thessalonians," p. 698.

70. See V. C. Pfitzner, *Paul and the Agon Motif* (Leiden: Brill, 1967), pp. 112-14. It is true that in a text like Col. 2.1 the agony can be entirely internal and spiritual, but this is not the case here. See Bruce, *1 and 2 Thessalonians*, p. 25. See especially the discussion in Rigaux, *Les Épitres*, pp. 404-5.

71. Malherbe, *The Letters*, p. 137.

In vv. 3-6 Paul will contrast his modus operandi with that of other orators and perhaps philosophers as well. He disavows impure motives (e.g., greed, the desire for praise), trickery, deception, flattery, and the attempt to be a people-pleaser. The disavowal of seeking praise rather than giving praise is a familiar motif in epideictic speeches and is another small clue to what sort of rhetoric we are dealing with in this document. Paul speaks of his *paraklēsis*, which here should be translated "appeal" and is "an exercise of the powers of persuasion, either in the way of (1) comfort, or (2) encouragement, or (3) exhortation, according as the reference is to (1) the past, what has happened, (2) the present, what is happening, or (3) the future, what will happen." Here the focus is on encouragement in the present.[72] Paul's appeal does not arise from "error," or one could translate *planēs* as "deceit," which seems more likely since Paul is listing moral rather than intellectual faults here (cf. 2 Tim. 3.13). Nor does it arise from impurity (i.e., unclean desires) of some sort, nor from guile. None of those are Paul's heart motives for doing what he has done in Thessalonike.

The social background here is that Paul is contrasting his behavior with that of the "many wandering charlatans [who] made their way about the Greek world, peddling their religious or philosophical nostrums and living at the expense of their devotees (like Lucian's false prophet Alexander)."[73] As Wanamaker rightly stresses, these verses do not indicate specific "opponents" or Christian competitors in Thessalonike but rather have a rhetorical function. Paul is simply contrasting his own motives and practice with that of popular rhetors and philosophers and hucksters of that era and realm (cf. Dio Chrysostom, *Oratio* 32.7-10; Lucian, *De morte Peregrini* 13).[74]

In v. 4 Paul speaks as an authorized agent of God, one approved and entrusted with the gospel. He speaks on the basis of that authorization but also in a way that comports with that authorization, not seeking to please human beings (Gal. 1.10; Col. 3.22). He was apparently accused by many of speaking in a manner that was pleasing to the crowds, and this accusation continued even after his death (cf. *Clementine Homilies* 18.10), but there is a difference between the manner and the matter of a speech. What Paul is referring to here is the substance of what he says. He is not denying that he used the art of persuasion, which conditioned how he spoke, nor is he denying that he could be flexible in his rhetorical approach to differing audiences (see 1 Cor. 9.19-23). Paul claims

72. Paul does not say either "our appeal was" or "our appeal will be," but simply "our appeal is not. . . ." He is talking about how he always operates — in a genuine and guileless and good way. See Marshall, *1 and 2 Thessalonians*, p. 64; Malherbe, *The Letters*, p. 139.

73. Bruce, *1 and 2 Thessalonians*, p. 26. See also A. Malherbe, "Gentle as a Nurse: The Cynic Background to 1 Thess. 2," *NovT* (1970): 203-17. The important thing to note is that Paul is contrasting himself with such people, not comparing himself with them in a positive way.

74. Wanamaker, *1 and 2 Thessalonians*, pp. 93-94.

that he is playing to an audience of One, however, in the sense that it is only from God, the tester of human hearts (see Rom. 8.27; Ps. 7.9; Prov. 17.3; Jer. 11.20; 12.3; 17.10), that he seeks validation. "God's testing and approval of Paul was directed to one purpose, namely God's intention to entrust him with the gospel" (cf. Gal. 2.7).[75]

The verb *dokimazō* means "test thoroughly and find fit for the assigned task."[76] Its second use in this sentence is in the present tense: God continues to test and approve Paul. The "heart" here is the seat of thought, feeling, and will: Paul has been tested thoroughly at the control center of his human personality. It is not just Paul's feelings that have been scrutinized but rather the whole inner self. There is perhaps a specific reason that Paul must stress in this discourse that he is not a people-pleaser. Epideictic rhetoric was the primary sort of rhetoric one used to please or entertain an audience, and though Paul is using this sort of rhetoric here, he wants to make it clear that God is the audience he is seeking to please in what he says.

Vv. 5 and 6 present us with a series of further negative qualifications in the form "nor . . . nor . . . nor," which will be followed by a positive statement in v. 7. Paul says literally "nor were we found employed in words," that is, that he did not make a living by being a rhetorician or speaker. Instead, he worked with his hands so that he could offer the gospel free of charge. *Kolakeias* refers to selfish employment and always involves selfish motives (cf. Theophrastus, *Characters* 2; Aristotle, *Eth. Nic.* 4.12). Nor did Paul dole out empty praise or flattery (a good reminder since he does praise the Thessalonians in this very context). He says that they already know this from their own experience. According to Plutarch, flattery is the opposite of bold or free speech (*parrhēsia*) and the latter characterizes the conversation of true friends (*Moralia* 48E-74E). Nor did Paul use a "cloak/pretext/motive for greed."[77] *Pleonexia* can refer to all sorts of covetousness, but in connection with proclaiming some message it surely refers to greed or the desire to bilk someone of their funds or resources through deception or flattery. Aristotle puts it this way: "The person who seeks to gratify people . . . for the sake of getting something for himself is a flatterer" (*Eth. Nic.* 4.6.9).

Nor did desire for glory/honor from any other humans ("not from you nor from others") motivate Paul's proclamation. The search for honor is a virtually universal activity in an honor and shame culture, so there was good reason for Paul to disavow it, as otherwise this motive might well just be assumed to be present. "This of course is not to say that Paul was not honored by them,

---

75. Wanamaker, *1 and 2 Thessalonians*, p. 95.

76. Best, *First and Second Thessalonians*, p. 96.

77. Wanamaker, *1 and 2 Thessalonians*, p. 97 makes the good point that the translation "motive" better suits the context as Paul is talking about real motives, not ostensible ones.

but it does mean that he and his colleagues did not insist upon deferential treatment. They did not stand on their dignity or status as it were, but (as Paul indicates in the following verses) earned the respect of the Thessalonians by their style of life among them."[78]

V. 7 indicates that as apostles, Paul and his coworkers could have thrown their weight around and made financial demands and so "been a burden to you." Instead "we were gentle among you." *Barei* here should be compared to its similar usage in Gal. 6.2, where it also refers to financial "burdens" (cf. 2 Thess. 3.8; 2 Cor. 12.16; Sir. 13.2; Neh. 5.18).[79] Especially relevant is 1 Cor. 9.1-6, where Paul says that apostles have the right to financial support. So here, as there, Paul is asserting a right that he chooses to forgo. This is the only reference to "apostles" in this letter, and it would seem to include Silas and possibly even Timothy, in which case Paul uses it here in its more generic sense of "agents" of someone.[80] On the other hand, a case can be made that Timothy was not present when Paul and Silas first went to Thessalonike but only visited later when Paul sent him from Athens (which he could do since he was not banned from the place like Paul and Silas). 1 Cor. 9.5-6 may imply that Barnabas had seen the risen Lord and was thus an apostle, and perhaps we may assume on the basis of 1 Cor. 15.7 that Silas had seen the risen Lord as well and was part of the group described as "all the apostles." Timothy by contrast was Paul's own convert. If these suppositions are correct, then Paul may be using "apostles" here, as elsewhere, of those who have seen the risen Lord and have been commissioned by him.[81]

The imagery and some of the ideas in this section of the *narratio* are reminiscent of a passage from Plutarch: "The very circumstances in which the unfortunate find themselves leave them no room for frank speaking . . . but they do require gentle usage and help. When children fall down, the nurses do not rush up to them to berate them, but they take them, wash them up, and straighten their clothes, and after all this is done, they then rebuke and punish them" (*How to Tell a Flatterer from a Friend* 69). *Trophos* can refer to either a nurse or a nursing mother. What favors the latter translation is the reference to "her own children" as well as classical usage of this term (cf. Theocritus 27.66; Sophocles, *Ajax* 849).[82] Paul's point is that the missionaries were gentle with their new converts in Thessalonike and did not burden them even with issues of hospitality and support. To the contrary, they nurtured and nourished them as a nursing

---

78. Wanamaker, *1 and 2 Thessalonians*, p. 99.

79. See the discussion in Witherington, *Grace in Galatia*, p. 423. The attempt by Malherbe to interpret this to refer to harsh words and demands of philosophers seems a less likely option since Paul will soon go on to speak of working with his hands. But see Malherbe, *The Letters*, p. 144.

80. See Bruce, *1 and 2 Thessalonians*, p. 31.

81. See the discussion in Wanamaker, *1 and 2 Thessalonians*, p. 99.

82. See rightly Lightfoot, *Notes*, p. 25.

mother would do. Paul in Gal. 4.19 also portrays his role in relationship to his converts as maternal, in that case laboring to give birth to his converts.[83]

Vv. 8 and 9 continue to convey the image of gentle and loving care and regard for the Thessalonians. The converts became very dear, indeed *agapētoi,* "beloved," to the missionaries, who shared with them not only the gospel but their own lives, who labored hard during both night and day[84] so they would not be a financial burden to the new converts. Here as throughout this section Paul is just reminding the Thessalonians of what they already know, as is characteristic of a *narratio* in an epideictic speech. The connection between preaching free of charge and hard manual labor to support oneself is clear in v. 9.[85]

The converts in Thessalonike are witnesses not only of Paul and his coworkers' maternal behavior but also of their paternal behavior, as Paul goes on to say in vv. 10-12, which comprise one long Greek sentence.[86] In order to heighten the rhetorical effect of what he is about to say Paul invokes both God and the Thessalonians as his witnesses in the present about the apostles' behavior when they were in Thessalonica.[87] Obviously the more gentle suggestions in 1 Thessalonians (cf. also 4.11-12; 5.14) about the need for all to work do not have the intended impact because Paul must take a more strident and direct tone in 2 Thess. 3.6-12. Paul will insist here that he and his coworkers behaved devoutly, uprightly, and blamelessly (all three terms are adverbs) while present in Thessalonike in regard to the way they related to their converts.

V. 11 has no main verb: "just as you know how . . . each one of you, as a father his children." The missing verb could be "treat" or "relate to," with v. 12 explaining what characterizes proper fatherly behavior toward one's children — encouraging, comforting, and appealing to/charging. As Chrysostom pointed out, when Paul wants to refer to his tenderness and affection for his converts he uses the image of the mother, but when he wants to dwell on instruction and advice he uses the figure of a father.[88] In the Greco-Roman world the mother

---

83. For this reason it is probably a mistake to press the "nurse" idea here, but see Malherbe, "Gentle as a Nurse," pp. 203-17.

84. For this same phrase about "toil and struggling" see 2 Thess. 3.8 and 2 Cor. 11.27.

85. I thus agree with Marshall's critique of R. Hock's notion that Paul works in the first instance to show his converts how he is like a philosopher living in the world with all its toil and putting his teaching into practice. See Marshall, *1 and 2 Thessalonians,* p. 72. Working to set a good example of Christians working may be a secondary motivation (cf. 2 Thess. 3.8), but here the primary motivation is clearly not to imitate philosophers. His concern is that the gospel be freely offered and freely received.

86. See Rigaux, *Les Épitres,* p. 425.

87. Wanamaker, *1 and 2 Thessalonians,* p. 104.

88. N. Petersen, *Rediscovering Paul* (Philadelphia: Fortresss, 1985), pp. 128-31 is quite right that the use of these paternal metaphors makes clear that a hierarchical relationship existed between Paul and his converts.

was normally in charge of the nurture of the child and the father in charge of moral instruction.[89] Paul then urges his converts to live lives ("to walk about"; cf. Prov. 28.6; Isa. 59.9) worthy of God because God is calling[90] them into his dominion and glory. As in Gal. 5.21 and 1 Cor. 6.9-10, entering or inheriting or obtaining the dominion requires being in the right moral condition.[91] Here *basileia* clearly refers to a future realm that one enters in due course, and when one has entered it one has entered into the very living presence of God (e.g., his glory).

V. 13 can be said to begin a new paragraph in the *narratio*. It reiterates to some degree what was announced in 1.5,[92] returning to the theme of thanksgiving. The new reason that Paul thanks God continually is that the Thessalonians received the preached word as the word of God and not merely as the words of humans. Paul speaks here literally of the "word of hearing" (cf. Rom. 10.17; Heb. 4.2) or, as I prefer to call it, "the heard word." "Of God" is in an emphatic position. With "as it truly is," Paul adds his testimony to that of the Thessalonian converts that the Word that they received and personally appropriated was God's Word. He and his converts are in agreement on this point. The context in which this Word is at work is among or in those who believe. "It is in believers that the Word is effective; those who accept it as the Word of God experience its transforming power, but where faith is lacking the Word is powerless."[93]

Some have considered vv. 13-16 an interpolation, though there is no textual basis whatever for such a conclusion,[94] and others have said that we see a deliberate rhetorical device here, either a digression or some sort of formal comparison.[95] For a passage to qualify as a digression, it would have to deal with a topic not previously covered and appear logically out of sync with what precedes and follows it. But is that really what we see here? Furthermore, does this passage follow the usual rhetorical approach Paul takes with digressions elsewhere?

Both praise and blame are appropriate in epideictic discourse, and we have both in this segment. Like the rest of this letter, it is clearly epideictic in character. Pauline digressions in other letters tend to break into a different sort

---

89. Wanamaker, *1 and 2 Thessalonians*, p. 106.

90. The textual evidence for the present participle (B, D, G, 33, 81) is stronger than that for the aorist.

91. See Malherbe, *The Letters*, p. 153. B. Witherington, *Jesus, Paul, and the End of the World* (Downers Grove: InterVarsity, 1992), 1ff.

92. Lightfoot, *Notes*, p. 30.

93. Marshall, *1 and 2 Thessalonians*, p. 77.

94. By this I mean there are no manuscripts which either omit or displace these verses.

95. Wanamaker, *1 and 2 Thessalonians*, pp. 109-10, following W. Wuellner, "Greek Rhetoric and Pauline Argumentation," in *Early Christian Literature and the Classical Intellectual Tradition*, ed. W. R. Schoedel and R. L. Wilken (Paris: Beauchesne, 1979), pp. 177-88.

of rhetoric from their contexts. For example, 1 Corinthians 13 is an epideictic digression in the midst of an otherwise deliberative discourse. In 2 Corinthians 10–12 Paul breaks into judicial rhetoric, arguing about things past, whereas what has preceded this segment is deliberative.[96] But here, vv. 13 and 14 reiterate themes already heard in 1.5-6. Both the reception of the word and the imitation theme were announced there and are replayed here. This is also true of the theme of suffering, which is mentioned in 1.6 and is found again in 2.14. Furthermore, Paul here is still reminding his audience of what has happened, as he was in ch. 1 at the beginning of the *narratio*. Reminder leads to praise and blame here.

The fresh note in this segment does not really come until vv. 15 and 16, where for the first time Paul turns to blaming someone for misconduct. These two verses could be seen as something of a very brief digression, but grammatically v. 15 is linked closely with v. 14 and v. 16 with v. 15, so it is not necessary to regard them as a digression. The remarks here grow quite naturally out of Paul's comparison between what happened to the churches in Judea and what happened in Thessalonike. Furthermore, Paul's reference to being blocked from speaking to Gentiles (v. 16) quite naturally prepares for his remark in v. 18 about being blocked by Satan from coming and speaking to the Thessalonians. So 2.13-16 fits quite nicely in its present context.

A rhetorical device is in play in v. 15, but it is not a digression but a *synkrisis*, a comparison. How does this work in a piece of epideictic rhetoric? Quintilian is quite clear that epideictic involves "the praise of famous men and the denunciation of the wicked . . ." (*Inst. Or.* 2.4.20ff.). One sets praise into bolder relief by contrasting it with blame of someone else. Hermogenes of Tarsus (second century A.D.) in fact says that the greatest opportunity to make praise effective is by using a comparison to show just how praiseworthy the subject of the encomium is.[97] In terms of overall rhetorical strategy, Paul has chosen to praise his audience's behavior, just as Quintillian urged should be done in epideictic speeches (*Inst. Or.* 3.7.24), thus helping secure their good will in light of what he will go on to urge on them in chs. 4 and 5.[98]

---

96. See the discussion in B. Witherington, *Conflict and Community in Corinth* (Grand Rapids: Eerdmans, 1995), pp. 429-64.

97. See the helpful and detailed discussion of Paul's use of this rhetorical device by C. Forbes, "Paul and Rhetorical Comparison," in *Paul in the Greco-Roman World*, ed. J. P. Sampley (Harrisburg: Trinity, 2003), pp. 134-71, here pp. 146-47.

98. There is a hundred pages of discussion and debate on this pericope in the volume edited by K. P. Donfried entitled *The Thessalonians Debate* (Grand Rapids: Eerdmans, 2000), pp. 31-131. Particularly helpful is the editor's own essay "The Epistolary and Rhetorical Context of 1 Thess. 2.1-12," pp. 31-60, as he recognizes how these verses fit nicely into a rhetorical *narratio*, in particular this one, and how recognizing the rhetorical conventions is a key to understanding this text and its function.

A Closer Look: Was Paul Anti-Semitic?

Certainly one of the major motivating factors for those who have seen this section of 1 Thessalonians as some sort of post-Pauline insertion is that it seems, at least in isolation and on first reading, to be a piece of anti-Semitic polemics.[99] This is especially thought to be the case when we compare this passage with Rom. 11.25-26.

One factor may be taken out of play immediately. There is no real textual evidence for an interpolation here, unlike, for example, John 7.53–8.11. Therefore one must hypothesize a very early interpolation indeed, prior to the use of this letter in the second century A.D.

Another factor needs to be taken out of play at the outset as well. Paul was a convert to the Christian sect of Judaism. Conversion radically changed Paul, as any fair reading of Galatians 1–2, 1 Corinthians 9, and Phil. 3.4-11 will show.[100] To suggest psychologically that he would be incapable of a polemic of this sort against Jews who were involved in either the process which led to Jesus' execution or the more recent persecution of Christians in Judea is to ignore the evidence of the polemics of many converts to Christianity from Judaism over the course of the last 2,000 years. Paul was certainly capable of polemics, and we should not rule out *ab initio* that this text might be from Paul simply because he was a Jew and that the text is polemical.

The judgment on Jews expressed in 1 Thess. 2.13-16 is in fact not very different from what Paul says in Romans 9–11. As T. Holtz points out, there is no doubt in Paul's mind as he writes Romans that judgment has fallen on Jews who have rejected the gospel. Paul even goes so far as to say that they have been broken off from the tree of the people of God, at least temporarily, so that they can be grafted back in by the mercy of God and through faith. Paul is certain that such a rejection brings immediate consequences of judgment. Paul is talking about the final judgment no more in 1 Thessalonians 2 than in Romans 9–11. Therefore, Holtz's conclusion is warranted: "such certainty has, on the other hand, never excluded Paul's conviction that God's grace which appeared in Christ releases even from this judgment."[101] Though Paul does not say so in 1 Thessalonians 2, that text, even with its polemics, does not rule out such a conclusion since Paul is talking about temporal judgment, not final judgment, there.

The emphasis in the passage is on the Thessalonians and their laudatory perse-

---

99. See for example the discussion of I. Broer, "'Der ganze Zorn ist schon uber sie gekommen.' Bemerkungen zur Interpolationshypothese und zur Interpolationshypothese und zur Interpretation von 1 Thes 2.14-16," in *The Thessalonian Correspondence*, pp. 137-59; in that same volume see also T. Holtz, "The Judgment on the Jews and the Salvation of All Israel: 1 Thes 2.15-16 and Rom 11.25-26," pp. 284-94. Further one should consider the arguments of D. Schmidt, "1 Thess. 2.13-16: Linguistic Evidence for an Interpolation," *JBL* 102 (1983): 269-79.

100. On the identity of Paul see Witherington, *The Paul Quest*, pp. 52-88.

101. Holtz, "Judgment on the Jews," p. 293.

verance despite their suffering the same thing that Jewish Christians had suffered in Judea at the hands of their fellow Jews. "The Jews" can mean nothing other than the particular Jews who did the persecuting. It cannot mean all Jews since all Jews were not persecuting Christians in Judea and some Jews were those being persecuted. Of course, when this verse was stripped of its original historical context and sense, and especially in view of its polemical tone, it lent itself to a tragic anti-Semitic use.

V. 15 needs to be seen in the long prophetic tradition of the critique of wicked Jewish leaders who persecute and execute the prophets (e.g., 1 Kgs. 19.10-14; 2 Chron. 36.15; Jer. 2.7-8; Ezek. 14.9-11; 34; Heb. 11.32-38).[102] Ultimately there would develop a martyrology of the prophets as we find in *Martyrdom of Isaiah* 5.1-14. Furthermore, there was also a tradition of prophetic proclamation that God would judge corrupt leadership in Jerusalem (e.g., Jeremiah 22; Hosea 5). Jesus is said to draw on this same critique in texts like Luke 11.47-51 and 13.34, which relate specifically to what was happening in Judea. We see a parabolized form of this tradition as well in the parable of the tenants (Mark 12.1-8 and par.).

This critique of wicked leaders cannot be globalized such that the one delivering it can be accused of critiquing all Jews. Paul's critique stands in this long tradition. Furthermore, he associates those who "killed the Lord Jesus" with those who keep him from speaking the gospel to Gentiles. Clearly in neither case can Paul be talking about Jews in general but rather those who oppose Jesus and the gospel.

It is sometimes objected that here Jews, or at least Jewish officials, are accused of killing Jesus. Paul had been to Judea prior to writing these letters, and Acts 22 is probably correct in saying he had been brought up in Jerusalem.[103] He knew quite well, especially if he was indeed a Roman citizen, as seems likely, that capital punishment in Judea was in the hands of the Roman governor. Furthermore, he was in a position to know who had instigated the action that led to Jesus' death. As with the prophets (2 Kgs. 19), it was not literally the Jewish leaders who killed Jesus, but they were the catalysts who set the judicial process in motion. We see this same way of putting things in Acts 2.36.

Analogy could then be drawn with later actions by Jewish leaders in Judea and in the Diaspora against Paul and others: "and drove us out" quickly follows the reference to Jesus' death.[104] The tense of the participle favors this translation rather than

---

102. The classic study of this phenomenon is O. H. Steck, *Israel und das gewaltsame Geschick der Propheten* (Neukirchen: Neukirchen, 1967).

103. See B. Witherington, *The Acts of the Apostles* (Grand Rapids: Eerdmans, 1998), pp. 668-69.

104. Some manuscripts (D, K, most minuscles) insert the word *idious* before "prophets" to make clear that Jewish prophets rather than Christian ones are in view. The shorter reading is to be preferred, supported as it is by ℵ, A, B, D*, G, I, P, 33, 81, and others. See Metzger, *TC*, p. 630. It may be doubted in so early a letter that Paul is thinking of Christian prophets (plural) being killed by Jewish authorities. There is of course the stoning of Stephen, which Paul himself had a part in, but it would be odd for Paul to be this vehement against other Jewish leaders who had a role in that and say or imply nothing about his own

"and persecuted us," since Paul continued to endure persecution. He alludes here, then, to the specific indignity suffered in Thessalonike.[105]

It needs to be remembered that this is a piece of epideictic rhetoric and one can expect a certain amount of hyperbole in this rhetoric when blame is being laid just as there is hyperbole in the praise. In fact what we have in vv. 15-16 is what is called *vituperatio* and was a stock sort of feature in polemics between social groups in conflict.[106]

"And are contrary to all humans" sounds something like what Tacitus says about Jews: "toward all others they cherish hatred of a kind normally reserved for enemies" (*Historia* 5.5.2). One may compare the words of Apion that Jews even swear by God to show no good will to any alien, least of all Greeks (Josephus, *Apion* 2.121). Juvenal likewise speaks of how unfriendly and inhospitable Jews were, denying even the normal acts of courtesy and hospitality to strangers (14.103-4; cf. Philostratus, *Apollonius* 5.33; Didodorus Siculus 34.1). Quintilian says in his discussion of epideictic rhetoric and dealing with blaming that "founders of cities are detested for concentrating a race which is a curse ('perniciosam') to others, as for example the founder of the Jewish superstition" (*Inst. Or.* 3.7.21). Anti-Semitism was widespread in the Roman world, and the Jewish religion was widely viewed as a "superstition."

Paul is not offering up that sort of polemic here or even a tirade that falls into the category of anti-Judaism. He is specifically concerned with the opposition of Jewish officials to the sharing of God's message, whether by Jewish prophets, Jesus, or Paul and his coworkers. It is this issue which raises his ire here. It is this sense that they act "contrary to (the good) of all." According to Acts, Paul often experienced this sort of hindering by Jews and others (Acts 13.45-50; 14.2, 19; 17.5-9, 13; 18.12). He would recount multiple beatings at the hands of Jewish officials in 2 Cor. 11.24, which lets us know, among other things, that he did not give up preaching in the synagogues wherever he went.

So Paul's criticism is theological rather than purely social,[107] but one can imagine the effect of such words on anti-Semitic Gentiles, indeed we know their effect on later anti-Semitic Gentiles such as the Nazis. Here is a text that needs to be handled extremely carefully and not ripped out of its immediate context.

The aorist verb *ephthasen* in v. 16 indicates that this wrath of God has already come. It does not indicate an ongoing process of judgment. Paul has something quite specific in mind, probably something that occurred in Judea, perhaps some of the reprisals already going on during the turbulent time leading up to the Jewish wars. The governor of Judea in A.D. 48-52, that is, as Paul wrote this letter, was Cumanus, whose rule involved one upheaval after another. Thousands of Jewish pilgrims were slaugh-

---

complicity in that crime. Nor do we have any evidence of deaths of Christian prophets before A.D. 50, unless Stephen and perhaps James the son of Zebedee are counted as such, even though neither one is called a prophet in the relevant literature.

105. See Wanamaker, *1 and 2 Thessalonians*, p. 115; Malherbe, *The Letters*, pp. 169-70.
106. See rightly Wanamaker, *1 and 2 Thessalonians*, p. 118.
107. Malherbe, *The Letters*, p. 170.

tered by this butcher during the Passover festival in A.D. 49 or 50 (Josephus, *War* 2.224-27; *Ant.* 20.105-12). Jews were expelled from Rome by Claudius in that same year. Cumanus committed a variety of other atrocities. Toward the end of his tumultuous rule, hostilities erupted between Jews and Samaritans, including a Jewish attack on Shechem with many innocent Samaritans killed. Cumanus responded with brutal force. Had the legate in Syria, Quadratus, not intervened, the Jewish war would have begun already in A.D. 51-52, as Tacitus says (*Annals* 12.54.3). After hearings before Quadratus, the high priests and other Jewish leaders were sent to Rome in chains. Herod Agrippa II intervened with Claudius and the emperor sided with the Jews rather than the Samaritans. Had this not happened, there is no telling what mayhem would have broken loose in Judea.

I would suggest that Paul has in view some of these events which had recently transpired in Judea — perhaps especially the carting off of the Jewish leaders to Rome. Paul might well have seen this as poetic justice as he remembered the execution of Jesus and the persecution of Jesus' earliest followers. In any case Paul has in view a temporal and temporary judgment which has already come in full or completely *(eis telos)* on the Jewish leaders of the opposition to the gospel in Judea. It is in this context that we should read 1 Thess. 2.13-16.

The Thessalonians became imitators[108] of the Christian assemblies in Judea[109] in that they suffered the same sort of things from "your own countrymen" as the Judean Christians did from "the Jews" (v. 14).[110] Lightfoot is surely right that we are meant to see a contrast here between "your own countrymen" and "the Jews." Both *symphyletos* and "own" make it very likely that we are talking primarily if not exclusively about Gentiles here. The

108. Notice the passive sense here: "you became imitators." See Wanamaker, *1 and 2 Thessalonians*, p. 112. Paul is not calling for imitation, which would be a deliberative rhetorical and ethical move. He is saying that unchosen circumstances caused a parallel to exist between the experiences of Christians in Judea and Thessalonike. See Marshall, *1 and 2 Thessalonians*, p. 78; Malherbe, *The Letters*, p. 167.

109. The addition of "in Jesus Christ" makes clear that we should not translate *ekklēsia* in a specifically Christian way as "church" because the qualifying prepositional phrase, not the noun, makes clear Paul is talking about Christian assemblies. "Judea" here is probably used in the Roman provincial sense, as Paul regularly uses geographical terms, which would then not include Samaria or Galilee. Against Wanamaker, *1 and 2 Thessalonians*, p. 112.

110. The plural "assemblies" here is interesting, as is the reference to Judea in general and not just Jerusalem in particular. We do find "assemblies" used of Jewish meetings in Acts 7.38, and one can compare the LXX of Ps. 22.22 where *ekklēsia* is used to translate *qahal*. However if we take seriously Paul's claim that at least the majority of his audience in Thessalonike turned from idols to the living God, it seems likely that they would have heard the term *ekklēsia* in light of their own background, which is to say in light of the use of the term for the Greek democratic assembly.

Gentiles who persecuted the Thessalonian Christians may be the "agora men" referred to in Acts 17.5 or some persecutors who came along later, after the time of Paul's visit.[111]

The rhetorical function of the analogy between persecutions in Judea and in Thessalonica is, as Chrysostom says, consolation and encouragement of the audience, which comports with the epideictic nature of this discourse (*Hom. on 1 Thessalonians* 3). It seems likely that Paul is alluding to a rather recent persecution of Christians in Judea, and it might be the one he alludes to in Gal. 6.12-13, not Paul's own persecution of Christians in Judea and elsewhere but a later persecution occurring in the A.D. 40s, closer to the time of the writing of Galatians in A.D. 49. Josephus tells us of an increase in Jewish zealotic activity around the time that Cumanus arrived as the new procurator of Judea in A.D. 48 (*Ant.* 20.105-6).[112] The "Judaizer" problem in Antioch and Galatia may have been a response to this persecution of Jewish Christians by Jews.[113]

Paul admires the Thessalonians' ongoing commitment to their Christian faith despite persecution. His comparison of them with the Judean Christians is implicit praise of them. "The willingness of the Thessalonians to convert to Christianity and to remain Christians in the face of strong coercion from their society indicates an acute sense of dissatisfaction with that society and their place in it. Undoubtedly they found in Paul's apocalyptic worldview an alternative symbolic world that made greater sense of their lives than the symbolic world they implicitly rejected in withdrawing from Roman civil religion. . . ."[114]

Vv. 15 and 16 should be seen in part as a form of the long-standing prophetic critique of Jewish leaders who rejected prophetic figures (see the discussion above).

The idea, reflected in v. 16, that there is a specific amount or quotient of sin that when fully committed will finally trigger the wrath of God, is found in Gen. 15.16; Dan. 8.23; 2 Macc. 6.14 (cf. Matt. 23.32; Rev. 6.11). It is here "the wrath," referring to the eschatological wrath of God, not just an ordinary tem-

111. It cannot be ruled out that there might be some Jews who were Macedonians who were involved in this persecution in Thessalonike, but the contrast between those who are ethnically Jews and those who are Macedonians suggests the view taken in the text.

112. See Bruce, *1 and 2 Thessalonians*, p. 46.

113. On this entire matter see R. Jewett, "The Agitators and the Galatian Congregation," *NTS* 17 (1970-71): 198-212, and also his *The Thessalonian Correspondence* (Philadelphia: Fortress, 1986), pp. 93-96. I would suggest that this link between Galatians and 1 Thessalonians on this matter is just one more reason to see Galatians as Paul's earliest letter, written closer in time to 1 Thessalonians rather than some of the later Pauline missives. Notice for example the similarity in phraseology between 1 Thess. 2.14 and Gal. 1.22: "the churches of Judea which are in Christ Jesus."

114. Wanamaker, *1 and 2 Thessalonians*, p. 114.

poral expression of divine anger.[115] The verb "has arrived/come upon" is clearly in the past tense, and so is not referring to some future event (such as the destruction of the Temple in A.D. 70). One could make a case that this wrath had "drawn near" rather than already begun in view of the use of similar language in regard to the kingdom in Matt. 12.28/Luke 11.20, but we have suggested a better view above. Nevertheless, Rom. 1.18–2.11 shows that Paul was perfectly capable of speaking of God's wrath as already active in the present.[116]

The meaning "at last" is not well attested for the phrase *eis telos*. Matt. 10.22 may suggest the translation "until the end" so that Paul would be talking about a wrath that lasts up until the end. The translation "forever/to the end" certainly has good biblical support in the LXX (Pss. 76.8; 78.5; 102.9). Some have referred to *Testament of Levi* 6.11, which speaks of God's wrath coming on the Shechemites for their sins "to the uttermost" *(eis telos)*. The meaning "completely" can be supported from Josh. 8.24; 2 Chron. 12.12; John 13.1. Malherbe is right to note that the parallelism between *pantote* and *eis telos* at the end of these clauses suggests a temporal sense to the latter.[117] The limit of the expression of this wrath however is "until the end or completion" (see Mark 13.12-13 on *eis telos* in this sense). One can fruitfully compare what is said here with Rom. 11.25-26.[118] The phrase does not mean "finally" or "forever" in 1 Thess. 2.16.[119]

115. There has been some discussion and suggestion that Paul might be depending on a Jesus tradition here — Matt. 23.31-36, where we do find reference to the murdering of prophets, the filling up of the fathers' sinful deeds, and judgment on such activity. See D. Wenham, "Paul and the Synoptic Apocalypse," in *Gospel Perspectives: Studies of History and Tradition in the Four Gospels*, vol. 2, ed. R. T. France and D. Wenham (Sheffield: JSOT, 1981), pp. 345-75, here pp. 361-62. This is possible, but if so Paul has modified it to suit his own circumstances.

116. See Witherington and Hyatt, *Romans*, pp. 58-70.

117. Malherbe, *The Letters*, p. 171. It could even be suggested, if one went with the translation "until the end," that Paul has in mind the same schema as in Romans 11 in which Jews are hardened by God until the full number of Gentiles come in and Christ returns at which juncture the Redeemer will transform all Israel, and they will be saved.

118. See T. Holtz, "The Judgment of the Jews and the Salvation of All Israel: 1 Thess. 2.15-16 and Rom. 11.25-26," in *The Thessalonian Correspondence*, pp. 284-94.

119. See Donfried, *Paul, Thessalonica, and Early Christianity* (Grand Rapids: Eerdmans, 2002), p. 207. I do not see any link in this text between the wrath of God and the death of Christ as an expression of that wrath, any more than there is any such link in Rom. 1.18-32. What is true from Paul's vantage point is that Christ's death and resurrection ushered in the eschatological age, and so eschatological wrath is part of the picture thereafter until the end. While Paul uses some apocalyptic ideas and language, his theology is not by and large apocalyptic in the way the book of Revelation or other apocalypses are. By this I mean that his letters are not filled up with the recounting of apocalyptic visions involving all sorts of multivalent symbols and images. One can say that in some ways he thinks like an apocalyptic seer about some issues, but he does not write like one on the whole. J. C. Beker and L. Martyn are wrong about Paul in this respect, though they are right that Paul has a concept of revela-

At v. 17 the subject changes to the recent past of Paul himself and his long-ing to see the Thessalonians. The change of subject is indicated by the emphatic "but we" which begins the sentence. Paul speaks as a parent when he says he is bereft of and separated from his converts and has a deep longing to see them (cf. Aeschylus, *Choephori* 249).[120] He has been separated from them "for the hour of a season," that is, for a brief period of time, "in face but not in heart." This only increased his deep desire to see his converts.[121] This verse surely sug-gests that 1 Thessalonians was written not very long after Paul was forced to leave Thessalonike. This expression of longing to see others and intent or hope to pay a visit is a regular feature of Paul's letters and has come to be called Paul's apostolic parousia (cf. Rom. 15.14-33; 1 Cor. 4.14-21; Phil. 2.19-24; Phlm. 21-22). Letters, emissaries, and personal appearances were the three ways Paul could guide and encourage his converts.

V. 18 says that "we," presumably including Silas and Timothy, all longed to come to see the Thessalonians, Paul especially "again and again."[122] What pre-vented him from coming? Paul says Satan prevented it.[123] In a sense this way of putting things is not unlike what we find in Acts 16.7, where we are told that the spirit of Jesus prevented the missionaries from going somewhere. Paul believes that supernatural forces are at work even in mundane events.

There has been much speculation about what he is referring to. Was it perhaps a recurring illness (cf. 2 Cor. 12.7; but in Gal. 4.13 it is the illness which leads Paul to proclaim in Galatia)? This might be a reference to the politarchs in Thessalonike having banned Paul from coming to the city, but this is uncertain. Elsewhere in Paul's letters Satan is the one who opposes and hinders the prog-ress of the gospel (cf. 1 Thess. 3.5; 2 Thess. 3.3; 2 Cor. 4.4). Particularly interest-ing is 2 Cor. 11.13-15, which suggests that the false apostles are servants and tools of Satan hindering Paul. This shows that Paul could see human beings as ma-nipulated by Satan to oppose Paul's work. Hence, it is possible this is an allusion to the politarchs' actions.[124]

The language of v. 19 is thoroughly epideictic. Paul shows how much he

---

tion of secrets and knowledge and of eschatological events that is like what we find in early Jewish and Christian apocalyptic.

120. Lightfoot, *Notes*, p. 36.

121. Here *epithymia* has a positive sense as in Phil. 1.23.

122. *kai hapax kai dis* means literally "and once and twice" but the sense is "more than once" or "again and again." See rightly Marshall, *1 and 2 Thessalonians*, p. 86. Wanamaker, *1 and 2 Thessalonians*, p. 121 makes the point that this phrase makes clear, along with 3.5 and 5.27, that Paul is the real or primary composer of this document and it is his voice that speaks here, though his colleagues would agree with him. See Malherbe, *The Letters*, p. 184, who stresses the personal, individual, and emotive nature of 2.18–3.5.

123. *Satanas* is, as here, the form used throughout the NT except perhaps in 2 Cor. 12.7.

124. See Bruce, *1 and 2 Thessalonians*, p. 55.

treasures his converts by lavishing on them even eschatological significance. They are Paul's hope and joy, but more to the point they are the crown or crowning achievement of his ministry which he hopes to lay at Jesus' feet and boast in when the Lord Jesus returns. The phrase "crown of boasting" is found in Prov. 16.31 (cf. Ezek. 16.12; 23.42 LXX). The crown, the *stephanos,* is the laurel wreath given to victorious athletes.

V. 19 then asks the rhetorical question what is Paul's hope, joy, and crown of boasting, parenthetically answering "is it not you?" This is the first occurrence of the term *parousia* applied to Jesus. The word literally means "presence" or "arrival" (see 2 Cor. 10.10). It was commonly used of the royal visits, which were accompanied by great ceremony. But it was also used of visitation by a deity who has come to help someone in need. This rhetoric of rulers and gods is applied to Jesus here and elsewhere in this letter. *Parousia* occurs some six times in 1 and 2 Thessalonians and only once elsewhere in Paul of Christ's return (1 Cor. 15.23). The emperor, like Jesus, was regarded as both ruler and god.[125] For example we have an inscription from Tegea dated A.D. 192-93 which reads "in the year 69 of the first *parousia* of the god Hadrian in Greece."[126] The rhetoric of emperor worship is being co-opted and applied to Jesus.

V. 20 adds the further confirmation and redundantly says — "yes, indeed, you yourselves (emphatic) are our glory and joy." Such lavish language and repetition is characteristic of the epideictic rhetoric of praise. "Glory" here refers to the eschatological glory which will manifest itself when Christ returns with the final review and rewards for all such ministerial labors.[127]

According to 3.1, Paul reached a point at which he could not stand not knowing what had happened to his new converts. Literally, he says he was no longer able to contain his desire to see his converts or hold out and endure it any longer without at least knowing that they were all right. The lesser of two evils was to be left behind in Athens alone while Timothy went and checked on them.[128] The verb *kataleipein* means more than "remain behind." Rather, it

---

125. We will say much more about Paul's parousia language, pp. 142-44 below.

126. See Bruce, *1 and 2 Thessalonians,* p. 57.

127. I am unimpressed with arguments that Paul is following friendship conventions here especially in regard to writing a letter to a friend. The friendship language never occurs, and furthermore, friendship conventions assume a peer relationship whereas Paul assumes a parental relationship to his converts, as we have already seen in various ways in 1 Thessalonians 1 and 2. Hierarchical relationships like that which Paul has with his converts followed different social conventions than friendship relationships. But see Malherbe, *The Letters,* pp. 179-81.

128. Commentators have speculated about the nature of the loneliness or "aloneness" of Paul. Does this reflect his lack of success in evangelizing in Athens? Or are we being told that he sent his coworkers off only shortly after he arrived in Athens? It is hard to know. See Best, *First and Second Thessalonians,* p. 130.

conveys the emotional sense of being left or bereft, as Aristotle's use of the term shows (cf. *Rhetoric* 2.4.26; 3.16.5).[129] Paul is a social animal and he is certainly not reluctant to show his feelings.

The sequence of events seems to have been as Lightfoot describes them: Paul was joined in Athens by Silas and Timothy, who had come there from Berea some time after Paul had arrived there. Paul then dispatched Timothy to Thessalonike and perhaps Silas back to Beroea and went on to Corinth alone. Timothy and Silas rejoined him in Corinth some time later (Acts 18.4-5).[130]

3.1a is virtually repeated in v. 5 in the first person singular. This has suggested to most commentators that Paul is the proper author of this document, though he continues to imply that he is speaking for more than just himself at various junctures.[131] This reflects his own collegial approach to ministry, though v. 5 makes evident that we should probably not think of Silas and Timothy as sharing in the authorship of this document.[132]

In v. 2 Timothy is called both "brother" and, more remarkably "a fellow worker with God." Paul likes to speak of the collegial nature of ministry and he uses the term *synergos* with considerable regularity (cf. Rom. 16.3, 9, 21; Phil. 2.25; 4.3; Phlm. 24). What is striking about the usage here is that Timothy is called not Paul's coworker but rather God's. This same idea is repeated in later letters as well (1 Cor. 3.9; 2 Cor. 6.1).[133] Whatever else one says about this, it makes clear that Paul thinks that ministry is a cooperative venture between God and some humans, and the latter have the inestimable privilege of working not only for but with God in spreading the Good News.

Timothy on this occasion was dispatched as a spreader of the Good News, to go spread some of that positive message in Thessalonike — strengthening and encouraging them in their faith.[134] Paul trots out Timothy's credentials

129. See Malherbe, *The Letters*, p. 190.

130. Lightfoot, *Notes*, p. 40.

131. In other words, while this is not quite a true plural, it is also not merely an epistolary plural. By this I mean that while only Paul is speaking, he believes he is speaking for his ministry team. See Wanamaker, *1 and 2 Thessalonians*, p. 127. We need not assume that Paul means that Silas also sent Timothy to Thessalonike or that Silas remained in Athens even though Paul says he was left alone. Paul was truly alone, and this likely means that Silas had been dispatched elsewhere. What is implied is that Paul is the head of the ministry team as it is he who sends Timothy because of his personal anxieties and concerns about the Thessalonians.

132. See Marshall, *1 and 2 Thessalonians*, pp. 89-90.

133. The idea was too striking for many scribes who either omitted *tou theou* (B, 1962) or substituted "servant/minister," *diakonon* (ℵ, A, P, and others), for "coworker." D*, 33, it, Ambrosiaster, Pelagius, and Ps-Jerome preserve the more difficult and surely the earlier reading, *synergos*. See Metzger, *TC*, p. 631 and the discussions in Best, *First and Second Thessalonians*, pp. 132-33, and Rigaux, *Les Épitres*, p. 468.

134. Again, epideictic rhetoric is about maintenance of already accepted truths and

presumably because Timothy was not well known and his authority not already fully received in Thessalonike.[135] There can be little doubt of Paul's fondness for, confidence in, and close relationship with Timothy, whom elsewhere he calls his "child" (i.e., his convert — 1 Cor. 4.17; cf. 16.10-11; Phil. 2.19-22). Faith is something that can be weakened or strengthened. It is not a static quantity or entity but rather a living and developing (or atrophying) thing. Here is the first place in this discourse where the gospel is called "the gospel of Christ," which could mean either about or from Christ.[136]

As v. 3 makes evident, Paul wanted to make sure none of his converts was agitated or shook up[137] by the trials or afflictions they were undergoing. He reminds them that Christians are destined or appointed for such suffering. He is not likely talking about his concern that they were shook up by Paul's (internal?) suffering.[138] Again he says "you know" (cf. v. 4). Paul does indeed believe that Christians, because they are Christians, are destined or appointed to suffer by God (cf. 2 Thess. 1.3-4 and 1 Thess. 2.14), much the same as Jesus was, passing through suffering on the way to final salvation on the day of judgment, to which they are also appointed (1 Thess. 5.9). "We suffer with him so that we will also be glorified with him" (Rom. 8.17).[139] He refers to suffering for the faith, an eschatological sort of suffering, not just any sort of pain that one might have.[140] Paul is even prepared to use his own sufferings and humiliations as a shaming device for converts who think they are immune or exempt from such things (1 Cor. 4.9-13). Clearly he did not operate with the modern theology which holds that one who has enough faith will always be well and exempt from all

---

values, hence strengthening and encouraging. Paul is not urging a change of praxis or belief here.

135. And perhaps because Timothy is the bearer of this letter back to the Thessalonians and its presenter and interpreter once he got there.

136. Bruce, *1 and 2 Thessalonians*, pp. 61-62.

137. The original or literal meaning of the verb here was "wagging," referring to a dog wagging his tail and thus indicating happiness or agitation (cf. Homer, *Odyssey* 16.4-10). The verb *sainesthai* occurs only here in the Greek Bible. It came to have the transferred sense of emotional agitation over something (see Diogenes Laertius, *Lives* 8.41) and hence was the equivalent of Latin *quasso* (see Cicero, *Tusculan Disputations* 4.29). See the discussion in Malherbe, *The Letters*, p. 192, and H. Chadwick, "1 Th. 3.3: *sainesthai*," *JTS* 1 (1950): 156-58 for evidence from the papyri that it can mean agitated or upset in a bad sense.

138. But see Malherbe, *The Letters*, p. 193. Against this Marshall, *1 and 2 Thessalonians*, p. 92; Rigaux, *Les Épitres*, pp. 471-72.

139. See the discussion in Bruce, *1 and 2 Thessalonians*, p. 63.

140. That is, Paul is talking about the kind of hostility to the word of God which will characterize the end times. See E. Bammel, "Preparation for the Perils of the Last Days: 1 Thessalonians 3.3," in *Suffering and Martyrdom in the New Testament: Studies Presented to G. M. Styler by the Cambridge New Testament Seminar*, ed. W. Horbury and B. McNeil (Cambridge: Cambridge University Press, 1981), pp. 91-100.

kinds of suffering.[141] Rather his ideas agree with Jewish apocalyptic texts that speak of the sufferings that the elect or faithful must undergo before the new age dawns (cf. Dan. 12.1; 2 *Baruch* 70.2-10; 2 Esd. 5.1-12; 13.30-31; 14.16-17).[142] This seems to be a view that Jesus also shared (Mark 13.7-8; cf. Phil. 1.16). Suffering thus becomes something of a confirmation that one is a Christian (cf. 2 Tim. 2.11-13). "Such suffering is not only evidence for the reality of their faith; it is an earnest of the coming glory (cf. 2 Thess. 1:4-10)."[143]

In v. 4 Paul reminds the audience that while he was with them he repeatedly told them[144] that there would be this sort of suffering or persecution, and it turned out that way, as they already knew. Part of Paul's pedagogy was to repeat in his letters what he had already taught in person.[145] In this case there was in addition the reinforcement of the Thessalonians' own experiences of suffering, both while Paul was with them and afterward. In substance we have in Acts 14.22 much the same message as here. This was a theme Paul often dwelled on.[146] Chrysostom draws an analogy with a doctor giving a prognosis: "It is much the same here. Paul knew beforehand and lets them know in advance that 'we are about to be afflicted, as it came to pass and you know.' He not only says that this came to pass but that he foretold many things, and they occurred as he predicted.' 'For we are appointed to these things.' Hence you should not be troubled and disturbed about the past, nor even about the future. If any troubling thing should happen, 'we are appointed for this very thing'" (*Homilies* on 1 Thessalonians 3).

V. 5 brings the thought to completion, returning to what Paul said in v. 1. Because of this situation of suffering Paul reached a point where he could stand the uncertainty no longer and so he sent to find out about their faith.[147] He reiterates an idea which he has expressed before: he was concerned lest the Tempter had tempted his converts and they had fallen under his sway with the result that all of Paul's apostolic labors[148] on their behalf turned out fruitless or "empty," that is, in vain (Phil. 2.16; 1 Cor. 15.58; Gal. 2.2; cf. LXX Job 39.16; Isa. 65.23; Jer.

---

141. Wanamaker, *1 and 2 Thessalonians*, p. 130, compares 2 Thess. 2.1-2, but there the shakeup is caused not by suffering but rather by the issue of the return of Christ and its timing.

142. See Best, *First and Second Thessalonians*, p. 135.

143. Bruce, *1 and 2 Thessalonians*, p. 63.

144. One could translate this "we kept on telling you in advance." See Malherbe, *The Letters*, p. 194.

145. See Marshall, *1 and 2 Thessalonians*, p. 92.

146. Lightfoot, *Notes*, p. 43.

147. Cf. the anxiety expressed in 2 Cor. 11.28 which Paul says is always with him.

148. Malherbe, *The Letters*, p. 195 rightly points out that the use of "labor" language is meant to convey the idea of strenuous and concerted effort to win people to Christ. See Rigaux, *Les Épitres*, p. 476.

51.53). This word of concern is directed to all the converts in Thessalonike and makes perfectly clear that Paul thinks it possible for Christians to succumb to temptation and make shipwreck of their faith (cf. 1 Tim. 1.19-20). On the Tempter we may compare 1 Cor. 7.5 (cf. 2 Cor. 4.4; Matt. 4.3; 1 Thess. 2.18; 2 Thess. 2.9-12).[149] In this case the mood of the phrase "would be in vain" is subjunctive, indicating a possibility rather than an already extant reality.[150]

The final section of Paul's narration of pertinent facts is found in vv. 6-10. Timothy has come to Paul and shared with him the "good news"[151] about the Thessalonians' faith and love and their standing firm in the Lord. Faith and love are two qualities frequently linked by Paul as characterizing the Christian life (cf. Eph. 1.5; Phlm. 5). But this was not all — the Thessalonians also had fond (literally "good") memories of Paul and longed to see him.[152] The news could hardly have been better.[153] As a result of this news, "now we live" (v. 8). It seems that this news set in motion almost immediately the writing of this letter that is so full of thanksgiving and emotion.[154] One certainly gets the impression that pastor Paul lived and died with his people's ups and downs. The "faith of his converts inspired him with new life."[155] As 2 Cor. 7.3, suggests his converts'

149. Wanamaker, *1 and 2 Thessalonians*, p. 132.

150. See Marshall, *1 and 2 Thessalonians*, p. 93.

151. Here is the only place in the Pauline corpus where a word like *euangelisamenou* is used of something other than the preaching about Jesus. See Luke 1.19; Heb. 4.2-6. This shows that Paul is perfectly well aware that this word is not a technical religious term, and of course, as we have noted before (see pp. 5-7 above), this language was already used in various contexts including in reference to the emperor. I agree with Wanamaker, *1 and 2 Thessalonians*, p. 133, that the temptation to over-theologize this word here should be resisted. See Rigaux, *Les Épitres*, pp. 477-78.

152. Malherbe, *The Letters*, p. 207 wishes to take this reference to "remembrance" in a semi-technical sense of pupils remembering their teacher and his teaching while he is absent (see Lucian, *Nigrinus* 6-7). The problem with this is that Paul speaks here not in a pedagogical way but in a personal way: they have fond or good remembrance of Paul himself. It is not about remembering Paul's teaching or that he was their teacher. The attempt to read this letter in light of treatises on moral philosophy while neglecting the clear rhetorical signals and epideictic nature of this material has numerous shortcomings, not the least of which is seeing Paul as a moral philosopher in this discourse rather than an apostle, rhetor, and apocalyptic seer.

153. The attempt to read this material in light of friendship conventions and letters between friends is somewhat askew because Paul does not have a peer relationship with his converts and does not use friendship language to describe the relationship. Rather, as we saw in 1 Thessalonians 1, he uses parental language. But see Malherbe, *The Letters*, p. 201. We should also avoid the implication, as Malherbe rightly warns, that Paul is using merely conventional language and is not sincere in what he says. The pastoral tone and spirit of this document makes clear nothing could be further from the truth.

154. Marshall, *1 and 2 Thessalonians*, p. 94; Bruce, *1 and 2 Thessalonians*, p. 66.

155. Lightfoot, *Notes*, p. 45.

weakness made him weak and their strengthening made him strong and re-
vived him (cf. all of 2 Cor. 7.3-7). One can compare Rom. 15.32; 1 Cor. 16.18;
2 Cor. 7.13; Phlm. 7, 20 to see how much Paul was invigorated by his converts'
spiritual growth.[156] "Distress" and "afflictions" are sometimes found together
in the LXX (Job 15.24; Pss. 24.17; 118.43; Zeph. 1.15), and they do not normally refer to purely internal sufferings (cf. Rom 5.3; 1 Cor. 7.26-28; 2 Cor. 1.8; 6.4; 12.10;
1 Thess. 1.6; 3.3). In light of Zeph. 1.15, we may think that Paul has eschatological
persecutions and sufferings in mind.[157]

The conditional clause with *ean* and the present indicative verb in v. 8 —
"if you continue to stand firm . . ." implies that it was possible they might not
stand firm, and so there is a hortatory character to such a phrase.[158] Paul did
not believe that one's faith comes prepackaged and complete at the point of
conversion. It is rather a living thing that grows or shrinks, can be little or great,
can be enhanced or diminished, and can even be said to be brought to completion (cf. Phil. 1.9; Col. 1.10; 2 Thess. 1.3).

Paul is overwhelmed with thankfulness to God, and there is no way to recompense God for all the joy with which he is rejoicing at the good news about
their steadfastness. "Paul means 'I am tremendously grateful to God — and yet I
realize that I am incapable of giving him the gratitude which he deserves'" (cf.
Ps. 116.12).[159] Rather than this news satisfying Paul, however, it has only intensi-
fied his desire to see his converts again, so he prays both "night and day" that he
might see them again and "supply what is lacking in/bring to completion the
shortcomings of your faith" (v. 10). Prayer at night indicates a deep concern for
the situation (cf. Pss. 42.8; 63.6; 77.2; 2 Macc. 13.10; 1QS 6.6-8). The earnestness of
Paul's praying is also shown by the word *hyperekperissou*, "exceedingly abundantly," which is the kind of hyperbole one would expect in epideictic rhetoric
(see similarly 5.13; Eph. 3.20). "Paul is fond of compounds expressing superla-
tiveness."[160] He is saying that he is making requests quite beyond all measure.[161]
Notice as well the rhetorical contrast between "in all the joy with which we rejoice" in v. 9 and "in all our distress and affliction" in v. 7. This sort of reduplication and amplification is also typical of epideictic rhetoric.[162]

What is said here begins to make the transition to the second part of this
discourse, where instruction and exhortation will be offered to strengthen the
existing faith of the converts in Thessalonike. The proper "transition" will come

156. Marshall, *1 and 2 Thessalonians*, p. 96.

157. Wanamaker, *1 and 2 Thessalonians*, p. 135.

158. We do not have here *ei* with the present indicative. See Malherbe, *The Letters*,
p. 203; Wanamaker, *1 and 2 Thessalonians*, p. 136; Rigaux, *Les Épitres*, p. 481.

159. Marshall, *1 and 2 Thessalonians*, p. 97.

160. Bruce, *1 and 2 Thessalonians*, p. 68.

161. Wanamaker, *1 and 2 Thessalonians*, p. 138.

162. See Wanamaker, *1 and 2 Thessalonians*, p. 137.

in the immediately following verses — vv. 11-13. For now we may stress with Marshall that "Christian growth is not produced 'automatically' by divine grace, so that the believer needs to make no effort, but rather the believer must be encouraged to show faith and love. Hence Paul can both pray to God for his converts and thank him for their spiritual progress and also urge them to grow in their faith and express delight when they respond to his urging."[163] Paul is not suggesting however that the Thessalonians have defects in their faith, only that they have deficiencies which need to be supplied.[164] Their understanding needs deepening and their adherence to core Christian values needs to be strengthened. The *narratio* contains implicit parenesis and prepares the hearers of the letter for the explicit parenesis to follow.

Bridging the Horizons

John Chrysostom, in reflecting on Paul's approach to ministry, says this:

> For Paul's work found its source in power, mighty power, power that surpassed mere human diligence. For Paul brought three qualifications to the preaching of the word: a fervent and adventurous zeal, a soul ready to undergo any possible hardship and the combination of knowledge and wisdom. Even with Paul's love of the difficult task, his blameless life would have accomplished little had he not also received the power of the Spirit. Examine the matter from Paul's own words: "That our ministry not be blamed." And again "For our exhortation is not founded on deceit, nor uncleanness, nor guile nor hidden under a cloak of covetousness." Thus you have seen his blamelessness. And again "For we aim at what is honorable, not only in the sight of the Lord but also in the sight of human beings." Without this Paul's work would have been impossible. People were not converted by Paul's miracles; no it was not the miracles that produced faith, nor did Paul base his high calling upon the miraculous but upon other grounds: a man must be irreproachable in conduct, prudent and discreet in his dealings with others, regardless of the dangers involved, and apt to teach. These were the qualifications that enabled Paul to reach his goal. (*Homilies* on Ephesians 6)[165]

---

163. Wanamaker, *1 and 2 Thessalonians*, p. 137.

164. See rightly Bruce, *1 and 2 Thessalonians*, p. 69. Paul is not correcting them so much as desiring to complete their understanding and basis for relating to God.

165. The translation is mine, but cf. that of P. Gorday, *Ancient Christian Commentary in Scripture* IX (Downers Grove: InterVarsity, 2000), pp. 63-64.

Chrysostom's reflections on Paul's ministry and the reasons for its success place the emphasis, of course, on the divine factor — God's divine power enabled Paul to accomplish these things. Yet at the same time Chrysostom emphasizes that it was not the miracles that Paul did that produced faith, but rather his good character and apt teaching. If these are the most essential characteristics of successful ministry, then there is hope for those of us who are not St. Paul and cannot conjure up miracles. But to good character and apt teaching Chrysostom adds zeal, a willingness to suffer or endure hardship, and both knowledge and wisdom. In other words, Chrysostom thinks that it takes more than an average person to accomplish such things as Paul did. Indeed, it requires a very exceptional person.

Some teachers have knowledge but are unable to turn that alloy into something more precious, namely wisdom. Still other teachers have zeal, but not a zeal that is "unto knowledge." This is especially dangerous in our age of biblical illiteracy, when earnestness is mistaken for truth over and over again. Still other teachers are willing to endure much for their task and their charges but have few rhetorical gifts and have not been properly trained. Still others have all the requisites mentioned but are of dubious character. Such folks become quite compelling false teachers. Yet there is something more that Chrysostom fails to mention here.

Throughout this section of 1 Thessalonians one is struck time and again by Paul's pastor's heart and by how much he loves his converts. He does indeed really relate to them as a parent to his beloved children. He worries about their safety, their perseverance in the faith, their health, and all the usual things a good parent worries about. In addition, he stresses that he treated them like the gentlest of nannies when he was with them, nursing them along slowly in the faith, not getting impatient with them. It is clear that he is elated when Timothy comes with the good report as to how the church in Thessalonike is doing. It takes a rare combination of gifts and graces, timing and opportunities, persistence and perseverance, and of course the power of God to produce a Paul. We would be fooling ourselves if we saw him as just another ordinary Christian who had an extraordinary experience of God. This is saying too little about this remarkable man.

But the early Christian movement did not require a legion of Pauls for it to grow, develop, and advance through time. It seems to have required only a few, who could then direct and empower willing coworkers and local converts in the right direction. There is no getting away from the hierarchical character of early church leadership structures, with apostles at the top, then coworkers just below that level, local church leaders below that, and finally everyone else. But this hierarchy was not based on gender, ethnicity, or social status. The criterion was proximity to Jesus, knowledge of his life and teachings, having seen the risen Lord or been converted and trained by those who did, and willingness to serve even under exigent circumstances, to mention but a few factors. The early Christian movement was not a democracy, nor did the local congregation have the final say over its own existence — the itinerant founding apostles and co-workers could intervene at any time and rearrange things.

Yet it is notable and truly remarkable just how much Paul tries to make room for the freedom of his converts. He prefers to persuade rather than command. He uses rhetoric rather than manipulation and strong-arm tactics to accomplish his ends, unless the congregation is really in extremis. He wants them to take up the tasks of Christian life and work freely, and he always speaks the truth to them in love, being gentle, though seldom subtle. When churches today look for leaders, do they pay attention to the qualities Chrysostom lists and Paul exhibited?

Another dimension of the materials we find in 1 Thessalonians 1–3 is, of course, their heavy theological content. Whether we are dealing with the election and perseverance of the saints or eschatology and the wrath of God, major issues are raised in this material which require thoughtful handling. Trying to teach what Paul says about election by cobbling together a few sound-bytes and ideas here and there does more harm than good for a congregation that is not well-versed in the Bible, which is to say most congregations in America. Special care is called for in handling 1 Thess. 2.13–16. Abuse of that text has led to no small amount of mayhem and anti-Semitism. If one does not know how to speak about that text prayerfully and with careful understanding of its rhetorical flavor, it would be best just to leave it alone. Better to preach or teach on some of the virtues Paul alludes to throughout this discourse.

In his wonderful book *The Spirit of Early Christian Thought,* Robert Wilken chronicles how it is that Christianity developed its own language and form of discourse, its own virtue list, while at the same time drawing on extant models, both Jewish and Greco-Roman. It was a both-and situation. But he reminds us at various junctures that it was not just a matter of borrowing ideas, or generating new ones, for that matter.

> Christian thinking is much too independent to be treated chiefly in relation to Greco-Roman thought. . . . Early Christian thought is biblical, and one of the lasting accomplishments of the patristic period was to forge a way of thinking, scriptural in language and inspiration, that gave to the church and to Western civilization a unified and coherent interpretation of the Bible as a whole. . . . The distinctive marks of early Christian thinking can be set down in a few sentences. Christians reasoned from the history of Israel and of Jesus Christ, from the experience of Christian worship, and from the Holy Scriptures (and earlier interpretations of the Scriptures), that is to say from history, from ritual, and from text. Christian thinking is anchored in the church's life, sustained by . . . devotional practices. . . . Theory was not

an end in itself, and concepts and abstractions were always put at the service of a deeper immersion in the "res," the thing itself, the mystery of Christ and of the practice of the Christian life. The goal was not only understanding but love. . . . Accordingly, the way to God begins not with arguments or proofs but with discernment and faith, the ability to see what is disclosed in events and the readiness to trust the words of those who testify to them.[166]

Just so, and this means that teachers and preachers must be ever so careful in stringing together series of texts or ideas without careful attention to nexus and context of the material and the part it plays in an ongoing discourse in a living movement. It is more about story than it is about syllogism, more about praxis than practical thinking, more about relationships than the history of ideas — relationships with God and others.

One who reads 1 Thessalonians with an open mind and heart cannot but be touched by the deep pathos of the text and the profound love and concern exuding from Paul as he guides and goads and praises and warns and frets and exults over his converts. Here we see Paul the pastor in his element. We would do well not to forget, then, that all of the content of this discourse is meant to serve pastoral purposes, which is still the most appropriate way for it to be used today.

---

166. R. Wilken, *The Spirit of Early Christian Thought* (New Haven: Yale University Press, 2003), pp. xvi-xviii, 7.

Transitus — Closing Wish Prayer — 3.11-13

The passage to be examined at this juncture serves as the conclusion to the *narratio* but also as a bridge passage or *transitus* to the exhortations that are to follow. In this regard it functions very much like material we find in that other great Pauline example of epideictic rhetoric — Ephesians — in Eph. 3.20-21. Part of the rhetorical function of this material is to get the audience into a reverential mode, which helps in making them receptive to the exhortations that will follow in 1 Thessalonians 4–5.

The already mentioned themes of Paul's desire to visit the Thessalonians again and his hope that their love and faith will increase are gathered up into a wish prayer which lays them before God. But this prayer is not just retrospective. At the end of this prayer in v. 13 Paul speaks of God strengthening the converts so they may be holy when Jesus comes with the holy ones. This is immediately followed in 4.1-12 with an exhortation about holiness, which in turn is followed in 4.13–5.11 by a discussion of what is true of the Christian dead and what happens when Jesus comes with his holy ones. Also "increase and abound in love" in 3.12 both prefigures 4.9-12 and also echoes love of the Thessalonians for Paul mentioned in 3.6-10. What precedes is thus brought to a close with allusions to some of its themes, and what follows is introduced as some of its key language is introduced.

Epideictic rhetoric focuses often on the arousal of the emotions, especially the deeper ones, and here Paul is indeed trying to not only set up an ethos of adoration and reverence for what must be heard next, but also pathos is involved as well (see Aristotle, *Rhetoric* 1.2.5; Quintilian, *Inst. Or.* 6.2.8). Paul is engendering good will here.[1] The wish prayer, the *transitus* between the *narratio*

---

1. See rightly A. Lincoln, *Ephesians* (Waco: Word, 1990), p. 171: "Here at the end, it in-

and the *exhortatio,* is in a sense a new *exordium* which again establishes rapport with the audience and makes them disposed to accept the following exhortations.[2] It also gives us a clear glimpse into Paul's prayer life and the kind of things about which he was apt to pray.

As Lightfoot points out, there is a rhetorical symmetry to Paul's treatment of these things, for just as the narration ends in this way, so also the second major division of the discourse ends in the same sort of fashion in 5.23-24, which begins with the identical *Autos de ho Theos,* "God himself," both dealing with the parousia of Christ and the Thessalonians' blamelessness on the day of his coming.[3] The more one studies the rhetorical structure of 1 Thessalonians the more one is impressed with the care given to the construction of the discourse and the following of rhetorical conventions.

Epideictic rhetoric was the rhetoric of sermons and 1 Thessalonians is a powerful sermon. Jewett's theory is that prayers like we find in these verses were originally offered at the end of the proclamation of the Word in Christian worship.[4] But in fact this discourse would have been part of an act of worship and this prayer would have concluded this part of the giving of the Word. So we do not need to suggest a different original social setting for this material, once we realize that it was part of a proclamation delivered orally to the Thessalonians.

But may God himself also our Father and our Lord Jesus make straight our road/ way to you. But may the Lord enlarge you and make you abound in love unto one another and unto all, just as also we unto you, unto the establishing of your hearts blameless in holiness before God and our Father in the coming of our Lord Jesus with all his holy ones [amen].[5]

V. 11 begins with the mention of God the Father and the Lord Jesus in tandem, and it is to be stressed that this wish prayer is directed to both. Both are viewed

---

creases the goodwill of the recipients by reminding them of the suffering apostle's ministry on their behalf. It underlines for the Gentile readers that they owe their participation in the salvation that had been promised . . . to the Gospel that was originally revealed to and proclaimed by Paul."

2. See Lincoln, *Ephesians,* p. 200.

3. J. B. Lightfoot, *Notes on the Epistles of St. Paul* (Winona Lake: Alpha, reprint), p. 48.

4. R. Jewett, "The Form and Function of the Homiletic Benediction," *Anglican Theological Review* 51 (1969): 18-34.

5. The evidence for and against seeing the "Amen" as original is rather evenly balanced, but in view of the close parallel of this section with Eph. 3.20-21 and especially Eph. 3.21, which ends with "Amen," it should probably be seen as original here. See Metzger, *TC,* p. 631. In epideictic rhetoric not only are prayers and doxologies appropriate and common, but introducing major themes in prayer, presenting them before God before offering praise, blame, or reminder for the audience's embracing of them is appropriate.

as proper objects of prayer, which is to say that both are viewed as part of the Godhead.[6] The verbs here are quite properly in the optative ("may"), but there is no doubt about the ability of the Father and the Lord to accomplish what is prayed for. Notice as well that the verb is singular while the subject is plural (cf. 2 Thess. 2.16). Lightfoot puts it this way: "It is worthy of notice that this ascription to our Lord of a divine power in ordering the doings of men occurs in the earliest of St. Paul's Epistles, and indeed probably the earliest of the New Testament writings: thus showing that there was no time, however early, so far as we are aware, when He was not so regarded."[7]

What is even more astounding is that Jesus' lordship and divinity are not argued for but simply assumed. While I would argue that Galatians may be earlier, the point Lightfoot is making still stands. There was already a very high christology in play even in the earliest NT writings. Paul envisions God removing the obstacles Satan put in Paul's path so that he may return to Thessalonike (see 2.18).[8] There was considerable precedent in ancient Israel and early Judaism for wish prayers of this sort (cf. Num. 6.24-26; Ps. 20.1-5; 2 Macc. 1.2-6), and we find such prayers with regularity in Pauline documents or documents from the Pauline circle (cf. 1 Thess. 5.23; 2 Thess. 2.1-2; 3.5, 16; Rom. 15.5-6, 13; 2 Tim. 1.16-18; Heb. 13.20-21).[9]

The two verbs which follow in v. 12 make clear that Paul is praying that the Thessalonians' love may increase and indeed abound as they are given a larger and larger capacity to love both each other and all others, with the love existing between Paul and his converts named as an example of what this should look like. Paul is not just encouraging "brotherly" love among Christians but also love for those outside the community, despite persecution and suffering. This is close to what we find in that other early Pauline letter, Galatians (Gal. 6.10).[10] The strengthening Paul will speak of in v. 13 "does not come directly from the loving: rather loving creates the kind of person whom the Lord can strengthen." Paul is trying to avoid inculcating a form of Christianity where the avoiding of personal sin is valued more highly than active love of others. Both are valued and held in tension, but it is primarily before God

---

6. C. Wanamaker, *Commentary on 1 and 2 Thessalonians* (Grand Rapids: Eerdmans, 1990), p. 141 points to Sir. 23.1-4 as background here, which may be of some relevance. What we see here, however, is that various divine names are parceled out between two persons, whereas only one is in view in the "Father/Lord" language in Sirach 23. One may compare also 1 Cor. 8.6, where again we see how the christological revolution in Paul's thinking changed the way he uses God language so that now Christ can be included in that sphere and way of talking.

7. Lightfoot, *Notes*, p. 48.

8. I. H. Marshall, *1 and 2 Thessalonians* (Grand Rapids: Eerdmans, 1983), p. 100.

9. See the detailed study of these sorts of prayers in G. P. Wiles, *Paul's Intercessory Prayers* (Cambridge: Cambridge University Press, 1974).

10. See rightly Wanamaker, *1 and 2 Thessalonians*, p. 143.

that humans need to exhibit holiness, while in relationship to others love should characterize one's behavior.[11] What Paul has in mind in relationships with both God and humans is holy love — not love without holiness and certainly not holiness without love.

V. 13 continues the thought of v. 12. Here as well it is the Lord Jesus who is establishing the converts' hearts — "the whole point of the passage requires that Christ should be regarded as the sole author of the spiritual advancement of the Thessalonians."[12] This establishing does not just involve the steadying of someone whose affections are uncertain or ambivalent. The aim of establishing the heart is that the converts might pass the eschatological test and be found blameless in holiness in the sight of God at the coming of Christ.

The idea is that those who meet Christ when he returns need to be in the same state of holiness as those who are returning from heaven with Christ (probably angels — see 2 Thess. 1.7; Dan. 4.10-13; Ps. 89.5; Zech. 14.5; *1 Enoch* 1.6-9; 1QH 3.22; 4.25; 1QM 3.25; cf. Jude 14; Mark 8.38; 13.27; Matt. 13.41; 25.31). The problem with arguing that saints are meant by "holy ones" here (cf. 2 Thess. 1.10; *Didache* 16.7; *Ascension of Isaiah* 4.14) is that the saints will reunite with Jesus when he comes, not before, according to 1 Thess. 4.16-17.[13] It seems likely that Zech. 14.5c underlies our text here. The language previously applied to the *yom Yahweh* and the theophanies of Yahweh in general are now being applied to Jesus. What all these OT texts have in common is that the theophany and judgment both occur on earth, not in heaven (Pss. 50.3; 68.1-7; 80.1; 82.8; 107.20; Isa. 26.19; 42.13; 63.9; 64.1; 66.18; Hab. 2.3; Zeph. 1.15; Mal. 4.1; this is even true of Dan. 7.13-14).[14] As we shall see when we examine 1 Thessalonians 4 and 2 Thessalonians 1–2, some of the imagery comes from theophany and judgment day material and some from language used of an emperor's visit to a city.[15]

It can be argued that "in holiness before God in the coming of our Lord" intends to convey the implication that when the converts appear before Christ they will be in the very presence of God. Put another way, when one appears before Jesus one also appears before the Father, and both together are the divine judges of the spiritual state of those who come into their presence. "The unity of the Father and Son in judgment is important. It means that we do not have to face any other God than the one who has revealed himself in Jesus." Furthermore, the prayer for growth in love is part and parcel with the prayer for holi-

---

11. E. Best, *First and Second Thessalonians* (London: Black, 1972), pp. 150-51.

12. Lightfoot, *Notes*, p. 49.

13. Against B. Rigaux, *Les Épitres aux Thessaloniciens* (Paris: Gabalda, 1956), pp. 491-92.

14. See the discussion in B. Witherington, *Jesus, Paul, and the End of the World* (Downers Grove: InterVarsity, 1992), pp. 145-78, and see F. F. Bruce, *1 and 2 Thessalonians* (Waco: Word, 1982), pp. 73-74.

15. See pp. 142-44 below.

ness since increasing in love amounts to increasing in holiness and moves toward the goal of blamelessness.[16]

We cannot finish this discussion without mentioning that Paul is envisioning that his converts will in due course fully reflect the character of God, who is holy (cf. Pss. 71.22; 89.18; Isa. 1.4; Jer. 50.9; Ezek. 39.7). The Thessalonians' coming to be "established without blame in holiness" means that they will be conformed to the character of God himself. "That this was of fundamental importance for Paul can be seen in 4.3, where sanctification or holiness . . . is said to be the will of God for the Thessalonians."[17] As it turned out, God would not answer the prayer to pave the way for Paul's return to Thessalonike for some time — after 2 Thessalonians had been written (cf. 1 Cor. 16.5; 2 Cor. 2.13; Acts 19.21; 20.1).[18]

Up to now in the discourse Paul has been primarily concerned about his relationship with the Thessalonians and the strengthening of it. Now he will turn in what follows to their relationships with each other and with the world.

16. Marshall, *1 and 2 Thessalonians*, pp. 101-2.

17. Wanamaker, *1 and 2 Thessalonians*, pp. 144-45.

18. See A. Malherbe, *The Letters to the Thessalonians* (New York: Doubleday, 2000), pp. 214-15.

The *Exhortatio* — A Call to Holiness and Hope — 4.1–5.15

Paul has established rapport with his audience, reminded them of their intertwined stories, and received the good news that they remained people of faith and love. It now remains for him to address the deficiencies alluded to in the *transitus* (3.10), the bridge between the narration of pertinent facts and the exhortation. These exhortations are in part reminders and further explications of what they have heard earlier about holiness (4.1-8), brotherly love and work (4.9-12), the Christian dead (4.13-18), the times and seasons of Christ's return (5.1-11), leaders, and living in a kind and peaceful fashion (5.12-15).

This will be quite appropriately followed by the *peroratio* (5.16-22), a closing wish prayer like the one which concluded chs. 1–3 (5.23-24), and then the usual epistolary elements which conclude such a Pauline letter (5.25-28). The notion that Paul is offering up a random and unorganized group of parenetic thoughts, a sort of miscellany, can be dismissed once one recognizes the rhetorical arrangement of the material. As we shall see, the content of the reminders and amplifications is pertinent to the Thessalonian situation even though corrections of problems are not offered here.

Exhortations were as appropriate in epideictic rhetoric as they were in deliberative rhetoric, but they served different functions in the different species of rhetoric. In deliberative rhetoric one urges a change in policy, practice, belief, or behavior in the near future. In epideictic rhetoric one urges growth and development of beliefs and behaviors one already has, at least in nascent form. Paul has set up a tone of thanksgiving and gratitude and has effected further bonding with his converts through his emotive rhetoric in chs. 1–3, and this in part served the rhetorical purpose of making the audience favorably disposed toward him and what he will urge in the second major portion of the discourse. "A frame of mind will have been developed among the recipients that should lead them to accept the paraenesis and, it is assumed, to practice the behaviour that it calls for. The recipients are meant to have been so strongly and favorably impressed with their Christianity as it has been presented in the *exordium* and *narratio* that they will be agreeably inclined toward a call to conduct their lives in a way seen to accord with that presentation."[1]

Paul then is not so much dealing with festering problems as filling up and filling out the audience's understandings of truths or teachings they have already embraced but may not have seen the full implications of. The apostle is not offering arguments or proofs for some singular thesis statement or opposing some group of antagonists. He is, rather, reminding and strengthening a commitment to a Christian way of believing and living into the future. The call to a further level of commitment to the core beliefs and values is appropriate at this juncture.

In terms of the topics usually addressed in epideictic rhetoric (including in its funerary form of eulogy, or even encomium) one was expected to praise key virtues and values and condemn vices that were destructive of the core values. One also, especially in a eulogy, would spend time on beliefs about the after-life, the fate of the dead, and the like. We find these very sort of topics in chs. 4–5 as Paul follows both the conventions and regular *topoi* of epideictic rhetoric.

Menander Rhetor notes the following points about epideictic rhetoric: (1) Encomia and thanksgivings about certain facts or events can be divided up into chronological sections and may well involve a variety of narratives of relevance (413.14-15; 414.7; cf. 1 Thessalonians 1–3). (2) Consolatory speeches could include materials dealing with the preferability of life after death to the present life (414.8-10; cf. 1 Thess. 4.13–5.10) and consolation for the bereaved, reassuring them of the blessed state of the deceased in that they now dwelled with the gods (421.14-17; 414.19-20; cf. 1 Thess. 4.13–5.10). (3) Such a speech could and should end with prayer, perhaps even a wish prayer (422.2-5; cf. 1 Thess. 5.23-24).[2] Epideictic rhetoric by its very nature often involved pertinent general instructions and reflections and wishes about fundamental matters rather than engaging in solving some particular problem.[3]

---

1. R. R. Jeal, *Integrating Theology and Ethics in Ephesians* (Lewiston: Mellen, 2000), pp. 177-78.

2. See the helpful discussion of all this in F. W. Hughes, "The Rhetoric of 1 Thessalonians," in R. F. Collins, ed., *The Thessalonian Correspondence* (Leuven: Leuven University Press, 2000), p. 107.

3. The failure to notice the rhetorical signals in the text is precisely why M. Dibelius and others made the mistake of thinking that all such NT parenesis was of a generic sort when they found that sort of parenesis in documents like Ephesians and 1 Thessalonians. Deliberative ethical teaching such as we find in 1 Corinthians or Romans is certainly not of this generic character. It should be noted as well that this is one of the things that distinguishes

Of course there were a variety of appropriate topics for epideictic rhetoric, as we have seen, and one need not address all or even most of them in any one discourse. Indeed, one needed to speak on the topics that would be most relevant or persuasive for the particular audience of suffering and bereaved folks and the particular occasion. There is then a sort of specificity to 1 Thessalonians within the parameters of the general topics of comfort, counsel, compassion, encouragement, and even exhortation one might choose to bring before those who were suffering, though the rhetoric is not like the specificity of deliberative rhetoric.[4] It is more a matter of dealing with first principles, or as Aristotle stresses, amplifying (*auxēsis*, or augmenting) and clarifying the implications of what one has already endorsed and embraced (*Rhetoric* 1.9.40).[5]

---

1 Thessalonians from 2 Thessalonians, which is indeed a problem-solving letter, a piece of deliberative rhetoric. It is interesting to compare and contrast the rhetoric of eschaton in 1 and 2 Thessalonians when the subject is treated in two different forms of rhetoric. See pp. 213-23 below.

4. See the discussion of E. Krentz, "1 Thessalonians: Rhetorical Flourishes and Formal Constraints," in K. P. Donfried and J. Beutler, eds., *The Thessalonians Debate* (Grand Rapids: Eerdmans, 2000), pp. 287-318.

5. See the discussion by F. W. Hughes, "The Social Situations Implied by Rhetoric," in *The Thessalonians Debate*, p. 251.

Part One:
The Call to Holiness and Brotherly Love —
4.1-8, 9-12

For the rest, then, brothers, we appeal to you and encourage you in the Lord Jesus, just as you received (instruction) from us on how it is necessary for you to walk and to please God, just as you are in fact walking,[1] in order that you would do so still better. For you know what instructions we gave you through the Lord Jesus. For this is the will of God — your sanctification, that you abstain from sexual sin, each of you knowing how to acquire his own vessel in holiness and honor, not in the passion of sexual desire as the pagans, those not knowing God, and not to go beyond and defraud his brother in this matter, for the executor of justice concerning these things is the Lord, just as also we forewarned you and testified. For God did not call us for impurity but in sanctification. Consequently the one disregarding is not disregarding humans but God, who also gave his Holy Spirit to us.

But concerning brotherly love it is not necessary to have to write to you,[2] for you yourselves were God-taught unto the love of one another. For also you practice it unto all the brothers in the whole of Macedonia. But we appeal to you to do so still better, and you should strive eagerly to live quietly and to attend to business the same way and to work with your [own] hands, just as also we charged you, in order you might walk properly in relationship to those outside [the community] and that you might have need of no one/nothing.

---

1. Some manuscripts omit this clause (D, K, L, some minuscles and the Textus Receptus), but it has strong external testimony (ℵ, A, B, D*, F, G, numerous others) and should be retained. See Metzger, *TC*, p. 632.

2. Literally "you have no need to write to you." The reading *exete* is likely original and should be retained. See Metzger, *TC*, p. 632.

In the first two sections of the exhortation (4:1-8, 9-12) Paul makes it quite clear that he is not dealing with new or different information, nor is he asking them to change course and go in a new direction. He reminds them that they have already been instructed by himself or even by God on these matters, and that he simply wants them to keep walking in the direction they are already going in these matters, only doing so "still better" (*perisseuete mallon,* vv. 1 and 10). This phrase binds these two sections together, and one can also say that the two sections stand in some natural contrast with each other: avoid defrauding your neighbors, rather practice brotherly love toward them living in peace with those outside. Paul is then reminding the Thessalonians what to do and what not to do in relationship to neighbors. There is a logical progression here, and in both sections the essential message is that one should conduct oneself in a holy manner in personal relationships.[3] The issue in play in vv. 1-8 is sexual ethics, not business matters. This explains the language about sanctification, passion, desire, and uncleanness and of course the exhortation to avoid *porneia.*[4] The remaining question then is what to make of *to heautou skeuos ktasthai* in v. 4. We will address that matter in some detail below.

To loipon, "for the rest/finally," is a clear marker of a division in the text. The problem with translating it "and finally" is that both here and in Phil. 3.1 it does not introduce the *peroratio* or the concluding remarks but simply indicates a significant shift in the subject matter. In Phil. 4.8 it does actually introduce the *peroratio* and so could be translated "finally" (as also in P. Oxy. 119.13). *To loipon* appears to be slightly stronger than just *loipon* (cf. 2 Thess. 3.1; 1 Cor. 1.16; 2 Cor. 13.11: probably introducing the *peroratio;* 2 Tim. 4.8).[5] My suggestion would be that here its use with *oun* gives the clue as to what is meant: "for the rest, then," that is, "as for the other topics which I need to address and have not yet."[6]

The construction of this first sentence is quite similar to what we find later in Col. 2.6 — "as then you have received Christ Jesus the Lord, walk in him." Paul

---

3. There may even be a connection with what follows, since someone who has lost their Christian spouse might make the mistake of going after another person's mate.

4. See the discussion in Witherington, *Women in the Earliest Churches* (Cambridge: Cambridge University Press, 1988), pp. 64-65.

5. See B. Rigaux, *Les Épitres aux Thessaloniciens* (Paris: Gabalda, 1956), pp. 495-96.

6. See J. B. Lightfoot, *Notes on the Epistles of St. Paul* (Winona Lake: Alpha, reprint), p. 51. F. F. Bruce, *1 and 2 Thessalonians* (Waco: Word, 1982), p. 78 suggests that it should not be confused with the genitival expression — *tou loipou* (Gal. 6.17; Eph. 6.10), which he says has a temporal sense — "the rest of the time." The problem with this conclusion is that in Eph. 6.10 it clearly introduces the *peroratio* and should be translated "finally," not "for the rest of the time," since it refers to the final bit of argumentation, and the same can be said of the occurrence in Gal. 6.17. I am not persuaded of the relevance of Hellenistic Greek usage of the term as a transitional particle to mean simply "therefore," but see M. E. Thrall, *Greek Particles in the New Testament* (Leiden: Brill, 1962), pp. 25-30.

requests and appeals here, rather than demands, as is appropriate in epideictic rhetoric dealing with a situation that is not a crisis and does not demand a heavy wielding of authority. Nevertheless, "in the Lord Jesus" makes it evident that this is a very serious appeal with Christ's authority behind it, or there is "a sense that Christ is thoroughly involved in the situation or action in question."[7] The same can be said for the use of *parangelia*, originally a word for a military command, in v. 2, a term that has an authoritative flavor to it (cf. 2 Thess. 3.4, 6, 10, 12; 1 Cor. 7.10, where the verbal form means "command"; 1 Tim. 1.18, where the noun means "instruction").[8] Furthermore, the use of *parakaleō*, "encourage," follows the style of rulers speaking to subjects. It "has neither the character of an order (as *epitassō*) nor of a supplication (as *deomai*)."[9] It is more than mere request, since Paul has authority as the founder of the Thessalonian congregation.[10]

Paul is clearly covering old ground here, and it is clear from his letters that ethical instruction was a regular part of his initial teaching of converts or potential converts (cf. 1 Thess. 4.6; 1 Cor. 6.9; Gal. 5.21). Furthermore, he commends the Thessalonians for already living the life he wants them to live. He wants them to make further progress and does not censure them for any lack of growth as Christians. They were relatively new Christians and had already suffered a good deal for their faith and had remained steadfast. To censure them at this juncture would not only be a bad rhetorical strategy; it might well alienate them from Paul at this crucial juncture in their spiritual journey. Paul then will encourage them to keep going in the right direction and remind them what that direction is. While he will appeal and exhort, v. 1 also stresses how it is "necessary" for them to walk (cf. 2 Thess. 3.7; Rom. 12.3). This is not optional, but rather required Christian conduct. "You know" in v. 2, as in 1.5 and 2.1, emphasizes that this is all reminder. "Remembering" is of the essence of discipleship, and the instructions given in these first two divisions of the exhortation serve the social function of helping to define boundaries and increase the internal cohesion of the community.[11]

---

7. J. D. G. Dunn, *Jesus and the Spirit* (Philadelphia: Westminister, 1975), p. 324.

8. Bruce, *1 and 2 Thessalonians*, p. 79. A. Malherbe, *The Letters to the Thessalonians* (New York: Doubleday, 2000), pp. 220-21 suggests that Paul is speaking more like Pliny, who in *Epistle* 8.24.1 says: "The love I bear for you obliges me to give you, not indeed a precept (for you are far from needing a preceptor), but a reminder that you should resolutely act according to the knowledge you already have, or also improve on it." There is a similarity in tone with Paul's remarks to be sure, but Paul *is* claiming to be their preceptor and says he has already given them precepts or charges when he was with them.

9. C. J. Bjerklund, *Parakalô. Form, Funktion und Sinn der parakalo-Sätze in den paulinischen Briefen* (Oslo: Universitetforlaget, 1967), p. 188.

10. E. Best, *A Commentary on the First and Second Epistles to the Thessalonians* (London: Black, 1972), 155.

11. See C. Wanamaker, *Commentary on 1 and 2 Thessalonians* (Grand Rapids: Eerdmans, 1990), p. 147.

Paul addresses his converts as "brothers" not only here but very frequently in all his letters. He believes in a literal spiritual kinship (not merely fictive kinship) created by the Holy Spirit's work in believers' lives such that they become part of one family, the family of faith. The spiritual use of the terminology is found only rarely in early Jewish sources (Exod. 2.11; Deut. 3.18 in the LXX; 2 Macc. 1.1), and we may suggest that it was Jesus' use of such terminology for his followers (see Mark 3.31-35) that prompted the frequency of usage by Paul and others. Perhaps, as Wanamaker conjectures, the use of Father language for God by Jesus and Paul and other early Christians also helps explain why "brother" and "sister" language is so common in early Christianity.[12]

V. 3 begins by identifying part of God's will[13] for all Christians, in Thessalonike and elsewhere: "your holiness/sanctification" (5.18 will mention a very different part of God's will for his people). In light of what follows in v. 3, it is perfectly clear that Paul is not talking about ritual purity but about moral purity. *Hagiosynē* (3.13) is the state of being holy, and *hagiasmos* is the process of being made holy.

Sanctification involves the avoidance of *porneia*, sexual sin.[14] This is part of the "separateness" that is at the core of the meaning of *hagiasmos:* holiness/set-apartness. There were numerous such prohibitions of *porneia* in early Judaism (*Jubilees* 20.3-6; 25.1; 39.6; Sir. 23.16-27; Philo, *De Specialibus Legibus* 3.51; *Testament of Simeon* 5.3; *Testament of Reuben* 4.6; cf. Exod. 20.14; Lev. 20.10-26; Rom. 1.24-26). *Porneia* has a root sense of prostitution (*pornai* being prostitutes), but it could sometimes have a specific reference to incest (see 1 Cor. 5.1; Matt. 5.32; 19.9), though often it was simply an umbrella term for any and all sorts of sexual sin, including fornication (cf. 2 Cor. 12.21; Gal. 5.19; Col. 3.5).[15] In

12. Wanamaker, *1 and 2 Thessalonians*, p. 147.

13. As Lightfoot, *Notes*, p. 53 points out, the omission of the definite article before *thelēma* indicates that the sanctification of the audience is not coextensive with the whole will of God, not even the whole will of God for this audience, but only part of it (cf. 1 Cor. 16.12; 1 Macc. 3.60). Lightfoot may also be right that Paul's reference to *porneia* and abstaining and what follows are perhaps an allusion to the decree in Acts 16.4 (cf. Acts 15.20, 29). This would also explain the characterization of conversion as a turning from idols in 1 Thess. 1.9. In other words, 1 Thessalonians, like 1 Corinthians, is written with knowledge of the decree and attempts to reinforce it. On this see B. Witherington, *The Acts of the Apostles* (Grand Rapids: Eerdmans, 1998), pp. 450-70.

14. See Rom. 6.22, where the goal of sanctification is said to be eternal life. In fact what is said is that having been set free from sin and free to serve God "you have your fruit unto holiness," and the result/goal is eternal life. Sanctification one has now as a fruit of salvation, but eternal life one has in the future as goal *(telos)* or completion of the process. It is surely implied that the latter goal is not reached without the former condition.

15. See J. Jensen, "Does *Porneia* Mean Fornication? A Critique of Bruce Malina," *NovT* 20 (1978): 161-84, refuting B. Malina, "Does *Porneia* Mean Fornication?" *NovT* 14 (1972): 10-17.

other words, in Jewish and Christian circles it referred to all sexual activity out-side marriage.[16] The definite article here before *porneia* probably means that it is used in its widest sense.[17] In Thessalonike *porneia* in a ritualized form was even part of religion in the cult of the Cabiri and in any case was widely toler-ated in many forms in the Greco-Roman world.[18] Christians needed not only to be sanctified but to play their part in consecration by abstaining from immoral-ity. "There are thus two aspects to sanctification, divine initiative and human endeavor."[19] Sanctification would inevitably set Gentile Christians apart from many of their former associates, especially in a seaport like Thessalonike.[20]

In the much controverted v. 4 Paul uses the term *skeuos*, "vessel," figura-tively, as he does elsewhere (2 Cor. 4.7; Rom. 9.21-23; 2 Tim. 2.20-21; cf. Heb. 9.21). Normally *ktasthai* had an ingressive sense — "acquire, take possession of" — rather than simply "possess, keep."[21] But we have examples in Jewish litera-ture (Sir. 36.24; Ruth 4.5 LXX) where *ktasthai gynaika* clearly means "take a wife." If *skeuos* is interpreted to mean "body," then the ingressive sense of the verb becomes impossible, and in any case "vessel" or the like used of a wife clearly has precedent in Jewish literature (see Prov. 5.15). This does not settle the issue of whether the verb has durative or ingressive force. If the former, then Paul is talking about honorable and holy conduct while married rather than taking a wife in a holy and honorable manner. Either reading is possible, but the ingressive reading perhaps has a bit of an edge.

Some scholars have however argued that *skeuos* is a euphemism for the male genitalia.[22] There are however serious problems with this view: (1) one has to read into the verb the concept of mastery and so render it "gain mastery/con-trol over," but in neither its ingressive nor its durative sense does *ktasthai* have that meaning. (2) Paul has other euphemisms for male genitalia: either "unpresent-able parts" or "less honorable parts" (1 Cor. 12.23-24). "Parts" is plural, but *skeuos* here is singular.[23] (3) The pronoun *heautou* is in the attributive position here ("his own"), which sets up a contrast with someone else's possession or *skeuos*.[24]

---

16. I. H. Marshall, *1 and 2 Thessalonians* (Grand Rapids: Eerdmans, 1983), p. 107.

17. See Malherbe, *The Letters*, p. 225. He is right to also point out that some scribes re-alized the breadth of the usage here and tried to make it clearer by adding "all" to the article (F, G) or by replacing the definite article with *pasēs* (ℵ, 104, 365 and several others).

18. See Rigaux, *Les Épitres*, p. 502; Bruce, *1 and 2 Thessalonians*, p. 82.

19. Malherbe, *The Letters*, p. 225.

20. See Best, *First and Second Thessalonians*, p. 160.

21. Malherbe, *The Letters*, p. 227.

22. See Wanamaker, *1 and 2 Thessalonians*, pp. 152-53; cf. Bruce, *1 and 2 Thessalonians*, p. 83; Marshall, *1 and 2 Thessalonians*, pp. 108-9.

23. In other words, one would have to argue that Paul is just talking about getting con-trol of the penis here, but he does not refer to the male apparatus in the singular elsewhere.

24. Malherbe, *The Letters*, p. 226.

This same sort of use of pronouns is found in 1 Cor. 7.2-4, where it is said that one's body belongs to one's spouse rather than to oneself. This makes explicable the use of "vessel" language of the spouse here. If Paul were simply talking here about gaining mastery over one's own desires and body rather than focusing on interpersonal behavior, he would not have used the pronoun as he does.[25] (4) the genitalia interpretation is largely based on the assumption that a text like 1 Sam. 21.5 provides the euphemism, which Paul then renders into Greek. But even if *keli* there is rendered "things" rather than "bodies," referring to the male genitalia, the noun is plural at least in its first occurrence, not singular as here.[26] So that is not likely to be the background to Paul's usage. We have in any case indisputable evidence of the use of *skeuos* for one's wife (or husband) in 1 Pet. 3.7. This matter is complex enough that it requires a more detailed discussion.

A Closer Look: Holy Wedlock and Unholy Alliances

Commentators have been divided throughout church history on the referent of *skeuos*.[27] In favor of the view that a man's own body is meant it is argued (1) that Paul is addressing all the audience, including the unmarried ("each of you"); (2) that this passage has notable parallels with 1 Cor. 6.12-20, where the reference is clearly to the believer's own body *(sōma)*; (3) in 2 Cor. 4.7 *skeuos* means "body"; (4) if Paul were referring to marriage he would seem to have a low or essentially sensual view of marriage and its function; (5) *ktasthai* need not mean "acquire," and there is some reason to think it can have the force of *kektesthai*, meaning "possess" or "gain mastery of"; and (6) Jewish ethics used *skeuos* of the body.[28]

Against this entire line of reasoning we may note: (1) in 1 Pet. 3.7 *skeuos* clearly refers to a wife, an argument which has even more force if in fact Silas had something to do with both of these documents (see 1 Pet. 5.12), or even if 1 Peter's author knows this particular Pauline tradition (cf. 1 Pet. 3.1-7 and 1 Thess. 4.1-8). If the latter is the

---

25. See rightly, Malherbe, *The Letters*, p. 226.

26. My OT colleague Bill Arnold furthermore suggests that *keli* in 1 Sam. 21.5 (21.6 in the Hebrew) may well refer to military weapons. The Hebrew word is generic and just means "things." It is not as specific as the Greek word translated "vessels."

27. Rigaux, *Les Épitres*, pp. 504-5 lists those who have taken each position. Theodore of Mopsuestia, Augustine, Aquinas, probably Lightfoot, and Best favor the allusion being to a wife, while John of Damascus, Theophylactus, Tertullian, Calvin, Beza, Dibelius, and Rigaux favor the reference to the man's own body.

28. While I agree with G. Carras, "Jewish Ethics and Gentile Converts: Remarks on 1 Thes 4.3-8," in *The Thessalonian Correspondence*, pp. 306-15, that Paul is both reflecting an indebtedness to general synagogue ethics about sexual morality and is also imposing that morality on Gentiles, Carras fails to note the telltale signs in which Paul has recontoured his Jewish ethic to fit his audience and their own largely Gentile ethos.

case, we would have early evidence that Paul's tradition was understood to refer to a wife. (2) The normal meaning of *ktasthai* is certainly "acquire," and, if that is the meaning here, it rules out the "body" interpretation. One does not "acquire" one's own body. (3) There are certain parallels between 1 Corinthians 7 and our text, and clearly 1 Corinthians 7 is about those who are or ought to be married. We have there much the same language as here: marriage is discussed in relationship to *porneia*, desire, uncleanness, and temptation. Paul says there that "because of sexual sin each should have his own wife" (1 Cor. 7.2). I submit that Paul is referring to the same matter here, though more generically or obliquely. (4) *Kektesthai* is used of marrying a wife in the LXX of Ruth 4.10 and Sir. 36.24. (5) *Pleonektein* can certainly refer to a man defrauding another through sexual activity, including adultery.[29] (6) Paul uses not *skeuos* but *sōma* when he speaks of a person's relationship to his own body, and the point there (2 Cor. 4.7) is the frailty of the human body, not its sexual character. (7) I can find no examples outside our current text where the translation "gain mastery of" is suitable for the use of *ktasthai*. The idea of mastery or control has to be read into the verb. (8) The language of honoring is present both here and in 1 Pet. 3.7. It would be strange to talk about honoring one's own body but quite appropriate to talk about treating one's spouse with honor. (9) Even if one translates *ktasthai* as having durative force and so meaning "keep, possess," this still suits the marital interpretation. There is in any case clear evidence of this verb being used of marriage (Musonius Rufus, fragment 12).[30]

Thus the sense here is: "your sanctification involves you knowing how to acquire/keep your own wife in a sanctified manner and in honor, not in the passion of desire, and does not involve defrauding your brother in this matter."[31] Paul's emphasis here on sexual matters is a product of his knowledge not only of the general ethos of permissiveness in the Greco-Roman world in such matters, but also his more specific familiarity of the ethos in port cities like Thessalonike. As I have said elsewhere, "in a permissive society it is easy to see how the intimate fellowship of early Christians who met in the confines of homes, shared in the Lord's Supper, greeting each other with a holy kiss, and allowed men and women to participate in all these activities *could* lead to an intimacy of the wrong sort between certain members of the Christian family."[32]

Chrysostom understands correctly Paul's line of thinking and remarks:

> To each man God has assigned a wife. He has set boundaries on nature and limits sexual intercourse to one person only. Therefore, intercourse with another is transgression, and taking more than belongs to one, and robbery. Or rather it is more cruel than any robbery; for we grieve less when robbed of our riches than when our marriage is invaded. . . . Paul does not mean by the use of the word

---

29. The defrauding language would seem less apt if homosexual activity were meant.
30. See Malherbe, *The Letters*, p. 226.
31. See the discussion in Witherington, *Women in the Earliest Churches*, pp. 65-69.
32. Witherington, *Women in the Earliest Churches*, p. 68.

"brother" that we are free to sleep with the wife of an unbeliever. Paul shows that God will avenge and punish such an act, not to avenge the unbeliever but to avenge himself. Why? You have insulted God. He himself called you, and you in turn have insulted him. Whether you sleep with the empress or your married handmaid, it makes no difference. The crime is the same. Why? Because he does not avenge the injured persons but himself. *(Homilies* on 1 Thessalonians 5)

This text then is a further piece of evidence that Paul advocated exclusive monogamy. Each man should have his own wife and have sexual relationships with his own wife and not invade someone else's marriage, but also should treat his own wife with honor and respect, not merely as a sex object. We have here the earliest evidence of Paul's views on Christian marriage and fidelity, and it comports with what we find him saying a bit later in 1 Corinthians 7 and much later in Eph. 5.21-33. It would appear that he formulated his views on this subject early on in his ministry and maintained them throughout his ministry.

V. 4 suggests that marriage should involve holiness and honor. Sanctification was not an abstract idea for Paul. As Malherbe stresses, "The realism with which Paul views holiness versus sexual immorality is evident from 1 Cor. 6.12-20. . . . In marriage, sanctification is so palpable a quality in the Christian that it extends in some way even to an unbelieving partner in marriage (1 Cor. 7.14). This is not the same as praying and thinking about God upon entering the wedding chamber (Tobit 8:1-10 . . .). It is from such a perspective of holiness that Paul's discussion of marriage should be viewed."[33] "Honor" was a regular subject of conversation when one considered a life partner in the Greco-Roman world (cf. Xenophon, *Hiero* 3.4; Plutarch, *Advice to Bride and Groom* 143B), but holiness or sanctification would be something rather new in the discussion for a Gentile unless one had previously been part of a synagogue discussion about this matter.

In v. 5 Paul associates immorality with pagan lack of knowledge of the one true God. This is a typical Jewish line of thinking, found especially in Wisdom literature (Wis. 14.12-27; cf. *Sibylline Oracles* 3.29-45), that associated idolatry with immorality or knowing the true God with sexual morality.[34] Paul will elaborate on this theme more fully in Rom. 1.24-27.[35] Paul contrasts his audience with pagans, not with Jews, probably because the majority of them came to Christian faith as pagans, not as either Jews or God-fearers.[36] He is thus deal-

---

33. Malherbe, *The Letters*, p. 228.

34. See Wanamaker, *1 and 2 Thessalonians*, p. 153.

35. On which see B. Witherington and D. Hyatt, *The Letter to the Romans* (Grand Rapids: Eerdmans, 2004), ad loc.

36. See pp. 73-74 above on 1 Thess. 1.9.

ing with temptations that Jews like Paul believed Gentiles often fell prey to, and no doubt they did. Paul's concern here is that lust will guide a person's decision about a mate and the course of one's relationship with one's mate. This, in Paul's view, is a mistake pagans were apt to make, and thus Paul is engaging in an attempt to resocialize his audience, getting them to rethink some of their basic assumptions and practices when it comes to marriage. After idolatry, sexual immorality and covetousness were seen as the major pagan vices (cf. Gal. 5.19-21; 1 Cor. 5.9-11; 6.9-10; 2 Cor. 12.20-21; Rom. 1.29-31; 2.21-22; 13.13).[37]

The grammatical construction *pleonektein ton adelphon* in v. 6 has a precedent in Dio Chrysostom, *Oration* 17.8. It is possible that the verb has the commercial sense of "defraud" here, not least because marriages in Paul's age were arranged and were viewed to a large extent as property transactions. To invade someone else's marriage was to defraud the husband of his property rights.[38] Nevertheless, Paul may be using the term in the same way as he uses *pleonexia* in 2.5, in which case the translation "act covetously toward the brother" may be correct.[39] The term in any case refers to the desire to possess more than one ought to in any sphere of life.[40] The Lord who is the avenger in these matters is Christ, rather than the Father (cf. 2 Thess. 1.8; 1 Thess. 2.19; 3.3). Paul perhaps draws on Ps. 94.1 here, but applies it to Jesus, as is his wont.[41] He places a strong stress on the fact that he has emphasized this matter before: "we warned you before and testified/kept on testifying."[42]

V. 7 involves an interesting contrast. Believers were not called or purposed for a life of debauchery and impurity. Rather a holy God called them in and for holiness. Paul "is not merely reminding them of their call but is drawing their attention to its moral consequences. . . . It is through God's call that they are sanctified (2 Thess. 2:13-14), that they became *hagioi klētoi* ('saints by calling'; 1 Cor. 2:2; 2 Cor. 1:1 . . .)."[43] It is by the ongoing work of the indwelling Holy Spirit that one continues to be in a condition that comports with one's calling, but clearly this condition must also manifest itself in the way a Christian wills and acts, and so there is a cooperative relationship between God and the believer in regard to sanctification, as this very exhortation makes evident. Sanctification is seen as the believer's responsibility in v. 3 and as God's action here. Both are true.

Paul punctuates this first exhortation with an exclamation point in v. 8 by saying that whoever rejects this teaching rejects not merely Paul or human

---

37. See Malherbe, *The Letters*, pp. 231-32.

38. See Best, *First and Second Thessalonians*, p. 166.

39. Best, *First and Second Thessalonians*, p. 166.

40. Rightly, Bruce, *1 and 2 Thessalonians*, p. 84.

41. Marshall, *1 and 2 Thessalonians*, p. 112.

42. *Dimartyrametha* could be a durative imperfect and hence the possible translation "kept on testifying."

43. Malherbe, *The Letters*, p. 234.

teaching but rather God and God's will and word for believers (cf. Luke 10.16). Paul believes he speaks God's Word and is God's agent to such a degree that to reject what he says is to reject God.[44] Paul finally reminds his audience that rejecting God in such matters of morality means also rejecting his gift of the Holy Spirit, and when the Spirit is grieved in a severe way the Spirit may leave (cf. Ezek. 36.27; 37.14, which may be alluded to here). Paul does not use here the aorist "gave," which would refer to either conversion or Pentecost, but "gives," which may have a non-temporal sense here (God in general is the giver of the Spirit).[45]

The Spirit is given in part to enable and empower an obedient or holy Christian life and is given to and inhabits the community, not just individuals (1 Cor. 3.16). The holiness of this Spirit is emphasized by the way this is phrased — "the giving of his Spirit, the Holy One, to you."[46] The serious tone of this section reflects the problem of sexual immorality recurring among Gentiles who had trouble leaving behind a lifestyle deemed acceptable in the larger culture. Paul is indeed seeking to inculcate a minority or counter-cultural ethic beyond anything even various Gentile moral philosophers of the age might have urged, including the Stoics.[47]

Having said how *not* to relate to one's "brothers and sisters" (vv. 1-8), Paul goes on to say how to relate to them: "Now concerning brotherly love . . ." Vv. 9-12 should be seen as a unit, with the correlation between working and brotherly love set up already in 2.8-9 in regard to his own conduct. Love of fellow believers is shown by not sponging off them when one can work and by not relying on patronage situations to take care of one's material needs. Brotherly love sets up parity relationships, not dependencies, and tends in the context of the Christian community to break down some of the social stratification found in that highly stratified society.[48]

The *peri de*, "but concerning," formula in itself does not indicate a response to an inquiry like the fuller phrase "now concerning the things you wrote" (1 Cor. 7.1).[49] It is a standard rhetorical marker which simply indicates

---

44. See pp. 83-83 above on 1 Thess. 2.13. Cf. Wanamaker, *1 and 2 Thessalonians*, pp. 157-58.

45. Rightly, Marshall, *1 and 2 Thessalonians*, p. 114.

46. Bruce, *1 and 2 Thessalonians*, p. 86.

47. One way the parallels with the moral philosophers is indeed instructive is in showing just how radical an ethic, by Gentile standards, Paul and other early Christians were insisting on. The Apostolic Decree of Acts 15 was as revolutionary a manifesto of freedom and at the same time a theological and moral constraint when applied to Gentiles as the modern Declaration of Independence was for eighteenth-century Americans or the Emancipation Proclamation in the nineteenth century.

48. See Malherbe, *The Letters*, p. 242 on this passage being a unit.

49. Rightly, Bruce, *1 and 2 Thessalonians*, p. 89.

that a new topic is being addressed, and we see it used again in this way in 1 Thess. 5.1 (cf. 4.13 as well).[50] Paul uses here a standard rhetorical device called "paralipsis" (cf. 5.1; 2 Cor. 9.1; Phlm. 19)[51] by telling his audience what he has no need to tell them, thus reminding them but also indirectly complimenting their knowledge and love.[52] Having arrived at the epideictic topics for exhortation, Paul marks off each one in an appropriate manner.

Paul exhorts them not to "brotherly love in general" but rather to love of their Christian brothers and sisters,[53] as is made clear with "love of one another" at the end of the verse. The term *philadelphia* originally referred to love of one's physical siblings, but early Christians such as Paul came to use it of their fellow believers (cf. Rom. 12.10; Heb. 13.1; 1 Pet. 1.22; 2 Pet. 1.7).[54] "It is interesting to note that '*philadelphia*', unlike *adelphoi*, constitutes an example of ancient inclusive language, since it was applied to both brotherly and sisterly love."[55] It is equally interesting that Paul deliberately refrains from using the friendship language of *philos* or *philia* and chooses rather to use family language, probably because he is trying to encourage treating fellow Christians not merely as friends, but rather in a more intimate way as family.

The Thessalonian Christians, Paul says, have no need for him to write about this love because they are "God-taught" a word found also in *Barnabas* 21. We may also compare *didaktoi theou* in John 6.45, but we have here what appears to be the first occurrence of *theodidaktos* in all of Greek literature.[56] The background seems to be Isa. 54.13: "all your sons will be taught by God."[57] Paul

---

50. On this see B. Witherington, *Conflict and Community in Corinth* (Grand Rapids: Eerdmans, 1995), p. 38, and for a detailed examination on the use of this phrase in Greek literature, including in rhetorical contexts, see M. M. Mitchell, "Concerning *peri de* in 1 Corinthians," *NovT* 31 (1989): 229-56.

51. Wanamaker, *1 and 2 Thessalonians*, p. 159.

52. See Best, *First and Second Thessalonians*, pp. 170-71; Malherbe, *The Letters*, p. 244.

53. Lightfoot, *Notes*, p. 59.

54. Marshall, *1 and 2 Thessalonians*, p. 114. The term *philadelphia* does not seem to have been extant much before the time of Paul unless 2 Macc. 15.14 is an example, and certainly it is not used in a spiritual way before our NT references. We do find it in *4 Macc.* 13.23-26; 14.1 and Philo, *Legatio ad Gaium* 87, 92, used of actual brothers (cf. also Plutarch's whole treatise on the subject of loving actual siblings or blood relations: *On Brotherly Love* 478A-92D). We do find *philadelphos* in Sophocles, *Antigone* 527 and in Xenophon, *Memorabilia* 2.3.17.

55. Wanamaker, *1 and 2 Thessalonians*, p. 160.

56. As has been demonstrated rather clearly it is unlikely that Paul is reacting against Epicurean notions in Thessalonike about those who are "self-taught," as the Epicureans sometimes proclaimed themselves. See rightly A. Smith, "The First Letter to the Thessalonians," in *The New Interpreter's Bible*, vol. XI, ed. L. E. Keck (Nashville: Abingdon, 2000), p. 720.

57. Paul may be calling the Holy Spirit "God" since he seems to be referring to some sort of inward instruction. See 1 Cor. 2.13.

could be suggesting that what he taught earlier was God's own teaching and word (see 1 Thess. 2.2-9).[58] The Thessalonians have been God-taught on this subject, unlike the general populace. Paul then is not addressing his audience in the way the moral philosophers addressed the general public on such matters. That his more limited audience is God-taught means that they have been taught how to love one another, not merely taught that they need to do so. Socially this exhortation was needed since the Christian community was composed of a disparate group of people of various sorts of social backgrounds and status who would not necessarily be inclined to love each other as brothers and sisters in the ethos they grew up in. Indeed, the more socially elite will have been taught to distinguish themselves from their social inferiors in various ways.[59]

V. 10 makes it apparent once again that Paul is urging the Thessalonians to continue doing what they are doing, even more so. In this case he trots out the example of their love for fellow believers in "the whole of Macedonia" (cf. 2 Thess. 1.3). Presumably he is referring to their hospitality toward traveling Christians from elsewhere in the province, but perhaps also to their aid for Christians in other cities (Philippi, Beroea).[60] Paul was good at building up social networks of mutual support between his churches through visits or financial commitments such as the collection for Judea (cf. Phil. 4.14-18). Just as 1 Thess. 1.8 proclaimed with good rhetorical hyperbole that the word about their faith had gone throughout the region, now it is their love that Paul urges them to spread around, as they are doing. Paul "shows himself to be the consummate pastor here because he sees the good and praises it but recognizes room for improvement."[61] Here again is clear evidence that this is for the most part a progress-oriented rather than problem-solving letter. They are to excel/abound more and more in what they already believe in and are doing. "Christian love should never become complacent as though a certain level of love were sufficient to please God."[62] The grammatical structure here is such that vv. 10b-12 are linked with what precedes in these verses — "abound" is the first of four or five straight subordinate infinitives dependent on the main verb "we exhort/appeal."[63]

Having spoken of the Thessalonian Christians' relationships among themselves (v. 9) and with fellow Christians in the region (v. 10), he turns to speak of how they are to relate to outsiders (vv. 11-12), and the advice basically is

58. See Riguaux, *Les Épitres*, pp. 517-18.
59. See Wanamaker, *1 and 2 Thessalonians*, p. 160.
60. See Best, *First and Second Thessalonians*, pp. 173-74.
61. Smith, "1 Thessalonians," p. 720.
62. Wanamaker, *1 and 2 Thessalonians*, p. 162.
63. Malherbe, *The Letters*, p. 245.

to live quietly, minding their own business, and working hard, even laboring with their hands. This is how the mandate in 3.21 that their love should increase not only to one another but to all is to be fulfilled.[64] In some ways this advice might have sounded counter-intuitive, at least to the elite.

Philotimeisthai ("aspire") was regularly used in political and philanthropic contexts of achievement of political ends by means of benefactions, that is, of aspiring to do just the opposite of living quietly. In fact, Plutarch says quite bluntly that those who manifest *philotimoi* and care about their reputation *(philodoxoi)* cannot lead a quiet life. It would be totally unacceptable to do so if one loved honor (*On Tranquility of Mind* 465F-66A).[65] The word's original sense, then, was pursuit or love of honor or distinction (see Thucydides 2.44, the speech of Pericles).[66] One would seek to promote the spread of one's name by acts of benefaction and getting one's name inscribed in stone on honor columns or in pavements. By the time, however, Paul used the term it often had the lesser sense of "aspire" or "earnestly endeavor" (see Rom. 15.20; 2 Cor. 5.9).[67]

Paul suggests that conventional forms of status-seeking and improving of honor ratings were to be left aside.[68] In other words, Paul and Plutarch would have quite dramatically disagreed on what amounted to honorable and decorous behavior. Christians are not called to establish their names in the public sphere and seek prestige. They are to be ambitious in a different and perhaps counterintuitive and "quiet" way. Paul is talking about not retirement but avoidance of conflict and doing purposeful work and community-building. Christians were to strive within and for the Christian community.

One can think of a good reason for this: Christians were being persecuted, and the lower profile they maintained the better it might go for them.[69] Paul is not countering apocalyptic lethargy brought on by the belief that Jesus was coming any minute, making work pointless.[70] He is dealing with social fac-

64. See Smith, "1 Thessalonians," p. 720; E. J. Richard, *First and Second Thessalonians* (Collegeville: Liturgical, 1995), pp. 219-23.

65. See the discussion in Malherbe, *The Letters,* p. 247.

66. See Lightfoot, *Notes,* p. 60.

67. See *New Docs* 1, p. 88 on the evolution of meaning of the term. Though Paul could be striving for a clear paradoxical remark — seek the honor of living quietly and attending to one's own affairs. There was no public display or honor in that! See Rigaux, *Les Épitres,* p. 520 on the history of usage.

68. See rightly, A. Smith, *Comfort One Another: Reconstructing the Rhetoric and Audience of 1 Thessalonians* (Louisville: Westminster, 1995), p. 40.

69. See rightly T. Still, *Conflict at Thessalonica* (Sheffield: Sheffield Academic, 1999), pp. 208-80.

70. But see R. Jewett, *The Thessalonian Correspondence: Pauline Rhetoric and Millenarian Piety* (Philadelphia: Fortress, 1986), pp. 96-102. It is striking that this pericope is separated from what follows by the *peri de* marker in 4.13, indicating a new topic is being discussed. Since

tors and forces not least of which is trying to help his Christians survive in a hostile environment.[71]

There may be another social factor at work as well. B. Winter has urged that we see hints here and in 2 Thess. 3.7-9 of Paul setting an example of avoiding entangling alliances with patrons and encouraging his converts to follow that example. They are to be quietly busy, not busybodies, which is to say not living on the dole of some patron and then spending their time spreading the patron's name around and seeking to win friends and influence people for the patron.[72] Christians, by contrast to the patron-client system, were all to work as they were able, avoid being a burden to others, and earn money to do good to others without thought of return. Love and doing good to all, especially the household of faith, rather than reciprocity, was to be their guiding principle. Perhaps especially there would be concern that Christians not be beholden to non-Christian patrons, who could demand all kinds of things of their time and work, some of which might be quite unethical and un-Christian. All of this raises some questions about manual labor which we must attend to at this juncture.

A Closer Look: A Christian Manual on Manual Labor?

Attitudes about work, especially manual labor, varied in the Greco-Roman world, as did attitudes about keeping busy with one's own business without being a busybody. These matters were interrelated, and there was a long history of discussion of such things. It is important on the one hand not to use sources like Dio Chrysostom's discussion on work uncritically as if it represented the overwhelming opinion of all ancients. Dio presents in *Oration 7* a defense of work, including "employments and trades," in the face of an elitist disdain for manual labor as well as for poverty. For example Plutarch says that "while we delight in the work [of craftsmen and artisans], we despise the workman"; "it does not necessarily follow that, if the work delights you with its graces, the one who wrought it is worthy of your esteem" (Pericles 1.4; 2.2). It was not just the rich who took such attitudes. There were also rhetoricians and philosophers who saw manual work as beneath their dignity. For example Philo, *Quod Deterius Potiori Insidiari Soleat* 33-34, mentions Sophists who boasted that they knew nothing of labor and found those who did such work as easy to despise. Dio, by contrast, urges that such work is appropriate for free persons (i.e., not just slaves) as it

---

Paul has not yet really addressed matters eschatological, his audience hearing this for the first time would not likely read eschatological matters into this discussion about behavior toward believers and others, which seems to be dealing with social problems that many Gentiles especially struggled with: sexual immorality, issues with work, and the like.

71. See Smith, "1 Thessalonians," p. 721.

72. B. Winter, *Seek the Welfare of the City* (Grand Rapids: Eerdmans, 1994), pp. 42-60.

will provide them with what is necessary in life and what is fitting. He even commends craftsmen (cf. 7.103-13, 124), but his focus is not on working with one's own hands but on gainful employment in general. Paul by contrast does focus on working with one's hands.

"Working with one's own hands" *(ergazesthai tais idias chersin hymōn)* seems to be a Jewish rather than Greek idiom, but is rare in the NT (cf. 1 Cor. 4.12; Eph. 4.28). "Work of one's hands" is only a bit more common (Acts 7.41; Heb. 1.10; 2.7; Rev. 9.20) but has OT precedents (Deut. 2.7-8; Job 1.10; Ps. 89.17; Isa. 2.8-9; Jer. 1.16-17; see also *Testament of Judah* 2).[73] This work ethic, if we may call it that, was common in Jewish contexts, and this is partly because work was not seen as mere drudgery but indeed as fulfillment of a divine mandate going back to Genesis 1. Gen. 3.17-19 makes not hard work or work by hand itself the curse, but makes the toilsomeness of work the result of God's cursing of the ground. A healthy work ethic was inculcated in Jewish literature throughout the ancient period, for example in Proverbs, and the lazy person was seen as one whose example was to be shunned (e.g., Prov. 10.4). Paul himself made it a regular practice to work with his hands (1 Thess. 2.9; 2 Thess. 3.8; 1 Cor. 4.12; Acts 20.33-34), and not just to avoid the need for patronage either, it would appear. It may well have been not only part of his practical approach to support his own ministry but also part of his outreach strategy. Especially during the games people would be in need of tents and the like.

It is not necessary to invoke the Stoic ideal of detachment, independence, and self-sufficiency *(autarkeia)* as a background to make sense of what Paul says about work in 1 and 2 Thessalonians. He did not in any case believe in self-sufficiency but in dependence on God and mutual love and service among Christians.[74] It is because of love of the other that one refuses to become either a parasite or sycophant and so engage in unhealthy non-parity relationships. Furthermore, because of love one will not stand idly by and watch the needy go hungry (cf. Eph. 4.28; 1 Tim. 5.3-8).[75] Furthermore, "Christians were to be productive members of society in which they lived and their activity was to contribute to the well-being, unity, and outreach of the fellowship."[76]

---

73. See Richards, *First and Second Thessalonians*, p. 220, whom I am following here.

74. See B. Witherington, *Grace in Galatia* (Grand Rapids: Eerdmans, 1998), pp. 428-29.

75. It is frankly amazing how Malherbe, *The Letters*, pp. 246-59 can work through this material and not even really discuss the Jewish view of manual labor and can simply dismiss rhetorical considerations and the social signals Winter has brought to light that indicate that Paul is concerned about parasitic relationships while putting forward the theory that Paul was concerned that the converts were lapsing into Epicureanism (p. 259)! This hardly explains why Paul has just said that their love and faith have been spreading throughout the region. Furthermore, the fact that they are still persecuted hardly matches with the idea that they are withdrawing into the ideal of a quietistic and private life. If Paul was worried about this, why would he urge them to strive to live quietly and mind their own business? This advice is totally useless if that is what they are already doing.

76. Richards, *First and Second Thessalonians*, p. 223.

This was a particularly difficult task in a time of persecution, and all the more so since Christians were to cut their ties with pagan temples and festivals and the like. How could they be a good example and witness to outsiders when they could not socialize much with them and sometimes received hostile reactions when they did bear witness? Paul's answer is that they can work hard, live quietly, and avoid entangling alliances while building up a positive Christian community known for its love and caring for each other. Paul is not really inculcating an introversionist sect here (he tells them to live quietly, not to be silent) but is limiting the ways Christians can engage with the larger culture and encourages them instead to focus during this hostile time on building up their own community. In the end, Paul modeled how working with one's hands could actually aid missions and evangelism rather than impede them, at least through an indirect witness.

There seems to be a certain contrast between the clauses in v. 11, with striving to live quietly and attend to one's own things being the private face of the Christian life, and working with hands the more public face. Some have pointed to Plato's remarks about retiring from public life and tending to one's own somewhat neglected affairs (*Republic* 6.496D), but Paul is not appealing primarily to elite persons, much less public officials.[77] He is appealing to all Christians in Thessalonike. V. 12 will call these two approaches to life an example of "decorous" behavior toward the outsider. The term *euschēmonos* is used by Paul to refer to proper or suitable conduct (Rom. 1.27; 13.13; 1 Cor. 7.36; 14.40), in this case "suitable" or "decorous" in the eyes of outsiders who are watching, apparently with a critical or even hostile eye.[78] Dio Chrysostom urges that one should avoid "unseemly" *(aschēmon)* work (*Oration* 7.110-25).[79] Paul is well aware that his charges are operating in an honor and shame context where the honor rating of one's occupation was as important as its practical value. Paul is urging a non-elitist approach to work, even manual labor. The final clause in v. 12 could be translated "lacking in nothing" or even "dependent on no one." The latter is probably correct here, but one can say that if a person lacks for nothing essential then there is no reason to be economically dependent on another.[80]

---

77. See Best, *First and Second Thessalonians*, p. 175.

78. Wanamaker, *1 and 2 Thessalonians*, p. 164.

79. One may compare the inscriptional evidence where it also refers to "decent" behavior. See *New Docs* 2, p. 86.

80. Marshall, *1 and 2 Thessalonians*, p. 117.

Part Two:
The Call to Hope and Alertness: The Tale
of Sleepers Dead and Living — 4.13–5.11

The second major portion of the *exhortatio* has, like the first, two parts that are related but do not involve straight repetition. The first has to do with the fate of the dead in Christ and the second with preparation for the coming of the thief in the night who will bring salvation and judgment to the world. In other words, we have reached the eschatological portion of the discourse. It was appropriate in epideictic rhetoric to speak of the fate of the dead as well as of the living, as epideictic was the rhetoric of funerals and encomiums. But Paul's focus is on the current state of the dead and the significance of the future for the present behavior of the living. He does not speak of the afterlife or the end of history for its own sake, but in service of the exhortation he is giving to his converts in Thessalonike. This shapes the character of his rhetoric here, which is about his converts being people of faith, hope, love, self-control, and alertness.

But I do not want you to be ignorant brothers, concerning those who have fallen asleep,[1] *in order that you may cease grieving/being sad as the rest having no hope. For if we believe that Jesus died and arose, so also God will bring with him those who have fallen asleep through/in Jesus. For this I say to you in/on the word of the Lord that we the living, those who are left around until the parousia of the Lord will not forestall those who have fallen asleep, for the Lord himself with a summons, with the voice of the archangel, and with the trumpet of God will come down from heaven and the dead in Christ will rise first, then we the living, those left around, together with them shall be caught up in the clouds unto the public*

---

1. Some Western and Byzantine witnesses (D, F, G, K, L, and others) have the perfect form of the participle ("have fallen asleep"), here conforming the text to Matt. 27.52 and 1 Cor. 15.20. The more unusual form is likely original. See Metzger, *TC*, p. 632.

welcoming of the Lord in the air and so we will always be with the Lord. So console one another with these words.

But concerning the times and seasons brothers, you have no need for me to write to you, for you yourselves know accurately that the day of the Lord as a thief in the night, thus it shall come. When they are saying "peace and security," then suddenly destruction will come upon them just as the birth-pangs of a woman having a baby in the womb and there will be no escape. But you brothers, you are not in the dark, in order that the day, like a thief,[2] overtake you, for all of you are sons of light, you are also sons of the day. You are neither night nor darkness. So then you should not sleep like the rest, but keep awake and be sober. For those sleeping sleep at night, and those getting drunk get drunk at night. But we being of the day, are sober, having put on the breastplate of faith and love and the helmet of salvation, for God has not appointed/destined us unto wrath but unto the acquisition of salvation through our Lord Jesus Christ, who died for us in order that whether we are awake or asleep together we shall enter into life/begin to live with him. Therefore encourage one another and build up one on one, just as also you are doing.

Paul will speak to his audience using Jewish concepts of death and resurrection, and more specifically Christian concepts about the return of Christ. But he also uses the language of the empire, so familiar to his audience, to speak of the coming of Christ with the slogan "peace and security" and the language of the royal visit to a city with the greeting committee going out to meet the ruler. But what sort of views would his audience have had about the dead and their fate? Why does Paul feel it necessary to make these sorts of remarks? While he believes his audience is familiar with the issue of the unknown timing of the second coming, he assumes that they do not know much about the fate of the Christian dead. What then did Gentiles of a largely pagan background believe about the dead?

A Closer Look: The Fate of the Dead

It is fair to say that Gentiles who had not been exposed to Judaism before they became followers of Jesus would have found the whole idea of the resurrection more than a little strange. It would have sounded more like corpses standing up than some positive form of afterlife. They were used to the Greek notion of the immortality of the soul, but that did not include the notion of a person coming back from the dead in

2. A few manuscripts (A, B, cop^boh) have *kleptas,* "thieves" in the accusative so that the text reads "surprise you like thieves ('do' or 'are surprised')." This reading, while more difficult, does not cohere with the context. See Metzger, *TC,* p. 633; A. Malherbe, *The Letters to the Thessalonians* (New York: Doubleday, 2000), pp. 293-94.

new and improved flesh, or at least not normally.[3] What then would have been the concerns of the Thessalonian Christians about their deceased brothers and sisters in Christ? Was it just a concern about them being left behind or left out when Christ returned?[4]

Greco-Roman peoples of various sorts did believe that a person survives death and goes into the underworld (see Plato, *Gorgias* 52D). Coins would be placed on the eyes to pay the boatman Charon to carry the person down and across the river Styx, avoiding the obstacles along the way, including Cerberus, the dog who guarded the gate into the underworld. There were stories such as the myth of Adonis, who as a child was so beautiful that Aphrodite hid him in a coffin and gave him to Persephone, the queen of the underworld. Aphrodite later wanted him back and struck a deal with Zeus whereby Adonis would spend one-third of the year with Persephone, one-third with Aphrodite, and one-third by himself. Adonis chose to add his third to Persephone's and so spent two-thirds of the year on Olympus and one-third in the underworld. While this story, unlike the story of Persephone, does not seem to be about the crop cycle, it is also not about what happens to normal human beings in the afterlife. As R. Bauckham also notes "the festival in July at which Adonis' death was mourned by women seems to have played no particular emphasis on his return from the underworld."[5]

We may leave out of account the stories of visions of the other world and the afterlife because they do not involve an actual death, nor do the stories of shamans who in some ecstatic state, after a ceremony of ritual death and rebirth, have their souls freed to journey to the underworld. The shaman characteristically goes on this journey to serve as a sort of shepherd or guide of a person's soul, or, in the case of the story of Orpheus, to actually rescue a deceased soul who is desperately missed (in this case the soul of Orpheus's wife).[6] What this story does show is the degree of sorrow and

---

3. There was the myth of Persephone being taken into the underworld by Hades and being allowed back into the world after her mother Demeter lobbied Zeus. This is an allegory about the seasons, and the compromise result was that Persephone was allowed to return to earth for two-thirds of the year but had to be in the underworld with her husband Hades the rest of the year. This myth was reenacted in the Eleusinian mysteries. Persephone going back and forth is connected to nature and the crop cycle, not to history and the afterlife of ordinary humans.

4. On the eschatology and afterlife language here in comparison to what Paul says elsewhere see J. Delobel, "The Fate of the Dead according to 1 Thes 4 and 1 Cor 15," in R. F. Collins, ed., *The Thessalonian Correspondence* (Leuven: Leuven University Press, 2000), pp. 340-47. Delobel thinks there is a consistency but differing emphases in how Paul thinks about the fate of the Christian dead in these letters. This is correct, and it helps Delobel's case if we recognize that some of the differences of expression in 1 Thessalonians 4–5 and 1 Corinthians 15 are due in some measure to the differences in rhetorical species between these two documents.

5. R. Bauckham, *The Fate of the Dead* (Leiden: Brill, 1998), p. 21.

6. See I. M. Linfarth, *The Art of Orpheus* (Berkeley: University of California Press, 1941), pp. 16-21; M. O. Lee, "Orpheus and Eurydice: Myth, Legend, Folklore," *Classica et Mediaevalia* 26 (1965): 402-12.

anxiety often expressed in the pagan world over the loss of a mate or another family member, something we can also readily see in the many grave inscriptions found in IG and SIG, and the depictions of sorrow in the grave art of the Greco-Roman world.[7] If Paul had read any of these inscriptions or seen any of the tomb art, it is no surprise that he might speak of pagans as those without a viable future hope.

Various other phenomena in the Greco-Roman world, however, attest to another side of what pagans believed about the afterlife. There were, for instance, attempts to obtain advice from the dead. We have the famous story of Odysseus going to Hades (*Odyssey* 11) to consult the dead seer Teireias, a story later revised by Virgil, who tells of Aeneas going to Hades to get advice from his father Anchises, who just happens to prophesy the future history of Rome (*Aeneas* 6). These stories bear a certain resemblance to 1 Sam. 28.6-25, though that story is about necromancy, not about a journey to Hades. What such stories share in common is that the Hebrew concept of Sheol seems no more positive than the Greek notion of Hades. The White Isles or Elysium was for "the few, the proud, the brave," the happy dead referred to by Pindar and Plato (*Phaedo* 112A-14C). As Bauckham points out, the function of all the stories of special journeys to Hades by illustrous figures was to give information about the fate of the dead, presumably because there was no little concern about what had happened to them in the afterlife.[8]

On the other hand, birthday parties were held for the deceased, complete with wine poured through a tube into the tomb in hopes that the deceased might also participate in the celebration (see CIL 6.26554).[9] The spirits of the dead were sometimes thought to stay in a sort of semi-existence near or in the tombs.[10] This practice is probably what Justin Martyr is referring to when he speaks of pagan magic at tombs, including the calling forth of spirits of deceased ancestors (*Apology I* 18). Romans also believed in the *genius,* the spirit of the *paterfamilias,* who might be prayed to or consulted, or was believed could inspire one and guide one to do the right thing. The Roman home shrines with death masks reflect this sort of belief. But this tells us nothing about whether the afterlife was viewed as pleasant for the deceased.

> No small part of old Roman piety consisted in a scrupulous reverence for the
> dead, and a care to prolong their memory by solid memorial and solemn ritual, it

---

7. I am thinking particularly of a particular sculpture in the Athens Museum of the soldier who dies in Asia Minor and never returns home. He is depicted on his tomb as sitting on a hill with his helmet off, looking toward Greece with absolute despair and sorrow on his face.

8. Bauckham, *The Fate of the Dead,* p. 29.

9. On the evidence for drinking tubes in tombs see K. Hopkins, *Death and Renewal* (Cambridge: Cambridge University Press, 1983), pp. 201-55, here p. 232.

10. R. M. Oglivie, *The Romans and Their Gods in the Age of Augustus* (London: Chatto and Windus, 1969), p. 75. For the various sorts of rituals for the dead that might be performed see Horace, *Odes* 1.28-34, and it may be that proxy baptism in Corinth should be seen in light of such practices. See B. Witherington, *Conflict and Community in Corinth* (Grand Rapids: Eerdmans, 1994), p. 294.

might be, to maintain some faint tie of sympathy with the shade which had passed into a dim and rather cheerless world. The conception of that other state was always vague, and *often purely negative*. It is not often that a spirit is sped on its way to join a loved one in the Elysian fields, and we may fear that such phrases, when they do occur, are rather literary and conventional.[11]

This sort of conclusion seems to be borne out by the famous inscription "I was not, I am not, I care not,"[12] which in fact seems to suggest that annihilation awaits one and all. On the whole the conclusion of Bauckham seems warranted:

> The old Homeric view was that the existence of the dead is undifferentiated: all share the same joyless gloom. The exceptions — on the one hand, Tantalus, Tityos, Sisyphus, who are punished eternally for their crimes against the gods, and on the other hand, a very few heroes of divine descent, like Menelaus, who are exempted from the common lot and dwell in the bliss of Elysium — are exceptions that prove the rule. But [stories of] the descent into Hades, so far as we can tell, reflected and encouraged a growing belief in retribution after death. The damned, who may be regarded either as those guilty of heinous crimes or as those who have not been initiated in the mysteries, suffer punishments, while the blessed enjoy themselves in a sunlit paradise.[13]

The function of the mystery rites, particularly the Eleusinian rites, seems to have been to assure a person of a tolerable or even blessed afterlife, one without punishments. The idea of such punishments for the wicked no doubt also increased the concern about the fate of the dead. Theocritus ably sums up the prevailing pagan attitude about death and the afterlife — "hopes are for the living, but the ones who die are without hope" (*Idyll* 4.42). Catullus (5.4-6) is equally succinct: "The sun can set and rise again/But once our brief light sets/There is one unending night to be slept through" (cf. Homer, *Iliad* 11.241). Lastly in the papyri (P.Oxy. 115, second century A.D.) we read "I sorrowed and wept over your dear departed one as I wept over Didymus . . . but really, there is nothing one can do in the face of such things. So please comfort each other." This expression is typical, as was the elaborate and often lengthy periods of mourning, the use of professional mourners to play sad music and weep at the grave, and the like in both Semitic and more Greco-Roman parts of the empire.[14] Pagan literature could bemoan the fact that while even crops rise again and renew themselves, as seemingly also the sun does, humans simply die. So nature mocks humans with its resilience. But by the time Christians begin to use these nature

11. S. Dill, *Roman Society from Nero to Marcus Aurelius* (London: Macmillan, 1904), pp. 256-57, emphasis added.

12. R. MacMullen, *Paganism in the Roman Empire* (New Haven: Yale University Press, 1981), p. 55.

13. Bauckham, *Fate of the Dead*, p. 29.

14. See W. K. C. Guthrie, *The Greeks and Their Gods* (Boston: Beacon, 1951), pp. 174-82, 260-95, 368-70.

analogies about dying and rising (see 1 Cor. 15.35-44; *1 Clement* 20), they are used in a positive way as pointing forward to the greater glory of resurrection.[15]

There was a variety of opinions about the afterlife in early Judaism. If, as is probable, a few of Paul's converts in Thessalonike were exposed to Jewish beliefs about the afterlife in the synagogue, it would have to have been Pharisaic beliefs they encountered for there to have been a meaningful point of contact with what Paul is saying here (cf. the confusion indicated in 1 Corinthians 15 with some actually saying "there is no resurrection of the dead"). More likely the vast majority of Thessalonian converts heard about these ideas first from Paul and his coworkers, and now he is further clarifying matters for them in this part of the exhortation.

In this sort of largely pagan environment, it is understandable that Paul as a pastor takes some pains to counter inconsolable grief and reassure his converts that for Christians the afterlife is positive, that it will be like a large family reunion and will involve a form of life more vital and alive than what those still living are currently experiencing. The spirit of the Christian belief, as opposed to the pagan belief, is aptly expressed by Chrysostom: "If then you seek [the deceased Christian], seek him where the King is, where the army of angels is; not in the grave, not in the earth" (*Homily* on 2 Cor. 1.6).

It is not necessary, then, to posit that Paul had failed to teach his converts about the afterlife when he was present with them under the assumption that the parousia was so imminent that such teaching was superfluous. His teaching here (see below) on the unknown timing of a thief breaking in during the night makes that suggestion highly improbable. Paul's premature exit from Thessalonike probably prevented adequate teaching, and some Thessalonian Christians had apparently died unexpectedly after Paul left, raising questions about the afterlife.[16] Paul does not need to reassure the audience that the parousia is coming. They already know about times and seasons of that event, that is, that it is unpredictable. He does need to offer further teaching about that event and teach for the first time about the fate of the dead as well, and more particularly show the connection between the fate of the dead in Christ, the resurrection of those dead, and the return of Jesus.[17] Of course in later centuries such questions were answered in a multitude of contexts to reinforce a strong belief in the afterlife. For example, from the inscriptional evidence we have IGA 5.423, which includes an epitaph which reads: "Before you say, grave, who or whose child lies here, this tombstone proclaims to all passers-by: here lies the body of ever-remembered Makaria; as is customary for the pious it [her body] tasted death, but she serves the heavenly city of the saints having as a reward for her labors heavenly crowns."[18]

---

15. See J. B. Lightfoot, *Notes on the Epistles of St. Paul* (Winona Lake: Alpha, reprint), p. 64.

16. See C. Wanamaker, *Commentary on 1 and 2 Thessalonians* (Grand Rapids: Eerdmans, 1990), pp. 164-66.

17. See rightly, Wanamaker, *1 and 2 Thessalonians*, p. 166.

18. *New Docs* 3, p. 107.

In v. 13 Paul introduces a new subject using a phrase he was to employ more than once to start a new topic about not wishing his audience to be ignorant (cf. 1 Cor. 10.1; 12.1; Rom. 11.25). It is the equivalent of saying he wishes them to know (cf. 1 Cor. 10.1; 2 Cor. 1.8; Rom. 1.13, 11.25; Col. 2.1). The subject is of course related to what he has already said or suggested about the parousia in 1.10; 2.13; and 3.13.

Use of "sleep" as a euphemism for death can be found in both Jewish and Greco-Roman sources (cf. Gen. 47.30; Deut. 31.16; 1 Kgs. 2.10; Job 14.12-13; Ps. 13.3; Jer. 51.39-40; 2 Macc. 12.45; John 11.11-13; Acts 13.36; 1 Cor. 11.30; Homer, *Iliad* 11.241; Sophocles, *Electra* 509). We may compare *Psalms of Solomon* 17.50 and *4 Ezra* 13.24, which distinguish between the living who manage to experience the coming glory and the dead who miss out because they died before it came. In the non-Christian texts mentioned above "sleep" does not really tell us anything in particular about the condition or fate of the dead. It is more a comment on how they appear to the living after they die — namely motionless and quiet, like one sleeping. What we find beginning in Dan. 12.2 and continuing in *Testament of Judah* 25.4 and *Testament of Issachar* 7.9; 2 Macc. 12.44-45; and *1 Enoch* 91.10 and 92.3 however is a connection between sleeping and being awakened by the resurrection, an idea Paul further develops here and in 1 Cor. 15.20-21. The present participle here in 4.13 — "those who are falling sleep" — may imply that Paul is thinking not only of Thessalonian Christians who have already died but also of those who will die before the parousia.[19]

Statements such as Mark 6.39 — "she is not dead but rather sleeping" — suggest that perhaps it was primarily Jesus' teaching that led to the notion in early Christianity that death is like sleep in this respect: its effects are no more lasting or harmful than sleep if it is followed by resurrection.[20] In Jesus' teaching, too, the metaphor of sleep for death is not meant to be a comment on what the dead are currently experiencing (cf. the parable in Luke 16.19-31).[21]

Paul connects grieving with being like the remainder of humanity that has no hope.[22] His use of the present subjunctive implies the cessation of some-

---

19. This is perhaps a small grammatical point in favor of the notion that Paul is not envisioning a necessarily imminent parousia but rather a period when Christians will go on dying before Christ returns. But see the discussion in Malherbe, *The Letters*, p. 263.

20. See the discussion of these matters in B. Witherington, *Jesus, Paul, and the End of the World* (Downers Grove: InterVarsity, 1992), pp. 1-30.

21. On this parable see A. J. Levine and B. Witherington, *The Gospel of Luke* (Cambridge: Cambridge University Press, 2006), ad loc.

22. G. K. Beale, *1 and 2 Thessalonians* (Downers Grove: InterVarsity, 2003), p. 130 is probably right to suggest that 1 Thess. 4.13 should be seen as a continuation of 4.11-12 and the exhortation to watch how one behaves in public in the presence of non-Christians. Certainly behavior at a funeral would count in this category and should be seen as an opportunity to be a good witness.

thing.[23] The Thessalonians are grieving for those Christians they have already lost, and Paul wants them to stop grieving. As "To continue to endure misery for the departed is to act like those who have no hope" (*Chrysostom, Homily* 6 on 1 Thessalonians). Here is another small clue that this is epideictic rhetoric meant for the consolation and correction of those suffering loss.

Grieving is for those without hope, and indeed it is the natural reaction for those who have no positive view of the afterlife. Paul is suggesting that outside Christ there is no hope of life beyond death. He was certainly no universalist or pluralist in the matter of salvation. But it was not just that pagans had no hope of a positive afterlife. According to 1.10 and 5.9 (cf. Rom. 1.18-32, 11.7; Eph. 2.3) they faced the judgment of God both in the present and in the future. Things look bleak for pagans from Paul's viewpoint.[24] On the opposite end of the spectrum, Paul is assuming that for Christians an increase in hope will cause an increase in holiness in the lives of the believers. They will be in earnest about Christian behavior because they know what is coming.[25] He is also assuming that a proper knowledge of the fate of the Christian dead should put a stop to hopeless grieving. *Kathos kai* . . . really cannot be translated "to the same extent as the pagans." Paul is urging a cessation of grieving that was already happening.[26]

V. 14 may include a primitive Christian confession even though it is cast in the form of a conditional statement. What suggests this is the use of the proper name Jesus and *anestē*, which is not usually the verb Paul prefers (cf. 1 Cor. 15.3-4).[27] The verb however is in the present tense indicating a real condition.[28] It is however interesting that Paul says "we believe" rather than "we know," suggesting that he has in mind more than just the facts that Jesus died and rose from the dead. Faith was not required to affirm that Jesus had died. Usually Paul speaks of Jesus being raised from the dead (by God — cf. 1 Thess. 1.10; Gal. 1.1; 1 Cor. 15.15; 2 Cor. 4.14; Rom. 4.24; 8.11; 10.9; Col. 2.12), but this is surely implied here in view of the second half of the sentence.

What Paul is doing, then, in the second half of the verse, which is gram-

---

23. See Malherbe, *The Letters*, pp. 263-64.

24. In fact one could read the phrase "the rest/remainder" to mean all non-Christians, Jews or Gentiles, but perhaps Eph. 2.12 should be our guide to Paul's meaning here, especially if the vast majority of his Thessalonian audience were formerly pagan.

25. Beale, *1 and 2 Thessalonians*, p. 131.

26. Lightfoot, *Notes*, pp. 63-64. I quite agree with Lightfoot that had Paul been speaking to a group which had any significant number of Jews in it, especially Jews who already believed in resurrection, he could not and would not have put this contrast so strongly. See the discussion at length in B. Rigaux, *Les Épitres aux Thessaloniciens* (Paris: Gabalda, 1956), pp. 529-33.

27. F. F. Bruce, *1 and 2 Thessalonians* (Waco: Word, 1982), p. 97.

28. See Beale, *1 and 2 Thessalonians*, p. 135.

matically awkward, is showing what follows from believing Jesus died and rose. This belief has a consequence for what we believe about the fate of the Christian dead. The structure of the Greek as we have it favors linking "through Jesus" with "those who have fallen asleep."[29] Does having fallen asleep "through Jesus"[30] mean what Acts 7.29 suggests, namely that Jesus will receive the spirit of the Christian when she dies? Possibly. It is also possible that *dia* has the force of *en* here, in which case Paul is speaking about dying in the Lord, that is, dying as a Christian (1 Cor. 15.18).[31] In fact the aorist participle here, *koimethentas*, favors this interpretation since it refers to the moment, not the condition, of death — they died in the Lord.[32]

It is only deceased Christians that Jesus will bring with him or bring back from the dead when he returns at the parousia.[33] This may mean that they will be brought with Jesus from heaven, but it may simply mean they will be brought back from the dead, and so raised, when Jesus returns, as texts like 1 Cor. 6.14 and 2 Cor. 4.14 suggest.[34] Paul seems to assume that the concern in Thessalonike was not about resurrection per se but about the relationship of the Christian dead to the parousia and whether they would participate in the greeting party in the air when Jesus returned and would be with him forever.[35]

V. 15 has been a flashpoint in the discussion of Pauline eschatology at least since the time of A. Schweitzer. Here, it is said, we have proof positive that Paul believed that he would live to see the parousia of Jesus. But this overlooks at least a couple key factors: Paul did not know in advance when he would die,[36] and he argues that the second coming will happen at an unexpected

---

29. See I. H. Marshall, *1 and 2 Thessalonians* (Grand Rapids: Eerdmans, 1983), p. 124.

30. See the full discussion in E. Best, *A Commentary on the First and Second Epistles to the Thessalonians* (London: Black, 1972), pp. 188-89, and Rigaux, *Les Épitres*, pp. 536-37.

31. Bruce, *1 and 2 Thessalonians*, p. 98.

32. See rightly Wanamaker, *1 and 2 Thessalonians*, p. 169.

33. Here, as in 1 Corinthians 15, Paul operates with a concept of the resurrection of the righteous. Thus there he can talk about Christ as the firstfruits and those in Christ as the latter fruits of the resurrection. This is in part because for Paul the resurrection of the believer means full conformity to the image of Christ, something the dead outside Christ will not receive when Christ returns. See the discussion in Witherington, *Jesus, Paul, and the End of the World*, pp. 181-222.

34. Malherbe, *The Letters*, pp. 266-67 suggests the translation "gathers through him" as though God will use Jesus to function as angels are elsewhere said to function, gathering the elect (Matt. 24.31), or perhaps "gathering together to meet him," but this places an unbearable strain on the phrase "in him." God is performing the action here. Jesus is instrumental to or the context of the action. Thus it is not about believers being gathered or gathering themselves together. It is better to translate the verb as "bring" or "lead."

35. See Wanamaker, *1 and 2 Thessalonians*, p. 169 and pp. 125-28 above.

36. One thing this text probably does suggest is that Paul was in good health at the time and did not anticipate his imminent demise.

time, like a thief in the night. It could be soon, it could be later, and in either case the indeterminacy of the timing is what fuels exhortations that one must always be prepared and alert. Since Paul does not claim to know the specific timing of either his own death or the return of Christ, he could not have said "we who are dead and not left around to see the parousia of the Lord. . . ." In short, he does not know that he will *not* be alive when Jesus returns, and so the only category in which he can logically place himself and the Christians he writes to here is the "living."[37]

What these verses surely do imply is that Paul thought it *possible* that he might be alive when Jesus returned.[38] As Best rightly suggests, Paul, until he was much older and near death, always had both possibilities before him. We do not hear the language of possible survival until the parousia in the later Pauline letters because one of the two unknowns, the timing of Paul's death, was becoming more likely to precede the other, the parousia. He did not change his view of the second coming or consider it delayed in the later Paulines because without knowledge of when it was supposed to happen one cannot could speak of it as "delayed." Paul's imagery of the thief implies a denial of knowing with that sort of precision.[39]

The meaning of "in the word of the Lord" has been debated. Some have argued that it refers to a saying of the historical Jesus and should be seen on a par with other Pauline texts such as 1 Cor. 7.10; 9.14; or 11.23. Unlike at least the first of those suggested parallels, we do not have here a direct quotation of a saying of Jesus. Various possible sources of this verse in the Jesus tradition have been suggested, but with the possible exception of Matt. 24.30, the parallels are

37. See the more detailed discussion in Witherington, *Jesus, Paul, and the End of the World*, pp. 181-220.

38. As Best, *First and Second Thessalonians*, pp. 195-96 rightly suggests, Paul always had both possibilities before him, both that of living until the parousia and that of dying first and rising at the parousia when Jesus returned.

39. Even in the Corinthian correspondence Paul considers both the possibility of being alive at the parousia and the possibility of being raised from the dead (cf. 1 Cor. 15.52 to 1 Cor. 6.14; 2 Cor. 4.14, 5.1; contrast Phil. 1.20, where death seems possibly imminent, but see Phil. 4.5). It is interesting that Chrysostom suggested that Paul was referring not to himself but to those who would be alive at the parousia (*Homily* 7 on 1 Thessalonians). But this resolves the tension in a way that Paul does not. Paul did, at least early in his ministry, conjure with the possibility of being alive when Jesus returned, or, put another way, he certainly did not envision Christ's return happening a very long time after he had died. Even Lightfoot, *Notes*, p. 66 says: "The Apostles certainly do speak as though there were a reasonable expectation of the Lord's appearing in their own time. They use modes of expression which cannot be otherwise explained. Such is the use of the plural here. . . . Nor does it imply more than a reasonable expectation . . . but nothing approaching to a certainty, for it is carefully guarded by the explanatory *hoi zōntes, hoi perileipomenoi*, which may be paraphrased, 'When I say "we," I mean those who are living, those who survive to that day.'"

at the level of ideas, not actual wording (cf. Matt. 10.39; 16.25, 28; 20.1-2; 24.31, 34; 25.6; 26.64; Luke 13.30; John 5.25; 6.39-40; 11.25-26).[40]

Another view is that Paul is citing an otherwise unknown saying of Jesus, one not found in the canonical Gospels. This is certainly possible but is a conjecture that cannot be verified.[41] Rigaux suggests that Paul is referring in general to the eschatology of Jesus such as found in Mark 13/Matthew 24, but this would suggest that Paul had extensive knowledge of the Jesus tradition, which many scholars doubt.[42] What we *can* say about the echoes and allusions to the Jesus tradition in Paul with some assurance is that he almost always feels free to paraphrase that tradition or put it in more Pauline wording, rarely quoting it verbatim.[43] Here it could be argued Paul combines a saying of Jesus with his own reflections on Dan. 7.13-14 and 12.2-3. This lack of direct quotation makes it difficult to know when Paul has or has not drawn on a saying of Jesus.[44]

A different line of approach has suggested that "in the word of the Lord" refers to a prophetic word revealed to Paul himself by the risen Lord.[45] This is certainly possible and has in its favor the fact that the very same phrase, *legomen en logō kyriou* appears in the LXX to indicate when someone speaks for God (cf. 1 Kgs. 21.35; 13.1-5, 32; Hos. 1.1; Ezek. 34.1; 35.1). But this hardly explains the echoes from the Synoptic material that we do find here. 1 Cor. 15.51-52 can be pointed to as a close parallel to v. 16, but not v. 15, and there Paul refers to a "mystery," which would seem to mean a revelation he received directly from God.

Perhaps the least problematic solution to this conundrum is to recognize that Paul saw himself as a prophetic interpreter of both the sayings of the historical Jesus[46] and of the OT and also as one who received direct messages from the risen Lord himself. In 1 Thess. 4.15–5.7 Paul does seem to draw on the Jesus tradition as found in Matthew 24, but in vv. 16-17 he also draws on both his own reading of Daniel and prophetic insight that he himself had been given by the risen Lord. The following chart shows the various parallels:

40. On this phrase not necessarily referring to a word of the historical Jesus see J. Delobel, "The Fate of the Dead according to 1 Thess 4 and 1 Cor. 15," in *The Thessalonian Correspondence*, pp. 340-47, here p. 341.

41. See, e.g., L. Morris, *The First and Second Epistles to the Thessalonians* (Grand Rapids: Eerdmans, 1991), pp. 140-41; J. Jeremias, *Unknown Sayings of Jesus* (London: SPCK, 1964), pp. 80-83.

42. Rigaux, *Les Épitres*, pp. 535-39.

43. See the discussion on the use of two sayings of Jesus in Galatians 6 in B. Witherington, *Grace in Galatia* (Grand Rapids: Eerdmans, 1998), pp. 430-40.

44. One could perhaps point to 1 Thess. 1.8, where "word of the Lord" refers in general to the gospel rather than some specific saying of Jesus.

45. See the discussion in Malherbe, *The Letters*, p. 268.

46. On Paul as a prophet see B. Witherington, *The Paul Quest* (Downers Grove: InterVarsity, 1998), pp. 130-73.

	1 Thessalonians	Matthew
Christ returns	4.16	24.30
from heaven	4.16	24.30
accompanied by angels	4.16	24.31
with a trumpet of God	4.16	24.31
believers are gathered to Christ	4.17	24.31, 40-41
in clouds	4.17	24.30
at a time unknown	5.1-2	24.36
coming like a thief	5.2, 4	24.43
unbelievers are unaware of		
coming judgment	5.3	24.37-39
judgment is like a mother's birth-pangs	5.3	24.8
believers are not to be deceived	5.4-5	24.43
and are to be watchful	5.6	24.37-39
warning against drunkenness	5.7	24.49[47]

These parallels should not be minimized, and they make it likely that Paul is drawing on the general sense and trajectory and imagery of some of that Synoptic material.[48] We can say with more assurance that the rhetorical function of citing a "word of the Lord" here is to console and reassure the audience about the fate of their deceased brothers and sisters and the equal participation in the parousia event of those who have died.[49]

Danielic material is also in the background here. Dan. 7.13-14 is part of

47. Here I am following Beale, *1 and 2 Thessalonians,* p. 137 and D. Wenham, *Paul* (Grand Rapids: Eerdmans, 1995), pp. 303-14, who should be consulted at length on the whole matter of Paul's use of the Jesus traditions (see his "Paul and the Synoptic Apocalypse," in *Gospel Perspectives,* ed. R. T. France and D. Wenham [Sheffield: JSOT, 1981], pp. 345-75).

48. I say that despite the conclusions of C. M. Tuckett, "Synoptic Tradition in 1 Thessalonians?" in *The Thessalonian Correspondence,* pp. 160-82. Tuckett comes to a basically negative conclusion on whether such a tradition underlies the eschatological material in 1 Thessalonians 4–5, though he admits that perhaps 5.2 derives from a Jesus saying.

It is interesting that Paul, like James, seems to know the Matthean, rather than Lukan, and at times even the Markan form of the Jesus tradition. In my view this is likely because the Matthean form of the tradition more often preserves the original wording of a saying of Jesus than does Luke, even sometimes more than Mark, though by no means always. I do not doubt that Matthew uses Mark, but sometimes he retrojects a saying of Jesus from Mark back into a more Semitic form of expression, perhaps following his oral tradition, and sometimes this is likely to be closer to what Jesus actually said. See B. Witherington, *The Gospel of Matthew* (Macon: Smyth and Helwys, 2005), Introduction. In other words, the matter is complex.

49. See rightly, Wanamaker, *1 and 2 Thessalonians,* p. 171. This reassurance may have been particularly needed by any in Thessalonike who knew teaching such as that found in 2 Esd. 13.24, which states that those who survive to the end are more blessed than those who die before it.

the famous oracle about "the one like a son of man" (*bar enasha*). Though it has been debated whether this figure goes up into the clouds and heaven to meet the Ancient of Days or comes with the clouds to meet the Almighty on earth for the day of judgment, in view of v. 14 it must surely be the latter. The kingdoms "under heaven" are handed over to the "son of man" figure and to the saints, and all rulers will worship and obey this figure. It is surely not envisioned that these non-Jewish kingdoms and rulers are in heaven and are ruled from heaven. The rule, like the final judgment, takes place on earth. Furthermore, the son of man figure comes with the clouds of heaven, an image of clouds coming down from above, not rising up from the earth with someone ascending with them.

Dan. 12.1 speaks of a major distress "at that time" from which God's people will be delivered.[50] This is followed in v. 2 by the promise that multitudes who sleep in the dust will awake, some to everlasting life, others to everlasting shame. It seems very likely that Paul has some of this material in mind in 1 Thess. 4.15-17, though typically, as he does with the Jesus tradition, he has made the material his own, using his own way of phrasing things.

His "we the living, those who are left around/remain" is important since it means that he envisions Christians still living on earth when Jesus returns. It also may suggest that he thinks the majority of Christians will be dead when Christ returns.[51] But what sort of return is Paul envisioning here? Can it be a secret or invisible return? Do we have some sort of theology of a pre-tribulation rapture here with Jesus not actually coming to earth? The details of the text as well as the use of the language of the royal visit to a city surely rule out such a view.

We should probably take vv. 14 and 15 together, with v. 15 providing the reason believers can be confident about the resurrection of deceased Christians, namely that Jesus himself spoke of this matter and affirmed this truth.[52] The verse goes on to say that the living will not have precedence or any advantage over those who have died in participation in the parousia event.[53] All believers will be on the same footing, or one might say, on the same cloud, when Jesus returns.

As v. 16 makes quite clear, Paul connects the resurrection of believers who are dead with the parousia and with the meeting of Christ in the air. The parousia precipitates these other two events. Paul does not mention the resurrection of unbelievers at this juncture. He takes that to be a separate event that occurs on a different occasion (contrast *4 Ezra* 4.1-5). V. 16 also makes as clear as

---

50. See below on 2 Thessalonians 2, pp. 207-15 below.

51. When one talks about a remainder the implication seems to be that a minority of the total number is referred to. See Marshall, *1 and 2 Thessalonians*, p. 127.

52. Beale, *1 and 2 Thessalonians*, p. 135.

53. See Bruce, *1 and 2 Thessalonians*, p. 99.

one could want that we are dealing with a public event, one announced not only by a loud command, as on a battlefield,[54] and the voice of the archangel (see Jude 9; *1 Enoch* 20.1-7; *4 Ezra* 4.36), but also by the trumpet call of God, though these may be three ways of referring to the same sound.[55] The images are martial, as if Jesus were summoning his army.

The meeting place is said to take place in the clouds or in the air, not in heaven. Paul considers the dead in Christ to be persons who can be "awakened" or "addressed." He is probably drawing on the *yom Yahweh* traditions, which referred to a trumpet blast announcing the event (cf. Isa. 27.13; Joel 2.1; Zech. 9.14; 2 Esd. 6.23; *Sibylline Oracles* 4.174; 1 Cor. 15.52). But it was also the case that a royal visit to a city would be announced by a herald (see Ps. 24.7-10) and might well also be announced by a trumpet blast meant to alert those in the city that the king was coming.

This imagery is pursued further in v. 17 with the use of the term *apantesin*. For example, Cicero says of Julius Caesar's victory tour through Italy in 49 B.C.: "Just imagine what a meeting/royal welcome (*apantesis*) he is receiving from the towns, what honors are paid to him" (*Ad. Atticus* 8.16.2; cf. 16.11.6 of Augustus: "the municipalities are showing the boy remarkable favor. . . . Wonderful *apantesis* and encouragement"). This word refers, then, to the actions of the greeting committee as it goes forth from the city to escort the royal person or dignitary into the city for his official visit. "These analogies (especially in association with the term *parousia*) suggest the possibility that the Lord is pictured here as escorted the remainder of the journey to earth by his people — both those newly raised from the dead and those remaining alive."[56] Chrysostom picked up these nuances quite clearly:

> For when a king drives into a city, those who are honorable go out to meet him; but the condemned await the judge within. And upon the coming of an affectionate father, his children indeed, and those who are worthy to be his children, are taken out in a chariot, that they may see him and kiss him; but the housekeepers who have offended him remain within. (*Homily* 8 on 1 Thessalonians)[57]

---

54. Cf. Prov. 30.27 LXX; Thucydides, *Historia* 2.92.

55. Bruce, *1 and 2 Thessalonians*, p. 101. Notice however this epitaph from the late second century: "Neither gold nor silver but bones lie here awaiting the trumpet call (*phōnēn salpingos*). Do not disturb the work of God the begetter" (*IK* 31, ll. 126-27 [§177] in *New Docs* 9, p. 102).

56. Bruce, *1 and 2 Thessalonians*, p. 103.

57. Notice as well that going out to meet the dignitary is a great public honor and carries the implication that this authority figure will deal with the dishonorable thereafter when he comes inside the city or home.

Paul's Thessalonian audience may have missed some of the allusions to the OT, but they would not have missed the language used here about a royal visit, indeed an imperial visit (cf. also Acts 28.15).[58] They would remember the visit of Pompey and later Octavian and others in the days when Thessalonike could even be talked about by Pompey as the capital in exile.[59]

Donfried sums up the implications of this imagery:

> If 1 Thessalonians is at all representative of [Paul's] original preaching then we certainly do find elements which could be understood or misunderstood in a distinctly political sense. In 2:12 God, according to the Apostle, calls the Thessalonian Christians "into his own kingdom"; in 5:3 there is a frontal attack on the *Pax et Securitas* program of the early Principate; and in the verses just preceding this attack one finds three heavily loaded political terms: *parousia, apantesis,* and *kyrios. Parousia* is related to "the 'visit' of the king, or some other official." When used as court language *parousia* refers to the arrival of Caesar, a king or an official. *Apantesis* refers to the citizens meeting a dignitary who is about to visit the city. These two terms are used in this way by Josephus (*Ant.* XI.327ff.) and also similarly referred to by such Greek writers as Chrysostom. The term *kyrios* especially when used in the same context as the two preceding terms, also has a definite political sense. People in the eastern Mediterranean applied the term *kyrios* to the Roman emperors from Augustus on. . . . All of this, coupled with the use of *euaggelion* and its possible association with the eastern ruler cult suggests that Paul and his associates could easily be understood as violating "the decrees of Caesar" in the most blatant manner.[60]

Donfried goes on to suggest that the dead in Christ in Thessalonike were victims of the persecutions elsewhere alluded to in this letter, which is certainly possible. Bruce has pointed out that in Acts 7.60 Stephen was stoned and then "fell asleep" (*ekoimethe*).[61] This language in the context of persecution could refer to one who suffered death through persecution. We may need to take seriously that when it was suggested that Paul and his coworkers had violated Caesar's decrees this had severe repercussions not only for them but also for their converts. Some lost their lives. No wonder Paul was so concerned about them!

But he does not back down from his anti-imperial rhetoric as he writes

---

58. See the references in Rigaux, *Les Épitres,* p. 198, to the use of the term of Cleopatra, Germanicus, and others.

59. See pp. 3-4 above.

60. K. P. Donfried, "The Imperial Cults and Political Conflict in 1 Thessalonians," in *Paul and Empire,* ed. R. A. Horsley (Harrisburg: Trinity, 1997), pp. 215-23, here p. 217.

61. F. F. Bruce, *The Acts of the Apostles,* rev. ed. (Grand Rapids: Eerdmans, 1988), pp. 327-28.

this letter, that is, his co-opting of imperial rhetoric to apply it to Jesus. The borrowing of imperial rhetoric is especially apparent in the Thessalonian correspondence. *Parousia* shows up four times in 1 Thessalonians (2.19; 3.13; 4.15; 5.23), twice in 2 Thessalonians (2.1, 8), and only once elsewhere in Paul (1 Cor. 15.23).[62] H. Koester has helpfully pointed out that the problem in Thessalonike is certainly not the delay of the parousia, but rather concern about the fate of the Thessalonian Christian dead, concern exacerbated by persecution and possibly even martyrdom. Will the dead Christians join the living in the great welcoming of the return of their Lord?[63] Paul's answer is an emphatic yes. But in the course of giving that assurance and making some remarkable christological and eschatological assertions, he is also busily deconstructing the extant pagan value system so that his converts will not lapse back into allegiance to it. N. T. Wright puts it this way:

> Paul's opposition to Caesar and adherence to a very high, very Jewish Christology were part of the same thing. Jesus was Lord — kyrios, with all its Septuagintal overtones — and Caesar was not . . . neither the recognition that Paul's main target was paganism, and the Caesar-cult in particular, nor the equal recognition that he remained a thoroughly Jewish thinker, should blind us for a moment to the fact that Paul still held a thorough and stern critique of non-messianic Judaism. . . . If Paul's answer to Caesar's empire is the empire of Jesus, what does this say about this new empire, living under the rule of its new Lord? . . . This counter-empire can never be merely critical, never merely subversive. It claims to be the reality of which Caesar's empire is the parody. It claims to be modeling the genuine humanness, not least the justice and peace, and the unity across traditional racial and cultural barriers, of which Caesar's empire boasted.[64]

It is particularly in the more eschatological sections of Paul's letters that the imperial cult language shows up. The imperial cult was an eschatological institution itself suggesting that a human being, namely the emperor, was divine and was walking around on the earth bringing the final form of peace and security to earth (see Virgil's *Aeneid*), a thought fully embraced in the eastern

---

62. One has to wonder whether Paul was reflecting on Claudius's crackdown on Jews and Christians in Rome in A.D. 49 and its aftermath as his reign deteriorated into bad government in his last years (49-54). The crackdown gave officials and others in a city like Thessalonike license to treat Paul and his coworkers and converts as they apparently did.

63. H. Koester, "Imperial Ideology and Paul's Eschatology in 1 Thessalonians," in *Paul and Empire*, pp. 158-66, especially pp. 158-59. See also the excursus on imperial eschatology as reflected in 1 Corinthians 15 in Witherington, *Conflict and Community in Corinth*, pp. 295-98.

64. N. T. Wright, "Paul's Gospel and Caesar's Empire," in R. A. Horsley, ed., *Paul and Politics: Ekklesia, Israel, Imperium, Interpretation* (Harrisburg: Trinity, 2000), pp. 160-83, here pp. 182-83.

part of the empire. Paul came into the same segment of the empire suggesting that another God was walking on the earth and offering kingdom, and had even come back from the dead. In such an environment this was an explosive message with considerable political implications. This message qualified as subversive, violating Caesar's decrees.[65]

It should be clear from the beginning of v. 16 that Christ is said to come *down* out of heaven and meet his followers somewhere else, in this case in the atmosphere, where there are clouds. There is likely an echo of Mic. 1.3 here: "For behold the LORD is coming forth out of his place, and will come down and tread upon the high places of the earth." Clouds are regularly said to accompany a theophany, when God comes down to the human level, not when humans are taken up into the presence of God in heaven (see Exod. 19.16; 40.34; 1 Kgs. 8.10-11; Ps. 97.2). Trumpet blasts also accompany theophanies (Exod. 19.16; Isa. 27.13; Joel 2.1; Zech. 9.14).[66] The meeting does not take place in heaven, so there is no rapture into heaven here.[67]

Paul adds, as the ultimate reassurance about the dead in Christ, that they will rise *first*, after which, according to v. 17, living Christians will be snatched up bodily (cf. Rev. 12.5; Acts 8.39; Wis. 4.11)[68] together with them in the clouds to meet the Lord in the air and be with him forever.[69] Far from the deceased Christians being left out of the parousia party, they will be first to be involved. It will be the ultimate family reunion with the king.

There may be echoes here of promises made sometimes in Greco-Roman

65. See pp. 7-8 above.

66. See Marshall, *1 and 2 Thessalonians*, p. 129. The clear implication is that the parousia of Christ is the coming of God to earth.

67. The term "rapture" does not appear in the NT. It comes from the Latin term *raptus*, "snatched," which is a rendering of the Greek here. The idea is present in *4 Ezra* 6.26; 14.9 and also in Gen. 5.24 LXX, where it is used of Enoch being taken up into heaven. The word itself however in either Greek or Latin does not carry the connotation of "into heaven," as the texts which speak of death doing the snatching or the land of the dead being the place one was snatched to make clear.

68. Interestingly and ironically this verb is used in Plutarch, *Letter to Apollonius* 111C-D, 117B; Lucian, *Funerals* 13, of the action of death itself. Inscriptions as well refer to fate snatching away loved ones into the realm of the dead (IG 2.1062a,3; 11477,9; 4.620,2; 5.733,12). See Malherbe, *The Letters*, p. 276; A. Smith, "The First Letter to the Thessalonians," in *The New Interpreter's Bible*, vol. XI, ed. L. E. Keck (Nashville: Abingdon, 2000), p. 725. *4 Ezra* 5.42 is interesting for it says "just as for those who are last there is no delay, so for those who are first there is no haste." Paul is using funerary language, another little clue that the rhetoric here is epideictic in character.

69. As Lightfoot, *Notes*, p. 69 makes very clear, the classical distinction between the pure ether of heaven and the atmosphere, which has clouds in it, is preserved here (e.g., Homer, *Iliad* 8.558; 17.371): "Thus then *eis aēra* here denotes that the Lord will descend into the immediate region of the earth, where he will be met by his faithful people."

contexts and epitaphs that the deceased would be with the "heroes," perhaps even in the Elysian fields. How much better to be with the Lord himself than just with the heroes.[70] Menander Rhetor in fact instructs that in an epideictic or consolatory speech one should speak of the departed as dwelling with the gods (*Division of Epideictic Speeches* 3.414.17-19; 421.17-18). In fact this became a stock element in funeral oratory and consoling letters (Cicero, *Tusculan Disputations* 1.75; Propertius, *Elegies* 4.11.99-102; Seneca, *Consolation to Marcia* 25.1; 26.3; Plutarch, *Letter of Condolence to Apollonius* 108D; 120BC; 121F). Paul then is following a familiar rhetorical convention here, and v. 18 follows naturally from v. 17.

Paul does not tell us here what he thinks happens next after the reunion in the air. That information he conveys in 1 Corinthians 15, and both here and there he says nothing about non-believers participating in this resurrection. He separates what will happen to believers and what will happen to non-believers when Christ returns. Note the reference to future wrath in 5.9. What Paul most wants to convey about what happens at the parousia is that the dead Christians will not only not be left out or disadvantaged, but will in fact take precedence. In a culture where pecking order was important, it would have reversed normal expectations to suggest that the dead had an advantage over the living.

A Closer Look: *Parousia*

It has been argued that *parousia* refers merely to a "presence" here and that what is envisioned is not a descent but rather an unveiling, with a removal of the barrier between earth and heaven, like the raising of a curtain.[71] The Greek text of 4.16, however, speaks of Jesus coming down from heaven. As for the meaning of *parousia*, Paul can use it in non-eschatological contexts to mean both "presence" (2 Cor. 10.10; Phil. 2.12) and "coming" (1 Cor. 16.17; 2 Cor. 7.6-7). But how is he using it in an eschatological context like 1 Thessalonians 4?[72]

We must bear in mind that the word had come to have special association with the arrival of significant persons already in the Hellenistic period and when coupled here with the language of coming down is hardly likely to mean anything else here. In fact most commentators say that every time this word appears in an eschatological context it means "coming" or "arrival," and they have the majority of the evidence on their side. As Best says, the word in its primary sense has a sense of movement.[73] A good example of the usage in a Hellenistic context in connection with an arrival and a

70. See Malherbe, *The Letters*, p. 278.

71. Beale, *1 and 2 Thessalonians*, pp. 138-40.

72. The detailed and careful discussion of the parousia in Rigaux, *Les Épitres*, pp. 195-280, should be consulted.

73. See the excursus in Best, *First and Second Thessalonians*, pp. 349-54.

greeting of a royal figure can be found in Josephus, *Antiquities* 11.26-28, where a priest is said to be awaiting the *parousia* of Alexander in order to go out and meet (*hypantesis*) him.

We must also keep in view that everywhere else in the NT the term is used in the eschatological sense of the coming or arrival of the Lord/Son of Man (Matt. 24.27-39; Jas. 5.7; 2 Pet. 1.16; 3.4; 1 John 2.28). Best concludes "The secular significance of parousia reinforces the conception of a coming of Christ which is a public event, in which he returns from 'outside' history to end history and which therefore eliminates any idea of a gradual development of events within history which themselves share the End."[74]

It is true that no one spoke of a "second coming" before Justin Martyr in the second century A.D. (*Dialogue* 14.8; 40.4; 118.4). Furthermore, *parousia* does not carry the connotation of "return" and is never used of the incarnation before Ignatius, *Philippians* 9.2.

Finally, it seems clear that the concept enshrined in this term is found in the Aramaic prayer *marana tha*, "come, O Lord" (1 Cor 16.22). 1 Thessalonians always uses *parousia* in connection with the term "lord" (2.19; 3.13; 4.14; 5.23). We must conclude, then, that the translation "presence" here in 1 Thessalonians 4 suits neither the eschatological context nor the history of the use of the term when speaking of "lords" or royal figures.

V. 18 involves an exhortation to encourage and comfort one another with these eschatological promises, the very sort of rhetoric that would be appropriate in an epideictic attempt to help the bereaved (cf. 5.11). With hope in the parousia and coming resurrection "not only could they expect to see their loved ones again but also they could expect a grand and permanent reunion for all the believers" and with Jesus.[75] The Thessalonians were to actively convey this consolation to each other (cf. P.Oxy. 115: *paregoreite oun heautous*). It was not just a matter of hearing and heeding what Paul said. They were to participate in their own healing.

The second division of the eschatological parenesis begins at 5.1. The use of *peri de* and "brothers" makes it clear that Paul sees this as a new topic or a new angle on a previously discussed topic, and here it is clearly one which is related to what has just been said about the parousia. But here the rhetorical function of the eschatological material is a bit different. Rather than consolation through new information this segment is more about exhortation based on the eschatological knowledge the audience already has.

This section has three divisions marked out by the word *de* ("but"): "but

74. Best, *First and Second Thessalonians*, p. 354.
75. Smith, "1 Thessalonians," p. 725.

concerning" (v. 1), "but you" (v. 4), and "but we" (v. 8). Their three related topics are the sudden and for some unexpected coming of the day of the Lord, when unbelievers will be judged (vv. 1-3), the preparation of believers for that day (vv. 4-7), and the necessary faithfulness of God's people, all of which is the basis for encouraging one another (vv. 8-11). The structure of this material is carefully wrought with the section ending with an inference drawn in v. 11 from what has just been said.[76]

There are obvious similarities with Rom. 13.11-14 in the use of the language of waking, sleeping, and sobriety. That the eschatological clock is ticking and the end possibly nearer than one thinks is clearer in Romans 13, which shows that no easy evolutionary schema of development will work when analyzing Pauline eschatology. Romans was written after 2 Corinthians, and yet Paul is still talking about the return of Christ and how the day of the Lord is possibly imminent.[77]

The attempt to take 1 Thess. 5.1-11 as if it were referring to events after the catching up of believers into the air rather than the parousia like 4.13-18 though in a different way (parousia = day of the Lord) must be said to be special pleading. The exhortations in 5.1-11 would be pointless if believers were not to be still on earth until the day of the Lord. The repetition of "with the Lord" in 4.17 and 5.10 and the similar endings directed toward the immediate audience in 4.18 and 5.11, along with the broader context and the content of these passages, indicate that Paul is speaking of the one and only second coming in both.[78] While 4.13-18 examines the second coming from the angle of the coming rescue of believers, 5:1-11 examines the same event from the perspective of judgment on unbelievers.[79] In this regard the latter is closer to 2 Thessalonians 2.

Chronoi kai kairoi is an important phrase in early Jewish and early Christian literature (Acts 1.7; 1 Pet. 1.11; Ignatius, *Polycarp* 3; cf. Neh. 10.34; 13.31; Dan. 2.21; Wis. 8.8; Eccl. 3.1; Demosthenes, *Olynthiac 3* 32). It is too simple to say that *chronos* refers to a longer period of time and *kairos* to a shorter one. *Chronos* is the general term for "time," whether long or short, and refers to the date of something if a particular event is in mind. *Kairos* can refer to place or time and has the sense of the fit measure, the appropriate or propitious moment or the right place. In short, *chronos* refers more to the quantity of time while *kairos* refers to the quality of time, and since the propitious moment is usually a brief

---

76. On this structure see B. Rigaux, "Tradition et redaction dans 1 Th. v.1-10," *NTS* 21 (1974-75): 318-40; E. J. Richard, *First and Second Thessalonians* (Collegeville: Liturgical, 1995), pp. 260-61; Beale, *1 and 2 Thessalonians*, p. 143.

77. See rightly Malherbe, *The Letters*, p. 289.

78. See rightly, Smith, "1 Thessalonians," pp. 725-26; T. Howard, "The Literary Unity of 1 Thessalonians 4.13–5.11," *Grace Theological Journal* 9 (1988): 163-90, rebutting the dispensational reading of these texts.

79. Rightly noted by Wanamaker, *1 and 2 Thessalonians*, pp. 177-78.

one, it often does refer to a short length of time, though this is incidental to its real thrust. The gist of the phrase here then is that the audience has no need to be informed about how much time must pass before the big event or what significant occurrences will mark or punctuate it.[80] Paul refuses to set up timetables because he cannot do so.[81] The timing has not been revealed. Indeed, what had been revealed is that no one knows the timing of this event, not even Jesus during his ministry (Mark 13.32).

V. 2 then tells us nothing about when Jesus will come, but rather how: in a sudden and unexpected manner.[82] Paul is describing here a sudden intrusion into human history, catching many unaware and unprepared. The controlling metaphor "thief in the night" goes back to the Jesus tradition (cf. Matt. 24.43; Luke 12.38-39; 2 Pet. 3.10; Rev. 3.3; 16.15) and stresses both the suddenness and unexpectedness of the event, but also its unknown timing. It also has an aura of threat or unwelcomeness to it, at least for the unprepared.[83] Strictly speaking it is the day of the Lord, not Jesus, that is said to come like a thief, but it is Jesus elsewhere.[84]

Paul uses several related phrases to refer to this coming event: "the day" (1 Thess. 5.4; 1 Cor. 3.13; Rom. 2.5; cf. 13.12), "that day" (2 Thess. 1.10), "the day of the Lord" (1 Thess. 5.2; 2 Thess. 2.2; 1 Cor. 5.5), "the day of our Lord Jesus Christ" (1 Cor. 1.8), "the day of the Lord Jesus" (2 Cor. 1.14), "the day of Christ Jesus" (Phil. 1.6), or simply "the day of Christ" (Phil. 1.10; 2.16). Paul has adopted and adapted the *yom Yahweh* traditions from the OT and applied them to Christ, for now it is Christ who will bring the final redemption and judgment to earth.[85] If

80. See rightly, Lightfoot, *Notes*, pp. 70-71. It is of course possible, since this is epideictic rhetoric, that Paul is using these terms as virtual synonyms, and so we would have an example of pleonasm or fullness and redundancy of expression. See Marshall, *1 and 2 Thessalonians*, p. 132. However, throughout the history of Greek usage, including in modern times, these two words when juxtaposed had distinct meanings. Today *chronos* refers to the year, *kairos* to the time. See Rigaux, *Les Épitres*, pp. 554-55 on this whole discussion.

81. When we examine 2 Thessalonians 2 (see pp. 205-15 below) we will point out that Paul is capable of talking about events that must precede the parousia as a way of making clear that the end is not yet at hand. But he does not speak of these events as sign markers or events which trigger the return of Christ and so must be closely juxtaposed in time with the parousia.

82. The Greek phrase *en tachei* can be used either adjectively or adverbially. It can mean "soon," but it can also mean "suddenly." Too often scholars have simply ignored the latter possibility (literally "in quickness"), overlooking the fact that the controlling metaphor in regard to the coming of the Lord/Son of Man was "thief in the night," a metaphor which suggests suddenness and an unexpected time.

83. See Marshall, *1 and 2 Thessalonians*, pp. 133-34.

84. See the discussion in Rigaux, *Les Épitres*, p. 557.

85. Of course he is probably not the first one to make this transfer. It seems to go back to Jesus and what he said about the coming of the Son of Man for judgment (Mark 14.62).

one compares 1 Thess. 4.14-17 and 5.2, it becomes clear that "the day" is the same as "the day of the Lord," which in turn is the same as the parousia.

It is not surprising that Paul speaks of "the day of the Lord" most often in connection with judgment since this phrase was used in the Hebrew Scriptures and the LXX most often to speak of coming judgment (cf. Rom. 2.5).[86] Zeph. 1.15-18; 2.2-3; and 3.8 (cf. Amos 5.18-20; Obad. 15; Joel 1.15; 2.1-2, 31-32; Zech. 14.1-21) stresses the idea that the day of the Lord is a day of God's judgment, though in Obadiah and Zechariah it is also a day of deliverance. Paul says that his audience knows very well (the phrase is emphatic: "you yourselves know very well") about this matter.[87] There is a note of irony here. The audience knows very well that the timing of the parousia has not been revealed and so is unknown and unpredictable.[88] In addition, Paul says that this day will come like an event at night![89]

It has sometimes been conjectured that with "when they say peace and security" Paul is drawing on an OT phrase, perhaps Jer. 6.14 or Ezek. 13.10.[90] The latter text condemns false prophets for crying "peace" when there is no peace, but says nothing about security, though the comments about the whitewashed wall may imply such a concern. Jer. 6.14 is of the very same ilk, criticizing false prophets for crying "peace, peace" when there is no peace. Clearly Paul's phrase is not a direct quotation of an OT phrase and his audience could not be expected to recognize such an allusion anyway. "When they say . . ." is also an odd way to refer to these false prophets, but it makes perfect sense if Paul is quoting here a cliché or proverb familiar in his audience's world. As Malherbe notes, the diction is not Pauline — Paul does not use either *legosin* or *eirēnē* (here in the political sense of cessation of hostility and violence) in quite this sense elsewhere, and he does not use *asphaleia* at all elsewhere.[91] There is some likelihood that at least the second half of this sentence echoes the Jesus tradition, specifically material found in Luke 21.34-36, but again that material does not account for the combination of "peace and security," and Paul would hardly introduce a word of Jesus with "when *they* say." "They" suggests outsiders, not insiders.

There were inscriptions all over the empire attributing to Rome and its army the bringing of "peace and security" to one region after another. For example, in Syria we have an inscription which reads "The Lord Marcus Flavius Bonus, the most illustrious Comes and Dux of the first legion, has ruled over us

---

86. See the discussion in Witherington, *Jesus, Paul and the End of the World*, pp. 163-65.

87. Lightfoot, *Notes*, p. 71 takes this to mean that they knew the saying or parable of Jesus about this.

88. Wanamaker, *1 and 2 Thessalonians*, pp. 178-79. *Akribōs* occurs only here and in Eph. 5.15 in Paul and refers to investigating something with great care and so knowing beyond reasonable doubt. See Josephus, *Against Apion* 2.175.

89. Malherbe, *The Letters*, p. 290.

90. See Lightfoot, *Notes*, p. 72.

91. See Wanamaker, *1 and 2 Thessalonians*, p. 180.

in peace and given constant peace and security to travelers and to the people"
(OGIS 613). Velleius Paterculus says "On that day there sprang up once more in
parents the assurance of safety of their property, and in all men the assurance of
safety, order, peace, and tranquility" (2.103.5). He adds that "The Pax Augusta
which has spread to the regions of the east and of the west, and to the bounds of
the north and the south, preserves every corner of the world safe/secure from
the fear of banditry" (2.126.3). Tacitus speaks of the time after the year of the
three emperors as a time when security was restored and adds that the "security
of peace" includes work without anxiety in the fields and in the homes
(*Historia* 2.21.2; 2.12.1). Not to be plundered by robbers either at home or on
journeys is "peace and security" (Josephus, *Antiquities* 14.158-60, 247). A variant
of this slogan, "peace and concord," is found in inscriptions dating back to 139
B.C. and referring to a pact between Rome and the cities of Asia "preserving
mutual goodwill with peace and all concord and friendship" (SIG 685.14-15).[92]

Paul must have thought "What foolish slogans and vain hopes when the
day of the Lord is coming." He is critiquing the slogans and propaganda about
the Pax Romana. It is on those who offer this rhetoric that destruction will
come, which may suggest that Paul foresaw the same future for Rome and those
who cooperated with it as John of Patmos does in Revelation 6–19.[93] Paul does
not want his audience to be beguiled by such rhetoric, especially after he has
been expelled and they have suffered persecution from those who are supposedly the bringers of "peace and security." It is the imperial propaganda and
prophecies that Paul is offering a rebuttal to here.

What is predicted for those who offer this slogan is sudden destruction
coming on them much like a birth pang suddenly seizes a pregnant woman (cf.
Ps. 48.6; Isa. 26.17; 66.8; Jer. 30.6-7; Mic. 4.9; *4 Ezra* 16.35-39; *1 Enoch* 62.1-6). The
wording here is closely parallel to Luke 21.34-36.[94] Paul stresses that there can be
no escape from this coming destruction for "them." He is not a crusader against
the empire in the sense of someone leading a social movement for reform.
Rather, he is a believer that God in Christ will intervene once and for all and
right the wrongs that Paul and his audience have been experiencing because of
their witness. God in Christ is the one who will bring justice, peace, and security once and for all, not the emperor with his slogans. Paul will say more on
this theme in 2 Thessalonians 2. The rhetorical effect of what he has said here is
to create a sense of urgency in regard to heeding his exhortations. "Paul in no

---

92. For more of this sort of evidence see the detailed discussion in K. Wengst, *Pax
Romana and the Peace of Jesus Christ* (Philadelphia: Fortress, 1987), pp. 19-26, and in regard to
our text pp. 77-78.

93. But see below on the issue of the "Restrainer," pp. 208-11 below. On Revelation see
B. Witherington, *Revelation* (Cambridge: Cambridge University Press, 2003), *ad loc.*

94. See Marshall, *1 and 2 Thessalonians*, pp. 134-35.

way seeks to decrease, let alone defuse, the eschatological pressure felt by the Thessalonians."[95]

The "they" of v. 3 will now be contrasted with "but you brothers" in v. 4,[96] and vv. 4-5 make a clear contrast between believers and unbelievers. With the darkness and light metaphors Paul in essence says that his converts are neither in the state of darkness, nor is the darkness the source of their existence.[97] They should not be surprised by the coming of the day of the Lord even if it arrives at an unexpected time. "Unpredictable events have different effects on those who are unprepared for them and those who are ready for them."[98] Believers are children of the day, sons of light (cf. Luke 16.8; John 12.38; Eph. 5.8). The self-descriptive language of the in-group here is much like what we find at Qumran (1QS 3.13–4.26; 1QM 1.1-3). A saying of Euripides helps us understand the force of the imagery here: "Night is the time for thieves, daylight is the time for truth" (*Iphigenia in Taurus* 1025-26).[99]

V. 5 calls the audience both sons of light and sons of the day. Here we see the two poles of Paul's eschatology. The light has already dawned in Christ, and the Thessalonian Christians are already children of light, transformed into new creatures.[100] But they await the day. Provisionally they are called "sons of the day," reassuring them that they will be participants when Jesus returns.[101] Paul says that "all" his audience are sons of light and sons of the day. He does not hold to a concept of an invisible elect in the midst of the church. He assumes that his whole audience believes in Jesus and so is among the elect and will be sons of the day.[102] But before they arrive at that day there is much to prepare for and much to persevere through. They must remember that they are no longer of the night nor of darkness.[103] They are not in a benighted condition and so should not be caught out by the coming of the day.

Knowledge is power, but it can also be used for motivation, and in v. 6 Paul turns to his exhortation based on what the Thessalonians know about the eschatological situation. With *Ara oun* ("so then") as a marker that he is turning to a logical conclusion or a moral consequence of what he has just said,[104] Paul draws

95. Best, *First and Second Thessalonians*, p. 208.

96. Rigaux, *Les Épitres*, p. 557.

97. Smith, "1 Thessalonians," p. 726.

98. Marshall, *1 and 2 Thessalonians*, p. 136.

99. See Lightfoot, *Notes*, p. 74 on this quotation.

100. Best, *First and Second Thessalonians*, p. 210.

101. See Beale, *1 and 2 Thessalonians*, pp. 144-45.

102. See pp. 65-67 above on Paul's conception of election.

103. On the parallel construction see Rigaux, *Les Épitres*, p. 563; Wanamaker, *1 and 2 Thessalonians*, p. 183.

104. This is Paul's usual rhetorical marker indicating that a conclusion or an application based on what has been just said is forthcoming (cf. 2 Thess. 2.15; Gal. 6.10; Rom. 5.18;

an ethical conclusion about how Christian behavior should differ from that of "the rest."[105] Lightfoot distinguishes between sleepers and drunkards. The former, he says, are the careless and indifferent, the latter the profligate and reckless.[106] It is interesting that Paul uses the metaphor not only of being awake and sober but of wearing certain clothes, or, as we might say, keeping our day clothes on, to describe the state of preparedness of Christians for the parousia.[107] Vv. 6-8 use four hortatory subjunctives to bring home this application.[108] Paul uses the terminology for sleep in three different ways: in v. 6 it is metaphorical, in v. 7 it is literal, and in v. 10 it is a euphemism for death as it was in ch. 4.[109]

The exhortation here probably owes something to Jesus' words in Mark 13.34-37 (cf. also Matt. 24.42-43), and in any case Paul is not saying what Clement of Alexandria later said, namely "we should sleep half-awake" (*Christ the Educator* 2.9.79). No, Paul is calling for his converts to remain awake, alert, and sober (cf. Eph. 5.14). Malherbe insightfully notes that while in those Synoptic texts alertness is mainly grounded in ignorance of the timing of the second coming, here it is mainly grounded in one's Christian identity — a Christian is of the light and enlightened and as such should always remain morally and spiritually alert.[110] *Nepein* occurs only here and at 2 Tim. 4.5 in the Pauline corpus, and it means literally "be sober," though it could be translated "be self-controlled." It is no good being awake but drunk. One will still not be prepared for the "thief" in that condition. So Paul is urging both intellectual and moral preparation and readiness for the parousia. The opposite would be moral and spiritual sleep or unconsciousness. Plutarch the moralist also urges his audience to be awake and sober and contrasts this with being asleep or drunk, using these same terms (*To an Uneducated Ruler* 781D).

V. 7 is a sort of gloss on or illustration of what Paul has just said, explaining that sleepers and those who get drunk generally do so at night.[111] The implication is that Christians are not of the night, nor should they be given to these sort of "night moves." "What is true at the level of everyday human experience applies on the religious and ethical plane."[112] Christians are held to God's twenty-four hours of daytime.

7.3; 8.1, 12). It is notable that only Paul among the NT writers uses this rhetorical marker. See Marshall, *1 and 2 Thessalonians*, p. 137.

105. V. 6 is then a continuation of v. 5.

106. Lightfoot, *Notes*, p. 75.

107. See Beale, *1 and 2 Thessalonians*, p. 149.

108. See Wanamaker, *1 and 2 Thessalonians*, p. 184.

109. See Malherbe, *The Letters*, p. 295.

110. Malherbe, p. 295.

111. See Rigaux, *Les Épitres*, p. 565. Drunkenness during the day was less common and considered more reprehensible (cf. Isa. 5.11; Acts 2.15; 2 Pet. 2.13).

112. Wanamaker, *1 and 2 Thessalonians*, p. 185.

V. 8 states the consequences of being daytime people. We must be awake and sober and put on the appropriate clothing to deal with the "slings and arrows of outrageous fortune." The famous triad of faith, hope, and love occurs again (cf. 1.3; 1 Corinthians 13). The armor imagery is further developed in Eph. 6.14-17. Both texts are indebted to Isa. 59.17, where it is God who wears the helmet of salvation.

The terminology is probably chosen carefully. The most vulnerable part of a person in a life-threatening situation is the head. *Sōtēria* can mean "rescue," "help," "healing," or "deliverance" in a mundane or profound sense. But here the helmet is the *hope* of salvation. What protects the believer against a mortal blow to his faith is to some degree the hope of salvation. If one has no hope or trust that God will one day make things right, then one's faith is fragile and can be overwhelmed by the problems and injustices of the present.[113] But this hope not only protects in the present, it gives courage in the face of the coming judgment of God, knowing that one will be saved or rescued from that maelstrom.[114]

Beale argues that the use of the aorist participle *endysamenoi* in 5.8 "indicates not that believers make their own efforts to put on armor, but that as 'sons of light' they have already been clothed with the armor. That is, although Christians have been clothed with the armor of faith, love and hope in Christ (as 1:3 affirms) they need to grow in these virtues and in their identification with Christ."[115] But 1.3 says nothing about where the faith, hope, and love have come from. Indeed, that verse focuses on the labor and endurance that come from those virtues. In Rom. 13.12-13 Paul does talk about the efforts Christians make to put on the armor. Furthermore, Paul regularly uses the language of "putting on" to refer to human activity (cf. Gal. 3.27; Eph. 4.24; Col. 3.10, 12). Attempts to blunt the hortatory character and force of 1 Thess. 5:8 and Paul's theological ethics in general should be resisted. As Eph. 6.11-17 later shows, such texts are all about exhortations to take up and put on and bear witness to and exhibit these qualities of the Christian life, and it is assumed that effort is required by the Christian to accomplish this aim. Here the aorist participle could mean "having put on," referring to an action the converts have taken in the past, or, if pure *Aktionsart* is in

---

113. Faith and love are grouped together here in connection with the metaphor of the breastplate. Lightfoot, *Notes*, p. 76 points out that faith is not fulfilled except by love. Malherbe, *The Letters*, p. 298 notes the singular position of "hope" here. It is probably singled out because hope is what these converts under fire were most in need of.

114. Bruce, *1 and 2 Thessalonians*, p. 112. Notice the reference in Gal. 5.5 to awaiting the hope of righteousness. The consummation of everything for believers comes when Christ returns and they are transformed into his likeness. This is clearly a reference not to Christ's righteousness but to the believers', which they will not fully obtain or reflect until the return of Christ and their bodily transformation.

115. Beale, *1 and 2 Thessalonians* p. 151.

view, it may be an exhortation to a single action: "put on." Either is possible here,[116] but in either case we are talking about human actions.[117]

V. 9 reassures the converts that God did not appoint them to suffer judgment and wrath in the future, but rather to receive salvation through "our Lord Jesus Christ." The sentence begins with *hoti*, "because": the converts are to put on the armor *because* God did not appoint them for wrath. Their destiny is different from that of those referred to as sleeping or drunk in v. 3.[118] But of course destinies and destinations can change. Those in darkness may finally see the light, and those in the light may make shipwreck of their faith. One reason Paul insists on speaking of salvation as something to be obtained[119] in the future is precisely because Christian behavior can affect the outcome until one dies or Jesus returns. Salvation is a gift, whether one is talking about initial or final salvation, but when one is referring to the latter it is a gift given to those who have persevered, have put on the armor, have stayed alert, have remained faithful and true, and the like.

Ethetō, "appointed," here as elsewhere indicates God's soteriological purpose. It is believers that God appoints or destines for final salvation (cf. 1 Pet. 2.8). This passage is somewhat like Rom. 8.28-29, and in both cases the language of destining is used to reassure Christians, those who love God, about their future. The subject is not about destining or electing some to be believers.[120] Sal-

---

116. On the translation "putting on" see Malherbe, *The Letters*, p. 297, who like Marshall sees this action as coincident in time with being sober or alert.

117. But see Smith, "1 Thessalonians," p. 727. As is well known, Greek verbs focus more on the kind rather than the time of action, and the aorist normally conveys the sense of punctiliar activity or the onset of something, whether it begins in the past or the present. Notice for example how at 1 Thess. 5.10 the aorist verb *zēsomen* refers to a future event, and it may be ingressive there: "we will begin to live with him." By contrast the present tense often conveys ongoing activity: "I believe" means "I continue to believe/keep believing." In hortatory contexts participles are often used to exhort the audience to do something or to continue to do something.

118. See Malherbe, *The Letters*, p. 298.

119. The word *peripoiēsis* is rare, and often refers to a possession (Eph. 1.14; 1 Pet. 2.9), but in 2 Thess. 2.14 and Heb. 10.39 it refers to obtaining, though Rigaux, *Les Épitres*, pp. 570-71 thinks the sense there is "preserve." But what would it mean to preserve salvation through Jesus?

120. It is of a piece with the quotation above from Beale that he goes on to argue: "Why is the apostle persuaded that the majority in the church at Thessalonica will be adequately prepared for Christ's return? Paul is convinced that most of his readers are elect (1.4) and that therefore *God did not appoint them to suffer wrath but to receive salvation* (5.9)" (p. 153). But the texts cited by Beale say nothing about "the majority" of the audience being elect or "some" of them being destined to obtain salvation. Paul addresses the entire Thessalonian congregation in this fashion throughout this letter. He does so because he believes that God desires that all should be saved and that God has appointed all believers to avoid wrath and

vation is obtained through the Lord Jesus. He is the medium or agent of salvation and one who is not connected to him cannot obtain final salvation. It is his work on the cross that makes possible the giving of the gift of salvation.

The idea here is that God has provided believers with the necessary "equipment" so that, if they will put on the armor, stay awake and alert, and so persevere, they may obtain the gift of final salvation. Paul "does not suggest that God's plan is fulfilled independently of the action of [human beings]. . . . Paul's exhortations to vigilance would be nonsensical if vigilance was the product of some inward causation in the believer by God or if there was no possibility of disobeying the exhortation."[121]

V. 10 flows logically from v. 9 and is important because it shows that Paul already had an understanding of the salvific nature and importance of Jesus' death and of how it was the key to believers being joined together and with Christ at the eschaton. It is disputed whether the crucial preposition here was originally *peri* or *hyper.* ℵ, B, and ms. 33 alone have *peri,* but 𝔭30, A, D, and many others have *hyper.* The number, geographical spread, and diverse text types represented by the latter favor *hyper,* which more clearly makes evident the beneficial nature of Christ's death: "he died *on behalf of* us."[122] This surely implies also that he died *instead of* us — that is, his death is vicarious, though this is not explicit here. In any case this theology is expressed more fully elsewhere (cf. Gal. 1.4; Rom. 14.9; 2 Cor. 5.15, 21). There may be something to the suggestion of M. D. Hooker that Paul has the idea of interchange in mind here — Christ became what we are and died, so that we might become what he is and live.[123] This idea is certainly in the mind of Irenaeus when he reflects on the meaning of Paul's letters and the Christ event (*Adversus Haereses* 5 preface). That Paul does not have to elaborate on the significance of Jesus' death here suggests that his audience has already been instructed on this matter, which was perhaps the most scandalous part of the Good News, namely the death on the cross of the Savior.[124]

---

obtain salvation. Beale also says (p. 152) that the reason things turn out as they do for believers is clear: "God's sovereign determination of someone for his own particular purposes." But unfortunately for Beale's view the language of election, appointing, destining is used in a variety of ways in Paul, and indeed in the NT, and in no case is it used in a way that suggests that humans are predetermined for salvation or wrath regardless of their own volition or desire, as if only God's will were involved in such crucial matters or affected the outcome of these things. See pp. 65-68 above and see Witherington and Hyatt, *The Letter to the Romans,* on Rom. 8.27-30.

121. Marshall, *1 and 2 Thessalonians,* pp. 139-40.

122. One may compare 1 Tim. 2.6: "he died on behalf of all." Jesus did not die just for the elect.

123. See M. D. Hooker, "Interchange in Christ," *JTS* n.s. 22 (1971): 349-61; "Interchange and Atonement," *BJRL* 60 (1977-78): 462-81.

124. Bruce, *1 and 2 Thessalonians,* p. 114.

The *hina* clause describes the purpose of his death: he died *in order that* a people, made up of both deceased and living believers, will one day live with him (see Rom. 14.8). Though Paul does not normally use waking and sleeping in tandem as metaphors for the living and the dead, it is fitting that he does here as he draws the eschatological section of the exhortation to a close.[125] Here again he touches in a reassuring way on the matter discussed in ch. 4, namely that deceased believers, along with those who are alive when Jesus returns, will enter into life or begin to live together with the Lord when he returns. "In Paul 'life' means more than 'existence with'; it implies 'resurrection life'; Paul envisages the Christian as entering into the resurrection life which depends on Christ's resurrection, and the Christian's life is transformed when this happens (1 Cor. 15; Phil. 3:21 . . .)."[126]

The parallels between 1 Thess. 4.14-18 and 5.10-11 make quite clear that Paul is not addressing sequential events in 4.14-18 and 5.1-11. The two sections also share the closing exhortation "encourage one another,"[127] but here Paul adds the exhortation to "build each other up," preparing for what he will say in 5.12-22,[128] and concludes with the reassurance "just as also you are doing."[129] Once again Paul makes it clear that this is a progress-oriented letter rather than primarily a problem-solving letter. Paul wants his audience to continue to believe and do what they already believe and are doing. This is a word of encouragement and consolation and as such follows the conventions of epideictic rhetoric, even in the exhortations, which are gentle and affirming, building on what is already the case and on values the audience already affirms.

Paul views his congregation in Thessalonike as not dysfunctional, even under fire, and so he is able to build on what is already true of them and what he has previously taught and done in their midst. He here encourages them to take up the tasks of being mutual encouragers and strengtheners of one another (cf. 1 Cor. 14.13), so seeking to strengthen the internal bonds of their small Christian community. The Christian does not build up himself. This is, rather, an action done in relationship to one another (cf. 1 Cor. 4.6 on the phrasing). It is a group-building exercise.[130] It is possible, as Malherbe has suggested, that the odd Greek phrase *eis ton hena* should be translated "one on one" rather than "one another," in which case Paul is saying that the building up should

---

125. See Wanamaker, *1 and 2 Thessalonians*, p. 189; Marshall, *1 and 2 Thessalonians*, p. 141.

126. On the verb as subjunctive and ingressive see Best, *First and Second Thessalonians*, p. 219 following ℵ and B rather than the future indicative, which is less well attested.

127. The parallels also include references to Jesus' death in 4.14 and 5.10 and the phrase "together with . . ." in 4.16 and 5.10. See Beale, *1 and 2 Thessalonians*, p. 155.

128. Smith, "1 Thessalonians," p. 727.

129. See Rigaux, *Les Épitres*, p. 574.

130. Best, *First and Second Thessalonians*, pp. 220-22.

take place in a more intimate way rather than just as a group or in a group meeting.[131] "In 2:11, Paul claimed that he had treated his converts *hena hekaston* as individuals; now he wants them, as individuals, to build up other individuals."[132] This indeed prepares us for the last of the exhortations in ch. 5 and the peroration which follows them.

Bridging the Horizons

We learn much about Paul's prayer life from a close examination of 1 Thess. 3.9-13. To judge from 3.9 and the thanksgiving sections in almost all Paul's letters, prayers of gratitude or thanks were a major part of his prayer. This was, of course, because he was utterly convinced that God was intervening in human history all the time and that God responded to the entreaties of his people. But there is something else to note about v. 9: Paul refers to joy in the presence of God when he prays. This at the very least refers to passions being involved and experienced in prayer, but it may also be referring to how prayer was for Paul not merely a time of speaking with God but rather a time of meeting with God, communing with God, experiencing God.

3.10 refers to intercessory prayer, in this case prayer offered repeatedly, indeed frequently (both day and night), that Paul might see his converts again and "supply what is lacking in your faith." This implies that Paul believes God is in charge of human history and can make it possible for him to see his converts again, but at the same time that he has a vital role to play in those converts' lives, in this case shoring up their fledgling faith. It is not all up to God. It also involves Paul's efforts. But just as clearly vv. 12-13 indicate that God makes their love increase and strengthens their hearts. Both the apostle and God are involved in their spiritual growth.

3.11 speaks of God clearing a path so that Paul may come to the Thessalonians. This suggests there were obstacles in the way. 2.16 spoke of human obstacles such as non-Christian Jews or Gentiles, but Paul can also speak of Satan as such an obstacle in 2.18. Clearly, though, Paul sees God as more powerful than any such obstacles. Prayer then becomes the means by which Paul participates in God's working out of his divine will and plan.

On August 13, 1979, my wife was in the hospital in Durham, England, "great with child." The doctor had just informed us that Ann would have to be in-

---

131. Malherbe, *The Letters*, p. 301. See the parallel in Theocritus, *Idylls* 22.65, where it seems clearly to mean "one on one."

132. Malherbe, *The Letters*, p. 301.

duced, as her blood pressure had become alarmingly high. She was very upset as we sat down to do our nightly reading of a chapter in the Bible, in this case a chapter from the doom and gloom portions of the middle of Ezekiel. Ann, a biologist, was distraught after all the child-birthing classes about having to have drugs to induce labor, and was worried about what it could do to the baby. We read along in the chapter, and in the midst of the doom, gloom, and prophecies of judgment, something suddenly stood out: "and I will multiply your kindred . . . and I will keep you safe . . . and you will come home soon. . . ." I realized that this was a promise given to Israel in exile over 2,500 years ago, but it was a word of knowledge that spoke to us directly. I told my wife not to worry, that the baby was coming, and that all would be well. I went back to the caretakers cottage at Elvet Methodist and kept my day clothes on, pacing the floor. I had no car and no phone and did not know when my neighbor, who did have a car and a phone, would show up. But I was certain he would, coming to take me to the hospital. He was surprised to find me fully dressed and ready to go when he knocked on the door. Like Paul's exhortation to the Thessalonians to keep awake and keep their Christian clothes on (cf. Rev. 19.7-8; Matt. 24.45-46) because Jesus would return, I was forewarned and so I stayed awake, alert, and fully dressed, for though I did not know when my neighbor would arrive, I was confident he would. Such was the situation in Thessalonike as Paul was addressing and forewarning the Christians there about what would come.

In his delightful and humorous small study *Epistles to the Apostle: Tarsus — Please Forward*, Colin Morris imagines what the letters written to Paul might have looked like. Two such letters he imagines coming from a Christian in Thessalonike and then from lawyers in Thessalonike writing on behalf of this socially well-to-do client who feels he has been taken in by the promise of Jesus' return, possibly imminent, which has led him to sell everything. Now he is the laughing stock of the town:

> My dear Paul,
>
> The followers of Jesus in this city are in receipt of your letter [i.e., 1 Thessalonians] which was read out in church a month ago and which appears to confirm a widely held view here that Our Lord will be returning in glory at any moment to take believers such as my humble self back with him to heaven. Being a hard-headed businessman I took your words with the utmost seriousness. To prepare myself and my family for the Day of the Lord, I sold my business at a knock-down price and gave the proceeds to the poor — and that let me add, was a tidy sum, but I assume we won't need cash in heaven!
>
> So here I am with my bags packed, my property disposed of, and myself, my wife and my children taking it in shifts to scan the skies for some-

thing unusual to appear. In fact every time I hear a trumpet, I nearly jump out of my skin! And what has happened? Nothing.

I can't help but feel that I've been made to look an utter fool in the eyes of my friends and business acquaintances. They all think I've gone stark, raving, mad. Meanwhile the man who bought my business, far from suffering the catastrophe reserved for the wicked, is making a handsome profit and living in my house, which is one of the finest in the city. He is allowing us to camp at the bottom of my, or rather his, garden, with passers-by leaning over the fence gawping at us and making the most offensive remarks. Not a pleasant predicament for a former Mayor to be in. Not that earthly honours matter, of course. But one has one's legitimate pride.

Would you kindly tell me what I do next? The tax people are pestering me for last year's assessment and I haven't a lead shekel to pay them with. Being a man of God you are probably unaware that disposing of one's assets in the interests of religion which is not recognized by the State does not qualify one for retrospective tax exemption. So I am in a pretty pickle, let me tell you!

I feel strongly that the financial implications of the Second Coming should have been given more serious consideration by the Apostles — though I suppose that tent-makers like yourself and former fishermen and so on could hardly be expected to appreciate the ramifications of big business. Indeed I doubt your incomes are substantial enough to attract any tax at all. How fortunate you are!

I am in a most embarrassing situation, what with a nagging wife, children who have got completely out of hand because they prefer earthly pranks to what they imagine will be heavenly boredom. You don't need me to tell you that we Christians in Thessalonica have suffered much persecution. But it is one thing to suffer for the Faith; another to be made to look ridiculous.

However, I do not intend to move from this spot until Jesus comes to collect me. Meanwhile it would be quite dishonest of me not to express grave concern at the most unbusinesslike way in which this whole matter is being dealt with.

I await an early reply, otherwise I shall be forced to turn the whole matter over to my lawyers.

> Paphlos
> former Managing Director
> Paphlos Importers Limited

When Paul responds with some of the material we find in 2 Thessalonians 1–2 indicating certain things must happen before Jesus comes, a response that is deemed unsatisfactory, this prompts the letter from the lawyers, who say:

In our view Mr. Paphlos has been the victim of a fraudulent deception and we are instructed by him to require you to make good your promise regarding this "Heaven" within thirty days or we shall be forced to take further action to obtain compensation for our client in order that he may resume the style of life to which he was accustomed before he fell under your influence.

Yours etc.,
Flaccus and Florus
[attorneys at law][133]

The wit involved in Morris's imaginary letters is evident, but they capture some important truths as well. First, eschatology can unsettle people if it is not explained clearly and fully, and can lead them to rash decisions. I am thinking of the Korean Christians who believed the "prophetic word" that Jesus would return in October 1992 and who acted precisely as described in these letters above. When Jesus did not show up, some of them committed suicide. The important point to be noted here is that Paul did not set any dates and indeed discouraged such speculations by using the thief in the night metaphor to indicate the suddenness and unpredictable timing of Jesus' return. Yet still Paul was and is continuing to be misunderstood. Obviously eschatology in the wrong hands is a dangerous commodity.

Second, Morris's letters also remind us that Paul's letters were part of an ongoing conversation on important matters. Though 1 Thessalonians is not likely a response to letters from Thessalonike, it is a response to oral communication Paul had with Timothy as he reported back about the situation in that city, no doubt informing Paul of what sort of encouragement and consolation the Christians there could use as they continued to endure persecution. Paul's letters are all ad hoc and are all meant to be words on target. If we do not attempt to reconstruct the context and setting in which they are spoken, we are bound to misunderstand what Paul says here, as did those Korean Christians.

Grief is natural in response to loss of someone or something. Just as evidence of burial rituals in an archaeological site is a sign of truly human existence, so, too, grieving is a universal human phenomenon. One thing that distinguishes Christianity is that Christians are called on to grieve differently from non-Christians. They are not to grieve as people who have no hope or faith in the afterlife or the resurrection.

Grieving may be natural, especially when one has loved someone or something profoundly and then it or they are gone suddenly, but it sometimes becomes egocentric in Christian contexts. One is grieving only for oneself and one's own loss if one truly believes the deceased has "gone to a better place" or is

---

133. C. Morris, *Epistles to the Apostle* (London: Hodder and Stoughton, 1974), pp. 15-19.

"in a better condition." This is in some ways unlike pagan grieving, where one is presumably grieving both for the deceased and for oneself. But one could argue that even pagans, if they truly believed in the immortality of the soul, were also grieving mainly for themselves. Yet in the contrast between two very different forms of afterlife (immortality of the soul and resurrection of the body) lies some profound differences in the way death, and so grieving, ought to be viewed. Let us consider some reflections by Frederick Buechner.

> Those who believe in the immortality of the soul believe that life after death is as natural a function of man as digestion after the meal. The Bible instead speaks of resurrection. It is entirely unnatural. Man does not go on living beyond the grave because that's how he's made. Rather, he goes to his grave as dead as a doornail and is given his life back by God (i.e. resurrected) just as he was given it by God in the first place, because that is the way God is made. . . . The idea of immortality of the soul is based on the experience of man's indomitable spirit. The idea of resurrection of the body is based on the experience of God's unspeakable love.[134]

What is especially helpful about these remarks is that they stress that Christians ought to look at life and ought to grieve, not only as those who have hope but also as those who have a memory that God has already raised Jesus from the dead and are prepared to trust that a loving God can do it again. Grieving, while trusting God, does not allow us to sink into prolonged self-pity or fear that after all one who has died is truly gone forever. In Christ there is no such thing as a lost loved one — they may be gone to be with the Lord, but they are not lost. The Christian knows right where to find them.

If there really is an all-powerful God of love whose character is revealed in Jesus, this ought to make a world of difference in the way a Christian approaches death or reacts to another Christian's death. Henri Nouwen put it this way: "Learning how to die has something to do with living each day in full awareness that we are children of God, whose love is stronger than death."[135] Learning how to grieve and how to comfort others who grieve, having something hopeful and meaningful to say, requires a similar awareness.

134. F. Buechner, *Listening to Your Life* (San Francisco: Harper, 1992), pp. 235-36.
135. H. Nouwen, *Turn My Mourning into Dancing* (Nashville: W. Publishing Group, 2001), p. 101.

Part Three:
Honor the Workers and the Work — 5.12-15

The last section of the exhortation before the final peroration, which brings the discourse to a climax, focuses on issues that affect community life and have to do with its leadership structure and its witness and ethos. This section is very brief, suggesting that Paul has now dealt with the main burden of what he wanted to share with his converts in Thessalonike. Nevertheless, it is important as it addresses the issue of leadership in a fledgling community.

But we appeal to you brothers, to acknowledge those working among you and those leading you in the Lord and advising you, also to have a regard for them beyond measure in love because of their work. Live at peace with/among them.[1] *But we urge you brothers to admonish the undisciplined/disorderly, console the faint-hearted/little-spirited, stand by the weak, be patient with all. See that no one returns wrong/injury for wrong/injury, but everyone continue to pursue the good unto one another and unto all.*

V. 12 has to do with appreciation and acknowledgment of the Christian workers in Thessalonike, whomever they may be. This verse then shares much in common with 1 Cor. 16.18 (cf. 1 Corinthians 1), only here Paul does not mention anyone by name, and we are probably right to think that the leadership structure is more primitive and new than the one in Corinth. Lightfoot is likely right that Paul is probably not thinking of three different sorts or kinds of leader — workers, leaders, and advisors. Rather, "worker" is the more general term (cf. *synergos* and 1 Cor. 16.16; Rom. 16.6, 12), which is followed by two of

---

1. See pp. 161-62 below on the textual variants.

the functions of the leaders — leading and advising.[2] There may be a rough parallel to Eph. 4.11, which speaks of shepherds/pastors who also teach.

Paul makes no appeal here to leaders he has appointed.[3] While it is not impossible that *proistamenos* means those who preside over others,[4] in Rom. 16.1-2 the cognate noun *prostatis* refers to Phoebe as a patron of Paul, not as someone who presides over him. Furthermore in Rom. 12.8 the verbal form is surrounded by terms referring to sharing one's material resources and showing mercy in practical ways (e.g., forgiving debts). In the Pastoral Epistles the term refers to looking after one's own household (1 Tim. 3.4, 5, 12), to caring for and prompting good works (Tit. 3.8, 14), and once to elders who "preside" or are "over" others (1 Tim. 5.17).[5] One may conclude the term is used in a general sense here of "leaders," but it seems more likely to have the special sense of patrons/caregivers/protectors.[6]

Perhaps we are to envision house church leaders who have become the patrons and protectors of some of the less well-off believers. Thus 1 Cor. 16.15-16 provides a true parallel here, and we may envision that social status and condition sometimes provided the means and opportunity to become the leader of a house church. "Such a non-egalitarian form of leadership should not surprise us as this is precisely the way leadership in the Diaspora synagogues emerged and it reflects the hierarchical character of Greco-Roman society."[7] Patrons frequently gave their clients advice and even admonitions, and we may envision this being the case with Christians as well. The owner of the house was the leader of the house church, and since his fellow Christians were seen as brothers and sisters, it would be natural for such a person to give them familial advice and even to exhort them once in a while. Paul here is giving permission for the Thessalonian leaders to do what he has been doing for some time in this letter, and he is asking for the audience to respect and acknowledge their authority, leadership, and work. He is not excluding others from doing some of these things (see v. 14 on admonishing). He is simply af-

2. J. B. Lightfoot, *Notes on the Epistles of St. Paul* (Winona Lake: Alpha, reprint), p. 79. The grammatical clue that this is right is that only "worker" has the definite article before it.

3. C. Wanamaker, *Commentary on 1 and 2 Thessalonians* (Grand Rapids: Eerdmans, 1990), p. 193.

4. See B. Rigaux, *Les Épitres aux Thessaloniciens* (Paris: Gabalda, 1956), pp. 577-78.

5. See F. F. Bruce, *1 and 2 Thessalonians* (Waco: Word, 1982), p. 119.

6. See I. H. Marshall, *1 and 2 Thessalonians* (Grand Rapids: Eerdmans, 1983), p. 148. The plural form here rules out the suggestion that Paul has a particular leader in mind. A. Malherbe, *The Letters to the Thessalonians* (New York: Doubleday, 2000), pp. 310-11 is right that the focus here is on functions rather than offices, but Paul is not merely talking about functions, he is talking about persons who can be singled out because they regularly perform certain functions for other church members.

7. Wanamaker, *1 and 2 Thessalonians*, p. 194.

firming those who are doing these things regularly and have taken the lead in doing so.

V. 13 confirms that Paul is concerned with the respect the Thessalonian leaders are getting, or not getting. He insists that they should be very highly esteemed in love. But he is not cultivating a cult of personality. This esteem is to be given "because of their work."[8] Nevertheless, it should not be grudging or partial but full-fledged.[9] There was a danger that these leaders, especially if they were of higher social status, as seems likely, would be respected because of their social position and who they were in the city. Paul will have none of that. They are to be respected for their Christian work.

Paul immediately adds "live in peace with one another/with them." This is not an unconnected thought. The number one thing that divides congregations is dissension or division over leadership.[10] 1 Corinthians 1 provides a good example where rivalry issues are in play and some are identifying themselves with one leader or another. Paul knows that the Thessalonian congregation cannot afford, especially with the external pressure and persecution, to be internally divided. In the Greco-Roman world rivalry conventions regularly came into play, a problem that quite readily affected the church (cf. the many exhortations to peaceable behavior: 1 Cor. 13.11; Rom. 12.18; Eph. 4.3; 2 Tim. 2.22; Heb. 12.14; Jas. 3.18). Thus, if they will all love their leaders, this will provide an environment where they can more easily live in peace with one another.

But it is likely that the proper reading of the second clause is "live in peace among/with *them*" that is, the leaders, as the reading with *autois* is well supported by 𝔭30, ℵ, D*, F, G, P, 81, 104, 1881*, and various other manuscripts. This rendering also makes the best sense of the sentence.[11] The exercise of authority, especially in a new situation, almost always prompts resentment. This would be all the more the case in a small community of believers who were vying for esteem from fellow in-group members and for self-esteem in an adversarial situation.[12]

In vv. 14-15 Paul turns to an equally brief final exhortation about how to

---

8. Rightly Bruce, *1 and 2 Thessalonians*, p. 119.

9. Marshall, *1 and 2 Thessalonians*, p. 148.

10. G. K. Beale, *1 and 2 Thessalonians* (Downers Grove: InterVarsity, 2003), p. 162.

11. But see the discussion in Wanamaker, *1 and 2 Thessalonians*, pp. 195-96. The issue here is whether *autois* has a rough or a smooth breathing. If the latter then the reading suggested above is right. E. Best, *A Commentary on the First and Second Epistles to the Thessalonians* (London: Black, 1972), p. 228 points out that we would expect *meta auton* if "with them" were Paul's meaning. But if Paul in fact means "among them," *en* is the proper preposition. The issue is how they will live in the midst of such leaders, not so much how they will relate to them. Some might be uneasy or uncomfortable with the social elite taking such leadership roles and begrudge them such positions.

12. Rigaux, *Les Épitres*, p. 581.

treat one's fellow Christians who are not leaders. The reference again to "broth-ers" indicates a new set of remarks set off from what has just been said. Here it needs to be stressed that "Paul knows nothing of an inert mass, the congrega-tion, on which the ministry operates."[13] The congregation performs some of the same functions of exhortation as the leaders do.

Ataktos is the opposite of *taktos,* which has the sense of "ordered" or ac-tion that is "required" or "prescribed" (*taxis* means "proper order"). Thus *ataktos* in Greek literature outside the NT can refer to people who fail to keep in line, in rank, or in their proper position, and so to the disorderly or unruly.[14] It is not used in the NT outside 1 and 2 Thessalonians. It is argued that in 2 Thess. 3.6-11 the cognates are used of those who are idle[15] and that this may well be the meaning here as well, providing a good link with 1 Thess. 4.11.[16] But use of the word in both Greek and Jewish literature outside the NT does not encourage us to render the word as "idle" (e.g., *Testament of Naphtali* 2.8–3.3). Idleness, of course, is one form of being out of order or acting inappropriately, but in 2 Thess. 3.6 the adverb *ataktōs* is used not only of what some Christians are fail-ing to do (work) but also of what they are doing (being busybodies). Laziness or idleness is not the main issue, but rather being out of line in their behavior. 2 Thess. 3.6 thus defines *ataktōs* as not living according to the received teaching. "Had Paul merely been concerned about the idleness of such people, however, he would have used the more common words for idleness, such as *argoi* or *apraktoi* to describe them."[17] On the whole then, the translation "disorderly" or "unruly/undisciplined" should be preferred here also.[18] The unruly behavior of such people is not more clearly defined here, as it is in 2 Thessalonians 3.

The second group spoken of in this verse are those who are literally called "the little-souled." *Oligopsychoi* occurs only here in the NT. Perhaps the least in-adequate English translation in this context is "faint-hearted." Aristotle says about such people that they are diffident and have a sense of inadequacy, con-trasting with the great-souled person, who is self-confident and self-sufficient (*Nicomachean Ethics* 4.3.3-7). The LXX as well uses this term of the faint-hearted or even the anxious (Isa. 25.5; 35.4; 54.6; 57.15; Sir. 4.9; cf. *1 Clement* 58.4). Such a person needs to be encouraged. The verb is *paramytheisthe,* which surely means "encourage" here (cf. 2.12).

The verse concludes with exhortations to help the weak and be patient

---

13. Best, *First and Second Thessalonians,* p. 223.
14. So Rigaux, *Les Épitres,* pp. 582-83.
15. See pp. 246-50 below.
16. See Marshall, *1 and 2 Thessalonians,* pp. 150-51.
17. Malherbe, *The Letters,* p. 317.
18. See the helpful discussion in Beale, *1 and 2 Thessalonians,* pp. 163-65. Bruce, *1 and 2 Thessalonians,* pp. 122-23.

with all these types of people, indeed with everyone. It is unlikely that "weak" here refers to weakness in faith, since Paul has just spoken of emotional and spiritual weakness. It probably has more to do with physical weakness, perhaps as a result of abuse or persecution.[19]

Makrothymia really means having a slow fuse or a great capacity for containing one's *thymos* (i.e., anger or profound passion). 1 Cor. 13.4 speaks of this quality as a manifestation of love, and it is part of the fruit of the Spirit in Gal. 5.22. The LXX uses this term to characterize God's way of relating to his people, "slow to anger and abounding in mercy and *patience*" (Exod. 34.6; Ps. 102[103].8; Joel 2.13; cf. Hos. 11.8-9; Rom. 2.4; 9.22).[20]

If there is some order to the sorts of persons Paul has referred to in this verse, we may note that he moves from behavioral, to emotional/spiritual, to physical maladies, covering all the bases. He has now concluded the more specific exhortations and is prepared to move to his peroration.

19. Beale, *1 and 2 Thessalonians*, p. 166.
20. See Malherbe, *The Letters*, pp. 318-20.

The *Peroratio* — Parting Shots — 5.16-22

The material we find in 5.16-22 quite nicely meets the requirements for a *peroratio* in epidectic rhetoric. Since epideictic rhetoric has no arguments, properly speaking, one would not expect a summing up or recapitulation of previous arguments. Rather, there is a compact group of final exhortations that builds on the exhortations that have come before, which is precisely what we find here. It is also the function of the peroration to appeal to the gut, to appeal to the deeper emotions that stir the audience — the emotions of love and hate, fear and anger, grief and consolation. In epideictic or funerary rhetoric one would expect that the final harangue would comport with the decorum and conciliatory tone of such rhetoric, which is the case here. Though Paul will give both positive and negative injunctions here, none of them could be said to be offensive, abrasive, or even controversial. He must appeal to values he shares with his Christian converts in Thessalonike and undergird those values and virtues as he closes his discourse.

These final exhortations almost all have to do with one's relationship with God. Paul now directs his audience away from the focus on their relationships with other humans to God and the gifts and character he is instilling in them. "The *peroratio* draws the audience members into action that is surrounded by *pathos*."[1] Just so, but it is also action taken in the context of a belief that they are surrounded and protected by the Almighty, through prayer, the Spirit, and the word of revelation.

In a sense this peroration is much like the one in Ephesians, also an epideictic piece, where Paul lifts his audience's sights from the mundane to fo-

---

1. R. R. Jeal, *Integrating Theology and Ethics in Ephesians* (Lewiston: Mellen, 2000), p. 198.

cus on the conflict with supernatural powers.[2] Perorations were meant to refresh the memory and influence the emotions (Aristotle, *Rhetoric* 3.19.1-6; Quintilian, *Inst. Or.* 6.1.1; *Rhet. ad Her.* 2.30.47), and amplify key concerns (Aristotle, *Rhetoric* 3.9.1; *Rhet. ad Her.* 2.20.47-49).

Hyperbole was in order in an epideictic closing (notice the several instances of "all" at the outset of this rapid-fire peroration), and recapitulation as well, so we note how Paul brings his audience full circle back to where he started with them in the *exordium* — back to prayer and thanksgiving — as he begins this section. Paul lists in a sense the spiritual disciplines and considerations that his converts must look to if they are to persevere despite pressure and persecution. They must continue without ceasing to return to the font, to the source of the Spirit and spiritual vitality, over and over again — to God. In this rousing fashion Paul bolsters, encourages, and consoles the faithful and helps them to keep walking in the right paths despite obstacles, grief, and problems.

Rejoice always; pray constantly; in all things give thanks, for this is the will of God in Christ Jesus for us. Do not quench the Spirit, do not ignore/despise prophecies; but test them all, hold fast to the good, from every evil form [of utterance] keep away.

On first glance, it might appear that this is a random sequence of final exhortations fired off in closing. But appearances can be deceiving.[3] The whole first part of the peroration has to do with prayer, which is said to be God's will for Christians. The whole second part is about prophecies, which are to be tested, but those that pass the test are to be held to as "the good."[4] The final warning perhaps has to do with false prophecies and staying away from those sorts of sources of spiritual pollution and influence, but we will say more on this in a moment.

One may ask at this juncture, however: what is the connection between prayer and prophecy? The answer is clear enough — God's answer to prayer can come in the form of prophecy, a revelation from above. When one is under pressure or persecution one is quite naturally driven to prayer, but one may also be driven to consult oracles as well. Paul has no problems with Christian prophecy. Indeed, he encourages his audience not to quench the Spirit. But even Christian prophecy needs to be sifted and tested (see 1 Corinthians 14).

---

2. See Jeal, *Integrating Theology and Ethics,* pp. 196-97.

3. C. Roetzel, "1 Thess. 5.12-28: A Case Study," in *Society of Biblical Literature Annual Papers,* ed. L. McGaughy (Chico: Scholars, 1972), p. 375 calls it "shotgun parenesis."

4. A. Malherbe, *The Letters to the Thessalonians* (New York: Doubleday, 2000), p. 328 rightly notes that Paul follows the rhetorical rule of three, binding together three exhortations in vv. 16-18.

What Paul does have a problem with is a Christian in desperation seeking out a pagan oracle or soothsayer, perhaps as a form of necromancy, out of desire for contact and reassurance about the Christian dead (see 1 Thessalonians 4). Admittedly this line of thinking is somewhat speculative, but as we shall see there is a train of thought in these final exhortations and it has to do with the vitality and viability of prayer and prophecy as useful spiritual resources for the Thessalonian Christians in their current situation. In other words, far from these last exhortations being random and generic thoughts fired off at the last minute, there is a connection between this material and what has come before in this discourse.[5]

The first exhortation in v. 16 might well have seemed counter-intuitive. What did persecuted and pressured Christians have to rejoice about, and how could they be expected to rejoice *constantly*? This injunction to rejoice is not uncommon in Paul's letters (see especially Phil. 2.18; 3.1; 4.4). He is not asking his converts to rejoice because of their circumstances but rather to rejoice in the Lord (see Phil. 4.4; Rom. 14.17). Joy is not caused by circumstances but has to do with one's relationship with God and the adoration and praise and sheer joy that arises out of that communion with God. It is no accident that the exhortation to rejoice is coupled with the one to pray. Adoration results in joy in the Lord and prompts further prayer.

But how is it possible to pray constantly, as v. 17 urges (cf. Rom. 12.12; Eph. 6.18)? "It is not in the moving of the lips, but in the elevation of the heart to God that the essence of prayer consists. Thus amidst the commonest of duties and recreations of life it is still possible to be engaged in prayer. And in this sense the command to pray without ceasing must receive its noblest and most real fulfillment. . . . It is in the Spirit alone that it is possible to 'pray without ceasing.'"[6] Since Paul goes on to speak of thanksgiving, we may assume that he is referring to petitionary and intercessory prayer here.[7] Thus we have here a discourse in miniature about the three major forms of prayer — adoration, petition, and thanksgiving.

V. 18 says that they should give thanks, not for all circumstances but "in all circumstances," which is a very different matter (cf. Col. 3.17; Eph. 5.20). Or it is possible that Paul means that they are to find ways to give thanks in every as-

---

5. See C. Wanamaker, *Commentary on 1 and 2 Thessalonians* (Grand Rapids: Eerdmans, 1990), p. 199: "Each of the three actions that he commands in vv. 16-18 either has its source in God, as in the case of the first one, or is directed toward God, as in the case of the last two."

6. J. B. Lightfoot, *Notes on the Epistles of St. Paul* (Winona Lake: Alpha, reprint), p. 81. Cf. G. G. Findlay, *The Epistles to the Thessalonians* (Cambridge: Cambridge University Press, 1925), ad loc, who says that prayer is "a stream always flowing, whether sensibly or in the background of consciousness; it forms the undercurrent of thought, which imparts its direction and tone to everything upon the surface."

7. I. H. Marshall, *1 and 2 Thessalonians* (Grand Rapids: Eerdmans, 1983), p. 155.

Corinthian congregation in regard to prophecy. It is a misreading of 1 Cor. 14.1 to suggest that the Corinthians were not enamored with prophecy. They were, but it appears that they were even more enamored with speaking in tongues and perhaps other spiritual gifts as well, and so Paul encouraged them to be more eager to prophesy.[20] Here Paul appears to be referring not to the despising, disdaining, or quenching of one's own prophetic utterances, but rather acting in a way that puts a damper on others offering such prophecies.[21]

But at the same time the Thessalonians were not to accept uncritically just anything that anyone who claimed to be a prophet said. Rather, they were to critically sift or test everything. *Panta* is neuter plural; it is the prophecy not the prophet that is to be tested.[22] The verb *dokimazō* was used of the proving or testing of precious metals and the like and then came to be used metaphorically as here (cf. Xenophon, *Cyropaedia* 4.30). "Proving" something, if it passed the test, then led to "approving" it (Plutarch, *Moralia* 18F). It is in this latter sense that the word is used in a similar context in 2 Thess. 2.2, where Paul warns this same audience about errant prophecies. Weighing the words of prophets is also referred to in 1 Cor. 14.29, and testing the spirits (1 Cor. 12.10) is shown in 1 John 4.1 to amount to a weighing of what is said in the prophecy.

The idea behind all this is that there are various sources of prophetic inspiration, divine and infernal, since there are both the Holy Spirit and other sorts of spirits, and so the utterances must be tested. Prophecy cannot simply be accepted just because it is a spiritual phenomenon and involves inspiration from some higher power or being. Pagans, just as much as Jews and Christians, believed in the reality of prophecy, that it could reveal hidden truths about the past, present, or future.[23] In such an environment one had to have criteria to discern what was from God. Perhaps the Thessalonians were too ready to be skeptical about the whole phenomenon. But Paul was not, as his own claim to be a prophet (1 Cor. 14.19) shows.[24]

Real prophecy does what Paul himself has been doing in 1 Thessalonians:

20. See the discussion in B. Witherington, *Conflict and Community in Corinth* (Grand Rapids: Eerdmans, 1994), pp. 274-90.

21. See Malherbe, *The Letters,* p. 332.

22. When it is the prophet that is being tested, the test regularly applied is in regard to behavior and character. See Matt. 7.15-23; *Didache* 11.3-11. The assumption of Paul here and elsewhere (e.g., Rom 12.6; see B. Witherington and D. Hyatt, *The Letter to the Romans* [Grand Rapids: Eerdmans, 2004], pp. 288-89 on that verse) is that true prophets could speak beyond the measure of their faith and inspiration, and therefore their words must be weighed and critically sifted.

23. See the excursus on pagan prophecy in Witherington, *Conflict and Community,* pp. 280-90.

24. See the discussion in B. Witherington, *The Paul Quest* (Downers Grove: InterVarsity, 1998) of Paul as a prophet. See pp. 77-80 above.

to upbuild, encourage, and console (1 Cor. 14.3, 31).[25] Paul has spoken of this when he reminded them from the very start of the letter that when he came to them he spoke prophetically in powerful words of the Holy Spirit (1 Thess. 1.5), and they in fact received those words as the very word of God, not merely the words of human beings (2.13). Thus, once again, Paul the prophet is the demonstration of what sort of utterances they could trust, and what the content of them might look like in this letter. We should probably, therefore, see these exhortations in 1 Thessalonians 4–5 as Pauline prophetic utterances, meant to be both heard and heeded, after proper weighing of course.

After "testing," the resulting action according to v. 21 should be to "hold fast to the good."[26] *To kalon* here can be distinguished from *to agathon* in that it refers to something that is good in itself while the latter refers to what is good in its results or practical effects (Aristotle, *Rhetoric* 1.9.3; cf. Xenophon, *Memorabilia* 3.5.28). "They can hold fast to it, in the sense that they take the message to heart, believe it and act upon it."[27]

The exhortation to embrace and hold fast to "the good" in prophetic utterances leads to a warning against the opposite: they are to keep away from every form or sort of evil (v. 22). Whereas "the good" is singular, "evil" is plural since it has multiple guises and forms of expressions and types.[28] One might even translate the clause as "abstain from every evil kind (of prophecy/utterance)," thus linking it more clearly with what precedes.[29] The word *eidos* refers to the various kind or species or type of something (Thucydides, *Historia* 2.50).[30]

25. See Wanamaker, *1 and 2 Thessalonians*, p. 202.

26. Noting the adversative *de* which binds vv. 20 and 21 together by way of contrast.

27. Marshall, *1 and 2 Thessalonians*, p. 159.

28. Lightfoot, *Notes*, pp. 86-87.

29. See Bruce, *1 and 2 Thessalonians*, p. 126; Marshall, *1 and 2 Thessalonians*, p. 159; Beale, *1 and 2 Thessalonians*, p. 174.

30. It is surely going well beyond the evidence here to argue that there was an organized charismatic opposition to the leadership in the Thessalonian church as R. Jewett, *The Thessalonian Correspondence: Pauline Rhetoric and Millenarian Piety* (Philadelphia: Fortress, 1986), pp. 175-76 suggests. As Wanamaker, *1 and 2 Thessalonians*, p. 203 says, Jewett seems to be reading the Corinthian situation into the one at Thessalonike. But surely the two situations were very different. Paul never had to tell the Corinthians "don't quench the Spirit."

The Invocation/Wish Prayer —
The God of Peace Who Sanctifies — 5.23-24

Invocations or wish prayers are not epistolary forms per se, though they may appear in letters. They come from liturgical and rhetorical contexts. More specifically, they come from funerary contexts, though we can find invocations in perorations of all three rhetorical species. Cicero provides a classic example[1] where in a peroration he invokes the various gods of the temples that a certain praetor being prosecuted had despoiled (*Verrine Orations* 72). Quintilian says that invocations are a very appropriate part of the peroration: "the invocation of the gods usually gives the impression of the justice of his cause."[2] He also stresses that perorations should be "as brief as possible" (*Inst. Or.* 6.1.2), as this one in 1 Thessalonians is. It is thus not at all surprising that Paul would include an invocation especially in a piece of epideictic rhetoric, just as a rhetor would, having just performed a eulogy or encomium, invoke divine blessing and comfort on his audience.

Epideictic rhetoric was often the most religious form of rhetoric since it regularly involved panegyrics of the gods themselves and praise for the blessings that a god bestowed (see Quintilian, *Inst. Or.* 3.7.3-4). Paul's invocation is rhetorically quite appropriate at this juncture and brings the epideictic rhetoric of this discourse to a proper close. Just as Paul concluded the *narratio* with a brief wish prayer that begins in the very same fashion as this one (3.11-13), so here he concludes the rest of the rhetorical divisions of the discourse with a

---

1. Which Quintilian hails as one of the finest examples of how to form an apt peroration (*Inst. Or.* 6.1.3).

2. See the discussion in A. Smith, "The First Letter to the Thessalonians," in *The New Interpreter's Bible*, vol. XI, ed. L. E. Keck (Nashville: Abingdon, 2000), p. 735, n. 140.

wish prayer of about the same length. Thus he provides models of prayer for those whom he has exhorted to pray.[3]

May the God of peace himself sanctify you so that you may be whole and preserved completely — spirit, life, and body, blameless at the parousia of our Lord Jesus Christ. Faithful is the one calling you, who also will do it.

The connection in v. 23 between the God of peace (cf. Rom. 15.33; 16.20; Phil. 4.9) and sanctified believers is noteworthy. Real holiness does not cause divisions but rather brings peace to God's people. As Bruce says, Paul seems to be reiterating in different words the theme of the wish prayer in 3.11-13, with sanctification being the last main theme there.[4] The two adjectives *holoklēron* and *teleios* occur together in Jas. 1.4 as well. The former denotes the presence of all the parts and the latter full development or completion of the whole. These two terms are often used in conjunction with sacrifices, which must be whole, complete, perfect, unblemished (cf. Philo, *De Virtutibus* 4, 14; *De Cherubim* 29; *De Agricultura* 29). Paul has in mind the condition of believers who must be presented or must present themselves as living sacrifices at the parousia of Jesus.

The tripartite division of human nature in this verse has often been commented on, not least because it appears nowhere else in the NT, and indeed nowhere else in prior Greek literature in this precise form.[5] Heb. 4.12 distinguishes between *psychē* and *pneuma* (cf. Phil. 1.27; 1 Cor. 14.45). The threefold division here was picked up by some of the early Church Fathers (cf. Irenaeus, *Adversus Haereses* 5.6). Lightfoot concludes that Paul means by "spirit" here the higher inner faculties (equivalent to "mind") and by "soul" the lower inner faculties

3. F. F. Bruce, *1 and 2 Thessalonians* (Waco: Word, 1982), pp. 128-29. Note how the epistolary elements, such as a final request for prayer (very different from an invocation of God directly) and the final greeting, mark the end of the peroration. They were indeed normal elements at the end of a Greco-Roman letter, while an invocation was not. Thus those who include 1 Thess. 5.25-28 in the peroration must not have examined perorations very closely so as to distinguish them from closing epistolary elements.

4. Bruce, *1 and 2 Thessalonians*, p. 129.

5. See A. Malherbe, *The Letters to the Thessalonians* (New York: Doubleday, 2000), p. 338. It does however appear in subsequent papyrological evidence, particularly Christian evidence from Egypt where the trichotomy is used to refer to the whole person. This includes P. Harr. 107 (111) and P.Oxy. 8 (1911) 1161 (IV). The latter has the same words in the same order as here. P. Coll. Youtie 91 from the fifth or sixth century involves a Christian amulet requesting Christ heal the whole person — soul, body, and spirit. See *New Docs* 1, pp. 102-3. Examples like this probably show the ongoing influence of the Thessalonian text in Christian communities in Egypt. Interestingly, in IGA 5.656 a person named Maria has her whole being described as "spirit and flesh," and then the former term is equated with "soul" (*psychē*). See *New Docs* 3, p. 111.

(i.e., the impulses and affections, "the centre of . . . personality").[6] Similarly, Marshall suggests that "soul" means human personality and is distinguishable from "spirit," which is the non-physical part of personality.[7]

The problem with such conclusions is that elsewhere Paul uses *psychē* of the natural self, indeed the life-force. It is almost synonymous with our word "being." Thus in 1 Cor. 2.14 the *psychikos* person is not the "soulish" person but rather the natural person as opposed to the spiritual person (*pneumatikos*). 1 Cor. 15.44-46 uses the same terminology to contrast the natural body with the spiritual body and adds that Adam became a living being, *psychēn zōsan* (quoting Gen. 2.7 LXX). In other words, *psychē* does not mean "soul" in the sense of the word with which we are familiar. It refers, rather, to something natural and physical or material such as the natural animating principle — life breath. So it is unlikely that Paul uses it here of something non-material.[8] That is what *pneuma* refers to — the non-material part of the human being which one gives up or gives back to God at the point of death. In any case, together these terms refer to the whole person, and the fact that God must sanctify, transform, and preserve the whole person before and at the parousia, for Paul is envisioning persons in resurrection bodies, who therefore will indeed be perfect and blameless living sacrifices offered up to the Lord Jesus.[9]

In a pagan sacrifice, everything depended on the absolutely perfect execution of the ritual. If the knife slipped, if the right words were not pronounced at the right time and in the right way, or if the animal was uncooperative, then one had to start over. But here (v. 24) the mostly Gentile audience is reassured that God is at work, that the sanctifying is something he is doing and will do in and for believers, just as he will raise them from the dead at the right time, and that God is faithful (cf. 1 Cor. 10.13 for the association of God's calling and faithfulness).[10] God's will is sanctification for the believer (1 Thess. 4.1), and God is busy performing his will within the believer. Similar ideas are seen in Phil. 1.6, 10-11.

The present tense participle "calling" is used, probably to indicate that God continues to call believers to sanctification and on to final salvation (cf. 1 Cor. 1.8-9). The completion of the process of sanctification and full conformity to the image of Jesus comes only through the divine action of God when

6. J. B. Lightfoot, *Notes on the Epistles of St. Paul* (Winona Lake: Alpha, reprint), p. 89, cf. p. 88.

7. I. H. Marshall, *1 and 2 Thessalonians* (Grand Rapids: Eerdmans, 1983), p. 163.

8. Cf. the discussion in B. Rigaux, *Les Épitres aux Thessaloniciens* (Paris: Gabalda, 1956), pp. 599-600, and D. B. Martin, *The Corinthian Body* (New Haven: Yale University Press, 1999).

9. See the helpful caution in Bruce, *1 and 2 Thessalonians*, p. 130, against over-reading these three terms.

10. In other words God will equip and purify the person in accord with what he has called him to do and be.

he raises the dead and indeed preserves and perfects in body and every other dimension of human personality the one whom he has sanctified and raised. It is
not up to human performance, but rather God's gracious action.[11] The prayer
that the converts may be preserved without fault at the parousia suggests that
they must be perfected before they appear before Jesus, perfected in body by
resurrection and perfected in spirit either at the resurrection or before.[12] Thus
Paul has reminded his audience in this brief peroration of the main resource
they have to allow them to persevere through their trials — God and his saving
activity in their midst.[13] We may think here of Augustine's famous prayer: "give
me the grace to do as you command, and command me to do as you will" (*Con-
fessions* 10.29).

11. See C. Wanamaker, *Commentary on 1 and 2 Thessalonians* (Grand Rapids: Eerdmans, 1990), p. 207: "Those Thessalonians aware of their own human limitations might well
have wondered how they could be kept blameless until the coming of Christ. In order to
avoid raising any doubts in their minds about their prospects at the judgment Paul reassures
them by immediately adding . . . 'the one calling you is faithful, who will indeed do
[this].' . . ."

12. See the discussion in G. Beale, *1 and 2 Thessalonians* (Downers Grove: InterVarsity,
2003), p. 176: "This may mean . . . that we are perfected immediately before the final judgment and have nothing for which to be judged. . . . Probably, however, the thought includes
both the process of sanctification and the perfect culmination of sanctification at the end of
history, both of which ensure safe passage through the narrow gauntlet of judgment." These
remarks are helpful, but they overlook 1 Corinthians 3, where Christians are told that their
works will be tested and judged, and 2 Cor. 5.10, which is perfectly clear that there will be rewards and punishments for all when "we" appear before the judgment seat of Christ, rewards
and punishments based on the deeds done in the body. The "we" here probably means "we"
Christians.

13. Smith, "1 Thessalonians," p. 736.

Epistolary Closing — 5:25-28

When Paul gets to the end of this letter he becomes even more succinct. There are very few epistolary elements here. There is nothing about travel plans, no reference to greetings from or to particular people, nothing about the process of writing (cf. Gal. 6.11).

Brothers, pray for us. Greet all the brothers[1] with a holy kiss. I adjure you by the Lord to have the letter read to all the brothers. The grace of the Lord Jesus Christ be with you.[2]

Paul begins these parting remarks with a request for prayer, which not only gives his audience an immediate opportunity to fulfill some of the prior exhortations but also humanizes Paul, making him approachable since he, too, and Timothy and Silvanus stand in need of prayer. This seems to have been a common practice of the apostle as he concluded a discourse (cf. 2 Thess. 3.1-2; Rom. 15.30; Col. 4.3-4).

In v. 26 we find what was to become a standard item in Paul's letters, the

---

1. Some manuscripts (א, A, K, P, and others followed by the Textus Receptus) add "holy" before "brothers," but this is probably not original since we find such a phrase nowhere else in Paul's letters. See Metzger, *TC*, p. 623.

2. Many manuscripts, including various excellent ones, add "Amen" at this juncture (so א, A, K, L, P, and numerous others). But the reading without it is well supported, and it is easier to explain the addition of it as the document came to be used in worship than its omission. See Metzger, *TC*, p. 634. It is interesting that some later manuscripts add a subscription telling us that this letter was written from Corinth (cop[bo eth], Euthalius), or more frequently Athens is the guess (A, B, K, L, 1908, many minuscules, and the Textus Receptus). These are of course later scribal guesses.

holy kiss (1 Cor 16.20; 2 Cor. 13.12; Rom. 16.16; cf. 1 Pet. 5.14). Basically this was how guests were greeted, and since the Christians met in a home some of the customs of family hospitality were carried over into the practice of the Christian assembly, not least because Christians were viewed as a family of sorts, the family of faith.[3] The kiss is to be holy or chaste, and thus perhaps on the cheek rather than on the mouth.[4] This had nothing to do with the sort of kissing referred to in the later Gnostic literature which was believed to convey esoteric knowledge or wisdom.

This practice of the holy kiss was, however, perpetuated and became widespread in the mainstream early church in connection with the Lord's Supper, beginning at least in the late second century (Justin Martyr, *Apologia I* 65; Tertullian, *De Oratio* 18; *Apostolic Constitutions* 2.57; Cyril of Jerusalem, *Catechism* 23; Chrysostom, *Homily* 22 on Matthew; Clement of Alexandria, *Paedagogus* 3.2.81).[5] By the time of Hippolytus it came in some circles to be called the kiss of peace (*Apostolic Traditions* 4.1; 18.3; 22.6), but was segregated by sex. In Paul's world a kiss was also a sign and means of reconciliation and so served as a deterrent to factionalism.[6] Outsiders in attendance would see in the kiss that the church was some sort of familial group or association.[7] Chrysostom notes "Because absent [Paul] could not greet them with the kiss, he greets them through others, as when we say, 'Kiss him for me'" (*Homily* 11 on 1 Thessalonians). Finally, the kiss was also a token of how Paul thought his converts should appropriately express their love for each other.

The adjuring in strong terms by Paul personally (noting the switch to the first person singular) in v. 27 to have this letter read to all has led to various conjectures such as that Jewish and Gentile Christians met separately in Thessalonike. It probably suggests no more than that there were already several house churches in Thessalonike and Paul wants to make sure they all get the entire message.[8] It may well be that the first person singular reflects Paul's taking up

3. See the discussion in B. Witherington, *Conflict and Community in Corinth* (Grand Rapids: Eerdmans, 1994), pp. 318-24.

4. The kiss of deference on the hand or even the foot is not what Paul has in mind, but rather the normal family greeting. See rightly E. Best, *A Commentary on the First and Second Epistles to the Thessalonians* (London: Black, 1972), pp. 245-46.

5. It may even be the case that this is when the act was practiced in Paul's churches (cf. 1 Cor. 16.20-22), which would presumably be when all Christians in town would be together and so could hear the reading of the letter together.

6. Cf. our phrase "kiss and make up." See W. Klassen, "The Sacred Kiss in the New Testament," *NTS* 39 (1993): 122-35.

7. See G. Beale, *1 and 2 Thessalonians* (Downers Grove: InterVarsity, 2003), p. 177.

8. It is worth noting the difference between what we find here and in Matt. 5.34. Paul is not strengthening a statement of his own by invoking the divine name. See rightly, F. F. Bruce, *1 and 2 Thessalonians* (Waco: Word, 1982), p. 135.

of the pen for the final remarks in the letter (cf. 2 Thess. 3.17).[9] These words of encouragement and exhortation are not for an elite group, such as the leaders, but for everyone, and Paul's strong adjuration is meant to elicit something like a tacit promise from the audience to do what he asks.[10] The "injunction to have the letter read conveys the authority of the words of the foundational leaders for all the members of the church."[11] The adjuration also makes certain that the document is read aloud (cf. Justin Martyr, *Apologia I* 67) and therefore not controlled by some subset of the whole.[12]

The final grace word in v. 28 is simple and direct. The grace of Christ is for all the Christians in Thessalonike,[13] and Paul wishes that grace for them all, especially during this time of trial. The Pauline final benedictions differ very little from one letter to the next — they all involve Jesus and grace (2 Thess. 3.18; Rom. 16.20; 1 Cor. 16.23; Gal. 6.18; Phil. 4.23; Phlm. 25). Paul began the letter by wishing them God's grace, and he concludes in the same fashion. Since this document was read in worship, we may assume that the end of the letter is liturgically shaped to suit the end of the worship service.[14] This stands in contrast to and replaces the normal closing greeting in a secular letters, which was simply "farewell" (cf. Acts 15.29; 2 Macc. 11.38).

Bridging the Horizons

There is, to say the least, confusion in the Protestant churches about prophecy. On the one hand we have those who want to suggest that there is no living voice of prophecy in the church today (it being eclipsed by the canon or dying out in the apostolic era). One of the more incredible forms these arguments take is based on an interpretation of 1 Cor. 13.9-10 which assumes that "the perfect" is a reference to the canon. Paul's Corinthian converts could not possibly have understood Paul to mean that since there was no NT canon, indeed would not be

9. See pp. 259-61 below.

10. See I. H. Marshall, *1 and 2 Thessalonians* (Grand Rapids: Eerdmans, 1983), p. 165. It means something like "I am putting you on your oath as Christians that you will do this." See A. Malherbe, *The Letters to the Thessalonians* (New York: Doubleday, 2000), p. 342.

11. A. Smith, "The First Letter to the Thessalonians," in *The New Interpreter's Bible,* vol. XI, ed. L. E. Keck (Nashville: Abingdon, 2000), p. 736.

12. See C. Wanamaker, *Commentary on 1 and 2 Thessalonians* (Grand Rapids: Eerdmans, 1990), p. 209; B. Rigaux, *Les Épitres aux Thessaloniciens* (Paris: Gabalda, 1956), p. 605.

13. Not just for some select group within the whole audience such as "the elect," for Paul does not distinguish between the whole audience and "the elect." He assumes they are all in Christ and need to hear what is said here and by God's grace can heed it.

14. See Wanamaker, *1 and 2 Thessalonians,* p. 209.

for several more centuries. Paul is referring to the eschaton, when believers will see Christ face-to-face. Short of the second coming, Paul expects prophecy to be a valid and useful spiritual gift. These cessationist folks might do well to listen to what Paul says about quenching the Spirit and despising prophecies. Another hermeneutical move that has the same effect is to identify prophecy with preaching or pneumatic exegesis, but in fact Paul's letters encourage neither such identification. Prophecy is by definition an inspired word from God for which the prophet is just the mouthpiece. It does not involve reflections on or exegesis of preexisting texts.

At the other end of the spectrum are those who appear to think that almost anything spiritual they say is a prophecy, especially if it has to do with the future, and that therefore it must be viewed as unquestionably true. Paul would not have agreed with this view either, for he speaks directly about sifting or weighing of NT prophecy in 1 Corinthians 14, and in Romans 12 he urges that a person should not prophesy except in proportion to one's faith. It could be 80% inspiration but 20% perspiration, and so it required sifting. NT prophecy thus has a different character from the sort of OT prophecy which involved the formula "thus says Yahweh . . . ," after which God's words are conveyed apparently verbatim. The NT era is more about the fulfillment of prophecy than the generating of new prophecies, and what new prophecies there are are mostly of temporary significance even after their substance is sifted, to judge from the paucity of prophetic books in the NT. More along these lines should perhaps be said at this juncture to prevent confusion.

It is clear enough from Paul's letters that he believed that OT prophecies were and would be fulfilled in Christ and in his community and not elsewhere. He believed, like the author of 1 Pet. 1.10-11, that the prophets of old were serving and speaking to and for believers. Even the promises of salvation for Israel are said in Romans 11 to be fulfilled in and through Christ, largely when he returns. In other words, the hermeneutic in operation where the NT deals with OT prophecy is focused on fulfillment. The OT prophecies were intended for the community of Jews and Gentiles united in Christ and will not be fulfilled outside the action of Christ and the people of Christ. The dispensational hermeneutic which suggests that OT promises and prophecies should be parceled out between non-Christian Israel and the church is nowhere to be found in the NT and especially not in Paul, whose christocentric vision of things is paramount and controls all else.

I have undertaken elsewhere a detailed diachronic study of biblical and extra-biblical prophecy from before the OT era until well into the Middle Ages.[15] Here I will just stress a few matters of definition. Apparently almost all ancient cultures had persons who exercised roles we would call prophetic.

---

15. *Jesus the Seer: The Progress of Prophecy* (Peabody: Hendrickson, 1999).

Prophecy did not begin with the period of the Israelite monarchy, nor did it end when that monarchy was eclipsed, for even in Israel prophecy in some forms carried on beyond that period of time. Nor were the prophets of Israel, any more than the NT prophets, operating in a cultural vacuum. It was possible for a Balaam or a Jonah or a Paul to cross cultural boundaries and still be recognized as some sort of prophetic figure. This is because the social functions and roles and to some degree even the forms and contents of the messages of prophets were the same throughout antiquity in the eastern end of the Mediterranean. Whether we are talking about the period of the Babylonian Empire or that of the Roman Empire, certain traits marked out prophetic figures such that they could be recognized throughout the region as some sort of spokesperson for the divine and could cross cultural and ethnic boundaries and still function. Indeed prophecy was such a cross-cultural phenomenon that Babylonian kings might well have Jewish prophets serving in their court, and Roman emperors might well listen to the word of an eastern and Jewish prophet before making a major decision. If one wants to understand biblical prophecy, one must be prepared to fish with a large net.

There is a difference between a mediator or an intermediary and a prophet. There are times and places where a prophet is simply a mouthpiece for some deity and in fact does not intercede with the deity on someone's behalf. The flow of communication is in one direction and is not prompted by any attempts at consultation by a human party. On the other hand, there are obviously also times when a prophet does beseech the deity or inquire of the deity on behalf of some human person or group, but this is not a specifically prophetic role. Priests, kings, or sages might also play such a role. Petitionary prayer or discourse is not a distinctively prophetic function.

Therefore, I am somewhat leery of calling a prophet an intermediary, for that term suggests an ambassador who exercises shuttle diplomacy between two parties. Some central or institutional prophets did tend to function that way a good deal of the time, perhaps especially if there were no adequate priests who might serve the function of approaching the deity and requesting things. But this does not adequately describe the actual distinctive social function of prophets and prophetesses, which was to speak oracles, a late word from God, to some person or group. Whether one is talking about the Mari prophets, Israelite prophets, or the later Christian prophets, their chief and distinctive task was to speak for or even as the instrument of the deity.

We must also make critical distinctions between the prophetic experience, the prophetic expression, the prophetic tradition, and finally the prophetic corpus. We do not have direct access to the first three of these things when we are dealing with the ancient prophets, but we do have the literary residue in different forms, whether the tablets from Mari, the Israelite prophetic books, the quotations of oracles in the NT, or the records of the pronouncements at Delphi. It is important to keep this point in view because confusion has sometimes been created by treating these four things together.

For example, we have very few direct transcripts of prophetic experience, though we do from time to time find some later reflections on what happened. A good example of this difficulty is found in the book of Revelation. Here we have John of Patmos relating things he saw and heard, not, however, as a transcript of an experience, but as a form of exhortation and consolation to a remote group of Christian disciples. In other words the literary residue is not a transcript but a later reflection on and presentation of the content of an earlier experience. What is also intriguing about this particular case is that apparently the oral prophetic expression and the period of transmission of tradition stages are skipped altogether. This material was not delivered orally by the prophet to anyone, for he was marooned, indeed probably exiled, at the penal colony on Patmos. Rather, he put the material into an epistolary framework and sent it off as a circular letter to some churches in western Asia Minor with which he was associated. In other cases there may have been an initial proclamation followed by a long period of oral transmission of specific prophetic traditions before they became part of a prophetic corpus. One must be sensitive to what we are actually dealing with when we approach the final form of the prophetic materials.

It is debatable whether we should see creative later editing and expansions on prophetic tradition as prophecy. For example, some of the creative exegesis of prophetic texts we find at Qumran do not necessarily qualify as prophecy itself, but rather as attempts to contemporize or apply former prophecies to a later audience. It is more a matter of hermeneutics than new revelation from God, more a matter of creative reinterpretation or *relecture* than inspiration. Prophets should also not be confused with their scribes or recorders when they had them. Baruch was not Jeremiah.

At its core prophecy is a living word from some deity, and a prophet is the messenger who delivers it. This is what Paul does not want the Thessalonians to quench, and this is what the modern church ought to avoid quenching as well. If it is true that the people perish without vision, then it would be well if the church would not marginalize, ignore, or deny the existence of our seers and prophets. In this fashion we will be heeding the exhortation Paul gives in 1 Thessalonians 5 and elsewhere.

COMMENTARY ON
2 THESSALONIANS

Epistolary Prescript — 1.1-2

The epistolary prescript in 2 Thessalonians is only a little more elaborate than the one in 1 Thessalonians, with a somewhat more extended grace wish and the addition of "our Father" in the address itself.

Paul and Silas and Timothy, to the assembly of the Thessalonians in God our Father and the Lord Jesus. Grace to you and peace from God the Father and the Lord Jesus Christ.[1]

However long after the writing of 1 Thessalonians this document was penned, Paul is still with Silas and Timothy, who appear again in the prescript. This in itself favors the conclusion that 2 Thessalonians was written not that long after 1 Thessalonians.[2]

The phrasing here is interesting — "the assembly of the Thessalonians in our God. . . ." This might mean "those assembling in the name of our God. . . ." It probably reflects the fact that Paul believed that whenever a group of Christians assembles God is present in their midst, and indeed they are present in the omnipresent God's midst. It is interesting that Paul here as in 1 Thessalonians does not speak of the assembly in a place (Thessalonike), but rather the assembly of a people, Thessalonians. This may indirectly support the contention that the audience is overwhelmingly Gentile,[3] otherwise we might expect to hear

---

1. Many good and early witnesses have "our Father" here as in the address, but B, D, P, and some others leave out "our." It is hard to decide whether it belongs here, as in v. 1, or not. See Metzger, *TC*, p. 635.

2. See A. Malherbe, *The Letters to the Thessalonians* (New York: Doubleday, 2000), p. 379.

3. On which see pp. 73-75 above.

about Jews and Gentiles, or "saints and believers" united in Christ. But there is the additional factor that rhetorically this helps Paul indicate that God has formed a people in Thessalonike, his own people. They are God's option in this city. The fact that *ekklēsia* is singular here may support the notion that there was only one house church meeting thus far in Thessalonike, but not necessarily as it could be a collective noun.

There may be, as Donfried has intimated, another reason for Paul's choice of this means of addressing his audience.[4] Already in the time of Augustus (Octavian) coins were minted in this city which depicted the head of Julius Caesar with a laurel wreath and the inscription *THEOS* on one side, and a head of Octavian bareheaded with the inscription *THESSALONIKEŌN*. Here already a Roman ruler is designated a god for the first time on a Thessalonian coin, and the city is claimed by the emperor Octavian as well. There is a later coin with Augustus with the laurel wreath and the same legend on the obverse and one even later with Tiberius and the same inscription. Paul doubtless saw some of these coins. Could he be claiming that Jesus was claiming the Thessalonians for himself and that the Father and the Lord were their God, in contradistinction to Caesar? In light of other evidence in both epistles that Paul is co-opting imperial rhetoric and applying it to Jesus, this seems very likely. No wonder Paul was thought to be violating the decrees of Caesar. He is calling the assembly of Thessalonian believers to order, and they are meeting in the name of and under the protection of the grace and peace of the Father and Son rather than the "peace and security" of the emperor.[5] Paul has made clear in 1 Thessalonians 1 that the Thessalonians have changed their allegiance from idols to the one true God, and this way of addressing them is a good way to reinforce that. Paul's ecclesiology is counter-cultural to say the least.

It is with two coworkers that Paul addresses the congregation, so it is one group of Christians writing to another, though clearly we are meant to think Paul is the dominant voice, as 3.17 will make evident. Here already at the outset he stresses what he and his audience share in common, namely faith in "God *our* Father." This small but subtle difference from 1 Thess. 1.1 is perhaps deliberate, as Paul must exhort his audience more strongly here than in 1 Thessalonians and so must go the extra mile to stress the connection and rapport he has with them as members of the same family of God. Otherwise the stronger exhortation might alienate an audience already under fire. This is how Paul begins in his other largely deliberative discourses as well (cf. Rom. 1.7; 1 Cor. 1.3; 2 Cor. 1.2; Gal. 1.3; Phil. 1.2; Phlm. 3).

The grace wish is distinguished from that in 1 Thesslonians by the addi-

---

4. See Donfried's essay on early Pauline ecclesiology and 1 and 2 Thessalonians in *Paul, Thessalonica, and Early Christianity* (Grand Rapids: Eerdmans, 2002), pp. 139-62.

5. See pp. 5-6 above and pp. 213-15 below, and Donfried, pp. 142-43.

tion of the phrase beginning with *apo*. This more extended form was to become Paul's standard form (e.g., 1 Cor. 1.3; Phil. 1.2). Paul sees himself as an emissary of both the Father and the Lord and brings greetings and peace from them both. Both are viewed as divine, and Paul sees himself as one who announces, indeed even conveys, their unmerited blessings and peace.[6] The addition of the phrase here can be seen as yet another piece of Paul's rhetorical strategy to establish good rapport with the audience before dealing with the problems, which is the strategy he follows in all his other deliberative missives as well.

---

6. See Malherbe, *The Letters*, p. 380: "This is part of Paul's tendency to ascribe qualities to Christ that are also used of God." Even more emphatic about the theological implications that Christ is viewed as God here is B. Rigaux, *Les Épitres aux Thessaloniciens* (Paris: Gabalda, 1956), p. 608. It is God alone who is the source of the *ḥesed* and shalom he is talking about, and Paul includes the Lord Jesus in his definition of God.

The *Exordium*/Thanksgiving Prayer — 1.3-10 — The Destiny of the Sacred Sufferers and the Terrible Tormentors

The *exordium* in 2 Thessalonians consists of one long Greek sentence. It begins like a thanksgiving prayer, but by v. 5 it has become didactic in character, seeking to offer some teaching on the coming judgment of God when the oppressed will be vindicated and the oppressors excluded from the dominion of God. This admirably foreshadows the discussion in ch. 2 and also serves to make the audience well-disposed to hearing what is to come, calming their fears and concerns about the future as they continue to suffer.[1] "The sole purpose of the *exordium* is to prepare our audience in such a way that they will be disposed to lend a ready ear to the rest of our speech" (Quintilian, *Inst. Or.* 4.1.5; cf. Cicero, *De Inventione* 1.20).

In deliberative rhetoric one seeks to persuade the audience to take some action in the future, which involves here a reassessment of eschatological expectation and a stiffened policy toward the "disorderly."[2] It was not necessary to introduce all one's points or arguments in the *exordium*. "It is important that the points which seem most likely to serve our purpose should be selected for introduction in the *exordium*" (*Inst. Or.* 4.1.23). Quintilian also stresses the need for the appeal to the emotions in the *exordium* and especially in deliberative oratory to make the audience favorably disposed to what will follow (*Inst. Or.* 3.8.12). He says that a particular act of persuasion "may justify an appeal to compassion with regard to what we have suffered in the

---

1. See C. Wanamaker, *Commentary on 1 and 2 Thessalonians* (Grand Rapids: Eerdmans, 1990), p. 215.

2. Cf. R. Jewett, *The Thessalonian Correspondence: Pauline Rhetoric and Millenarian Piety* (Philadelphia: Fortress, 1986), p. 82; G. A. Kennedy, *New Testament Interpretation through Rhetorical Criticism* (Chapel Hill: University of North Carolina Press, 1984), pp. 19-20.

past or are likely to suffer" (*Inst. Or.* 4.1.27), which aptly describes part of what Paul is doing here.

Deliberative oratory always deals with subjects about which there is some doubt in the audience (*Inst. Or.* 3.8.25), and that admirably describes the rhetorical situation in Thessalonike in regard to matters both eschatological and ethical. It is also the task of deliberative discourse to magnify or minimize the importance of a subject from the very outset in the *exordium* (Aristotle, *Rhetoric* 3.14.12), something Paul certainly does by vividly portraying here the eschatological outcome for tormentors and faithful sufferers and hence the importance of right belief about eschatological matters.[3]

Finally Quintilian adds that one of the more effective rhetorical devices to secure goodwill at the outset of a discourse is "rhetorical expressions of wishing" (*Inst. Or.* 4.1.33). The exordium here leads directly into an expression of Paul's wishes for his converts (vv. 10-11), which further establishes goodwill with the audience before the first argument begins in ch. 2. These wishes take the form of a *propositio* built on the *exordium* and flowing naturally from it while being a separate Greek sentence.[4]

We ought to give thanks to God always concerning you, brothers, just as is worthy/ fitting, because your faith is flourishing and the love of each one of you is increasing for all of you unto one another, with the result that we ourselves boast in you in all the assemblies of God, of your fortitude and faithfulness in all your persecutions the sufferings which you endure, [here is] evidence of the just judgment of God unto you considered worthy of the dominion of God, for which you also suffer — since in the righteous God's estimation he will requite/recompense your afflicters with affliction and you who have been afflicted [he will give] relief/rest with us in the revelation of our Lord Jesus from heaven with the angels of his might in a fire of flame, giving punishment to those who do not acknowledge God and those not obeying the Good News of our Lord Jesus, men such as these pay the penalty of eternal doom from the presence of the Lord and from the glory of his power, when he comes to be glorified in his holy ones and to be marveled at among all those who believe (note that our witness was believed by you), in that day.[5]

This *exordium* can be divided into two parts by subject matter (vv. 3-4 and vv. 5-10), though there is just one long complex Greek sentence.[6] It moves from thanksgiving to the didactic rather quickly.

3. See the discussion of the *exordium* in 2 Thessalonians in F. W. Hughes, *Early Christian Rhetoric and 2 Thessalonians* (Sheffield: Sheffield Academic, 1986), pp. 34-36.

4. On the proposition see pp. 199-201 below.

5. Happily there are no textual problems in this section, though there are some grammatical quandaries.

6. B. Rigaux, *Les Épitres aux Thessaloniciens* (Paris: Gabalda, 1956), p. 612.

One of the regular subjects of deliberative oratory was piety toward the gods. Everyone ought to praise, thank, and offer sacrifice to his or her god. It is then in no way surprising that Paul would begin a piece of deliberative oratory in v. 3 with a statement that both he and his audience "ought to give thanks," which he will repeat at 2.13. Such appeal to obligation or duty was at the heart of a good deal of deliberative oratory. R. D. Aus may be right that the phrases *eucharistein opheilomen* and *kathōs axion estin*, which distinguish these verses from the opening thanksgiving in 1 Thessalonians, are liturgical expressions (*1 Clement* 38.4; *Barnabas* 5.3; 7.1; Hermas, *Similitudes* 9.28.5; cf. Philo, *De Specialibus Legibus* 1.224; 2.173, 185; on the latter phrase cf. 1 Cor. 1.6; 11.1).[7] The "ought" points to the divine, while "as is fitting" points to the human side of the obligation.[8] The Thessalonians' conduct had, at least in part, merited giving God thanks and thus it was fitting to give such thanks. Paul thus begins on a note of religious duty, both his own and that of his audience, which is appropriate in deliberative discourse, as is reference to what is "fitting" or "suitable."[9] Recognizing the rhetorical species of 2 Thessalonians provides an explanation for the difference from the parallel in 1 Thessalonians 1, which opens an epideictic discourse, involving the rhetoric of praise and blame, not advice and appeals to duty.[10]

7. R. D. Aus, "The Liturgical Background of the Necessity and Propriety of Giving Thanks according to 2 Thess. 1.3," *JBL* 92 (1973): 432-38. Cf. for example the much later Anglican and Methodist liturgy: "It is very meet, right, and our bounden duty that we should at all times in all places give thanks." It is interesting and perhaps relevant that this sort of language of "ought" and "fitting" in regard to thanksgiving shows up in Hermas in connection with suffering (*Similitudes* 9.28.5).

8. So J. B. Lightfoot, *Notes on the Epistles of St. Paul* (Winona Lake: Alpha, reprint), p. 97. E. Best, *A Commentary on the First and Second Epistles to the Thessalonians* (London: Black, 1972), p. 249 points out that *ophelein* refers to a special personal obligation rather than one arising out of the nature of things, which would presumably be expressed by the verb *dein*.

9. Here the non-rhetorical explanation of the difference from the opening in 1 Thessalonians 1 seems weak or forced. But see C. R. Nicholl, *From Hope to Despair in Thessalonica: Situating 1 and 2 Thessalonians* (Cambridge: Cambridge University Press, 2004), pp. 145-46. Nicholl thinks that Paul is responding to something of an anxiety attack the Thessalonians are having because they assume that the day of the Lord has come and gone and they have been "left behind." There is perhaps some truth to this conjecture since Paul is trying to reassure his converts in the face of some confusion and doubts. See I. H. Marshall, *1 and 2 Thessalonians* (Grand Rapids: Eerdmans, 1983), p. 170.

10. On the rhetorical species of 1 Thessalonians see pp. 21-30 above. Some commentators have mistakenly deduced that the author is expressing a cooler tone here, as if giving thanks were seen as a mere duty rather than a real response to the good spiritual things happening among the Thessalonians. Besides the fact that Paul's passion comes immediately to the fore in the compound verb in v. 3b and in the following passionate explanation of eschatology (see Marshall, *1 and 2 Thessalonians*, p. 170), this deduction about the tone here totally

Paul is thankful for the flourishing faith and increasing love for each other that the Thessalonians are exhibiting. "Flourishing" and "increasing" are in the present tense. They represent an ongoing and growing phenomenon. *Hyperauxanein* "implies an internal, organic growth, as of a tree."[11] Paul likes compound verbs and nouns, and here one could translate "grows greatly."[12] "Faith" refers in part to the inward or spiritual growth and fortitude under pressure of the Thessalonians, but "love" refers to the outward manifestation of care and concern for each other.[13] This Christian love was exhibited by "each one of all of you for one another."[14] Paul has no notion of an elect group within the congregation who are the true Christians. Rather, he assumes that all of them are fully Christian and that all exhibit the fruit of the work of God's Spirit in their lives.[15] It may be significant that in 1 Thess. 3.10 Paul spoke of their lack of faith but here of its flourishing. Apparently the mission of Timothy to strengthen their faith (1 Thess. 3.2, 5) had had good effect. Or again in 1 Thess. 3.12 Paul prayed that their love might abound to each other, and here he says that this has transpired.[16] Presumably, then, something good happened in the interim between these two letters which led to the strengthening and exhibiting of the Thessalonians' faith under pressure and persecution.

Hōste at the beginning of v. 4 introduces a result clause.[17] The faith and love of the Thessalonians has resulted in Paul's boasting about them to other Christians, especially about their perseverance and faith through many trials. Paul finds remarkable the fact that they are persisting in these Christian virtues

---

misses the fact that Paul is deliberately sending the right rhetorical signals and thus indicating that this is a deliberative piece of rhetoric, signals he wants his audience to pick up from the outset.

11. Lightfoot, *Notes*, p. 98.

12. Best, *First and Second Thessalonians*, p. 250.

13. See Rigaux, *Les Épitres*, p. 613.

14. There may be a touch of rhetorical hyperbole in saying that each one of them was loving all of them (see 2 Thess. 3.11 especially and A. Malherbe, *The Letters to the Thessalonians* [New York: Doubleday, 2000], p. 385), but such is the nature of the *exordium* in a rhetorical discourse. It establishes rapport and makes the audience well disposed for even a bitter pill which they may be asked to swallow thereafter.

15. Best, *First and Second Thessalonians*, pp. 250-51 rightly notes that an imitator of Paul trying to sound "Pauline" would be unlikely to have had Paul's skill in creating and using compound verbs and nouns (here "flourishing" is a NT hapax legomenon, noted as typically Pauline by Chrysostom in his second homily on 2 Thessalonians), and would have been more likely to use the characteristic Pauline triad of faith, hope, and love, whereas here we only have faith and love.

16. See F. F. Bruce, *1 and 2 Thessalonians* (Waco: Word, 1982), p. 144.

17. The translation "therefore" is not very felicitous here as it suggests a logical conclusion, when in fact what we have is a response by Paul that is a result of the faith and love exhibited by the Thessalonians.

despite the newness of their faith and the pressure being exerted on them to abandon it. Here again Paul uses a compound verb, *enkauchasthai* (found only here in the NT but cf. Rom. 11.18; in the LXX Pss. 51.3; 73.4; 96.7; 105.47), indicating boasting in something or someone specific, in this case the Thessalonians. Paul does not have a problem with boasting or praising, so long as it is "in the Lord" or "of the Lord" and not "in the flesh" or "of the self."

Paul speaks of boasting in oneself apart from God's grace, in God and in one's accomplishments or attributes in a manner he considers legitimate "because it is done within the broader framework of understanding that anything truly worthy of boasting about has its source in God's grace (2 Cor. 10.8-13; 12.5-9; see also 1 Cor. 4.7)."[18] Paul also follows some Greco-Roman social conventions about inoffensive self-praise and sometimes engages in self-praise in a deliberately ironic fashion, boasting in weaknesses and disasters and trials.[19] Paul is quite happy to boast to others about the virtues of his own converts (cf. 2 Cor. 7.14; 9.2), and in fact boasts to one group of converts about another in order to urge them all to a higher level of Christian belief and living. 2 Cor. 8.1-5 would certainly include a boast about the Thessalonians.[20]

V. 4, like 1 Thess. 1.8, reminds us that the social networks among the Pauline churches were considerable and quite active. These sorts of remarks, while they may involve some rhetorical hyperbole, should not be passed off as mere exaggeration or effusiveness. They reflect the fact that Paul was well-connected, as were various of his churches, and information traveled widely and reasonably quickly, thanks to the aid of many traveling Christians, especially Christians among the social elite.[21] Paul was at the center of this social network and was intentional about strengthening it and keeping it informed.[22]

---

18. G. Beale, *1 and 2 Thessalonians* (Downers Grove: InterVarsity, 2003), pp. 182-83, note on 1.4.

19. On which see B. Witherington, *Conflict and Community in Corinth* (Grand Rapids: Eerdmans, 1994), pp. 432-40.

20. See Bruce, *1 and 2 Thessalonians*, p. 145. Here Paul boasts about perseverance whereas the boast in 1 Thess. 1.7-9 has to do with their preaching rather than their conduct under pressure. There is then no reason to follow Wanamaker and others and suggest that these references to boasting suggest that 2 Thessalonians is the earlier letter.

21. In his recent study on the Pauline onomasticon E. A. Judge has shown that the vast majority of the people mentioned seem to be Gentiles, and a goodly number of them Roman citizens. Of course Paul's churches were not just or even perhaps in the main made up of members of the social elite, but there were a goodly number of the elite in Paul's churches, including in Thessalonike probably. It is in no way surprising that Latin names predominate in a Roman colony city like Philippi whereas in Thessalonike Greek names are in the strong majority. See E. A. Judge, "Latin Names around a Counter-Cultural Paul," in *The Bible and the Business of Life: Essays in Honour of Robert J. Banks's Sixty-fifth Birthday*, ed. S. C. Holt (Adelaide: ATF, 2004), pp. 68-84.

22. See Rigaux, *Les Épitres*, p. 616.

We have here the general phrase "the assemblies of God" referring to multiple local assemblies of believers (for the plural cf. 1 Cor. 11.16). Paul likely has in view here all the assemblies which he has founded or is founding (including those in Corinth or Ephesus, where he may be at present; cf. Rom. 16.4: "the assemblies of the Gentiles").[23] The linking of "steadfastness" with *pistis* suggests that Paul has in mind with the latter faithfulness rather than just faith (cf. 1 Thess. 3.5; 1 Pet. 1.5-9; Heb. 6.12; Rev. 13.10). As Best rightly points out, "Calvin wrongly suggested that *endurance* is the fruit of *faith*; it is also incorrect to understand the two words together as meaning 'your firmness in faith'; *faith* and *endurance* are rather here parallel concepts for they have a common article, and the single *hymōn* applies to both as does the following phrase *in all the.* . . ."[24]

The terms *diogmois* and *thlipsesin* are virtual synonyms, used together here for the sake of amplification or rhetorical effect (see Rom. 8.35; Mark 4.17), though the first probably has a bit more specificity (cf. Rom. 8.35 to 2 Cor. 12:10),[25] focusing on external persecutions, while the latter refers to trials of various sorts.[26] Together they refer not only to outward pressure to conform, but probably to real persecution resulting in physical as well as mental and emotional suffering. These actions are being exerted precisely because of the Thessalonians' new-found Christian faith. In other words, this is a religious persecution, to which, Paul is about to say, God will necessarily respond. The final clause, "which you are (continuing) to suffer," indicates clearly that the situation has not improved since Paul left or since he wrote 1 Thessalonians. But equally, his converts are continuing to endure despite the persecution.

V. 5 begins with the word *endeigma*, which can be translated "sign,"[27] "indication," "guarantee," "proof," or "evidence," but the specific meaning here, along with the meaning of this entire verse, is much controverted.[28] This precise word is found nowhere else in the NT. It can be taken as either nominative or accusative. As is widely agreed the verse is elliptical, and most commentators have filled it out with something like *ho estin*, "this is . . . " which makes it retrospective. But one of the clear problems with the retrospective interpretation of "the just judgment of God" is that "it is difficult to conceive in what way the Thessalonians' perseverance presages the righteous judgment of God without introducing extraneous ideas into the text such as the notion

23. See Marshall, *1 and 2 Thessalonians*, p. 172.

24. Best, *First and Second Thessalonians*, p. 253.

25. See Malherbe, *The Letters*, p. 388.

26. Lightfoot, *Notes*, p. 99.

27. Possibly the related term *endeixis* means "sign" as in "sign of destruction" in Phil. 1.28. Cf. Rom. 3.25-26; 2 Cor. 8.24. These two words however are not simply synonyms. See the discussion in Lightfoot, *Notes*, p. 100. As Wanamaker, *1 and 2 Thessalonians*, p. 221 points out there are notable differences between the Philippian text and 2 Thess. 1.5.

28. See Nicholl, *From Hope to Despair*, pp. 149-50 on this word.

that God has granted the Thessalonians the ability to persevere and remain faithful."[29]

Exactly so, which is why another reading that is prospective is more likely. I would suggest that something like *hode estin*, "here is . . . ," should be supplied at the beginning of the verse, that Paul is using *endeigma* in its rhetorical sense of "evidence,"[30] and that the sense of the verse is: "Here is evidence of the just judgment of God . . . ," followed by the evidence in question. The sufferers need some sort of reassurance that God's justice will in due course be done and they will be vindicated. This reassurance is given in vv. 6-10, where a theology of recompense is enunciated in a way similar to what we find in Luke 16.25. Present suffering and future glory are regularly contrasted in the NT (cf. Luke 6.20-26; Matt. 5.10-12; Acts 14.22; Rom. 8.17; 2 Tim. 2.11-12; 1 Pet. 1.6; 3.14; 4.13-14; Jas. 1.2, 12). It is a theme or set of ideas Paul shares in common with other NT authors.[31] Furthermore, "just judgment" is also found in John 5.30 and 7.24, where it refers to Jesus' judgment. A close parallel can be found in Rom. 2.5, where the final eschatological judgment is in view, as it is here.

The "evidence" Paul is referring to is for the long-suffering believer. It is not a sign to unbelievers. In v. 5b Paul speaks of these Thessalonians as those who are deemed worthy by God of participating in the coming dominion of God on earth. *Kataxiothai* here, as in Luke 20.35; Acts 5.41; and *4 Maccabees* 18.3, likely has a passive sense, referring to how God thinks of someone.[32] The parallel with Luke 20.35 is especially close. It is for nothing less than the full establishment of God's perfect will and righteous eschatological reign on earth that the Thessalonians suffer. It is an honor to do so.

They are not deemed worthy of the dominion merely because of the fiat of God. Paul has in mind here, rather, the aforementioned faithfulness and endurance of these believers. They have manifested the character of those whom Paul says elsewhere will be able to inherit, enter, or obtain the dominion of God (e.g., Gal. 5.21; 1 Cor. 6.9-10, contrasting the kind of behavior which will keep a person, even one who professes belief, out of the coming dominion). "The kingdom of God is entered through tribulation (Acts 14.22) but the kingdom cannot be said to be the purpose of the tribulation on the part of those who inflict it or even on the part of those who endure it."[33] The characteristic reversals

29. Wanamaker, *1 and 2 Thessalonians*, p. 221; contrast Rigaux, *Les Épitres*, p. 620.

30. *Pistis* is the Greek rhetorical term for "proof," a different term altogether.

31. See texts like *Psalms of Solomon* 13.9-10; 2 Macc. 6.12-16; 2 Baruch 13.3-10; 78.5. Cf. Heb. 12.3-11 for the developing reflections on the theology of suffering and eventual vindication. See J. M. Bassler, "The Enigmatic Sign: 2 Thessalonians 1.5," *CBQ* 46 (1984): 496-510.

32. See Best, *First and Second Thessalonians*, p. 255. It could, however, mean "made worthy," which is the sense preferred by Malherbe, *The Letters*, p. 395, and then one could see the suffering as the "perfecting" or "making worthy" of the believer for the dominion.

33. Bruce, *1 and 2 Thessalonians*, p. 149.

of the day of the Lord are enunciated here so that it will be easier to demonstrate in ch. 2 that that day certainly has not yet come. There may well have been some in Thessalonike who saw their current severe suffering as evidence that the day of the Lord had passed them by.[34]

A simple contrast is indicated in vv. 6-7 — first the lost then the saved — and then further in vv. 8-9, where the fate of the lost is enunciated and then contrasted with those mentioned in v. 10 as saved. This is as stark a depiction of what happens on judgment day as any found in the Pauline corpus, and ch. 2 will build on it, making clear that Paul really does believe there are eternal consequences to having and persevering in faith in Christ or refusing to do so.

Eiper at the beginning of v. 6 is a conditional particle meaning "if (as is the fact)" or "since," not implying any doubt about the proposition that follows.[35] Again here we have the language of rhetoric: the speaker states rhetorically in the form of a hypothesis something that he actually takes to be a recognized fact.[36] Paul also uses *eiper* as a preamble to a hypothesis that he believes to be true in Rom. 8.9, 17; 1 Cor. 8.5.[37] We are thus justified in rendering the text "since it is just before God to repay those troubling you with trouble."

The verb *antapodynai* in itself does not have a pejorative sense. It could refer to a negative (as here) or a positive (as in Luke 14.14) recompense. Paul, as Rom. 12.19 (cf. Heb. 10.30) suggests, is likely thinking of the paradigmatic statement about God being the one who takes vengeance in Deut. 32.35. In the LXX of that verse the verb is *antapodosō*.[38] For Paul here, God's justice or judgment involves both vindication and vengeance (cf. *4 Ezra* 10).[39]

Some have objected to the sentiments expressed in these verses because they seem incompatible with the notion of a loving God. It is of course quite clear from numerous Pauline texts (e.g., Rom. 5.8-10) that God loves us while we are yet his enemies, ungodly, and sinners.

> The God whom Paul is describing is a God who does offer love and reconciliation to his enemies, but if they refuse this offer and continue in opposition to his goodness and love, then it would seem inevitable that, having refused mercy, they must face justice. Nothing in the NT suggests that God's love is indifferent to justice, and that he bestows a free pardon on his ene-

---

34. See Bassler, "The Enigmatic Sign," p. 508.

35. See, e.g., Theodoret, *Interpretation of the Second Letter to the Thessalonians* on 1.6. Chrysostom says that Paul uses this particle because it indicates something that should be seen as self-evidently true (*Homily* 2 on 2 Thessalonians).

36. Best, *First and Second Thessalonians*, p. 256.

37. See Bruce, *1 and 2 Thessalonians*, p. 149.

38. Some have seen echoes of Isa. 66.4-6 LXX here, but we could as well point to Ps. 137.8 on the issue of God as recompenser. It is not an uncommon biblical idea. Cf. Obad. 14.

39. See Wanamaker, *1 and 2 Thessalonians*, p. 224.

mies at the cost of failing to defend the persecuted against the persecutors.[40]

The issue of fairness in God's judgment is certainly not raised by this text since
Paul will go on to say that the judgment is falling on those who refuse to acknowledge God or obey the Gospel, which implies that they have had opportunity (and presumably the ability) to respond positively to God and the gospel.
Paul paints a picture of a courtroom with God as the judge. What is implied as
well is that God's judgment is redemptive, that in the same act in which he
judges the tormentors he also vindicates the tormented. There are two sides to
this coin of judgment. Sometimes this notion is pushed even further in apocalyptic literature (e.g., Revelation 6–19) in which rescuing the tormented or oppressed takes the form of the judgment and even death of the tormentors or oppressors. Paul in fact will go further than this and discuss the "eternal
destruction" of the wicked.

The God who will give recompense to the tormentors will also give rest or
relief to the Thessalonians and to Paul. *Anesis* is not "rest" in the normal sense
of that word, but rather relief from suffering, as in 2 Cor. 2.13; 7.5; 8.13 (cf.
Josephus, *Antiquities* 12.112; 16.22). Paul is not dealing with rewards for suffering
but just simply the cessation of suffering (cf. *4 Ezra* 7.36-95; *2 Baruch* 73.1).[41] It
is different from *eirēnē* in v. 2, which has a more positive sense. Paul brings himself into the equation at this juncture as well, and as 3.2 will make clear (cf.
1 Thess. 2.15; 3.7), with good reason. He, too, has suffered persecution even in
Thessalonike. "Paul was conscious of a fellowship in suffering between himself
and this church at the particular time of writing" (cf. 2 Cor. 1.7; Phil. 1.30).[42]

This relief, however, is not in the present but will come when Christ returns.[43] Until then, believers may expect tribulation and suffering to continue.[44] And what a return it will be. Here it is described as Jesus being revealed
(*apokalypsis*) from heaven in blazing fire and with his angels. "Revealed" is used
in this same sense of the parousia in 1 Cor. 1.7, and the cognate verb is used in
2 Thess. 2.3-8 (cf. Rom. 8.18; 1 Cor. 3.13; 1 Pet. 1.5; 5.1). It means that Jesus will be
clearly visible. He will come "from heaven," the exact same phrase as in 1 Thess.
4.16, from God's dwelling place with divine authority to judge. The day of
Yahweh has become the day of the Lord Jesus in Paul's thought world. Christ is
coming with a heavenly retinue — "with the angels of his might," which may

40. Marshall, *1 and 2 Thessalonians*, pp. 174-75.
41. Marshall, *1 and 2 Thessalonians*, p. 175.
42. Marshall, *1 and 2 Thessalonians*, p. 175.
43. This would surely seem to imply that Paul thought that this return might transpire
during the lifetime of his currently suffering audience.
44. Paul is possibly drawing on the Jewish tradition that the coming of Messiah would
be preceded by a time of heavy suffering and tribulation for the faithful. See 1QH 3.2-18.

mean the angels through whom he will exercise his judicial might.[45] This is probably who was meant by "all his holy ones" in 1 Thess. 3.13 (cf. Matt. 25.31; Zech. 14.5; *1 Enoch* 1.9). But this is not all.

Jesus is also returning "in fire of flame."[46] It is interesting that the same phrase is used to describe the burning bush in Acts 7.30 (cf. Isa. 29.6; 30.30; 66.15; Dan. 7.9; Ps. 104.4).[47] There are therefore overtones of theophany in this phrase, but Paul is probably also thinking of coming judgment here and wishes to speak of it in a dramatic and rhetorically effective way (cf. Dan. 7.9-10; Isa. 66.15-16). In fact, this particular phrase could arguably be said to modify what follows in v. 8, which would connect it more clearly with the idea of judgment (cf. Rom. 2.5).[48] In any case, Paul is making as clear as he can that he is talking about the coming of God, involving theophany, divine judgment, and full retinue, not someone less than God.[49] Increasingly as this *exordium* progresses, Paul draws on more and more phrases and ideas from Isaiah (especially Isaiah 2, 44, and 66).

V. 8 emphasizes the result of Jesus' return for unbelievers — namely "punishment" (a possible translation of *ekdikesis*). There is an echo here of 2 Sam. 22.48 (= Ps. 18.47) where God is described as the one who avenges (*didontos ekdikesin* here, *didous ekdikeseis* in the LXX),[50] and in light of Rom. 12.19 it is likely that vengeance rather than punishment in general is meant here as well.

Judgment is reserved not just for tormentors of Christians but for all who do not know God and do not obey the gospel. The definite article is repeated — "those who do not know God and those who do not obey the gospel" — but the attempt to see here two distinct groups (Gentiles and Jews?) is misguided, not least because Jews can also be called those who do not know God (Jer. 4.22; 9.3-6; Hos. 5.4; of Gentiles in Ps. 79.6; Jer. 10.25; cf. 1 Thess. 4.5) and disobedience to or rejection of the gospel also characterizes Gentiles in Rom. 11.30-32.[51] We

---

45. Malherbe, *The Letters*, p. 399.

46. Some manuscripts have "in flame of fire" as a slight correction (B, D, G, and a few others).

47. On the possible echoes of Isaiah 66 throughout this section see R. Aus, "The Relevance of Isaiah 66.7 to Revelation 12 and 2 Thessalonians 1," *ZNW* 67 (1976): 252-68.

48. See Wanamaker, *1 and 2 Thessalonians*, pp. 226-27. What favors this connection with v. 8 is the echo of Isa. 66.16. For a full chart comparing vv. 7-12 with OT and intertestamental parallels see Rigaux, *Les Épitres*, p. 624.

49. See rightly Lightfoot, *Notes*, p. 102.

50. See Beale, *1 and 2 Thessalonians*, p. 187.

51. See rightly Best, *First and Second Thessalonians*, p. 260; Wanamaker, *1 and 2 Thessalonians*, p. 227 against Marshall, *1 and 2 Thessalonians*, pp. 177-78. I doubt however that Wanamaker is right that there is intended to be an implied threat here to Christians who disobey Paul's commands, suggesting that they will miss out on salvation if they disobey. That is not the focus of the remarks here. Lightfoot, *Notes*, p. 103 suggests that the first group

have thus two phrases in synonymous parallelism here, as in Ps. 36.10 and Jer. 10.25a.[52] Paul's connection here of ignorance and disobedience suggests, as does Rom. 1.18-32 (cf. Rom. 10.16),[53] that he is thinking not about people who are merely ignorant of God and the gospel, but rather of those who ignore God, refusing to acknowledge him, and those who disobey the gospel, though they have at least heard it or heard about it.[54] The tormentors had to have had some knowledge of what it was the Christians they were persecuting believed, and it is these tormentors especially that Paul has in view here. But in the end those punished are punished because of the way they have responded to God and his salvation, whether directly or indirectly, not merely because of how they have responded to some Christians.

V. 9 goes on to make clear the eternal consequences of God's judgment.[55] For those who reject God and the gospel the penalty is *olethron aiōnion*, which is in apposition to *dikēn*. We find this same phrase in 4 *Maccabees* 10.15 and in the NT at 1 Thess. 5.3; 1 Cor. 5.5; 1 Tim. 6.9. The concept of eternal punishment is found also in 1QS 2.15; 5.13. The semantic field in which it operates can be seen when we compare the reference to destruction in Rom. 9.22; Phil. 1.28; 3.19 (cf. *Psalms of Solomon* 2.31-34), eternal fire in Matt. 18.8; 25.41; Jude 7; 4 *Maccabees* 9.9, eternal chastisement in Matt. 25.46; 4 *Maccabees* 10.11, or eternal judgment in Heb. 6.2; 1 *Enoch* 91.15.[56] Eternal destruction, then, is the opposite of eternal life.[57] As Malherbe says, the phrase here then means everlasting or perpetual ruin, not annihilation.[58]

Compared to some Jewish apocalyptic sources Paul's language is mild, as he does not relish nor dwell on descriptions of the damned and their pains, but rather in essence describes their condition and eternal separation from God and God's people.[59] V. 9 appears to contain an echo of Isa. 2.10, 19, 21, where it is

---

is the same as those described in Romans 1 as rejecting natural revelation, while the second group comprises those, both Jews and Gentiles, who hear and reject the gospel. This is not impossible, but if so, Paul does not make these distinctions clear here.

52. See Malherbe, *The Letters*, p. 401.

53. On which see B. Witherington and D. Hyatt, *The Epistle to the Romans* (Grand Rapids: Eerdmans, 2004), pp. 58-72.

54. See rightly Bruce, *1 and 2 Thessalonians*, p. 151: "It is not inadvertent ignorance that is meant but inexcusable refusal to know God for which the pagan world is condemned . . ."; also Marshall, *1 and 2 Thessalonians*, p. 178; Best, *First and Second Thessalonians*, p. 261.

55. This verse begins with the word *hoitines* which refers to a particular class of people just referred to — those who ignore God and reject the gospel. See Rigaux, *Les Épitres*, p. 630; Lightfoot, *Notes*, p. 103.

56. See the discussion in Rigaux, *Les Épitres*, pp. 630-31.

57. See Marshall, *1 and 2 Thessalonians*, p. 178.

58. Malherbe, *The Letters*, p. 402.

59. The word "eternal" indicates the finality of the outcome. See Bruce, *1 and 2 Thessalonians*, p. 152.

predicted that the unrighteous will try to hide themselves in rocks from "the presence of the fear of the LORD and from the glory of his might." Paul omits the reference to fear, thus strengthening the contrast and parallel construction with what will be said of the believers.[60]

The presence, glorious appearance, and might of the returning Christ is for the lost judgment from which they seek to hide, but the very same characteristics of Christ's presence have a very different effect on the saved: glorification, perfection, and transformation into Christ's likeness. The light and power that blinds one illumines another (see 2 Cor. 4.4-6).

Ultimately, whatever the immediate effect of the return of Jesus on the lost and on the saved, Paul wants to emphasize that eternal exclusion from God's presence is the long-term consequence for one and the eternal dwelling in the presence of God and of his blessing for the other. Those who want to ignore and be separated from God in this life will continue to be so in the next, and those who long to obey God and to be in his presence in this life will do so forever in the next (4.17). In each case the outcome is appropriate and fits the response in this lifetime. And one can say that to experience forever the absence of the God who is holy love is hell indeed. Paul is not an early advocate of a second chance beyond death. This lifetime is the time when the critical response to God must be made.

V. 10 rounds off the *exordium* on a more positive note. Paul wishes to leave in the minds of his suffering converts a positive image of what awaits them when Christ returns. The focus is on Jesus, not on them. When Jesus comes, he comes to be glorified in the presence of the saints and to be wondered at by all who have believed. "The holy ones" here are surely the saints rather than the angels.[61] It may be that a distinction is being made between two groups here — "the saints" being Jewish Christians, while "the believers" are Gentile Christians (in which case the phrases about being glorified and being wondered at are another example of parallel construction).[62]

"Glorified in his saints" alludes to Ps. 88.6 LXX (89.7) and "marveled at. . ." likely draws on Ps. 67.36 LXX (68.35). This former could mean that the saints reflect Jesus' glory in their lives or that he will be glorified in their presence. Alternately, it could mean that the saints will glorify Jesus when he comes, taking "in" in the instrumental sense of "by."[63] This last seems most likely here, since the parallel clause speaks of something believers do, "marvel" at the Lord.[64]

60. Malherbe, *The Letters,* pp. 402-3.

61. Bruce, *1 and 2 Thessalonians,* p. 152.

62. Paul does elsewhere use "holy ones" for Jewish Christians, for example in Romans 16 and in Ephesians.

63. See Wanamaker, *1 and 2 Thessalonians,* p. 230.

64. Marshall, *1 and 2 Thessalonians,* p. 180.

"In that day" goes with both phrases, punctuating the timing when this glorifying and marveling will take place, and likely is an echo of Isa. 2.11, 17. Isaiah 2 and 66 have been alluded to in various ways in this section.[65] Here is more evidence that Paul has a Scripture-saturated mind and way of expressing himself, but it is not at all clear that his audience, being mostly former pagans, would have recognized the echoes.[66] But he has made abundantly clear in these verses that if all these things accompany the day of the Lord, then certainly it has not yet transpired. This prepares perfectly for the first argument, a refutation, in ch. 2.[67]

The *hoti* clause is parenthetical, reminding the Thessalonians that Paul's witness about Jesus and such matters was believed by them when he was present.[68] This reassures them that they are among those who are included, that they have already truly believed. The implication is that they should continue to trust his witness and be persuaded by his rhetoric in this discourse about such future matters and about the effect of their current belief and behavior on those matters.[69] As Wanamaker says of this awkward phrasing, "If 2 Thessalonians were a carefully composed pseudonymous letter based on 1 Thessalonians . . . such an awkward parenthesis would be inexplicable."[70]

65. Beale, *1 and 2 Thessalonians*, pp. 190-91.

66. See pp. 36-40 above on the audience.

67. Malherbe, *The Letters*, pp. 404-5.

68. See Best, *First and Second Thessalonians*, pp. 266-67. I agree with Best that Paul is the author of this material in vv. 7-10 based in OT allusions, though he may have used some of it before.

69. As Best, *First and Second Thessalonians*, p. 266 suggests, the misplacement of this clause gives a hint that Paul is dictating here and that the scribe does not correct Paul's diction but simply takes it down as Paul speaks. Wanamaker, *1 and 2 Thessalonians*, p. 231 points to the apt parallel in 1 Cor. 1.6.

70. Wanamaker, *1 and 2 Thessalonians*, p. 231.

Propositio — 1.11-12 —
Persuasion by a Praying Proposition

There were various forms and sorts of "propositions" or thesis statements in Greco-Roman rhetoric, and much depended on what the exigency was that the rhetor needed to overcome and deal with. Did the problem turn on a definition of fact, or was there an issue involving a dispute over events or behavior? Different problems required different sorts of approaches to persuasion. As Quintilian says, propositions can be single, double, or manifold (*Inst. Or.* 4.4.5) and it was not necessary for them to focus on single concerns or theses. Sometimes there could be a proposition for each of the major arguments or proofs (*Inst. Or.* 4.4.7). In ch. 2 the issue will turn on a definition of fact: has the day of the Lord happened already? If not, what is the evidence against it having already transpired? But Paul must also deal with the issue of the idle, which involves a dispute about what amounts to correct Christian behavior. He must persuade his audience to change both some of their beliefs and some of their behavior. 1.11 alludes to the issue of behavior, which will be discussed in ch. 3, while v. 12 alludes to the issue of eschatological belief and so leads directly into the first argument, in ch. 2.

Unto which end also we pray always concerning you all, in order that our God might count you worthy of the calling and might fulfill/complete every good desire of goodness and work of faith in power, in order that the name of our Lord Jesus may be glorified in you, and you in him, according to the grace of our God and the Lord Jesus.[1]

One of the more effective ways of changing behavior is to let people overhear one's prayers for them. Like the parent who prays "dear Lord, if only my child

---

1. There are no real textual issues in these verses.

would live up to his potential" while the child can overhear it, Paul here offers a public wish prayer to be read out before the congregation. Its rhetorical function is not just to convey information about Paul's prayers but also to instigate transformation. One "states in prayer what one hopes will happen as a result of the prayer."[2]

In particular, Paul wants the audience to be persuaded that they must continue to behave faithfully and with endurance so that one day they will be counted worthy to be included in God's dominion. He wants them to desire "every good purpose" and asks that God will empower them to fulfill "every act prompted by their faith" (cf. 1 Thess. 1.3), a way of phrasing things that suggests a bringing to conclusion a process which has already begun.[3] Paul wants the name of Jesus to continue to be glorified by them and through their conduct. Their belief and behavior should continue to be like their initial response to Paul's witness. The reference to mutual glorification alludes to the eschatological scenario already referred to in vv. 7-10, to be unpacked more fully in ch. 2. But this wish prayer can only be fulfilled if there are some changes in belief and behavior in the Thessalonian Christian community.

V. 11 is clearly connected to vv. 5-10 by the *eis ho* at its outset. Paul's prayer then has to do with behavior and belief in the interim that will allow his converts to arrive at the parousia among the saved and receive the eschatological benefits just listed. Here, as Lightfoot points out, calling seems to refer to something in the future, namely being worthy of being called into the dominion of God when Jesus returns (Matt. 22.3, 8; cf. especially Phil. 3.14; 1 Cor. 1.26; 7.20 on Paul's varied use of "call" language).[4] The day of the Lord as Paul has described it in vv. 7-10 is closely related to how life is lived in the present. God's calling is to both that consummation and to holy living now. Paul's prayer is therefore that the Thessalonian Christians will be found worthy of this calling. God alone can declare them worthy (cf. 1 Thess. 5.24) if they live in a manner worthy of the calling (cf. Eph. 4.1).

Paul prays that both the desires and the actions of the Thessalonians will be perfected so that they will long to do the good[5] and will be faithful to carry out such desires. God "completes" or "fulfills" these things in the sense that he enables and empowers them to come to fruition.[6] Here again is a prayer which involves both God's action and the actions of the Thessalonian converts as

---

2. I. H. Marshall, *1 and 2 Thessalonians* (Grand Rapids: Eerdmans, 1983), p. 182.

3. See Marshall, *1 and 2 Thessalonians*, p. 182.

4. J. B. Lightfoot, *Notes on the Epistles of St. Paul* (Winona Lake: Alpha, reprint), p. 105. See the discussion in B. Rigaux, *Les Épitres aux Thessaloniciens* (Paris: Gabalda, 1956), pp. 638-39.

5. Notice how Paul uses *eudokia* of human willing in Rom. 10.1; Phil. 1.15; 2.13. See C. Wanamaker, *Commentary on 1 and 2 Thessalonians* (Grand Rapids: Eerdmans, 1990), p. 234.

6. A. Malherbe, *The Letters to the Thessalonians* (New York: Doubleday, 2000), p. 411.

prompted and empowered by God. 1.11 thus points forward to the parenetic material to come in 2.13–3.5.

There are two goals to what was described in v. 11: the glorification of the name of the Lord Jesus in these converts' lives and activities (cf. Isa. 66.5) and in due course the glorification of them in him (v. 12). This language of interpenetration is similar to that of John 13.31; 17.1, 10, 21-26 and reflects the belief that the Lord Jesus is a divine being in whom or in whose presence and glory the converts can dwell. The bringing of glory to the name of God and the Lord here and now suggests that "glorified" bears an ethical sense, as in 2 Cor. 8.3.[7] Christ and his "name" are glorified here and now when the converts behave (and believe) as described (cf. 1 Thess. 2.12; Matt. 5.16; 1 Pet. 2.12; 4.16).[8] Wanamaker makes the interesting point that while Christ is absent in heaven, it is his name which is glorified on earth, but it will be his person which is glorified when he returns.[9] Paul concludes the prayer by making clear that none of this is possible except by the grace of God and the Lord being active not only at the point of initial salvation but throughout the Christian life until one reaches the eschatological goal.[10]

Vv. 10 and 12 are quite similar except that v. 10 deals with the initial act of faith while v. 12 deals with perseverance in acts of faith until the eschaton.[11] We have here a reiteration of some of the ideas in 1 Thess. 2.12: "live lives worthy of God, who calls you into his dominion and glory."[12] Christ's glory becomes ours in a derivative sense (cf. 1 Cor. 2.7).[13] The hearers have now been prepared for the corrections of eschatology and ethics which follow in chs. 2–3, where Paul will seek to dissuade and persuade his audience about several important matters.

Bridging the Horizons

Greg Beale makes an interesting analogy between what happens when one goes to a sporting event and seeks to get into the stadium and what happens when one enters the dominion of God. To enter the stadium one needs both money

---

7. Malherbe, *The Letters*, p. 411.

8. E. Best, *A Commentary on the First and Second Epistles to the Thessalonians* (London: Black, 1972), p. 272.

9. Wanamaker, *1 and 2 Thessalonians*, p. 235.

10. That there is only one article before "God" and "Lord" might suggest the translation "the grace of Jesus Christ our God and Lord." See F. F. Bruce, *1 and 2 Thessalonians* (Waco: Word, 1982), pp. 156-57. But if so this is an unusual way of putting it, and in any case Paul elsewhere uses "Lord" without the definite article to refer to Jesus (cf. 1 Thess. 4.1; 2 Thess. 3.4, 12). But see Tit. 2.13 and cf. 2 Pet. 1.11.

11. Marshall, *1 and 2 Thessalonians*, p. 183.

12. See G. Beale, *1 and 2 Thessalonians* (Downers Grove: InterVarsity, 2003), p. 194.

13. See Rigaux, *Les Épitres*, pp. 640-41.

and the ticket which one buys with the money, for it is the ticket which allows one to enter the stadium. Beale compares this to the price Christ has paid for our entrance into the dominion, but the ticket to get in is the good works which Christians must manifest, including persevering in the faith until the end. "Therefore, both faith in Christ's work *and* human works are absolutely necessary for being considered worthy of [final] salvation."[14]

Beale rightly adds that ultimately it is the "money" which made possible the "entrance"; the ticket is not an equal cause of getting in. Yet God has set up the rules such that one cannot get in without a valid "ticket," which involves human effort and activity. This I think fairly represents the balance of Paul's view of the matter. While believers are not saved *by* their works, properly speaking, not even by their own efforts at persevering, nevertheless God has so arranged it that they are not saved to the uttermost and so enter the dominion without such efforts and activities either.

We live in a culture that demands justice, fair play, one's rights. This is all well and good if one is talking about ordinary rights and wrongs. But one demands justice of God at one's own peril, since "all have sinned and fallen short of the glory of God." If God were to be merely just, no one could be saved. Salvation is not a matter of justice or fairness but a matter of grace, of God's undeserved benefits.

One of the major ethical themes in Paul's letters is that vengeance is God's and that God must be allowed to repay. Humans may plead with God for vindication, but they should never try to exact revenge or take vengeance on another person. To do so only sets in motion a horrible and potentially endless cycle of reprisals, such as we see today in Israel with Jews and Palestinians. In 2 Thessalonians 1 Paul promises that God will someday right the wrongs and redress the balance of justice, as a means of helping his converts through trials and persecution. They are to have faith and endure. But elsewhere he goes further to speak more directly about an ethic of nonviolence in response to violence, indeed of an ethic of killing enemies with kindness, so to speak.

In Rom. 12.14, 16-21 we hear this ethic spelled out in some detail. What is most interesting about Paul's use of such an ethic is that it is not just a matter of pragmatism or quietism, trying to keep his tiny minority of converts in Thessalonike and elsewhere out of harm's way, although that is one of the aims of this ethic. It is in fact more a matter of principle, grounded in Paul's reading of Jesus' ethical teaching.

Rom. 12.14 refers to blessing rather than cursing one's enemies and seems to be a paraphrase of the Q saying of Jesus found in Matt. 5.44/Luke 6.28. In fact, this text and the Q saying are the only two occurrences of this contrast between blessing and cursing in the NT. The participles have disappeared in Romans, which

---

14. Beale, *1 and 2 Thessalonians*, pp. 184-85.

may that suggest Paul is using a different source at this juncture. It would appear that in vv. 14-21 Paul has turned from how Christians treat each other to how they relate to the world, which may persecute or harm them. Blessing was a boundary-removing act, just as cursing was a boundary-defining act. Invoking God into one's relationships was a powerful thing to do. Again, what Paul is asking is counterintuitive, and Paul believes that such things are possible precisely because the eschatological Spirit, with its character-forming power, dwells within the Christian community. What Paul is asking is not natural, but rather supernatural. There is little evidence from early Judaism that non-retaliation was a code early Jews lived by outside the community of Jesus. What few such exhortations there are refer to not taking vengeance against fellow Jews.[15] Jesus' exhortation goes further than that. Paul treats Jesus' words as something familiar, as a living tradition, so that there is no need to cite it verbatim or identify the source.

Rom. 12.15 is perhaps less abnormal ethically, but Paul is urging that one truly and actively enter into other persons' joys and sorrows. We find such exhortations in Jewish wisdom literature (Sir. 7.34). He is not talking about ritualized celebrating or mourning as a cultural duty. Just as he says that loving must be done sincerely (v. 9), so also must these activities. What is inculcated here is at the opposite end of the spectrum from the Stoic notion of impassiveness.

Rom. 12.17 is emphatic about not returning evil for evil. It should never happen that way with Christians. Here we have an echo of Matt. 5.38-42/Luke 6.29. Is it an accident that the two allusions to the Jesus tradition found in close quarters here are also found together in Q? Perhaps not, since it seems likely Paul is drawing on early Christian sources here. He wants to stress that Christians should not engage in shameful behavior. One should strive to do what is considered honorable by all human beings. The verb here means "take thought of in advance." Paul is calling for Christians to do their best to adhere to the best of the Roman cultural virtues and so provide a point of contact and be a source of honor and witness for the Christian community in Rome.

Christians were called to strive to be at peace, so far as possible,[16] with all persons, not seeking to vindicate oneself (Rom. 12:18). This seems to allude to Matt. 5.9. Christians were to break the cycle of negative reciprocity in the form of honor challenges and enmity conventions.[17] They were to leave such vindicating, much less vindictiveness, out of their codes of behavior. Instead, they

---

15. See K. Yinger, "Rom. 12.14-21 and Nonretaliation in Second Temple Judaism: Addressing Persecution within the Community," *CBQ* 60 (1998): 74-96. There is of course also the record of the more normal response, for instance when the Maccabees call down curses on their tormentors as they go on to martyrdom (2 Maccabees 7).

16. Notice the note of realism here on Paul's part. He knows that it will not always be possible to live at peace with a neighbor.

17. On which, see my *Conflict and Community in Corinth* (Grand Rapids: Eerdmans, 1994), pp. 154-61.

were to leave room for the just judge, God, and God's wrath to deal with situations that required such measures.

There is an echo in Rom. 12.19 of Lev. 19.18, but also of Matt. 5.39 in regard to non-retaliation. The reference to wrath here reminds us of what is said in Rom. 1.18-32, but it also prepares us for what will be said in 13.4, and this theme is more fully developed in 2 Thessalonians 1–2. From Rom. 13.4, one may conclude that Paul believes that authorities do have a limited right to exercise force and do so as agents of God, but Paul does not believe that private individuals, in particular Christians, should try to take justice into their own hands.

Rom. 12.20 also involves quotations, in this case Prov. 25.21-22 and Matt. 5.44 on providing food and drink for the enemy.[18] "Heaping burning coals on the head" is usually thought to connote a sort of killing with kindness, so to speak. It probably refers to some sort of shaming convention meant to drive a person to remorse and better behavior,[19] or could it be a metaphor for what the penitent feels and does? There is some evidence of an ancient Egyptian practice in which penitents would literally carry a tray of burning coals on their heads.[20] Rom. 12.21 may provide an explanation in speaking of not succumbing to evil but overcoming it with good. "This is not merely prudential; it is the way God himself has proceeded against his enemies (cf. v. 8). The mercy of God . . . will triumph over the rebellion and disobedience of men (9.32); the mercy of those on whom God has had mercy may similarly prove victorious."[21]

I have brought in this subject here because it seems clear, now that I have worked through the exegesis of the whole Pauline corpus, that Paul consistently pursues an ethic of nonviolence where it is rhetorically appropriate to do so. This does not by any means suggest that he gave up on justice or an ethic of justice. He simply instructs Christians to leave justice in God's hands, the same hands that sent Jesus to die for the sins of the world. In Paul's view the world's Savior will also be the world's Judge when Jesus returns.

---

18. On the advice about treatment of enemies in early Jewish and Greco-Roman literature cf. Seneca, *De Ira* 2.34.5; Epictetus, *Encheiridion* 42; *Epistle of Aristeas* 225-27; *Testament of Benjamin* 4.2-3; *Joseph and Aseneth* 23.9. What these texts show is that a merciful ethic in regard to enemies did exist in early Judaism and paganism, even if L. T. Johnson, *Reading Romans: A Literary and Theological Commentary* (Macon: Smyth and Helwys, 2001), p. 196 is correct about the majority of the evidence in saying: "The moral code of the ancient world — that of both Judaism and Hellenism — recognized the validity of having enemies and of paying back harm done to oneself or one's loved ones."

19. See K. Grieb, *The Story of Romans* (Louisville: Westminister/John Knox, 2002), p. 122.

20. See W. Klassen, "Coals of Fire: Signs of Repentance or Revenge?" *NTS* 9 (1962-63): 337-50. After saying "overcome evil with good," it is surely unlikely that Paul with this metaphor wants to encourage any form of vengeance.

21. C. K. Barrett, *A Commentary on the Epistle to the Romans* (London: Black, 1957), p. 223.

Refutatio — 2.1-12 — Prelude to the Parousia

One of the most striking features of the rhetoric of 2 Thessalonians is that the arguments start with refutation rather than confirmation. In Galatians and Romans refuting arguments come after the *probatio* rather than before (e.g., Gal. 4.21–5.1; Romans 9–11). Quintilian in fact says that refutation should normally come after the confirming arguments (*Inst. Or.* 5.13). Paul must have seen some urgency in this refutation because something was deeply troubling and worrying the Thessalonians. Nicholl shows at some length that the Thessalonians were worried about the eschatological state of affairs not only because some of their fellow believers had died but also because, in view of their ongoing suffering, they had begun to question whether they had been left out or left behind, the glory train already passing them by.[1] In the face of this deteriorating situation, Paul feels he must strike at the root of the problem — a false claim about the timing of the day of the Lord.

Quintilian also says that as a rule no strong appeals to the emotions should be made in a refutation (*Inst. Or.* 5.13.1). The argument should be crisp, clear, and logical. Paul's argument here in fact is something of a blow-by-blow preview of coming attractions arranged in logical order. Here we have "logos," actual argumentation, rather than the appeal to the emotions usually associated with the *exordium* or the peroration.

One of the favorite, and often the first, of rhetorical strategies when it came to a rebuttal was to deny the facts the opponents are touting are actually "the facts" (*Inst. Or.* 5.13.4). This is precisely what Paul does here. Someone has said that the day of the Lord had already come. Paul denies this by trotting out a

---

1. C. R. Nicholl, *From Hope to Despair in Thessalonica* (Cambridge: Cambridge University Press, 2004), pp. 219-21.

series of examples of events which have not yet or not yet fully transpired and which must precede the day of the Lord. Paul does not appeal to just one such event but in fact several, mounting a multi-pronged attack on the claim.

It would appear that Paul does not think that whoever it was that said that the day of the Lord had already happened had presented a series of arguments in favor of that notion, since Paul follows the procedure Quintilian suggests for those who do not present a strong multi-pronged case for a position. In such an instance one can simply take up the other argument or arguments en masse and refute them all at once rather than having to dismantle them point-by-point (*Inst. Or.* 5.13.11). In such a case as Paul is dealing with, it was sufficient to show that the claim was false because it contradicted the facts or some other evidence the audience had not yet considered (*Inst. Or.* 5.13.17).

In his ground-breaking rhetorical treatment of 2 Thessalonians, F. W. Hughes correctly argued that we have a refutation in 2.1-12, but he also argued that we have in vv. 1-2 a *partitio*, followed by the argument proper in vv. 3-15. Hughes is right that we do have a brief statement in vv. 1-2 of the problems to be dealt with in this first argument, but while the argument proper begins at v. 3, the argument does not extend beyond v. 12. In vv. 13-17 we have a separate section on thanksgiving followed by another wish prayer which should not be seen as part of the refutation itself.[2] They are rather attempts to bring the first portion of the discourse to closure with prayer of various sorts. The matter is once more left in the hands of God.

L. Hartman is one of the few scholars who has rightly posed the question of the relationship between chs. 1 and 2. He stresses rightly that it should be posed as one concerning the rhetorical organization of the letter. He recognizes that the thanksgiving functions as an *exordium* or rhetorical *proemium* hinting at the subject to be discussed and making the audience favorably disposed toward the speaker. "Chapter one prepares for chapter two. It introduces the general subject of the present tribulations regarded in an eschatological perspective, and it does so in a subtly admonishing manner. As such it also functions as . . . a *captatio benevolentiae*. After this preparation chapter two presents the specific problem and an argument for its solution is given."[3] Hartmann further notes that the close connection between these two chapters is cemented rhetorically by the way the concluding wish prayer in 2.16-17 takes up the same concepts as that found in the wish prayer in 1.11-12 — *pistis, klēsis, doxa, agatha,* and *erga*.[4] What this suggests is

---

2. See F. W. Hughes, *Early Christian Rhetoric and 2 Thessalonians* (Sheffield: Sheffield Academic, 1986), pp. 56-58.

3. L. Hartman, "The Eschatology of 2 Thessalonians as Included in a Communication," in R. F. Collins, ed., *The Thessalonian Correspondence* (Leuven: Leuven University Press, 2000), pp. 470-85, here pp. 477-78.

4. Hartman, p. 478, n. 40.

not that Paul is blending epistolary elements with rhetorical elements but rather that as a pastor he is blending elements of Christian worship and spiritual life with his use of rhetoric. The pastoral approach and the rhetorical construction both affect how this material is presented and developed.

But we appeal to you brothers, concerning the parousia of our Lord Jesus and our being gathered together with him, that you not be quickly driven from sound judgment[5] nor be alarmed/disturbed either through a spirit or through a word or through a letter as if from us to the effect that the day of the Lord has come. Let no one deceive you in any way, because unless the apostasy has come first, and the person of lawlessness,[6] the son of destruction has been revealed. . . . The adversary and one exalting himself over every so-called god or object of worship, with the result that he himself sits down in the Temple of God, claiming himself that he is God. Do you not remember that when I was with you I kept on saying this to you? And now you know what is holding him back, so that the revelation of him [will come], only at the proper time. For the mystery of lawlessness is already at work, only the Re-strainer until now is holding him back from the midst. And then the Lawless One will be revealed, whom the Lord Jesus will kill/destroy with the breath/spirit of his mouth and will annihilate [him] by the manifestation of his parousia, whose is the parousia according to the activity of Satan in all power and signs and pseudo-wonders, and in all allurement to wickedness of those of destruction, in return for which/because of this they did not receive/welcome the love of the truth unto their salvation. And because of this God sent them a force of delusion unto their believ-ing the lie, in order that all may have been judged who did not believe the truth but rather took pleasure in wickedness.

No part of 2 Thessalonians has received more attention than 2.1-12, and under-standably so. Most often the scholarly debate has had to do with its compatibil-ity with the material found in 1 Thessalonians 4–5. Some have found it difficult to reconcile the language of possible imminence in 1 Thessalonians with the discussion of necessary preliminary events, particularly the apostasy and the appearance of the man of lawlessness, in 2 Thessalonians.

These discussions have almost never taken into consideration rhetorical factors, nor have they adequately dealt with the juxtaposition in early Jewish

---

5. F. F. Bruce, *1 and 2 Thessalonians* (Waco: Word, 1982), p. 163 has the translation "shaken out of your wits," which gets at the sense of the matter.

6. There is a major textual issue here as to whether the text originally read "person of lawlessness" (*anomias,* ℵ, B, various minuscules, and Church Fathers) or "person of sin" (*hamartias,* A, D, G, K, L, P, and an equally good list of minuscules and Church Fathers). While the latter is more widely attested, the former word is rarely used by Paul and it seems to comport better with the context. See Metzger, *TC,* 2nd ed., p. 567 where this reading now gets a B rating (in the earlier edition it had a C rating).

apocalyptic of the language of imminence with discussion of preliminary eschatological events. Indeed, we see this in the NT — for instance in Mark 13.
What is usually never spelled out in such discussions, Jewish or Jewish Christian, is the amount of time between the preliminary events and the parousia or
end. Nor is it spelled out in 2 Thessalonians.[7]

Furthermore, as E. Krentz has pointed out, too often the discussion of the
material in 2 Thessalonians 2 has been done in an abstract and contextless way. But
"2 Thessalonians does not present abstract or theoretical theology; it is rather a response to human need, hope, and aspiration in a time of persecution. The fundamental conviction that God is a God of justice who will vindicate his suffering
church underlies this theology and gives it unity."[8] L. Hartman sounds the same
appropriate note when he says "the author is less a theologian who tries to come to
grips with a theological problem, that is, the delay of the parousia, than he is a
pastor who wants to strengthen the faithful in their afflictions."[9] Before dealing
with the details of this rhetorical argument in 2 Thess. 2, it will be well to come
to grips with the largest conceptual challenge first: who or what is the Restrainer?

A Closer Look: Exercising Restraint: Apocalyptic Answers to Difficult Questions

There have been almost as many conjectures about "the Restrainer" as there have
been commentaries on 2 Thessalonians. This is, of course, a sign of scholarly uncertainty about the referent, and it is interesting though strange that many of those who
are most adamant that 2 Thessalonians is post-Pauline are least sure about a specific
referent of this figure or have concluded that no particular referent is in view. Apocalyptic symbols and terminology are often deliberately vague so they may be
multivalent, but they are seldom nonreferential.[10]

One must take into account the social situation that is generating the problems
that Paul is addressing in 2 Thessalonians. Nicholl has admirably summed them up

---

7. Against for instance H. Koester, "From Paul's Eschatology to the Apocalyptic Schemata of 2 Thessalonians," in *The Thessalonian Correspondence*, pp. 441-58, who follows
W. Trilling's influential studies *Untersuchungen zum zweiten Thessalonicherbrief* (Leipzig: St.
Benno, 1972) and *Der zweite Brief an die Thessalonicher* (Neukirchen: Neukirchen Verlag,
1980). See also C. H. Giblin, "2 Thessalonians 2 Re-Read as Pseudepigraphal: A Revised Reaffirmation of *The Threat to Faith*," in *The Thessalonian Correspondence*, pp. 459-69.

8. E. Krentz, "Traditions Held Fast: Theology and Fidelity in 2 Thessalonians," in *The
Thessalonian Correspondence*, pp. 505-15, here p. 505.

9. Hartman, "The Eschatology of 2 Thessalonians as Included in a Communication,"
p. 472. See also A. Malherbe, *The Letters to the Thessalonians* (New York: Doubleday, 2000),
p. 415 on how the pastoral tone and intent of the material shapes it.

10. See B. Witherington, *Revelation* (Cambridge: Cambridge University Press, 2003),
pp. 32-40.

and has made clear that the same developing social situation undergirds 1 and
2 Thessalonians. Paul is dealing with "an immature persecuted Gentile community
having difficulties with manual laborers exploiting richer community members and
having problems processing Jewish eschatological ideas, awaiting word from Paul
concerning the timing of the Day of the Lord and shaken by the deaths into thinking
that God was angry with them,"[11] or if not angry, at least had found them unworthy
to participate in the eschatological glory.

Paul says that his audience "knows" about the *katechon*, "the Restrainer." If we
take this at face value, not assuming that it means that they *should* know (which is not
impossible), then this matter had been discussed or alluded to previously. This comports with the fact that Paul is offering a rebuttal here and a further eschatological
clarification of the audience's situation, not breaking entirely new ground.

In the relevant papyri *katechō* regularly has the sense of restraining or holding
in captivity (e.g., P.Oxy. 101.3644.30; P. Giess. 70.3; P.15a; and many other examples).[12]
In the NT itself this verb means "hold fast" (e.g., Rom. 7.6; 1 Cor. 11.2; 1 Thess. 5.21; cf.
Luke 8.15) but can also mean "hold back/delay/restrain" (Rom. 1.18; Phlm. 13; Luke
4.42). The context in 2 Thessalonians 2 suggests that the meaning of the substantive
participle is "restrainer." Paul is talking here about two parousias — the parousia of
the Lawless One and the parousia of Christ. The Restrainer is on the opposite side of
the struggle to the Lawless One, holding back the Lawless One's appearance. It appears that "the Restrainer's present activity functions to hold back the rebel's revelation until the appointed time and to prevent the premature unleashing of Satan's full
power and full deception."[13] Who then is this Restrainer, and what does his identity
suggest about who the Lawless One is?

One of the earliest conjectures about the Restrainer was offered by Tertullian
(*De Carnis Resurrectione* 24) followed by Hippolytus (*Commentary on Daniel* 4.21).
Their view was that it was the Roman emperor or empire, a view still followed in our
era by some exegetes.[14] The problem with this is that, as we have already seen, Paul offers up some not so subtle anti-imperial rhetoric in his various letters, including
1 Thessalonians.[15] This suggestion has been broadened so that what is referred to is a
human ruler in general or perhaps the principle of law and order.[16]

11. Nicholl, *From Hope to Despair*, p. 218.

12. See the list in Nicholl, *From Hope to Despair*, p. 227 n. 10.

13. Nicholl, *From Hope to Despair*, p. 228.

14. See C. Wanamaker, *Commentary on 1 and 2 Thessalonians* (Grand Rapids: Eerdmans, 1990), pp. 256-57.

15. See pp. 142-45 above. It would also be very surprising to hear such a positive evalua-
tion of Rome if this document had been written in the late first century when in Christian
circles there had been a history of persecution and we have negative responses to empire and
emperor such as we find in Revelation.

16. See for example, J. B. Lightfoot, *Notes on the Epistles of St. Paul* (Winona Lake: Alpha, reprint), p. 114; E. Richard, *First and Second Thessalonians* (Collegeville: Liturgical, 1995),
pp. 338-40.

A more specifically "Christian" identification of the Restrainer has taken a variety of forms including the Holy Spirit, Paul, or the proclamation of the gospel. On the other end of the spectrum is the suggestion that what is meant, shockingly enough, is Satan or "the rebellion."[17] None of these suggestions seems to take adequately into account the Jewish apocalyptic context of this material, or the earlier Jewish apocalyptic prophecy, which might also be relevant.

For example, it seems reasonably clear that Paul is alluding to texts like Dan. 9.27; 11.31; and 12.11 in his description of the desecration of the Temple of God in 2 Thess. 2.4. He likely knew of Antiochus Epiphanes and his desecration of the Jewish Temple and about the near desecration of the Temple by Caligula in the A.D. 30s. Finally, he may well have known of the Jesus tradition in Mark 13.14. These sorts of echoes in 2 Thess. 2.4 should prompt a search in other early Jewish and Jewish Christian literature for the identity of the Restrainer. The material in Daniel joins Paul's anti-imperial rhetoric and Paul's knowledge of figures like Antiochus and Caligula to make it all the less likely that Paul saw the Roman Empire or emperor as a positive restraining force of evil. In Revelation 17–18 and *Sibylline Oracles* 8.37-193 Rome is certainly portrayed in a negative light. Indeed, it is likely, if Paul was paying close attention to Daniel 7–12 and to other early Jewish apocalyptic ideas, that he might argue that the anti-God Lawless One might well be a future Roman emperor, especially since Dan. 7.24-25 suggests that this anti-God ruler would have Israel within its boundaries and jurisdiction.[18]

The problem with the suggestion that Paul might be the Restrainer is that Paul does allow that he may live until the Lord returns in 1 Thessalonians 4–5, and furthermore he does not envision a time when the gospel will be removed from the scene. Indeed in parallel material in Mark 13 we are told that the gospel must be proclaimed throughout the many nations before the end can come. But here in 2 Thessalonians 2 the Restrainer is removed and is succeeded by a time of lawlessness and by the Lawless One, prior to the return of Christ. Similarly, the Restrainer cannot be the Holy Spirit, who can hardly be said to be removed from the scene by some greater power, since there are no traditions in the NT about the Spirit ever being withdrawn again after Pentecost. The Lawless One does not supplant God or the Spirit since God is still at work in the world in 2 Thess. 2.11. Nor can the church be in view since the theology of the rapture of the church out of the world before or during the final tribulation has no grounding in early Jewish and Jewish Christian texts. Indeed, it is an idea which arose for the first time in the nineteenth century.[19] The suggestion that Satan himself is the Restrainer must fall on the hard rock of what 2 Thess. 2.9-10 says, namely that the Lawless One comes on the scene by the power and instigation of Satan. The Lawless One does not supplant Satan but is rather his

17. On this suggestion see E. Best, *A Commentary on the First and Second Epistles to the Thessalonians* (London: Black, 1972), pp. 299-302.

18. See Nicholl, *From Hope to Despair*, p. 229, n. 19.

19. See my discussion of the history and problems with rapture theology in *The Problem with Evangelical Theology* (Waco: Baylor University Press, 2005).

agent in the world who signals not the removal of the satanic from the world but rather its furtherance.

Dan. 12.1-2 tells us that before the final resurrection at the eschaton the archangel Michael will arise. Michael is called "the great prince who protects your people." He will arise because there will be a time of unparalleled great distress. In widely diverse early Jewish and Jewish Christian literature Michael is seen as the most important archangel (*1 Enoch* 24.6; *Testament of Isaac* 2.1; *Ascension of Isaiah* 3.15-16; 1QM 17.7; *3 Enoch* 17.3). His major task is protecting God's people, and, indeed, he is seen as the military leader of the heavenly host (*1 Enoch* 90.14; *2 Enoch* 22.6-7; 1QM 17.6-8a). He is the one who will blow the trumpet and lead the charge at the final judgment (*Apocalypse of Moses* 22.1; cf. 1 Thess. 4.16). Furthermore, Michael is the primary opponent of Satan in this sort of literature (*1 Enoch* 69; 1QM 17.5-6; Jude 9; Rev. 12.7-9). Some of this literature even says that he defeats Satan in the end (1QM 13.10).[20] Rev. 20.1-3 depicts a mighty angel who has the power to restrain Satan, indeed chain him and throw him into a holding tank for the millennium where he cannot deceive the nations. That this angel is probably Michael can be seen from the parallel in PGM 4.268-72, the Paris magical papyrus where not only is *katechon* used of the restraining activity but Michael is the restrainer of the great dragon, Satan.[21] In Rev. 12.7-9 Michael fights Satan and casts him out of heaven, again making it probable that Michael is the one containing Satan in Revelation 20. I would suggest then that Paul is operating in 2 Thessalonians 2 in the same constellation of early Jewish and Jewish Christian ideas.

But what of the Restrainer being removed from the scene? Nicholl has shown that the LXX rendering of Dan. 12.1a refers to Michael standing aside or passing aside, which precipitates unprecedented tribulation for the people of God. This rendering of the text of Daniel would have been extant at least as early as the late second century B.C. and was surely known to Paul since he regularly draws on the LXX in his letters. The eschatological rebellion against God must be preceded by the removal of Michael, who contains or inhibits all such activities. Nicholl has shown that this interpretation of Dan. 12.1 was extant in Jewish circles at and before the time of Paul.[22]

If Michael is "the Restrainer" or restraining force (hence the neuter noun *katechon*) in view of the Danielic background, then the Lawless One must be a pagan ruler inspired and empowered by Satan. This comports with the whole drift of Daniel 7–12 and with Paul's anti-imperial rhetoric in 1 Thessalonians 4–5. Though Paul is referring to a desecration of the Jewish Temple as in Daniel and the early Christian traditions in Mark 13, he does not think that this Lawless One has appeared yet. That is, it is not Claudius. But Paul does see "the mystery of lawlessness" already at work. The

---

20. For this and much more see now Nicholl, *From Hope to Despair,* pp. 231-32.

21. While this papyrus dates from the third or fourth century, it is widely agreed by scholars that it contains many ideas and traditions from the time of Jesus and Paul and before.

22. See Nicholl, *From Hope to Despair,* p. 245.

apostasy and the Man of Lawlessness are yet in the future, and so therefore also is its sequel, namely the return of Christ.[23]

Perhaps it is in order to end with a conjecture. Had Paul lived long enough, would he have seen the destruction of the Temple in Jerusalem by Titus in A.D. 70 as a fulfillment of much of what he says here? Yes, I think that is possible, perhaps even likely. It would have been the destruction of the right temple by a pagan emperor claiming divine honors, even though he did not desecrate the Temple in quite the manner described in Daniel and here. Paul might also have given some thought to Nero being the anti-Christ figure who was not yet revealed at the time Paul wrote 2 Thessalonians.[24]

What then would he have made of the fact that Titus was not destroyed by the second coming of Jesus? I suspect that Paul would have fallen back on what he had already said in 1 Thessalonians 5: the timing of the coming of the thief in the night is unknown, even if one can see or foresee some of the preliminary eschatological events. Even in 2 Thessalonians 2 Paul is careful not to comment on the intervals between the removal of the Restrainer and the appearance of the Lawless One or between the latter and Christ's return.[25]

Since however, this is an apocalyptic scenario Paul is dealing with, he may well have added, had he lived to the end of the first century A.D., that Titus was but one manifestation, one incarnation of the Lawless One, perhaps only a foreshadowing of the final one. These apocalyptic symbols are after all multivalent: they can refer to any anti-God ruler, be it Antiochus Epiphanes, Caligula, Nero, Titus, Domitian, or their successors.

The argument which begins at 2.1 starts with an appeal rather than an exhortation or a command. The very nature of the art of persuasion is making effective appeals. Paul introduces an appeal or request similarly in 1 Thess. 4.1 and 5.12. Here Paul immediately reminds his audience about something he has clearly spoken of before: the parousia and the gathering of the believers to Christ at his coming. These subjects were addressed in 1 Thessalonians 5 and 4 respectively. As Marshall points out, one reason for the difficulty in deciphering this material and identifying the Lawless One is that "vss. 5-7 go back to the period before his appearance described in vss. 3-4, and vss. 9-12 go back to the period of his appearance before his destruction described in vs. 8."[26] In other

---

23. See the useful summary of interpretive options on "the Restrainer" in Best, *First and Second Thessalonians*, pp. 295-302.

24. See Bruce, *1 and 2 Thessalonians*, pp. 171-72.

25. It is of course supremely ironic that later Christian commentators such as Chrysostom saw the Roman Empire as the Restrainer preventing the coming of the anti-Christ (see *Homily* 4 on 2 Thessalonians).

26. Marshall, *1 and 2 Thessalonians*, p. 185.

words, we have a rhetorical and logical rather than a chronological arrangement.

We should compare the use of *episynagogēs*, which refers to a gathering together of a community, to the use of the verbal form of the word in Mark 13.27 and Matt. 24.31, where it refers to the gathering together of the believers at the coming of the Son of Man (cf. Heb. 10.25).[27] The parallel usage in 2 Macc. 2.7 refers to the regathering of Jews into the temporal kingdom after the Babylonian exile, as it does in the LXX at Isa. 43.4-7; 52.12; 56.8; Jer. 31.8; Ezek. 28.9; and Ps. 105.47 (the uncompounded form *synagein* in some of these places).[28] The more eschatological sense of "gathering" is hinted at in *Testament of Naphtali* 8.3; *Testament of Asher* 7.7 (cf. *Didache* 9.4; 10.5).[29]

Paul is alluding to 1 Thess. 4.17 in this use of the term and so is speaking of the same event as he spoke of there: the second coming of Christ.[30] The word itself, which is found only here in Paul, like the description in 1 Thess. 4.17, refers to an event which happens to the believers: they are gathered together. The initiative comes from God.[31] Paul links the coming of the Lord and the gathering together as almost a single event, as they share one article: "the coming and gathering. . . ."[32]

V. 2 describes the problem directly: a claim that the day of the Lord has already occurred.[33] Both here and in Gal. 1.6 Paul is concerned with a hasty (*taxeōs*) departure by young converts from the truth of some aspect of the gospel.[34] Paul assumes that three sorts of communication might be responsible for the Thessalonians being unsettled and upset: a spiritual word (i.e., a revelation or prophetic utterance; see 1 Cor. 14.12, 32; cf. 1 John 4.1-3), an oral message, or a letter purporting to be from Paul. The phrase "as from us" certainly qualifies

27. See the discussion in Rigaux, *Les Épitres*, pp. 647-48.

28. See Lightfoot, *Notes*, p. 108. One of the real weaknesses in the dispensational approach is that it takes "parousia" in 2.1 as referring to the secret rapture of the church but concedes that in 2.8 "parousia" refers to the second coming. But Paul uses this term consistently when speaking of Jesus to refer to the second coming, an all too visible event. The further proof of this comes not only because of the general use of this term to refer to a public event (see pp. 142-45 above), but also because in this very context in vv. 8-9 we can note how "parousia" is used in parallel with the verb "revealed" to refer to the very public coming of the Lawless One. See also Beale's critique, *1 and 2 Thessalonians*, p. 198.

29. See Best, *First and Second Thessalonians*, pp. 274-75.

30. It is truly remarkable that it was 2 Thess. 2.1-2 that caused J. N. Darby to become convinced about a rapture of the saints before the day of the Lord. See Bruce, *1 and 2 Thessalonians*, p. 163.

31. See Wanamaker, *1 and 2 Thessalonians*, p. 238.

32. Malherbe, *The Letters*, p. 415.

33. *Throeisthai* is also used in Mark 13.7; Matt. 24.6 to refer to being disturbed about eschatological matters, but this is the only occurrence in Paul's letters.

34. See Lightfoot, *Notes*, p. 108.

"letter," the nearest antecedent, but possibly it modifies all three sources.[35] In view of what is said in 2.5, it seems clear that we must take seriously the "*as if from us*" with regard to "a letter." Paul is not referring to 1 Thessalonians. It is not his own letter misinterpreted but a letter purporting to be from him that is at issue here. If he believed that the misunderstanding came from his previous letter, he would have sought simply to make clearer what he had said before, not alluded to three possible sources of misunderstanding.[36]

But Paul is convinced that misunderstanding has been created about the day of the Lord by some oral or written communication. We do not know who was providing this misinformation. Elsewhere in 2 Thessalonians Paul does not refer to false teachers or pseudo-prophets. One gets the feeling that Paul is not sure where this misinformation has come from.[37] His concern here is not to attack the source but to counteract the effects with sound teaching and arguments. It would appear that Paul has had to deal regularly with these sorts of misrepresentations, perhaps sometimes deliberate, sometimes accidental, on various occasions (cf. from a later period 2 Tim. 2.18; 2 Pet. 3.3-13). This is one reason that at the end of this letter he offers an authenticating signature. For a religion based on proclamation and communication of a message, misinformation and disinformation, especially if the source is trusted, is deadly.

In Paul's letters *ta enestōta* refers to things present (Rom. 8.38; 1 Cor. 3.22), while the cognate *enestos* simply means "present" (1 Cor. 7.26: "the present distress"; Gal. 1.4: "the present evil age"; cf. Heb. 9.9: "the present time"). The question that arises with what is claimed here is whether we should translate the verb *enistēmi* (here in the perfect tense *enestēken*) as "is already here" or "is near/imminent." The perfect tense in its normal sense would refer to an event which has happened in the past and has enduring effects into the present. It seems clear from the use of the cognates that Paul does not just mean something that is on the near horizon, so here the sense is "has already come (and so is here)."[38] "It does not mean 'is coming' (*erchetai*, 1 Thess. 5:2), 'is at hand' (*engiken*, Rom. 13:12), or 'is near' (*engys estin*, Phil. 4:5)."[39] Paul would hardly have had to go to these lengths or argue in this way if all that some were saying was that the day of the Lord might be or was near.[40]

35. See Malherbe, *The Letters*, p. 417; cf. Marshall, *1 and 2 Thessalonians*, p. 187.

36. See Best, *First and Second Thessalonians*, p. 279; Wanamaker, *1 and 2 Thessalonians*, p. 239.

37. See rightly Lightfoot, *Notes*, p. 110: "the whole sentence is couched in the vague language of one who suspected rather than knew. But he must at least have had reasons for believing that an illicit use has been made of his authority in some way or other. . . ." See also Rigaux, *Les Épitres*, pp. 650-52.

38. See rightly, Beale, *1 and 2 Thessalonians*, pp. 199-200 and the note there.

39. Malherbe, *The Letters*, p. 417.

40. See rightly Best, *First and Second Thessalonians*, p. 276.

But how could the Thessalonians have come to believe that the day of the Lord had already passed them by? If they were in the main former pagans this is understandable in the sense that they may well have spiritualized the notion of the second coming and the coming resurrection (cf. the possible parallel in 1 Corinthians 15), and deduced from all their sufferings that they must have missed this blessing. The concept of a bodily resurrection of a deceased person was a hard one for pagans to grasp, much less take seriously (cf. Acts 17.16-34).[41] It is understandable that they might well have spiritualized eschatological language of various sorts, much as many do today.[42] A possible parallel can be cited from the time of the emperor Septimus Severus, during whose reign a rather severe persecution of Christians which "disturbed the minds of many" and even encouraged the opinion that the parousia of the Antichrist was already approaching or imminent (Eusebius, *Hist. Eccl.* 6.7).[43]

Wanamaker is helpful however at this juncture when he points out that the Thessalonians "most likely understood [the day of the Lord] not as a literal twenty-four hour period but as the final period of the present order culminating in the coming of the Lord Jesus."[44] In other words, rather than spiritualizing things, they may have simply thought that their current sufferings were part of the day of the Lord, and that Jesus' coming must then be imminent, all being part of the final events.[45] This, too, is a possibility, though Paul does not give us enough information to be sure which interpretation of their error is correct.

Paul's chief concern, as v. 3 makes evident, is that his converts not be led astray by this mistaken notion of the day of the Lord having already come. The language here about deception is reminiscent of Mark 13.5, where we have the warning to take heed lest one is led astray. We have here an anacoluthon or incomplete sentence: "for unless the apostasy/rebellion comes first . . . ," something unlikely from a forger.[46] The rest of the sentence would read something like "that day will not come" (cf. NRSV).[47] *Apostasia* normally refers to a political or even military revolt in Greek literature, but in the LXX it can refer to a re-

---

41. See the discussion in B. Witherington, *The Acts of the Apostles* (Grand Rapids: Eerdmans, 2004), pp. 511-35.

42. Beale, *1 and 2 Thessalonians*, pp. 200-201.

43. See the discussion in Bruce, *1 and 2 Thessalonians*, p. 165.

44. Wanamaker, *1 and 2 Thessalonians*, p. 240.

45. See R. D. Aus, "The Relevance of Isaiah 66.7 to Revelation 12 and 2 Thessalonians 1," *ZNW* 67 (1976): 263-64.

46. See rightly Wanamaker, *1 and 2 Thessalonians*, p. 244. There are numerous such examples of incompleteness or scribal carelessness (or, better said, a scribe not having time to fix it because he is taking rapid dictation) in Paul — cf. 2 Thess. 2.7; Gal. 1.20; 2.4; 2.9; 5.13; 1 Cor. 1.31; 4.6; 11.24; 2 Cor. 8.13; 9.7; Rom. 4.16; 13.7. Notice that these are the letters generally referred to as the earlier Paulines. Perhaps later on Paul had more and better scribes.

47. See Marshall, *1 and 2 Thessalonians*, p. 188.

volt against or apostasy from the one true God (cf. Josh. 22.22; 2 Chron. 22.19; 33.10; Jer. 2.19; see especially 1 Macc. 2.15: defection from the Law during the Maccabean revolt; Josephus, *Vita* 43: the Jewish revolt against Rome).

The idea of a revolt against or apostasy from God during the eschatological age is not uncommon in early Jewish literature (*Jubilees* 23.14-21; 2 Esd. 5.1-12; *1 Enoch* 91.7; 93.9), including the NT (cf. Matt. 24.12; Acts 21.21 to 2 Tim. 3.1-9; Heb. 3.12). This activity is regularly associated with the rise of false prophets or teachers (Mark 13.22; 1 Tim. 4.1-3; 2 Tim. 4.3-4), as it seems to be here.[48] The issue is what is happening not so much in the community of faith as in the world in general, causing believers to have to swim against the tide of the culture.[49] As Marshall points out, it is remarkable that Paul does not more fully explain what he means by the apostasy or rebellion, which in turn suggests that he said something to his converts before on this subject,[50] perhaps along the lines of the Synoptic apocalyptic discourse in Mark 13, as he seems to draw on that material in 1 Thessalonians and elsewhere. Notice that Paul assumes that believers will be present when the "apostasy" hits.

There is some debate as to whether Paul is referring to one event (apostasy brought on by the appearance of the Lawless One, the Rebel), or a series of events (first rebellion, then the Lawless One appears), though it is clear enough that the word "first" refers to both of these phenomena as preceding the parousia of Jesus. The Lawless One will be described as doomed in vv. 6-7, for this is what "son of perdition/destruction" (a Hebraism) surely implies (cf. 1 Sam. 20.31 and John 17.12). Favoring the view that two eschatological phenomena are referred to is the parallel construction using two different verbs: the "rebellion" comes, but the Lawless One is revealed, presumably after the "rebellion" has been set in motion.[51] There are some intriguing parallels between our

48. See Rigaux, *Les Épitres,* pp. 654-55.

49. Beale, *1 and 2 Thessalonians,* pp. 203-4 points to the reference to the false teaching about the day of the Lord to suggest that what is meant is apostasy within the community of faith, but this teaching about the day of the Lord could just as easily have come from the synagogue as from within the church, and the reference to the delusion of the perishing does not suggest a group in the church but rather outsiders to the Thessalonian Christian community. We might add that Rom. 1.18-32 is a perfectly good example of a description of rebellion against God which could be called *apostasia,* and it is clear that there the subjects are not Christians. Finally, the largely Gentile Thessalonian audience could not have understood "Temple of God" as coded language for "the church of Christ" without further explanation. Best, *First and Second Thessalonians,* pp. 282-83 suggests that the apostasy could refer to Jews who reject the gospel (cf. Romans 11, where they are said to be temporarily broken off), which would comport with texts like *Jubilees* 23.14-23; *1 Enoch* 91.3-10; 1QpHab 2.1ff, which refer to an apostasy within Judaism.

50. Marshall, *1 and 2 Thessalonians,* pp. 188-90.

51. See Wanamaker, *1 and 2 Thessalonians,* p. 243.

text and *Psalms of Solomon* 17.11-22, which refers to Pompey's campaign in Judea in 63 B.C. and refers to him as "the lawless one" whose actions result in Jewish apostasy.[52]

From a rhetorical point of view, it is clear that we have here *not* the device known as personification (the impersonal process of rebellion encapsulated in the "figure" of a person — the man of lawlessness),[53] but rather a comparison, a rhetorical *synkrisis* of two parousias and two persons, the Lawless One and the lawful Judge/Ruler, Jesus.[54] At the outset Paul deliberately calls this Rebel a human being (*anthrōpos*, v. 3). The nature of a *synkrisis* is that it often involves a contrast by way of a comparison. Aelian Theon stresses that "comparison" is normally a form of speech which contrasts the better and the worse and that such comparisons can effectively be drawn between two persons (*First Progymnasta*).[55] There are, to be sure, some similarities between the two being compared, but by and large they differ in their actions and effects.

Quintilian makes clear that the best way to signal that a *synkrisis* is under way is to use the same language of both persons (*Inst. Or.* 9.3.32). Accordingly we note: (1) both the Lawless One and Jesus are said to have a *parousia* (vv. 8-9); (2) both are revealed or appear, having been hidden from human view (*apokalyptein* of Jesus in 1.7 and of the Lawless One in 2.3, 8; *epiphaneia* of Jesus in v. 8); (3) both are clearly powerful figures (vv. 2, 4, 7-9, 11); and (4) the Lawless One works in tandem with a supernatural figure, Satan, just as Christ works in tandem with God the Father in these eschatological events, and in both cases the two figures working together are distinguished from one another (i.e., the Lawless One is not Satan).

These parallels even in particular terms make it hard to deny either that the Lawless One is viewed as a person or that Paul is following the rhetorical conventions for *synkrisis* here. Rhetorical comparison was seen as one of the chief means of rebuttal and of amplifying and so making one's argument more persuasive (*Inst. Or.* 8.4.3). This "figure" or technique was probably familiar to all the Thessalonians, because such comparisons were a staple of even elementary education in the Greco-Roman world.[56]

So the Lawless One is some sort of rival savior or ruler figure (cf. 1 John 2.18). It may also be that we have here an echo of the concept of the man of Belial, for Belial is rendered in the LXX as both *anomia* (2 Sam. 22.5 = Ps.

52. See Wanamaker, *1 and 2 Thessalonians*, p. 245.

53. As suggested by Lightfoot, *Notes*, pp. 111-12.

54. On this subject we have a helpful detailed study by C. Forbes, "Paul and Rhetorical Comparison," in J. P. Sampley, ed., *Paul in the Greco-Roman World* (Harrisburg: Trinity, 2003), pp. 134-71.

55. See the full quotation of this section of this text in Forbes, "Paul and Rhetorical Comparison," pp. 143-44.

56. See Forbes, "Paul and Rhetorical Comparison," p. 134.

18.4[17.5 LXX]) and *apostasia* (1 Kgs. 21.13).[57] It is quite possible that Paul has in view some future pagan ruler who will recapitulate the sins of Antiochus Epiphanes, Pompey, and Caligula and perhaps even lead some Jews astray, as was the complaint in Daniel and the *Psalms of Solomon*. This might then be an allusion to one sort of act that the emperor cult could lead to and could lead even some Jews astray. "Lawlessness" is said to be characteristic of the influence of pagans on Jews in *Psalms of Solomon* 1.8; 2.3; 3.13 and specifically of Pompey's influence in 17.13-20.[58]

V. 4 provides us with echoes of Dan. 11.36, where the pagan king (e.g., Antiochus Epiphanes) tries to exalt himself in the Temple of the one true God. The degree of his arrogance is shown in the participle *hyperairomenos*, which means "hyper-exalting oneself." Whereas Daniel has "over every god," Paul has "over every so-called god" (cf. 1 Cor. 8.5 on this phrase) "and every object of worship." But this is not just about self-exaltation and self-deification; this is also about opposition: the verse begins with the reference to "the adversary" (*ho antikeimenos*).[59] Self-deification is seen in the man sitting down in the inner sanctum of the Temple of God. *Naos* refers to the inner sanctum or "holy of holies" in the Temple, and so we are to think of the ultimate defilement of the Temple of God, such as that accomplished by Antiochus Epiphanes and attempted by Caligula (Josephus, *Antiquities* 18.8.2). The definite article before *naos* makes it clear that Paul is referring to a particular Temple.[60] The earliest Christian interpreters of this text (e.g., Irenaeus, *Adversus Haereses* 5.30.4) understood quite clearly that the literal Temple in Jerusalem was meant.[61] Thereby, this man nominates/proclaims himself to be deity (cf. Ezek. 28.2, where the king of Tyre says, "I am god; I sit in the seat of the gods"). *Apodeiknunai* can have the sense of either nomination for an office or proclamation of a sovereign once he assumes power (see Philo, *In Flaccum* 3.2).

The deification of the Roman emperor is likely to supply some of the imagery here, though Daniel's broader reference to any pagan ruler is alluded to as well. This was an image the Thessalonians would be well familiar with from coins portraying the emperor on one side with the word *theos*.[62] It would be hard to overestimate the alarm it caused Jews when Caligula attempted to have his statue set up in the Temple in Jerusalem (see Philo, *Embassy to Gaius* 203-346). There was a near revolt in A.D. 39-40 in Judea over this act. But it was not

---

57. Bruce, *1 and 2 Thessalonians*, pp. 167-68.

58. See Malherbe, *The Letters*, p. 419.

59. In 1 Tim. 5.14 this very term is used of *the* Adversary, Satan, but here it is used of his minion or agent.

60. Best, *First and Second Thessalonians*, pp. 286-87.

61. The use of *naos* here is quite clearly different from the figurative use in 1 Cor. 3.16-17 (cf. 6.19); 2 Cor. 6.16 (and see Eph. 2.21).

62. See Lightfoot, *Notes*, p. 113.

just Caligula. There was also the episode of Herod Agrippa I in A.D. 44 receiving divine honors at Olympic-style games in Caesarea Maritima, appearing in gold clothing with the sun reflecting on him, being acclaimed the voice (and appearance) of god, and being struck down at that very occasion (Acts 12.21-23; cf. Josephus, *Antiquities* 19.343-47).

One could go all the way back to the time of Julius Caesar. Following Caesar's victory at Pharsalus in 46 B.C. statues of him were erected in various places, including Macedonia, with the inscription *THEOS EPIPHANĒS*, "God manifest."[63] Both words are used in Paul's argument. It was especially in the more Greek part of the empire, in places like Asia, Macedonia, and Greece that these sorts of proclamations and claims of the emperor were found, claims usually resisted in Rome by traditional Romans. Thessalonike was a Greek city, even in Paul's day.[64] As such its citizens were well familiar with the rhetoric of the imperial cult. Here Paul is opposing that rhetoric to his own claims about Jesus, the real God who will manifest himself at the second coming.

Claudius was emperor A.D. 41-54, during the time when 1 and 2 Thessalonians were likely written. A bronze coin was issued during that same time in nearby Philippi with the inscription *colonia augusti iulia philipensis* and on the other side portraits of Caesar and Octavian with the inscription *DIVUS AUG*, divine Augustus.[65] When Claudius died in A.D. 54 his successor and adopted son Nero had coins minted indicating the divine status of Claudius.

Coins were of course tools for the political and religious propaganda of emperors, and it is hard to miss how Paul's rhetoric here is a rather clear attack on all such rhetoric, counteracting it with claims he makes about Jesus and his royal coming or appearing, which will involve a direct attack on the self-exalting man of lawlessness.[66] It would be hard not to see this as a reference to a future emperor, especially with such a lawless emperor as Caligula as part of the living memory of all Jews of the period.[67] In the *Sibylline Oracles* (5.33-34) we have an allusion to Nero arrogating and exalting himself to the realm of the divine. These sorts of ideas were part and parcel of the ethos in which these letters were written.

Paul is using multivalent apocalyptic prophetic language throughout this

---

63. See the discussion in L. Kreitzer, *Striking Images* (Sheffield: Sheffield Academic, 1996), p. 81.

64. See pp. 3-8 above.

65. See the drawings and commentary in Kreitzer, p. 92.

66. See also pp. 142-46 above on Pauline anti-imperial rhetoric.

67. Here is where, with Marshall, *1 and 2 Thessalonians*, p. 191, we note that it is not very believable that a forger would write something like this after A.D. 70, when the Temple in Jerusalem no longer existed. It is true that Irenaeus uses this text, envisioning that the Temple will be rebuilt before this eschatological event, but that is from well after the first century and well after the time when the church had a large proportion of Jews, particularly Jews in Israel.

argument, language intended to be more evocative than literally descriptive. Had someone later objected that the Temple in Jerusalem was destroyed in A.D. 70 without Jesus' involvement, Paul could have insisted that that event was but a type of the final Temple desecration and parousia of Christ. But we cannot apply this "Temple language" to the church. Paul is speaking in a largely Gentile context, and his audience will surely hear him as referring to an actual temple, in this case the Temple of the one true God that still stood in Jerusalem. Paul nowhere in 1 and 2 Thessalonians refers to the church as "the Temple of God."[68]

V. 5 is simply a reminder that Paul spoke about some of these matters when he was with them — but to what extent we do not know and cannot tell. He reverts here to the first person singular: "don't you remember what *I* told you while I was with you?" (cf. 1 Thess. 5.1). This surely makes clear that Paul is the primary author of this material (cf. 2 Thess. 3.17), while Silas and Timothy are presumably simply offering the "amen" to Paul's teaching (cf. 1 Thess. 2.18; 3.5, though there it is made more abrupt and emphatic by the use of *egō*).[69] Paul refers back to his original oral teaching, not back to 1 Thessalonians. This need not mean that he had not yet written 1 Thessalonians, but in fact likely does mean that he does not think he addressed the issue of signs or precursors to the parousia in that letter. This is, of course, true. Neither ch. 4 nor ch. 5 of 1 Thessalonians speaks of earthly or historical events that lead up to the second coming. "Since they had received this instruction by word of mouth, a general allusion was sufficient to remind them of the details."[70]

The tone of the reminder here is more strident than the similar reference back to oral teaching in 1 Thess. 3.4 (cf. 4.2), suggesting that the situation deteriorated further after 1 Thessalonians was written.[71] The stridency can be seen in the imperfect tense of *elegon*, which means "I kept on telling you. . . ." By going back *ad fontes* to the original oral teaching, Paul circumvents anything the Thessalonians might have heard about these apocalyptic matters in the interim.[72]

---

68. See Marshall, *1 and 2 Thessalonians*, p. 192 and rightly Wanamaker, *1 and 2 Thessalonians*, pp. 246-47, against Beale, *1 and 2 Thessalonians*, pp. 206-11. See the stress of Best, *First and Second Thessalonians*, p. 287, who says that here "Paul does not conceive in any way of an apostasy within the church." We might add pastorally that for a group of Christians under persecution and experiencing anxiety it would hardly be encouraging to regale them with a description of how their congregation and others would fall apart at the seams, suffer major defections, and, worse, suffer the horrible influence of a lawless teacher who saw himself as a deity! 2 Thessalonians is not to be read in light of 2-3 John as it is dealing with a very different scenario. See the discussion in Rigaux, *Les Épitres*, pp. 660-61.

69. See Marshall, *1 and 2 Thessalonians*, pp. 192-93; Best, *First and Second Thessalonians*, p. 290.

70. Bruce, *1 and 2 Thessalonians*, p. 169.

71. Malherbe, *The Letters*, p. 421.

72. Malherbe, *The Letters*, p. 421.

V. 5 terminates the first major portion of Paul's argument. Vv. 6-12 constitute the second major salvo or part of this act of persuasion.[73] V. 6 introduces a new player in the apocalyptic scenario, the Restrainer. Yet Paul seems to be saying "and now you know what's holding the Lawless One back." In regard to the old debate about whether Paul is talking about a restraining force or a restraining person, the answer is simply Yes: there is a restrainer who is exercising restraining force, holding back the Adversary. Here the reference to something — *to katechon* (neuter article followed by the participle), the restraining force. In v. 7 Paul will refer to the person who is doing the restraining — *ho katechon* (masculine article followed by the participle).[74] This interpretation does justice to the grammar in both verses as well as to allusions to previously known figures in these verses, as we have discussed above.[75] The evidence as we have it shows that *katechein* was interpreted to mean "restrain" all the way back to the time of Tertullian in the second century A.D. and should not be interpreted to refer to a delay or a delayer, as if Paul were speaking about a delay in the parousia.[76]

That there is personal agency involved in this restraint is suggested even in v. 6 with its reference to "his time." God has orchestrated things such that the Lawless One will not be "revealed" until the Restrainer's "time." As in so much of apocalyptic literature God will use another personal agent, a powerful angel, to accomplish his purpose. Paul is probably referring to the angelic restrainer Michael.[77] Since v. 6 follows v. 5, the drift of the argument seems to be that Paul told the Thessalonians about this person when he was with them, and so they should remember. "Now" here is logical: "well then you know."[78] On the issue of an appointed or appropriate eschatological time see 1 Tim. 6.15 (cf. Acts 1.7; Mark 13.32; *4 Ezra* 4.34-37; 7.74; *2 Baruch* 21.8; 48.2-5; 56.2). "The function of this statement is to tap into the apocalyptic knowledge of Paul's readers in order to put the coming of the Day of the Lord in proper eschatological perspective."[79]

"The mystery of lawlessness is already at work" (v. 7) and thus precedes the appearing of the Lawless One, who is being held back from appearing by

---

73. See Rigaux, *Les Épitres*, p. 662.

74. This interpretation obviates the necessity of exegetical gymnastics such as suggesting that the force is suddenly without warning "personified" in the following verse. That is not how rhetorical "figures" work!

75. See pp. 218-20 above.

76. Wanamaker, *1 and 2 Thessalonians*, pp. 250-51.

77. For earlier attempts to explain the Restrainer in light of a Jewish apocalyptic background see O. Betz, "Der Katechon," *NTS* 9 (1962-63): 276-91. His argument however has the weakness that the Hebrew word *tamak* is never translated *katechō* in the LXX. For a list of at least seven options in regard to the Restrainer see Beale, *1 and 2 Thessalonians*, pp. 213-17.

78. Lightfoot, *Notes*, p. 113.

79. Malherbe, *The Letters*, p. 423.

the Restrainer, who is standing "in the midst." One may wish to compare "the mystery of our religion" in 1 Tim. 3.16 (cf. 3.9) for a similar Pauline usage.[80] Lawlessness, just like "restraint," has both personal and impersonal faces or dimensions.[81] *Mystērion* here surely has the sense not of something incomprehensible but rather of something hidden from plain view but nonetheless extant and at work. See for instance Josephus's reference to a "mystery of evil," a "secret evil," in the life of Antipater (*War* 1.470).[82]

There are interesting parallels elsewhere in early Jewish apocalyptic, for example in 2 *Baruch* 29.4, where we hear that the two great apocalyptic monsters, Behemoth and Leviathan, are being kept until the time when the Messiah will be revealed. Or we may compare Rev. 7.1-3, where the winds are said to be restrained until God's servants are sealed. The idea of the divine hand exercising control or restraint, often through an intermediary such as an angel, is characteristic of apocalyptic literature, which sets out to comfort the afflicted and pressured whose lives seem out of their own control. In this case the Restrainer is an angel, a protector of God's people.[83] "The apostasy has not taken place, nor has the Rebel appeared . . . but rebellion even now opposes God; this rebellion will culminate in the revelation of the man of rebellion, who will be utterly vanquished by Christ in his parousia."[84] When the Restrainer is taken off the scene, the "mystery" of lawlessness will become manifest in a public person — the Lawless One.[85]

V. 8 begins with "and then," indicating the sequel to the removal of the Restrainer. We thus arrive at the same juncture in time as in v. 3. Paul does not say how long the Lawless One will operate unhindered before Christ returns but only makes clear his ultimate downfall.[86] The final judgment of the Lawless One will be accomplished by word rather than by war. Similarly, in Rev. 19.21 the rider on the white horse (Christ) executes the kings of the earth and their armies by the sword of the word coming out of Messiah's mouth. In Rev. 20.7-10, the final judgment of Gog and Magog, who have gathered for battle, also happens by direct divine action, in this case fire from heaven. In early Christian apocalyptic scenarios there is no great final battle between human forces called Armageddon, only a final divine execution as here in 2 Thessalonians.

Vv. 8 and 9 use three disclosure words to speak of the revelation of a person: *apokalypsthesetai* and *parousia* of the Lawless One and *epiphaneia* and

---

80. See Lightfoot, *Notes*, p. 114.
81. Marshall, *1 and 2 Thessalonians*, p. 195.
82. Marshall, *1 and 2 Thessalonians*, p. 195.
83. See pp. 208-12 above.
84. Best, *First and Second Thessalonians*, p. 293.
85. Malherbe, *The Letters*, p. 423.
86. Marshall, *1 and 2 Thessalonians*, p. 200.

parousia of Christ. As we have already noted, Paul is offering a rhetorical comparison of the two figures being spoken of.[87] Such words were part of the language used to refer to the visitation of a god or a "divine" emperor to a city (see Diodorus Siculus 1.25).[88] Paul's usage is undoubtedly also connected with the usage in the LXX when it speaks of God's visitation, usually for judgment (cf. 2 Sam. 7.23; 2 Macc. 2.21; 3.24). The piling up of words to make clear the importance and gloriousness of Christ's return is typical of apocalyptic literature. *Epiphaneia* is used of the second coming again in 1 Tim. 6.14; 2 Tim. 4.1, 8; Tit. 2.13. If there is a difference of nuance between *epiphaneia* and *parousia*, it is that *epiphaneia* conveys the sense of a sudden or unexpected appearing.[89]

The slaying of the Lawless One "by the breath of his mouth" is likely an echo of Isa. 11.4 LXX: "and he shall smite . . . with the word of his mouth, and with the breath of his lips he shall slay the wicked."[90] In the somewhat later Christian apocalyptic work the *Ascension of Isaiah* 4.14 we find the following: "the Lord will come with his angels and with his armies of the holy ones from the seventh heaven with the glory of the seventh heaven, and he will drag Beliar into Gehenna together with his armies." We may also compare the earlier Jewish text *1 Enoch* 62.2: "the word of his mouth slays all sinners," or Wis. 11.19-20. In each case the destruction of evil comes by direct divine intervention, and in this particular text it is personal — the Lawless One is destroyed.[91]

The advent of the Lawless One is quite deliberately described in v. 9 in a way that parallels the (first) coming of Christ. Not only does this person have a "parousia," "he too works in obedience to a superior power; he too has his miracles and signs."[92] The language of power, signs, and wonders is used in 2 Cor. 12.12 of the distinguishing sign of the genuine apostle's work, so here Paul indicates that these are deliberately misleading or false signs (cf. Mark 13.22) and wonders (one could also compare Rom. 15.19, which again speaks of Paul's apostolic work; Acts 2.22 of these same three things characterizing Jesus' ministry and Heb. 2.4 for this same sort of language applied to God).

What is being claimed here is that just as God empowers Christ, so Satan empowers the Lawless One to perform pseudo-miracles and signs.[93] It is not suggested that these signs and wonders are not real, in fact their real quality is what is misleading about them.[94] Indeed, it is said that the Lawless One is

---

87. See pp. 142-45 above.

88. We may, as Lightfoot, *Notes*, p. 116 hints, have this choice of terms because of its familiarity to Paul's largely Gentile audience.

89. See Wanamaker, *1 and 2 Thessalonians*, p. 258; cf. Rigaux, *Les Épitres*, p. 673.

90. See Marshall, *1 and 2 Thessalonians*, pp. 200-201.

91. Malherbe, *The Letters*, p. 424.

92. Lightfoot, *Notes*, p. 116.

93. Marshall, *1 and 2 Thessalonians*, p. 201.

94. See Wanamaker, *1 and 2 Thessalonians*, p. 259; Malherbe, *The Letters*, p. 425.

equipped with "all power." These miracles are "false" in the sense of misleading and coming from a wicked source.[95] The text literally says that this "parousia is according to the energizing power of Satan." The same sort of thing is said about the beast and the false prophet in Rev. 13.2. Jesus himself warned about the appearance of false prophets and even false messiahs offering false signs and wonders to lead people astray before the coming of the Son of Man (see Mark 13.22).[96] Miracles were said to be performed by various emperors, and Caligula especially claimed to perform such things during his rule (Tacitus, *Annales* 4.81). Paul could well have seen Caligula as a type of false leaders to come. Since these wonders and miracles are said to accompany the coming of the Lawless One, Paul is then thinking of a period of time between the coming of the Lawless One and the return of Christ.[97]

V. 10 is simply a continuation of v. 9, making clear that it is "those who are perishing" who are likely to be deceived by these satanic miracles and all sorts of unrighteousness and must be held largely responsible for this outcome because they refuse to love the truth and thus be saved. As Lightfoot says, we have here the course of a soul perishing, descending into destruction. They begin by refusing to love the truth, become infatuated with this course of action, and by degrees reach a point where they actively champion falsehood and error.[98] In the end, as Romans 1 makes clear, God gives them up to a debased mind. Only here in the entire Bible do we find the phrase "love of the truth."[99] Paul speaks here of receiving or welcoming the love of the truth.[100]

V. 11 puts it even more dramatically: because they have refused to love the truth God sends them a powerful delusion so that they will believe the lie they have chosen, with a result (v. 12) that all who have gone down this road will be finally judged (i.e., condemned). Isa. 29.10 expresses this same kind of idea: God sends a spirit of torpor on unbelieving Israel to prevent them from seeing and hearing. In a sense Paul is saying that God allows those who refuse to love the truth to have the consequences of their choice, confirming them in their obduracy.[101] This is more than just a matter of God judging or punishing sin with sin (Deut. 29.4; Isa. 6.9-10). It is a matter of God giving people up to a debased mind, God saying "okay, if you insist, have it your way, including the consequences of such a choice." Here we have an example of God not only allowing

---

95. See the discussion in Rigaux, *Les Épitres*, p. 674.

96. It seems probable that here again Paul is drawing on his knowledge of the teachings of Jesus about the apocalyptic scenario. See pp. 131-40 above and see Bruce, *1 and 2 Thessalonians*, p. 173.

97. Best, *First and Second Thessalonians*, pp. 305-6.

98. Lightfoot, *Notes*, pp. 117-18.

99. See Wanamaker, *1 and 2 Thessalonians*, p. 261.

100. Malherbe, *The Letters*, p. 426.

101. See Beale, *1 and 2 Thessalonians*, p. 222.

sinners to violate his will but allowing them the consequences of those violations, which ultimately means judgment, condemnation. We may compare texts like 2 Sam. 24.1; 1 Chron. 21.1; 1 Kgs. 22.23; and Ezek. 14.9 in which God uses evil spirits to accomplish his purposes.

Since God does not desire that anyone refuse to love the truth, this tells us something about how God exercises his sovereignty.[102] There are things God causes to happen and things God allows to happen, and some of the latter are against his will.[103] 2 Cor. 4.4 states the matter more clearly: the god of this aeon has been allowed to blind the minds of unbelievers to keep them from seeing the light.[104] Here Paul is talking about the lost or perishing who refuse to love the truth, not about the Thessalonian believers.[105] This idea of a climax of wickedness in the last days before the parousia is also found in texts like *Psalms of Solomon* 17.23-29. "The thought is not of two pre-determined classes of people whose character and destiny is fixed by God, but is simply descriptive of the actual character of certain people as being on their way to destruction (and thus in a sense already experiencing something of that process) and of others as being on their way to salvation (and already experiencing the saving power of God)."[106]

As Lightfoot says, "truth" and "falsehood" cover not only the domain of theology, but also the domain of ethics,[107] for believers are called to embrace, love, and even do the truth and to shun all that is false and unrighteous. "Wrong-doing is a lie, for it is a denial of God's sovereignty; right-doing is a truth, for it is a confession of the same."[108] To take pleasure in wickedness is in effect clear evidence that one disbelieves the truth. Strong emphasis then is placed here on human responsibility for human lostness: the lost rejected the truth and took pleasure in its opposite, resulting in their condemnation.

The force and effect of this powerful rhetoric of rebuttal is severalfold. First, it makes clear that it is an error to say the day of the Lord has already come, so there is cognitive correction here. There may also be the suggestion that there is still time for further amendment of life. Second, this argument may

---

102. See Malherbe, *The Letters*, p. 427.

103. Rigaux, *Les Épitres*, pp. 678-79 rightly stresses that Paul is not an absolute dualist. There is only a limited dualism, such that God in the end superintends all and has no equals.

104. Best, *First and Second Thessalonians*, p. 310 is perhaps right that we are not meant to see a sequence here, first Satan deceiving the perishing and then God finishing them off with a delusion. Rather Paul is looking at the same event or process from two different sides. As Best rightly adds, what v. 11a suggests with "for this reason" is that God's action is consequent upon the human refusal to love the truth, not the cause of that refusal.

105. See Bruce, *1 and 2 Thessalonians*, p. 173.

106. Marshall, *1 and 2 Thessalonians*, p. 202.

107. Marshall, *1 and 2 Thessalonians*, p. 202.

108. Lightfoot, *Notes*, p. 118.

be meant to suggest that the tormentors of the Thessalonian Christians will eventually be dealt with by God. Third, there is meant to be some comfort here for believers under pressure and persecution that God is still in charge and that they are not among those who are perishing but rather among those who love the truth.[109] And love of the truth "implies much more than its admiration, whether intellectual, emotional, or aesthetic; it is committal to the truth. To accept the love of the truth is therefore equivalent to obeying the truth. . . . Truth is accepted not through compulsion of miracle but through love of it. Those who love the truth are saved."[110]

Bridging the Horizons

W. B. Yeats, in contemplating the scenario described here, wrote the following about what would happen when the Restrainer was removed:

> Things fall apart; the centre cannot hold
> Mere anarchy is loosed upon the world,
> The blood-dimmed tide is loosed, and everywhere
> The ceremony of innocence is drowned
> The best lack all conviction, while the worst
> Are full of passionate intensity.

This speaks to the fact that when the ethos of a culture changes it affects the whole culture, with even "the best" losing heart and lacking conviction. Paul sees this sort of outcome in the great "apostasy," for which the church will be around and will be affected and infected. Apostasy affects the church with the culture as a whole as it defects from the remnants of positive values that it clung to earlier.

Greg Beale in his treatment of 2 Thess. 2.1-12 aptly draws an analogy between the perishing and the famous frog in the kettle of water.[111] A frog is a cold-blooded creature and so is unable to detect gradual increases in temperature. If you place the frog in the pot when the water is a normal temperature for the frog and then gradually increase the heat, the frog simply adjusts and adjusts until he is boiled alive. In the "descent into destruction" those who first refuse to love the truth then take pleasure in wickedness, then finally become champions of unrighteousness and falsehood, gradually adjusting and adjusting until all that is left is their final judgment. The end result is not just a life of

---

109. Wanamaker, *1 and 2 Thessalonians*, pp. 263-64.
110. Best, *First and Second Thessalonians*, p. 308.
111. Beale, *1 and 2 Thessalonians*, p. 224.

chaos but finally a judgment of condemnation to an eternity of accepting the consequences for such actions. It is a fearsome and fearful prospect. Not only does sin punish sin, but ultimately God does as well. Charles Williams describes this whole process in graphic detail in his classic novel *Descent into Hell*. It is, and is intended to be, a frightening portrayal of spiritual deterioration.

It is not really a surprise that many people, even many church people, find this sort of apocalyptic material repugnant. Their vision of the ultimate religion is a no-fault religion where no one gets judged by God and no one is ever held ultimately responsible for their actions. This at least is how they want to be treated themselves, but strangely some of these same folks are the very people demanding justice when they have been injured, robbed, disenfranchised, bamboozled, and the like. But you cannot have it both ways. If God is a just and righteous God, then one can expect that justice will be fairly administered to all. Equally strange is the fact that the very people who refuse to believe that God will one day judge the living and the dead are those who stridently try to implement an ethic of justice in the form of the liberation of the oppressed here and now. This is simply a realized form of eschatology, with humans implementing it. But the question should be asked: Who do we really want exacting justice in this world? Fallible human beings who can get it wrong and often do since they are not omniscient or omni-benevolent, or an all-knowing and all-loving God who does not make mistakes when it comes to justice issues? It is precisely because of questions such as these that Paul implores his converts on more than one occasion to leave vengeance in God's hands.[112]

The movie *Kingdom of Heaven* has raised some of these very questions in a poignant way, in regard to the ethics of crusading and the Crusades. The story is grounded reasonably well in history, telling the story of the hiatus between the second and third Crusades when Saladin's forces surrounded the Holy Land and held an uneasy peace with Baldwin, the Christian leper king of Jerusalem. Peace was preserved by allowing persons of all monotheistic faiths who had a stake in Jerusalem free access to the city to live, work, and pray.

The film is laden with ironies of various sorts, not least of which is the portrayal of both Muslims and Christians fervently shouting and believing it was God's will that they murder the infidels on the other side, only to discover that in fact God thwarted both sides' efforts from time to time. Jerusalem is seen as the epicenter of kingdom of heaven, the ultimate irony since it is the site of so much unheavenly plotting, treachery, immorality, and murder, but then such is the very nature of war.

The film intends to force the audience to realize the inherent contradictions involves in fighting for the kingdom of heaven, a kingdom Jesus said would be established by love, even love of enemies, by turning the other cheek,

112. See pp. 122-25 above.

and by refusing to retaliate when harmed. It is a kingdom worth living and dying for, but its very nature is violated by killing for it.

It is no surprise that the central character in the movie, Balian, a blacksmith become a knight, becomes agnostic in the face of the machinations that go on in the name of God on both the Christian and the Muslim sides. Yet Baldwin is a wise king and there are reminders in his life and in the lives of others of real Christian values such as goodness and kindness, even to one's enemies, holiness, and always being prepared to tell the truth. In the end Balian resolves to defend the people of Jerusalem but not the bricks and mortar.

This is a wonderfully thought-provoking movie for people of all faiths and no faith, and it raises the question once more whether Christian crusades can be holy wars any more than Muslim jihads. Or is it in fact the case that there are no just wars, only wars that seem more and less justifiable to us, more and less unjust to human beings who have an infinite capacity for self-justification and protecting their own turf? *Kingdom of Heaven* throws down the gauntlet in a way Ridley Scott's earlier effort in *Gladiator* does not, forcing us to realize both the limitations and the great cost of violating one of the fundamental biblical commandments recognized and accepted by all three monotheistic religions: thou shalt not murder.

My own uneasiness with the ethic of war and kingdom that is often promulgated in my own country is expressed in the following poem.

Esse Quam Videre — To Be, Rather than to Seem

Take me to the just side of justice
And the right side of righteousness,
Not the vindictive side of vindication,
for otherwise — I do not wish to go.

Lead me to the passionate side of compassion,
And the gracious side of grace,
Not the condescending side of mercy
for otherwise I remain remote — for pity's sake.

Push me past the truant side of trouble
And the pleasant side of pain
Not allowing me to wallow in it —
Lest I marvel at my martyrdom

Carry me to the service side of serving
And the sacrificial side of sacrifice
Not the calculating side of caring
for otherwise my generosity remains too frugal.

Put me outside my selfish Eden
And beyond my creature comforts
Without raising Cain in my life
for I desire to be a remarkable, not a marked man.

Fill me with an inextinguishable blaze
A peerless and fearless love,
Not a faltering flame or a fumbling forgiveness
for I desire to be christened with real Christlikeness.

May the Spirit make me spiritual
And the Son shine in my life
And the Father find me faithful,
lest I miss the kingdom's goal.

What comports with the ethic of Paul when it comes to the matter of dealing with wickedness in the culture on a large scale is the prayer *Marana tha,* and the trust that Jesus will return someday, and when he does all manner of things will be well.

Prayer Matters — 2.13–3.5

One of the notable features of this deliberative discourse is the way that Paul, when he gets to a problem about which he must persuade his audience, surrounds the discussion with prayer. We have seen the thanksgiving and the wish prayer in ch. 1, but here we see it again after the first argument in 2.1-12. Here the prayer brings closure to the *refutatio,* provides a transition to the second argument, and energizes the Thessalonians to pray for Paul as well. One could skip from 2.12 to 3.16-18 without noticing anything missing, but all this prayer material in 2.13–3.5 belongs together.

We have seen the wish prayer in 1 Thess. 3.11-13 as a *transitus* to the next argument, and we should do the same here with 2 Thess. 2.16-17. That means that we should see 3.1-5 not as the final argument or peroration but as the final prayer section before the second argument (3.6-13) and the conclusion of the discourse. We could identify 2.13-15 as a brief second argument, as do Wanamaker and Hughes, complete with a final exhortation or even peroration in v. 15.[1] But we can call it only an indirect argument in that the prayer language encourages continued good behavior by the audience. It is better to see it in the pastoral way it was intended, as prayer which surrounds and undergirds the two major arguments of this discourse.

---

1. C. Wanamaker, *Commentary on 1 and 2 Thessalonians* (Grand Rapids: Eerdmans, 1990), pp. 264-66, who is simply following F. W. Hughes, *Early Christian Rhetoric and 2 Thessalonians* (Sheffield: Sheffield Academic, 1986), pp. 68-71.

Thanksgiving/Firm Living — 2.13-15

As Marshall suggests, this whole passage seems to be an antidote to the feelings of uncertainty that were generated by the false teaching about the day of the Lord.[1] It can also be thought of as a rhetorical relief pill after the intensity of the immediately preceding material on the end of things, settling the audience back down and allowing them to breathe again and have a sense that they are all right.[2]

But we ourselves ought always to give thanks to God concerning you, brothers beloved by the Lord, because God himself chose/preferred you, firstfruits[3] for salvation through sanctification of spirit and trust of the truth, unto which he also called you through our gospel, unto the acquisition of the glory of our Lord Jesus Christ. So then, brothers, stand firm and keep the tradition which you were taught, whether through word or through our letter.

1. I. H. Marshall, *1 and 2 Thessalonians* (Grand Rapids: Eerdmans, 1983), p. 205.

2. See rightly A. Malherbe, *The Letters to the Thessalonians* (New York: Doubleday, 2000), p. 438.

3. Here we have a classic example of the dilemma created by the Greek manuscripts not using separation of words, accents, or breathing marks. Did the text read *ap' archēs* or *aparchēn*? The former reading has strong support in א, D, K, L, and most minuscules. Against this reading is that it occurs nowhere else in Paul, for whom *archē* is always a word for "power," often supernatural powers (except in Phil. 4.15). By contrast Paul often uses the term "firstfruits," and in metaphorical senses (six places elsewhere than here; e.g., 1 Cor. 15.20-23 of Christ). Furthermore, copyists sometimes changed *aparchēn* to *ap' archēs* (Rev. 14.4; Rom. 16.5; see Metzger, *TC*, p. 6). Finally, one may add a theological argument for *aparchēn*. Elsewhere Paul does not speak of Christians being chosen from before the foundations of the world. Eph. 1.4 is about being chosen in Christ, by which is meant that Christ is chosen by God before the foundations of the world.

V. 13 is nearly identical with 1.3. Reduplication is a regular rhetorical de-vice meant to reinforce certain truths. The stress here, however, is on thanksgiving for God's activity in the converts' lives, whereas in 1.3 the stress was on their virtues. Paul here offers the comfort of the fact that God has cho-sen these converts to be saved in a certain way — through the sanctifying of their spirits and their trust/belief in the truth. This contrasts with what has been said in 2.10 about the perishing and their refusal to love the truth.

. As the translation above suggests, the proper rendering here is probably "firstfruits" (cf. Rom 8.23; 11.16; 16.5; 1 Cor. 15.20, 23; 16.15) rather than "from the beginning" since Paul does not refer elsewhere to a pre-temporal choosing of some to be saved (and others not). Furthermore, he is addressing those who are already Christians and is talking about their future salvation, or, put another way, the completion of the salvation process in their lives. God chose them to be the first converts in this city,[4] and the means by which they are to be saved to the uttermost will be both through the sanctifying work of the Spirit in their inner beings and through their own embrace and trust of the truth. "Through sanctifi-cation . . ." and "through trust . . ." are one phrase following the preposition *en*, which here has the sense of *dia* (through),[5] which in turn makes it all the more likely that both phrases refer to the effects of salvation on the inner person.[6]

An odd word for "elect/choose/take/prefer" is used here, *haireō*, and pos-sibly there is an echo of Deut. 26.17-18 LXX, where the context is one of cove-nanting, not unilateral choice by God. The people have declared that Yahweh is their God, and God has declared that they are his people, his treasured posses-sion. *Haireō* is a NT hapax in this sense, and elsewhere in the NT the cognate is used of human choosing (Phil. 1.22; Heb. 11.25).[7] It is possible that either the Holy Spirit or the human spirit is meant here (on the latter cf. 1 Thess. 5.23; 2 Cor. 7.1), but since "sanctification of spirit" and "trust of the truth" are paral-lel it is likely that Paul is referring to the effect of salvation on the human spirit (cf. 1 Pet. 1.2) and the belief in the truth that resides within the Christian as a re-sult of salvation.[8] It would be possible to translate this sentence "but God pre-

4. B. F. Lightfoot, *Notes on the Epistles of St. Paul* (Winona Lake: Alpha, reprint), p. 120: "The Thessalonians converted on his first visit (of which he speaks elsewhere as *archē tou euangeliou*, Phil. 4.15) might fairly be classed among the 'firstfruits' of Macedonia. . . ."

5. See Malherbe, *The Letters*, p. 437, and cf. Chrysostom's *Homily* 4 on 2 Thessalonians.

6. See Wanamaker, *1 and 2 Thessalonians*, p. 266.

7. See Lightfoot, *Notes*, p. 119.

8. E. Best, *A Commentary on the First and Second Epistles to the Thessalonians* (London: Black, 1972), pp. 314-15. Also slightly favoring the reference to the human spirit is the absence of the definite article and of "holy." One thing is clear from the way Paul puts things: God's choosing is not equivalent to salvation. Rather salvation is a result of God's preferring or choosing them to be saved in a particular way. There is a connection, and the choosing of course is related to both the means and the end of salvation.

ferred you firstfruits to be saved through the sanctifying of your spirits and trust in the truth."[9] The firstfruits were dedicated to God, and as such were the part that sanctified the whole. So here these firstfruits have been selected to be sanctified in spirit.[10] Paul may thus be playing on the firstfruits metaphor throughout this verse.[11]

V. 14 speaks of calling and the vehicle of calling — Paul's preaching of the gospel in Thessalonike. But it was ultimately God calling through Paul's preaching. It is not just that Paul was speaking for God. Rather, God was speaking through Paul (1 Thess. 1.5).[12] Here as elsewhere in Paul *euangelion* refers to the oral proclamation of the Good News.[13] Only in Irenaeus (*Adversus Haereses* 3.2.8) do we first see this term clearly used in reference to a written Gospel. The aim or purpose of the proclamation was that the converts might one day obtain the glory of Christ (cf. Rom. 8.17-18; 1 Cor. 15.43; 2 Cor. 3.18; Phil. 3.21),[14] a reference to the conclusion of the salvation process.[15] In fact it is a reference to believers obtaining the same glorious embodied condition Jesus himself has as a result of the resurrection (cf. 1 Corinthians 15). It is the very glory of Jesus that they will one day possess, and so they will have been made like him.[16] This

9. But see the discussion in G. Beale, *1 and 2 Thessalonians* (Downers Grove: InterVarsity, 2003), pp. 225-26.

10. But see B. Rigaux, *Les Épitres aux Thessaloniciens* (Paris: Gabalda, 1956), pp. 684-85.

11. See F. F. Bruce, *1 and 2 Thessalonians* (Waco: Word, 1982), p. 190.

12. Here is probably another instance where we see evidence that Paul saw himself as a prophetic figure, a mouthpiece for God. On this see pp. 82-84 above. Totally misinterpreting what is said here is Beale, *1 and 2 Thessalonians*, p. 228, who thinks the calling spoken of here is strictly the internal irresistible work of the Holy Spirit. But the text is perfectly clear: the call comes "through the Good News (i.e., proclamation of the gospel) of *ours*," just as 1 Thess. 1.5 also makes clear.

13. Wanamaker, *1 and 2 Thessalonians*, p. 267: "The Thessalonians were called by God . . . to share in salvation when Paul and his missionary colleagues were visiting their city to preach the gospel."

14. See Best, *First and Second Thessalonians*, p. 316.

15. Lightfoot, *Notes*, p. 121.

16. See rightly Wanamaker, *1 and 2 Thessalonians*, p. 269. Typically, Beale, *1 and 2 Thessalonians*, p. 227 suggests an alternative — namely that God calls persons so that God obtains (even more) glory for Jesus. One has to ask, is this really the way God works? Is God really a glory-grabber or really that egocentric? Surely it is us and not God that lacks glory (Rom. 3.23). Phil. 2.5-11 makes it clear that Jesus already has all the glory he needs, and indeed, far from the glorification of Jesus in the resurrection and his enthronement taking away from the glory of God, it adds to it. God does not need to add to his own or Jesus' glory. Instead as 1 Thess. 2.12 says, he calls believers to share his glory, or, more literally, as it is put there, to enter into God's dominion and glory. Obtaining glory is not in any case a zero-sum game. When humans are glorified in the resurrection this does not subtract from God's glory, but adds to it. Nor does God save human beings simply to increase his own or Jesus' glory quotient. God saves people for the very reason v. 13 mentions — because he loves us.

phrase is clearly parallel to 1 Thess. 5.9, which speaks of obtaining salvation through Jesus.[17]

An exhortation (v. 15) brings this thanksgiving prayer to a close and reminds us once more that these are more prayer reports than just prayers since Paul wants the audience to hear them and since he can exhort the audience while reporting the prayer. In other words, God is not the sole audience. Paul has said in 1 Thess. 3.8 that the audience's steadfastness in the faith is his very breath of life. The verb here is in the continuous present tense and means "continue to stand fast," referring to an ongoing vigilance and effort on their part. Only here does Paul use it without an object (cf. 1 Thess. 3.8: "stand fast in the Lord"; 1 Cor. 16.13: "in the faith"; Phil. 1.27: "in one Spirit").[18]

Paul has referred obliquely to his passing along of traditions to the Thessalonians in 1 Thess. 4.1 and this verse here is meant to recall 2 Thess. 2.2. The contrast in expression with that verse makes clear that only here is Paul referring to one of his own letters.[19] These traditions involved a variety of things, including the story of Jesus, as 1 Cor. 11.23-32 and 15.3-8 show.[20]

There seems to have been a distinction between the Good News received by revelation (Gal. 1.12) and received by tradition (1 Cor. 15.3). It is possible that the "letter" here is 1 Thessalonians, though we cannot be sure. "Traditions" seems to apply equally to what was heard orally and to at least some of what was written.[21] The important point is that standing fast is enabled by holding onto, embracing, believing, and keeping the traditions Paul has passed on to the Thessalonians orally and in writing.[22] If, as is likely, we should see this thanksgiving as bringing to a close the section on eschatology, then Paul may be thinking in particular of what he has passed on in regard to the future coming of Jesus and its attendant circumstances.[23]

---

17. See Bruce, *1 and 2 Thessalonians*, p. 191; Rigaux, *Les Épitres*, p. 686.

18. Wanamaker, *1 and 2 Thessalonians*, p. 268.

19. See pp. 213-14 above and Lightfoot, *Notes*, p. 122.

20. Marshall, *1 and 2 Thessalonians*, pp. 209-10.

21. Bruce, *1 and 2 Thessalonians*, p. 193.

22. Malherbe, *The Letters*, p. 440.

23. Wanamaker, *1 and 2 Thessalonians*, pp. 268-69. It is interesting that unlike in the Pastorals (1 Tim. 6.14, 20; 2 Tim. 2.2; Tit. 2.1-2) Paul says nothing here about passing on these traditions, just holding fast to them. Apparently that was a concern of later times. See Best, *First and Second Thessalonians*, p. 318. Paul of course does not have in mind the later Catholic idea of sacred traditions which were not written down. See Rigaux, *Les Épitres*, pp. 688-89.

A Closer Look: On Doing Theology in Ad Hoc Letters

The discussion of Pauline theology has been bedeviled by a variety of methodological problems, not the least of which is the tendency to treat Paul's letters as if they were either theological compendia or discrete theological exercises. Equally problematic is the attempt to discern some sort of evolutionary spiral of Paul's views, as if 1 and 2 Thessalonians represented the "early" and perhaps more capricious eschatologically-oriented Paul, while letters such as Philippians represent a more sober and realistic Paul. All such conjectures overlook some factors of decisive importance: (1) 1 Thessalonians does not represent the early Paul. By the time this letter was written Paul had been a Christian for a least a decade and a half if not more. Nor does it represent his nascent attempts to found churches, since it was written during Paul's so-called "second missionary journey." (2) Future eschatology is certainly just as much in evidence in 1 Corinthians and Romans as it is in 1 or 2 Thessalonians, and it is not absent from Philippians either. The attempt to find development in Paul's eschatological views is problematic at best. Furthermore, there is the issue of the rhetoric Paul is engaging in in a particular letter, which affects how he will express himself. In an epideictic discourse we would expect less focus on the future than in a deliberative discourse, and in fact that is usually how it plays out in Paul's letters. (3) Paul's letters are ad hoc documents. They do not contain his prepackaged theology. They contain his theologizing into specific situations. One has to take this into account at every turn when scrutinizing Paul's theological views. From a rhetorical point of view one proper question to ask as a starting point is how God or Christ fits into the stories Paul is telling in the narration portion of his letters. Paul theologizes out of and into a storied world, and it is important to analyze what roles he sees the divine playing in that world.

As Richard Hays has frequently pointed out, since theology and ethics are intertwined and interdependent in Paul, it is a mistake to analyze just the more theological remarks in isolation. For example, discussion of holy living and sanctification can focus on what God's Spirit is doing in the community and in the life of the believer or on how the community or individuals are living and behaving. Belief and behavior not merely affect one another but are reciprocals of a sort. Behavior is a working out of what one believes, so the community is to "work out its salvation with fear and trembling, for it is God who works in your midst to will and to do" (Phil. 2.12-13). The indicative is not merely the basis of the imperative but that which makes the imperative capable of being obeyed.

It is of course true that Protestant theologians have been especially leery of too closely identifying the work of God and the human response or speaking of the necessity of the latter in the process of human salvation. Paul, however, had no such qualms, which is not surprising since he was an early Jew and early Jewish thinkers were often more concerned with orthopraxy than orthodoxy. Paul seems equally concerned with both, and he believes that behavior can compromise or express belief. Indeed, he believes, just as other early Jewish thinkers believed, in the danger of apostasy, a theological topic not often discussed in musings about Pauline theology. It is not enough to say that Paul has an understanding of election, God's sovereignty, and God's final vindication of the saints at the second coming, subjects which all come up in the Thessalonian correspondence. The question is: what sort of concept of election, and how does it interact with Paul's ethics, especially the necessity of ethical behavior to final salvation?

In his rhetorically sensitive treatment of Paul's theology, K. P. Donfried observes that Paul responds to changes in the situation and thus, for example, offers up more future eschatology in 2 Thessalonians 2 to correct misunderstandings that may have in part been caused by a misreading of Paul's previous remarks, both when he was in Thessalonike and in 1 Thessalonians.[24] This means that we must be very cautious about reading Paul's letters in a post-Enlightenment history-of-ideas kind of way, looking for development of thought. It may be more of a matter of development of social and rhetorical situation than development of thought.

It is also important when one considers Pauline rhetoric to ask from time to time when Paul is using rhetorical hyperbole or other rhetorical devices. How does this affect his theologizing? His remarks cannot simply be taken flatly at face value. Of course there is some realization of this when Paul moves into a more apocalyptic kind of language such as in 2 Thessalonians 2, but one should always be alert to such things.

One must also be prepared to figure out the implications of Paul's frequent transfer to Christ of language previously applied only to God. The day of the Lord becomes the day of the return of Jesus, who will be the final executor of justice upon the earth. This happens not just occasionally but in all parts of 1 and 2 Thessalonians, beginning in the epistolary prescripts. Therefore, we must say that Paul is thinking of the Lord Jesus in the category of God, not merely as an agent of God. Somehow there has been a Copernican revolution in his thinking about what the terms "God" and "Lord" mean, and Jesus is included within those parameters.

And this Copernican revolution has also affected his thinking about ethics, because Paul honestly and earnestly believes that he and his converts live in the end times. He theologizes to comfort, to encourage, and to galvanize his converts into living in a more Christlike manner. He believes that there will be divine intervention again in the future which will bring final justice and final redemption. He believes that he and his converts stand between the great works of eschatological salvation with Christ's death and resurrection behind them and Christ's return before them. To place too much emphasis on only one of these poles is a mistake when it comes to Pauline theology, for Paul never gave up his blessed hope for the eschatological future.

J. M. Bassler, in her response to the writings of R. Jewett, E. Krentz, and E. Richard on the theology of the Thessalonian letters, remarks that these letters seem an odd

---

24. His treatment in *The Theology of the Shorter Pauline Letters* (with I. H. Marshall; Cambridge: Cambridge University Press, 1993), pp. 3-104 is certainly the best available in English that is sensitive to the contextual issues.

place to begin a quest for Paul's theology.[25] I disagree. They are an excellent place to begin for they remind us that not only does Paul do his theologizing in ad hoc letters, he does it in pastoral letters and in doxological contexts. He is no armchair theologian pondering out the meaning of theological minutiae. He is, rather, doing his best pastorally to shore up the beliefs and behavior of his converts so that they can endure as part of a countercultural movement under pressure and persecution. He deliberately draws on imperial rhetoric in his theological expressions and transferring it to Christ and the Lawless One because he believes that only Jesus is truly Lord and that the emperor has no right to command absolute allegiance, much less worship. Paul expects his letters to be read, indeed to be orally and rhetorically delivered in worship services, which is to say in the context of much prayer, singing, worship, and fellowship of various sorts. His theologizing in these letters is surrounded by and indeed bathed in prayers of thanksgiving, wish prayers, prayer reports, benedictions, and the like. There is a profound theology of trust and reliance on the Almighty in these sections of the letters which some have ignored as untheological. This is a huge mistake.

Paul is a pastoral theologian who lives what he preaches and believes what he says. Experience, not just understanding, is the basis of expression in so much of what he says. However uncomfortable some of us may be with this, it is still an essential feature to understanding Paul's theology. Nor should we overlook how much worship and Christian experience was the matrix out of which much Christian theological reflection in general came, as the recent studies of L. Hurtado and R. L. Wilken have reminded us.[26] One can only hope that these things will be better taken into account in the future when the subject is Pauline theology.

---

25. J. M. Bassler, "Peace in All Ways," in Bassler, ed., *Pauline Theology* I: *Thessalonians, Philippians, Galatians, Philemon* (Minneapolis: Fortress, 1991), p. 71.

26. R. L. Wilken, *The Spirit of Early Christian Thought: Seeking the Face of God* (New Haven: Yale University Press, 2003); L. Hurtado, *Lord Jesus Christ: Devotion to Jesus in Earliest Christianity* (Grand Rapids: Eerdmans, 2003).

Transitus: Another Wish Prayer — 2.16-17

This wish prayer looks back to the blessed hope Paul has been speaking of and forward to the exhortation about Christian deeds and words which is yet to come. It thus serves as something of a transitional section in the discourse. It is also nicely situated in the prayer section of the discourse which involves both the previous and the immediately following pericopes. That we are on the right track in viewing the structure this way, and in light of the structure of 1 Thessalonians, is shown by the fact that this passage is followed by the same sort of "final" request as in 1 Thessalonians (cf. 2 Thess. 3.1 to 1 Thess. 4.1).[1] The hortatory portion of the discourse does not really begin until 2 Thess. 3.6.

But may our Lord himself, Jesus Christ, and God our Father, the One who loved us and gave unfailing encouragement and good hope in grace, encourage your hearts and strengthen you in all works and good words.

We have in v. 16 a compound subject — the Lord and the Father act in concert. "For Paul, God and Christ together are the source of spiritual blessing."[2] The *autos* which begins the sentence is emphatic ("the Lord himself . . ."), and this seems to be a regular way to start a wish prayer (cf. 1 Thess. 3.11; 5.23; 2 Thess. 3.16).[3] The verb "has loved" is in the aorist here, perhaps alluding to a particular event in the past — the Christ event and especially the death of Christ.[4] But the verb that follows, "has given," is also aorist.

---

1. See J. B. Lightfoot, *Notes on the Epistles of St. Paul* (Winona Lake: Alpha, reprint), p. 122.
2. I. H. Marshall, *1 and 2 Thessalonians* (Grand Rapids: Eerdmans, 1983), p. 211.
3. See F. F. Bruce, *1 and 2 Thessalonians* (Waco: Word, 1982), p. 195.
4. See A. Malherbe, *The Letters to the Thessalonians* (New York: Doubleday, 2000), p. 442.

In a wish prayer such as this it is perhaps more likely that the aorist is used in a final sense, simply stating what has been and is the state of affairs. God has not stopped loving or giving. What God has given is both eternal or inexhaustible[5] encouragement or comfort[6] and good hope (cf. Rom. 15.4), two things much in demand by the Thessalonians, who have been persecuted and have lost loved ones. The phrase "eternal encouragement" is Paul's own, but he adds a phrase familiar to his audience:[7] "good hope" is not found elsewhere in the Greek Bible but is found in texts, inscriptions, and epitaphs as a way Greco-Roman people expressed their hope for a good afterlife (cf. Julian, *Epistles* 20.452C).[8] It refers back to the preceding discussion of the eternal future of the Thessalonians, which gives them hope. Lest we think that they have earned this future Paul adds "by grace." These gifts reflect the character of the giver rather than the merits of the recipients.[9] On the sequence of "encouragement and hope" one can compare Rom. 15.4-5 and 2 Cor. 1.3-11.

As v. 17 puts it, these gifts are meant to encourage their hearts, but also to ground them and establish them in every good work and word. This foreshadows the subject matter of the argument coming in ch. 3 about work. Like Moses in Acts 7.22, they are called to be powerful in deeds and words (cf. Luke 24.19). The repetition of "good" here is for emphasis.[10] "They have been given a good hope (v. 16) but they are not to let their minds linger on this and neglect their ordinary and everyday duties; a good hope ought to work itself out in a good life."[11] Or, put in other terms, God encourages these believers in part so that they will be stimulated to godly behavior.[12] Just as Timothy was sent to establish and encourage the Thessalonians (1 Thess. 3.2), so now God is invoked to do the same directly.[13]

---

5. So Lightfoot, *Notes*, p. 122.

6. *Paraklēsis* can mean either, and in view of the circumstances of the Thessalonians the nuance of comfort may be to the fore here. See Marshall, *1 and 2 Thessalonians*, p. 211, who in any case is surely right that "consolation" is not the appropriate translation here. Paul is talking about a blessing experienced within the believer's heart, as is shown by the word "hope" as well.

7. See E. Best, *A Commentary on the First and Second Epistles to the Thessalonians* (London: Black, 1972), p. 321.

8. For example, in the cult of Demeter and Persephone. See P. Otzen, "'Gute Hoffnung' bei Paulus," *ZNW* 49 (1958): 283-85.

9. See Lightfoot, *Notes*, p. 123.

10. A. Malherbe, *The Letters to the Thessalonians* (New York: Doubleday, 2000), p. 442.

11. Best, *First and Second Thessalonians*, p. 322.

12. C. Wanamaker, *Commentary on 1 and 2 Thessalonians* (Grand Rapids: Eerdmans, 1990), p. 272.

13. See B. Rigaux, *Les Épitres aux Thessaloniciens* (Paris: Gabalda, 1956), pp. 691-92.

Final Request — 3.1-5

The prayer mode of discourse continues with an imperative for the audience to pray for the apostle (v. 1) and another wish prayer (v. 5). In both form and diction this material continues the pattern of imitating or echoing some of the material in 1 Thessalonians, but it also prepares us for the second and last major argument of the letter in vv. 6-13.[1] Jewett is surely right that the *exhortatio* does not begin until v. 6 and thus that vv. 1-5 should be seen as the "final" section of this prayer interlude between arguments.[2] In this case *to loipon* introduces the last section of the three-part prayer segment,[3] not the final argument or exhortation itself.[4] The style of this material is somewhat rough, which is just one more good reason not to think of this letter as composed by a slavish imitator of Paul. Who would imitate Paul's lapses from good form?[5]

Finally, pray, brothers, for us, that the word of the Lord will make rapid strides and be honored/glorified just as it was among you, also that we may be delivered from perverse and evil persons, for not all are of the faith/to be trusted. But faithful is the Lord, who strengthens you and guards you from the Evil One. But we have been persuaded in the Lord about you, that what we commanded and you are doing,

1. A. Smith, "2 Thessalonians," in *The New Interpreter's Bible*, vol. XI, ed. L. E. Keck (Nashville: Abingdon, 2000), p. 764.
2. R. Jewett, *The Thessalonian Correspondence: Pauline Rhetoric and Millenarian Piety* (Philadelphia: Fortress, 1986), pp. 81-87.
3. Rigaux, *Les Épitres aux Thessaloniciens* (Paris: Gabalda, 1956), p. 693.
4. Against, Wanamaker, *Commentary on 1 and 2 Thessalonians* (Grand Rapids: Eerdmans, 1990), p. 273. It could even mean "for the remainder (of your prayers) remember us . . ." if we take *loipon* more literally than literarily.
5. With Wanamaker, *1 and 2 Thessalonians*, p. 273.

you also will go on doing. But may the Lord direct/straighten out your hearts unto the love of God and the endurance of Christ.

"Brothers, pray for us" seems to be imitating 1 Thess. 5.25, but there the content of the prayer is not indicated. The imperative in v. 1 is to pray that the Word of God[6] will both run swiftly (probably echoing Ps. 147.15 LXX) and be glorified everywhere, that is, be received and praised and honored everywhere, just as it already is among the Thessalonian converts. Thus Paul speaks of both the rapid spread of the proclamation and also its ubiquitous reception. This is no small prayer request. There is probably an echo of the Isthmian games here, which Paul probably witnessed while in Corinth: runners run so they may be honored or glorified by the crowd and the judges when they finish first in the race (cf. 1 Cor. 9.24; Gal. 2.2; Phil. 2.16).[7] Chrysostom says that Paul speaks of a race that is run unhindered (*Homily* 4 on 2 Thessalonians). Acts 13.48 is a close parallel in that it speaks of the glorifying of God's Word. Here alone Paul uses the running metaphor not of himself but of an impersonal subject, his message. There is perhaps also an echo of Wis. 7.24, where wisdom is said to run swiftly.

The second request (v. 2) is more personal: that Paul may be delivered from wicked and evil people who have no faith. If Paul was still in Corinth this may give us a clue to when he wrote this letter, as his trial before Gallio took place probably in late 51 or in 52 at the latest.[8] Paul may then have written this letter just before his trial, at which he was indeed delivered from his adversaries, in this case some Jewish opponents of the gospel, and was able to stay a bit longer in Corinth before heading east.[9] This conclusion is supported by what Paul has said in 1 Thess. 2.14-16.[10]

6. Here again synonymous with the gospel Paul is preaching. See pp. 73 and 136-37 above on 1 Thess. 1.8 and 4.15.

7. See G. Beale, *1 and 2 Thessalonians* (Downers Grove: InterVarsity, 2003), p. 237.

8. See B. Witherington, *The Acts of the Apostles* (Grand Rapids: Eerdmans, 2004), pp. 83-84.

9. I. H. Marshall, *1 and 2 Thessalonians* (Grand Rapids: Eerdmans, 1983), pp. 214-15 is surely right that Jewish opposition is likely in mind considering what we know from Acts 18 about Paul's time in Corinth. The attempt by Beale and others to see Christian false teachers being labeled here as evil is forced. Paul is not dealing with in-house opposition to any real extent in either 1 or 2 Thessalonians. The issue is an external source of pressure, persecution, and opposition finally consummated in the Lawless One, who clearly is not and never was a believer. As J. B. Lightfoot, *Notes on the Epistles of St. Paul* (Winona Lake: Alpha, reprint), p. 125 stresses, outsiders are meant, and it is arbitrary and not well-grounded in the text to find here a statement that not all who profess to be Christians are genuine Christians. See rightly E. Best, *A Commentary on the First and Second Epistles to the Thessalonians* (London: Black, 1972), p. 326 on who the opponents are here.

10. See Malherbe, *The Letters to the Thessalonians* (New York: Doubleday, 2000), p. 444.

We have a very similar request in 2 Cor. 1.8-11 (cf. also 2 Cor. 11.23-25; Rom. 15.31). Paul's language in a general sense sounds a note much like that of the psalmist (cf. Ps. 139[140].1; Isa. 25.4). The passive voice of "delivered" makes it clear that it is God whom Paul is looking to to provide deliverance.[11] Paul's view is that opposing the gospel is an act of "evil," not just ignorance. "Evil" is coupled with *atopos,* which literally means "out of place" and thus outrageous or perverse (cf. Luke 23.41; Acts 25.5; 28.6; Job 27.6; 34.12; 36.21; Prov. 30.20 LXX; Philo, *Legum Allegoriae* 3.53).[12] Actions against God's Word and emissary are out of place.[13] While there are perhaps some polemics involved, Paul is not just flexing his rhetorical muscles here. He really did face considerable and concerted opposition in Corinth and elsewhere. The final clause of the verse says that faith is not the response of all to the gospel. One may compare Rom. 10.16, where Paul says that not all have obeyed the gospel.[14]

In both content and tone vv. 3-4 foreshadow the final exhortation in vv. 6-13. There is, for instance, the concern about "doing" (see below on v. 13) and the issue of thoughtful concern for other believers (see below on vv. 7-9). Idleness is unacceptable when a fledgling church is facing such external difficulties.[15]

V. 3 stresses that while not all have faith, the Lord himself is always faithful, which echoes 1 Thess. 5.24 (cf. 2 Tim. 2.13). 1 Thess. 3.13 spoke of the converts' hearts being established, but here it is simply the converts who are said to be established (cf. 2 Thess. 2.17). There is also a promise that the Lord will guard them from evil (or more likely "the Evil One," in light of the definite article here and the apocalyptic tone of ch. 2; see John 17.15).[16] The verbs here should be seen as having ongoing force: the Lord will continue to strengthen and continue to guard.[17] "He will not only place you in a firm position, but also maintain you there against assaults from without."[18] Paul does not pray that they will be free from trials but that God will establish and strengthen them in the midst of trials so that they can endure them.[19] What Paul prayed for in 2.17 he is now confident of here.[20]

Paul has been persuaded in the Lord (v. 4; cf. Gal. 5.10; Rom. 14.14; Phil.

11. Wanamaker, *1 and 2 Thessalonians,* p. 275.

12. See Lightfoot, *Notes,* p. 125.

13. Beale, *1 and 2 Thessalonians,* p. 239.

14. F. F. Bruce, *1 and 2 Thessalonians* (Waco: Word, 1982), pp. 197-98.

15. Smith, "2 Thessalonians," p. 765. Beale's attempt (*1 and 2 Thessalonians,* pp. 244-46) to turn this into a discourse on perseverance of the saints engineered entirely by God totally misses the connections with what follows in 3.6-13.

16. We may have an echo of a saying of Jesus from the Lord's Prayer (Matt. 6.13). See the lengthy discussion in Lightfoot, *Notes,* pp. 126-27; Bruce, *1 and 2 Thessalonians,* p. 200.

17. Wanamaker, *1 and 2 Thessalonians,* p. 276.

18. Lightfoot, *Notes,* p. 125.

19. Best, *First and Second Thessalonians,* p. 327.

20. Malherbe, *The Letters,* p. 445.

2.24) concerning the audience that they are doing and will do (see 1 Thess. 4.1)[21] what needs to be done, that which Paul has commanded and charged them to do.[22] Paul has confidence in both the Lord and the Lord's work in the Thessalonian community.[23] Paul thus quickly turns from a request for himself to once more showing concern for his converts.[24] He indirectly commands the audience by speaking of confidence that they will act accordingly.[25] He usually speaks of "command" (*parangelia*; cf. 1 Thess. 4.1) when it comes to ethics or matters of church praxis.[26]

All of this prepares for Paul's exercise of his apostolic authority with more than one command in the following argument, for he knows that there is a problem in Thessalonike in regard to work. Some were carrying out his precepts on "doing," some were not. The situation required a remedy. As Wanamaker stresses, Paul is creating pathos here in his audience so that they will be emotionally inclined to hear and heed the final exhortation which follows.[27]

V. 5 presents us with one more final wish prayer before the last argument or act of persuasion. God is at work in the hearts of the Thessalonians, and here Paul prays that God will guide or direct their hearts (cf. 2 Chron. 12.14; 19.13; 20.33; Sir. 49.5) into "the love of God and the perseverance of Christ." Are these two genitive phrases objective or subjective? That is, is the subject just divine activity or human emulation of God's love and Christ's steadfastness/perseverance? God is clearly asked to guide here, that much is very clear. It is likely that "the love of God" here, as in 2 Cor. 13.13; Rom. 5.5; 8.32, is God's own love, but where is the locus of this love — in God or in the hearts of the Thessalonians? Rom. 5.5 surely suggests that the locus is the hearts of the Thessalonians. Thus Paul is indeed praying that his audience will behave such that they manifest the love of God in their community.[28]

Likewise, he is urging them to show the same steadfastness, perseverance, faithfulness, endurance as Christ.[29] This is not about Christ persevering with them, but rather their persevering or enduring like Christ, precisely because God has instilled in them the love and perseverance to do so.[30] It is God who is

---

21. Rigaux, *Les Épitres*, p. 698.

22. The tense of the verb here is perfect and does not favor the translation "confident." It is one thing to say "I have been persuaded," another to say "I have been confident," which might instill doubt rather than encouragement, which is the intent here.

23. Lightfoot, *Notes*, p. 127.

24. Marshall, *1 and 2 Thessalonians*, p. 215.

25. Marshall, *1 and 2 Thessalonians*, p. 216.

26. See Malherbe, *The Letters*, p. 446.

27. Wanamaker, *First and Second Thessalonians*, p. 278.

28. See Bruce, *1 and 2 Thessalonians*, p. 202.

29. See the discussion in Rigaux, *Les Épitres*, p. 700.

30. Of course they are directed into this love and steadfastness by God, and of course

directing (and enabling) their hearts into manifesting such divine qualities. Read this way, this verse is the perfect transition into the final argument in vv. 6-13. Strongly in favor of the translation "endurance" here is that this is what *hypomonē* means in 1 Thess. 1.3 and 2 Thess. 1.4. "The context necessitates that v. 5 encourage obedience in areas of Christian behavior."[31] Best suggests that the text is either referring to taking Christ's endurance as an example (cf. Jas. 5.11) or receiving the steadfastness he imparts.[32] There is no reason it cannot be both — they have been enabled by God's work in their hearts to emulate these divine traits (cf. Rom. 15.5). Lightfoot says it best: "Thus then *hē agapē tou Theou* here will signify 'the love of God,' not only as an objective attribute of deity, but as a ruling principle in our hearts."[33] Rigaux takes things a step further and sees here a call for the Thessalonians to take their share of the sufferings of Christ with endurance and patience (cf. 2 Cor. 1.5).[34] This, too, gives a logical sense in light of the context of persecution.[35]

---

they can and must rely on God's love and steadfastness, but the focus here is on their behavior, as the previous clause about doing and continuing to do shows. But see Malherbe, *The Letters*, p. 446.

31. Wanamaker, *1 and 2 Thessalonians*, p. 279.

32. Best, *First and Second Thessalonians*, p. 330.

33. Lightfoot, *Notes*, p. 128. In other words Paul, as Lightfoot suggests, may be taking advantage of the ambiguity of the phrase to offer a double sense.

34. Rigaux, *Les Épitres*, p. 700.

35. See Marshall, *1 and 2 Thessalonians*, p. 218.

Working Hypothesis — 3.6-12

Paul's arguments are sometimes theologically oriented and sometimes more ethically oriented. This last argument of 2 Thessalonians is clearly of the latter sort. 3.6 begins very much like 2.1, signaling the start of a new thematic and rhetorical section of the discourse. This is indeed a problem-solving discourse dealing with two very different issues: misinformation in regard to eschatology, dealt with at length in ch. 2, and misbehavior on the part of some Thessalonians, dealt with here. Almost everything else in this letter is some form of prayer. It may be true, as Wanamaker suggests, that this letter was written in haste to deal with the two aforementioned problems, which could explain its brevity and also some of its roughness of style and grammar.[1]

Attempts to connect the problem of idleness with the problem of eschatology fail to recognize that Paul deliberately separates these two issues by three segments of prayer. Furthermore, many have failed to pick up the rhetorical signals that make the two arguments in this letter quite different. The first is a rebuttal of some sort of false understanding or teaching, but the argument we find in ch. 3 is of a very different sort.[2] It is a correction of a certain kind of behavior, and the form of argument is *exhortatio* with the usual appeals to authority that characterize such rhetoric. Before detailed discussion of this section, then, two things, then, must be sorted out: (1) rhetorical analysis of what is going on in this argument and (2) analysis of the social problem and situation that Paul is addressing here.

---

1. C. Wanamaker, *Commentary on 1 and 2 Thessalonians* (Grand Rapids: Eerdmans, 1990), p. 280.

2. For a sound refutation of the connecting of eschatology and idleness in these letters see R. Russell, "The Idle in 2 Thess. 3.6-12: An Eschatological or a Social Problem?" *NTS* 34 (1988): 105-19.

In a deliberative argument such as we have in 2 Thessalonians or, for example, in Galatians (where a similar note is struck about the need for each Christian to work in 6.1-10),[3] it is not unusual to end the discourse with an exhortation. We see this same phenomenon in some of the orations of Demosthenes such as the one on concord included in *Epistle* 1.[4] Demosthenes closely links the concluding *peroratio* with a final exhortation which comes next. In the *peroratio* Demosthenes trots out the example of Alexander and argues that the key to his success was hard work — activity rather than inactivity. This is the same sort of rhetorical argument that Paul will make in both his final argument and in the final peroration at 3.13-15, which follows the argument on work and recapitulates and amplifies that argument.

There is then some precedent here for what Paul is doing, a precedent unlikely to be lost on Thessalonians, whose city was named after Alexander's half-sister[5] and who cherished the Alexandrian Greek tradition and knew well its legacy. It is hard to doubt that they would have known of Demosthenes' famous oration on concord. There is then some real rhetorical precedent not only for offering an exhortation but for raising the issue of activity or work at the close of a deliberative discourse. Perhaps Paul was counting on his audience's familiarity with such an argument to add extra clout to his argument here.

There is much that is pertinent to our discussion in what Aristotle has to say about arguing about ethics and the need to use deliberative rhetoric to that end (*Rhetoric* 1.1354a3-6). For example, Aristotle says that in order to be convincing when arguing about ethics, skill in rhetoric is necessary. Persuasion about ideas is one thing, persuasion about behavior something altogether different and often more difficult (1355b25-26). Two things are especially crucial in an argument about ethics that attempts to change longstanding behavior: the ethical behavior and ethos of the speaker himself (1377b28-78a19) and the authority of the speaker. As Quintilian insists, "what really carries greatest weight in deliberative speeches is the authority of the speaker" (*Inst. Or.* 3.8.12). It is no accident that not only by his conduct when present but also in his reminder of that conduct already in 1 Thess. 2.9[6] Paul has built up his own example and ethos in preparation for just the sort of argument which follows here, where again he will argue from his own behavior as a model for that of the audience. Paul's appeal to his authority is precisely what one would expect in such delib-

---

3. See B. Witherington, *Grace in Galatia* (Grand Rapids: Eerdmans, 1998), pp. 417-38.

4. See the detailed discussion in F. W. Hughes, *Early Christian Rhetoric and 2 Thessalonians* (Sheffield: Sheffield Academic, 1986), pp. 43-50.

5. See pp. 1-5 above.

6. On which see pp. 81-82 above. This is another small argument that it is likely that 1 Thessalonians preceded 2 Thessalonians, or else Paul would have to reestablish his own behavior as a model in this letter in order to effectively make this argument.

erative oratory about behavior. The time has come to insist on proper behavior in this matter lest the community be divided while under pressure.

The question of the ethos of a fledgling community like that of the Christians in Thessalonike and the sort of work ethic and character traits or virtues it was cultivating was an important one for those trained in the rhetorical tradition, as Paul surely was. This was so because a rhetor knew that a new community, especially a new religious community, would be judged primarily on the basis of its behavior — the tree would be judged by the fruit it bore, especially for a proselytizing religion like Christianity. Above all, concrete acts of misbehavior had to be recognized, identified, and corrected if the witness of the community was not to be spoiled.[7]

I would suggest that here, as in Galatians 5–6, Paul is drawing on familiar discussions in Aristotle about ethics, ethos, rhetoric, and in this case the ethics of work (see *Politics* 3.13.12B4a and Paul's quotation of it in Gal. 5.23). The topos he is focusing on here is idleness (a form of disorderly behavior for a Christian) and work, and Paul will follow the deliberative rhetorical strategy of appealing to the need for equity as honorable behavior: all should work if they wish to eat (see *Inst. Or.* 3.8.26 on equity). Honorable behavior was supposed to take precedence over that which is merely convenient, pleasurable, or expedient. Paul then is appealing to the highest ethical values already extant in this Greek city (see *Inst. Or.* 3.8.32-33). More could be said along these lines, but this is enough to show that Paul is following in the footsteps of those who have argued and persuaded on this sort of subject before.

What, however, of the social situation? Here we are helped by the work of E. A. Judge, B. Winter, and others.[8] Winter paints a detailed picture of a situation where, especially during persecution, Christians should seek to live quietly, and this meant not getting caught up in the obligations of clients to patrons, including political and civic obligations. The alternative was to work with one's hands and not be dependent on a patron for one's daily bread and living expenses. There was, as Winter shows, a long tradition going back to Plato that Paul is alluding to here. Plato insists that the virtuous person follow "this principle of doing one's own business" (*Republic* 433A-B). Indeed Plato says there that there was a popular adage that "to do one's own business *(to ta autou prattein)* and not be a busybody is just." In *Gorgias* 526C Plato praises Callicles for being a private man who minded his own business and was not a busybody.

As Winter points out, often the very reason that a client established a relationship with a patron was to avoid attending to the day-to-day affairs of their own lives so as to be an advocate and aide for the patron in various ways. "The extra-biblical examples . . . record the juxtaposition of 'minding one's own

---

7. See my discussion in *Grace in Galatia*, pp. 390-91.
8. See Russell, "The Idle in 2 Thess. 3.6-12."

business' with 'being a busybody.' These concepts clearly refer to *politeia*. Paul makes the same nexus in his subsequent discussion in 2 Thess. 3:11."[9] Paul's great concern is that Christians live in a way that commends itself to outsiders (see 1 Thess. 4.12) and does not simply fit into the social nexus of sponges, syco-phants, and hangers on and the patrons who support them. If prominent Christians were behaving like such, it would bring no credit to the community which was supposed to be modeled on equity and self-sacrificial behavior.

It is possible as well, as Winter goes on to say, that the effects of the fam-ine which hit the Greco-Roman world hard in A.D. 51 was also in play in Thessalonike, leading some to live off of whatever dole they could find or re-turn to a life of clientage.[10] In other words, 2 Thessalonians is written after the real effects of the famine had hit, and more needed to be said about work in this serious situation. These sort of reflections remind us once more, if we needed a reminder, that Paul is not firing off general ethical maxims at the end of his let-ters but speaking into quite specific social situations, even if we cannot always deduce precisely what that situation was.

The social scenario we are envisioning is, then, as follows: First, there is pressure and some periodic persecution affecting Christians in Thessalonike. When 2 Thessalonians is written this is still going on, though there appears to have been a lull when 1 Thessalonians was written. Second, this letter is written in haste to shore up the vulnerable areas and correct both a theological problem and an ethical problem, because the tiny community could not afford to frag-ment in view of the social animus against it.

Third, socially there are both elite and non-elite persons in this Christian community, and various of the non-elite persons are used to being clients of patrons, with perhaps some Christian patrons and perhaps some non-Christian patrons as well. Some of the urban poor in the congregation may well be living off the graciousness of some Christians, but is it really likely that these folks would simply refuse to work? Such a refusal was more likely from those used to be clients, a little higher up the status chain.[11] Paul had begun to sort this problem out when he was there, and he took it a step further when he wrote 1 Thessalonians. But now it must be dealt with head on, even to the point of ad-vising the shunning of a few Christians who will not work and support them-selves. Rhetorically speaking one's last argument is what one wants ringing in the audience's ears as they contemplate a response, and so it is clear that this ethical issue is of paramount importance to Paul at this juncture.

Fourth, the situation may have been exacerbated by a broader problem

---

9. B. Winter, *Seek the Welfare of the City* (Grand Rapids: Eerdmans, 1994), pp. 46-51, here p. 50.

10. Winter, *Seek the Welfare of the City,* pp. 54-57.

11. See the discussion in Russell, "The Idle in 2 Thess. 3.6-12," pp. 108-11.

especially affecting the non-elites, namely famine and the resulting food short-ages.[12] There may in fact be a clue about this in Acts 17.5, which refers to the "agora men." This suggests a situation in which a variety of people are out of work, and in the competition for the jobs of artisans and the like there would be an extra reason not to employ members of Paul's audience — they were part of a despised eastern religious cult. Perhaps, then, some Christians had turned to other Christians, and to non-Christians as well, for help by volunteering to be clients.

Fifth, Paul's larger concerns about this situation are that patronage situations create entangling alliances which are ethically compromising. For example, a client might be required to go to a ceremony at the temple of the imperial cult or make a sacrifice at one of the longstanding Greco-Roman temples in Thessa-lonike, thus compromising their exclusive allegiance to the biblical God (see 1 Co-rinthians 8–10). A client might in addition be expected to dine in pagan temples, where the meals were believed to be hosted by the resident deities, in order to be involved in business deals or campaigning and improving the honor rating of the patron in various ways. These sort of situations were deleterious to a Christian's theological and ethical commitments, and Paul wants them stopped.

And sixth, Paul may have felt some urgency about this matter, being in Corinth and seeing quite clearly firsthand what those sorts of compromising relationships were doing to his new converts there (again see 1 Corinthians 8–10). It was hard enough to resocialize adults into a new religious allegiance without having the added problem of strong temptations to go back to old pat-terns of living and behavior brought on by external pressure and the need to put food on the table.

But we charge you brothers, in the name of the Lord Jesus Christ to stay away from all of the brothers living in a disorderly/undisciplined way, and not according to the tradition which they received[13] *from us. For you yourselves know how it is nec-essary to imitate us, because we were not idle/undisciplined among you. Nor did we eat bread without payment at any of your houses, but in labor and toil night and day we were working in order not to burden any of you. Not that we did not have the authority/right, but in order that we ourselves might give you an exam-ple/model unto your imitating us. For also, when we were with you, we charged*

12. On the social effect of such conditions see P. Garnsey, *Famine and Food Supply in the Graeco-Roman World: Responses to Risk and Crisis* (Cambridge: Cambridge University Press, 1988).

13. There is a textual issue here. Should we read "you received" (*parelabete*) with B, F, G, 104, and others or "they received" (*parelabosan*) with ℵ, A, and others? Probably the less common and more surprising third person reading is correct. See Metzger, *TC*, p. 636. Paul is claiming that those who are idle have personally received the tradition about working and so know better.

you about this, that if anyone did not wish to work, neither should he eat. For we hear that some are living among you in disorderly fashion/idleness, not working but rather meddling. But such persons we charge and beseech in the Lord Jesus Christ that with quietness they be working to eat their own bread.

From stem to stern this argument or exhortation is about work and the need to follow Paul's example in working. The call for imitation was not only appropriate but common in deliberative rhetoric, and Paul avails himself of this rhetorical strategy here. He will not ask his converts to do anything he himself has not first modeled. In general he never brings up autobiographical things about his past or previous conduct except as part of persuading his audience to do something — in this case to go and do likewise.[14] It was the conviction of rhetors and sages that much hinged on the character and model of one's teacher. Mimesis or imitation was seen as an essential way of demonstrating that one had learned the lessons the teacher or rhetor was offering (see Cicero, *De Oratore* 2.87-97).[15] Thus Paul's exhortation here would appear to a largely Gentile audience as the action of a rhetor and/or teacher.

One can detect a certain progression from 1 Thessalonians to 2 Thessalonians on the issue of work and the idleness of some converts in Thessalonike. "What was at the earlier date a vague suspicion is now an ascertained fact. The disorderly conduct of certain members has become patent."[16] It is in this final argument in 2 Thessalonians that we have the most evident echoes of 1 Thessalonians.[17]

The initial charge here in v. 6 is a command backed up by the authority of Jesus himself (cf. 1 Cor. 5.4; Ignatius, *Polycarp* 5).[18] To disobey is to disobey the Lord himself.[19] Paul is, in the first instance, addressing those in the congregation who are behaving appropriately. The active verb *stellein* has as its literal sense the furling or rolling up of a sail or the girding up of a robe, but when used metaphorically it conveyed the idea of shrinking back, shunning, staying away from, or just avoiding (see 2 Cor. 8.20; Gal. 2.12; Mal. 2.5 LXX). Shunning is intended to make clear to the disorderly brother that his behavior is inappropriate and unacceptable.

14. On this matter see G. Lyons, *Pauline Autobiography: Toward a New Understanding* (Atlanta: Scholars, 1985).
15. See E. Fantham, "Imitation and Decline: Rhetorical Theory and Practice in the First Century after Christ," *Classical Philology* 73 (1978): 1-16, 102-16.
16. J. B. Lightfoot, *Notes on the Epistles of St. Paul* (Winona Lake: Alpha, reprint), pp. 128-29.
17. A. Smith, "The Second Letter to the Thessalonians," in *The New Interpreter's Bible*, vol. XI, ed. L. E. Keck (Nashville: Abingdon, 2000), p. 767.
18. F. F. Bruce, *1 and 2 Thessalonians* (Waco: Word, 1982), p. 204.
19. Wanamaker, *1 and 2 Thessalonians*, p. 281.

Ataktos comes from the military realm of speech and refers to insubordi-nate or disorderly conduct (cf. Xenophon, *Cyropaedia* 7.2.6; Demosthenes, *Third Olynthiac* 11).[20] Paul has probably chosen this word rather than the ordi-nary word for idleness to indicate that those who are behaving this way are do-ing more than being idle. They are out of order, for Paul has given them all quite specific instructions, even marching orders, with regard to work. Such people are not doing what they ought and are doing what they ought not. Therefore, the translation "idle" covers only half of their offense. They are not being good soldiers in Christ in acting in this way. As Wanamaker adds, in the context of work this word refers to a failure to fulfill one's duties and work obli-gations.

As v. 7 goes on to make clear, Paul has already indicated in the past the importance of following his lead when it comes to work. He includes his own personal example as part of the received tradition passed on to the Thessalo-nians.[21] As he has made clear in 1 Thess. 2.9,[22] he worked hard day and night with his hands when he was in their midst.[23] But here in v. 8 Paul mentions his working as part of a deliberative act of persuasion, appealing for imitation, whereas in the epideictic rhetoric of 1 Thessalonians such an appeal would have had less force and would perhaps even have been seen as inappropriate. In fact, he only appeals for imitation in letters that take the form of deliberative rheto-ric (e.g., 1 Cor. 4.16; 11.1; Phil. 4.9). *Dōrean* as an adverb means "freely," or "for nothing." There may be an echo here of Matt. 10.10: if the laborer deserves his food, then the converse is also true.

Paul states in v. 9 that it was not a matter of his not having the right or au-thority *(exousia)* to ask to be supported as their teacher and apostle (see 1 Cor. 9.3-18, especially v. 15). But he waived that right so as not to get caught up in pa-tronage relationships, something he wants his audience to avoid as well. But he is not content just to set such an example. V. 10 indicates that he gave them a

---

20. G. Beale, *1 and 2 Thessalonians* (Downers Grove: InterVarsity, 2003), pp. 164-65, 249 is quite right to emphasize this.

21. E. Best, *A Commentary on the First and Second Epistles to the Thessalonians* (Lon-don: Black, 1972), pp. 336-38.

22. Wanamaker, *1 and 2 Thessalonians*, p. 284 makes a telling point in that the phrase here is different enough from that in 1 Thess. 2.9, the latter having better grammar, that it is hardly likely that it was just copied by an imitator here from the Pauline original in 1 Thessalonians. The writer of 2 Thessalonians was writing in haste and from memory with-out the exact phrase before him in all likelihood. This is another small point in favor of Pau-line authorship of 2 Thessalonians.

23. On Paul as tentmaker see B. Witherington, *Conflict and Community in Corinth* (Grand Rapids: Eerdmans, 1994), pp. 208-9. This practice may have been also a viable strategy for making converts since there were Olympic style games here as at Isthmia, and various vis-iting people looking for temporary accommodations, such as tents.

maxim on the matter while he was with them.[24] This problem of idleness was a lingering one and had festered by the time 2 Thessalonians was written. Paul the sage had taught them: "if one is not willing to work, neither should they eat" (cf. Gen. 3.9; *Genesis Rabbah* 2.2 on Gen. 1.2; Prov. 10.4). This may well be a popular saying,[25] and Paul may be quoting another such saying in the next verse. Paul's exhortation is directed at those who refuse to work ("those who *will* not work"), not those who are unable to do so nor perhaps those who have been unable to find work in lean times.[26]

The plight of the urban poor in the Greco-Roman world was considerable, especially during famine. Rome had the grain dole, but not all other cities had such assistance for the poor. Those who had no savings to fall back on hired themselves out as day laborers (the "agora men" of Acts 17:5) or sought patronage if they had a skill or a trade. It would appear that Paul is mostly talking about the latter sort of folk in his critique here.[27] The force of his exhortation would presumably have also put a stop to Christians in the community being patrons of such folks.

V. 11 involves a play on words having the root meaning of "work."[28] The example that Quintilian cites of such word-play is similar: that of an orator who "non agere . . . sed satagere" (*Inst. Or.* 6.3.54), who is not merely doing his pleading but is overdoing it. Even closer to Paul's pun is a line in Demosthenes' *Fourth Philippic (soi men ex hon ergaze kai periergaze).*[29] This then may have been a saying familiar to the Thessalonians, making it all that much more rhetorically effective here as advice not just from Paul but also from previous sages.[30] The English translation "they are to be busy, not busybodies" conveys something of the sense, since the latter Greek word here has

24. Notice the imperfect tense of the verb: "we were commanding" or better "we used to command. . . ." See Wanamaker, *1 and 2 Thessalonians,* p. 285.

25. Cf. pseudo-Phocylides, *Sentences* 153: "Work diligently so that you can live from your own means." A. Malherbe, *The Letters to the Thessalonians* (New York: Doubleday, 2000), p. 452 is right that Paul is probably putting the maxim in his own language and not quoting.

26. I. H. Marshall, *1 and 2 Thessalonians* (Grand Rapids: Eerdmans, 1983), p. 224; Wanamaker, *1 and 2 Thessalonians,* p. 286. There was a disdain among the Greco-Roman elite for various forms of manual labor as beneath the dignity of a high-status free person. It is even possible that Paul is critiquing such persons here, but this is less likely than the view suggested in the text. See Best, *First and Second Thessalonians,* p. 338. It is less likely presumably because there were surely very few truly elite persons in this congregation, especially after the persecutions. Acts 17.4 suggests, however, that some high-status women had become Christians in Thessalonike.

27. See Wanamaker, *1 and 2 Thessalonians,* p. 282.

28. See rightly Bruce, *1 and 2 Thessalonians,* p. 207, who calls it *figura etymologica.*

29. Cf. Demosthenes, *Orations* 26.15; 32.28.

30. See B. Rigaux, *Les Épitres aux Thessaloniciens* (Paris: Gabalda, 1956), p. 711.

to do with meddling rather than minding one's own business and working
(cf. 1 Tim. 5.13).

It is not clear how Paul heard of this situation of idleness in Thessalonike,
presumably through some oral report from a Christian who came to Corinth
from Thessalonike. One reason Paul may have been sensitive about this point
and why he set such an example of work is that philosophers were notorious for
being busybodies and also for living off of patrons, whom they served as tutors
or rhetors (cf. Plutarch, *On Being a Busybody* 516A; Lucian, *Icaromenippus* 20;
Dio Chrysostom, *Oration* 80.1). Rebuttals to this charge by philosophers (e.g.,
Epictetus, *Discourses* 3.22.97) show that they were sensitive to this sort of
charge. Paul in any case was determined that no one would suggest such a thing
about him as a teacher and rhetor.[31] It is interesting that Plutarch in the aforementioned tract says that the busybody cannot endure *hēsychia* or quietness
(518E).

In v. 12 Paul charges those in question (cf. 1 Thess. 4.1)[32] to be quiet, settle
down, and earn their own food to eat. The way he puts it suggests that he is ex-
pecting those behaving appropriately to inform the others of this command, as
he calls them "such people" rather than addressing them directly. *Hesychia* refers to quietness, not silence. Paul is reinforcing here what he said in 1 Thess.
4.11. The opposite of meddling in other people's affairs and business is living
quietly and taking care of one's own. It should be noted that Paul is not as hard
on the idle here as he is on the misbehaving in 1 Corinthians 5–6. He does not
suggest they should be excommunicated and he still calls them brothers.
Shunning, then, is a step short of the extreme remedy and is meant to wake up
the idle, it would appear.[33] In order to reinforce and amplify this argument Paul
turns in vv. 13-15 to his peroration.

31. See the helpful discussion in Malherbe, *The Letters*, p. 453.
32. This combination is a strong form of charging or commanding. On connecting the
appeal with an "in order that" clause see 1 Cor. 1.10; 16.12, 15; 2 Cor. 8.6; 12.8; 1 Thess. 4.1.
33. Marshall, *1 and 2 Thessalonians*, p. 220.

Peroratio — 3.13-15 — On Shunning and Shaming without Excommunicating

A peroration could have several different functions. It could recapitulate the major points of a previous discourse (*Inst. Or.* 6.1.1), or it could amplify some particular previous argument (6.1.11) to reinforce a telling point that needed immediate application. The latter is what Paul does in 2 Thess. 3.13-15.

Almost always a peroration would use emotive language or an appeal to the deeper emotions, and this is evident here where Paul asks the portion of his audience that is behaving well to avoid the idle, while not treating them as non-believers or enemies. He is trying to arouse his audience to action without prompting them to over-do it. What he counsels is a difficult line to walk, especially if those to be shunned were family members or close friends. But here at the end Paul speaks of an isolated offender, of one person who is acting in this manner, and so seems to assume that this is an isolated problem. The appeal to avoid or to "shame" would prompt or stir up a variety of emotions and might even set into motion enmity conventions of various sorts. Shaming in an honor and shame culture could be a very effective behavior modification technique, but it would also arouse deep emotions and usually controversy.

The wisdom of Quintilian was that whichever form of peroration one chose, it needed to be succinct and to the point (*Inst. Or.* 6.1.2). Paul must insist on the exercise of discipline, but as a pastor he wants the erring person to be treated as still a brother. This mixture of justice and mercy at the end of the discourse should have stirred up feelings of admiration in the audience for Paul's even-handedness, for in fact he is the judge here, but he must persuade those enduring trials to behave in a specifically Christian manner despite their natural inclinations. This required no little skill in persuasion.

But for you brothers, do not slack off from/grow tired of well-doing. But if anyone does not obey our word through this letter, take note of this one, do not associate with him, in order that he might feel ashamed, but also do not regard him as an enemy, but admonish him as a brother.

At the close of this brief exhortation Paul returns to speaking to the majority of his audience, whom he now addresses directly. While v. 13 is transitional, looking backward and forward, we should probably see the return to address to the majority as the signal that we have reached the peroration. "You" at the beginning of the verse is emphatic. He urges them not to grow weary in well-doing,[1] or in acting in an honorable way. As Marshall points out the key term here means "treat well" (cf. Matt. 12.12; Luke 6.27; Acts 10.33; Gal. 6.9; Phil. 4.14).[2] It is possible that Paul says this out of concern that what he has just said might stifle real and much-needed charity and acts of compassion. In any case the working and orderly behavior of those he addresses is primarily in focus. They must set an example for the others.[3]

In v. 14 Paul asks not the leaders but the congregation as a whole to take note of or mark down the misbehaving (cf. *1 Clement* 43.1). Perhaps the leadership structures are not yet well developed (but see 1 Thess. 5.12), but more likely he wants the community to act in concert on this matter.[4] The advice here returns to that given at the beginning of the last argument in 3.6.[5] It is not clear how singling out the offender would take place, perhaps in the congregational meeting (cf. 1 Cor. 5.4, 12; 2 Cor. 2.5-11).[6]

What precisely does it mean not to associate with someone? The only other occurrence of the verb *synanamignysthai* in the NT is in 1 Cor. 5.9. In 1 Cor. 5.9-11 eating with someone misbehaving is banned, and this may well be in mind here as well. At the congregational meal, the offender must eat alone, an appropriate punishment for a person who has refused to work in order to eat (cf. 1QS 6.24–7.25; 8.21-24).[7] As Lightfoot says, the verb literally has the sense of mixing freely with some group or individual or engaging in close familial sort of discourse, as opposed to restricted access.[8] Another possibility would be that the offender would not be invited to a private Christian meal to prevent his

---

1. He gives the same exhortation in Gal. 6.9, another of his earliest letters.

2. I. H. Marshall, *1 and 2 Thessalonians* (Grand Rapids: Eerdmans, 1983), p. 226.

3. See the division of the text and the rationale in A. Malherbe, *The Letters to the Thessalonians* (New York: Doubleday, 2000), p. 458.

4. See pp. 159-62 above.

5. See Marshall, *1 and 2 Thessalonians*, p. 226.

6. See Malherbe, *The Letters*, p. 458.

7. E. Best, *A Commentary on the First and Second Epistles to the Thessalonians* (London: Black, 1972), p. 344.

8. J. B. Lightfoot, *Notes on the Epistles of St. Paul* (Winona Lake: Alpha, reprint), p. 134.

sponging off the host while doing no work.[9] The purpose of the avoidance in any case is that the person in question feel ashamed. This sort of punishment is meant to produce grief and amendment of life (2 Cor. 2.6-7; 7.10). It may well be that Paul is drawing on his experience in early Judaism, where such a person would be disciplined by the imposition of some sort of ban involving a breaking off of relations until there was repentance.[10]

As v. 15 makes clear, Paul does not want the congregation to give up on this erring Christian. It is clear from this verse that withdrawal cannot mean absolute avoidance in all respects because this person continues to be admonished (present continual tense of the verb here). The person is a "brother," but in 1 Cor. 5.11 Paul speaks of "someone called a brother."[11] Plutarch tells us that admonition, especially when coupled with withdrawal of some sort, could produce guilt, shame, and grief (*On Moral Virtue* 452CD). Marcus Aurelius (*Meditations* 6.20) gives the advice that if someone behaves rudely or roughly in the gymnasium one should "avoid him, but not as an enemy." The admonition in our text is directed to the will of the individual since it is his will to work which is in question.[12]

Polycarp (*Philippians* 11) in fact cites 2 Thess. 3.15 in remarking about two former church members who loved money too much and were shunned because of it. This citation is important, coming from about A.D. 110, as it shows that Paul's second letter to the Thessalonians was already known at that time and was in use as a letter of Paul. Polycarp cites 1 Thess. 5.22 at the same time and seems to assume that the church in Philippi, just up the road from Thessalonike, knows these letters.

Rom. 16.17-20 and Titus 3 then would seem to depict the next step in the process whereby someone was actually regarded as no longer a believer.[13] The former seems especially close to this peroration in 2 Thessalonians and signals a significant problem that needs to be overcome. At the same time Paul warns that personal feelings of hostility toward the person are not to enter into this disciplinary matter — he is not to be treated as an enemy.[14]

Paul's discourse thus ends on a solemn and serious note, which will be somewhat ameliorated by the closing benedictions. But as Chrysostom says, Paul does not want the offender treated as an outsider. "Do not disconnect

9. See Marshall, *1 and 2 Thessalonians*, p. 228.

10. On this see I. H. Marshall, *Kept by the Power of God* (Minneapolis: Bethany Fellowship, 1969), pp. 47-48.

11. See F. F. Bruce, *1 and 2 Thessalonians* (Waco: Word, 1982), p. 210.

12. Malherbe, *The Letters*, p. 459.

13. See the discussion in G. Beale, *1 and 2 Thessalonians* (Downers Grove: InterVarsity, 2003), pp. 260-63.

14. Marshall, *1 and 2 Thessalonians*, p. 229; B. Rigaux, *Les Épitres aux Thessaloniciens* (Paris: Gabalda, 1956), p. 716.

what is said here from what follows, where having said 'have nothing to do with him', he added 'do not look on him as an enemy, but warn him as a brother.' Do you see how he urges us to hate the deed but love the person? For indeed it is the work of the Devil to tear us apart, and he has always taken great care to destroy love, so that the means of correction will be gone, the sinner maintained in error and the way of his salvation blocked" (*Homily on 1 Corinthians* 33.5).

Epistolary Closing — 3.16-18

Like Paul's first argument, the second is surrounded by prayer. The worship elements here, including the wish prayer in v. 16 and the closing benediction, remind us that this document was intended to be read out as part of a worship service. Epistolary closing remarks are usually seen as a sort of miscellany of final remarks, and to some extent this is true here, but as for a Pauline closing, Paul always leaves his congregations with a final benediction or grace word.

May the Lord of peace himself give you peace through it all and in all ways.[1] The Lord be with all of you. The greeting is of my hand, of Paul, which is a sign in every letter. I write thusly. The grace of our Lord Jesus Christ be with you all.

Whenever there is discord or disobedience, peace is lacking in a congregation, especially in its wider sense of "shalom" or wellbeing, but Paul is praying here that the Lord will superintend even the disciplinary measures and bring a peaceful resolution of the problem. V. 16 wishes for peace in all circumstances and in all or every possible manner. The idle are not excluded from this peace wish. It is for all.[2] There may be an echo here of LXX Isa. 26.12-13 or Num. 6.26.[3] The parallel wish prayer in 1 Thess. 5.23 has "God of peace," and so it may be debated whether *kyrios* here refers to the Father or the Son. It is probably the latter

---

1. Some mss. (A*, D*, F, G, and various minuscules) have *topǭ* here rather than *tropǭ*. The former is found in 1 Cor. 1.2; 2 Cor. 2.14; 1 Thess. 1.8; 1 Tim. 2.8, but the less usual reading is to be preferred, not least because it has excellent support in ℵ, A, B, K, P, and many other manuscripts. See Metzger, *TC,* p. 638.
2. See J. B. Lightfoot, *Notes on the Epistles of St. Paul* (Winona Lake: Alpha, reprint), p. 135.
3. G. Beale, *1 and 2 Thessalonians* (Downers Grove: InterVarsity, 2003), p. 268.

since that usage is ubiquitous in Paul's letters, but if so this is the only place in the NT where Jesus is called "the Lord of peace."[4] The peace wish follows a warning passage, as if to balance it, not only here but in Gal. 6.16; 2 Cor. 13.11; and Rom. 16.20, and in each case Paul has been correcting problems before the conclusion of the document. We may surmise that Paul sometimes thought it wise to leave the real bone of contention until the end of the discourse.[5] The peace wish is important because Paul does not want enmity conventions to determine what is done in regard to the idle, which would cause mayhem and a reciprocity cycle of vituperation and further shaming, division, and alienation.[6]

The autograph offered in v. 17 comports with what we find in 1 Cor. 16.21 (probably the next extant letter Paul wrote) and in Col. 4.18. Paul probably does not mean that he offered an autograph at the end of every genuine letter since we have undisputed Pauline letters where he does not, and in some of those same letters, particularly 1 Cor. 16.21, Paul says the same thing as here. Presumably then this means that Paul took the pen from the amanuensis at this juncture in all his letters and *wrote something,* whether it involved his signature or not.[7] The idea was that people would recognize his handwriting and realize that he was the genuine author of the document and that he cared enough to conclude it in a personal way. *Houtos graphō* surely refers to the handwriting style itself ("thus I write" means "this is my [recognizable] handwriting").[8] In Gal. 6.11 Paul remarks on the size of his Greek characters. The final support from this conclusion comes from the fact that personal signatures were not a normal part of ancient Greek letters.[9]

A Closer Look: The Ancient Art and Labor of Letter Writing

"Something about the nature of early Christianity made it a movement of letter writers. We possess more than nine thousand letters written by Christians in antiquity."[10] One can readily see Paul as one of the instigators of this trend. But

4. See C. Wanamaker, *Commentary on 1 and 2 Thessalonians* (Grand Rapids: Eerdmans, 1990), p. 291.

5. F. F. Bruce, *1 and 2 Thessalonians* (Waco: Word, 1982), p. 212.

6. See A. Malherbe, *The Letters to the Thessalonians* (New York: Doubleday, 2000), p. 462; I. H. Marshall, *1 and 2 Thessalonians* (Grand Rapids: Eerdmans, 1983), p. 230.

7. See E. Best, *Commentary on the First and Second Epistles to the Thessalonians* (London: Black, 1972), p. 347.

8. Lightfoot, *Notes,* p. 136.

9. See Wanamaker, *1 and 2 Thessalonians,* p. 293.

10. S. Stowers, *Letter Writing in Greco-Roman Antiquity* (Philadelphia: Fortress, 1986), p. 15.

how should we view Paul as a letter writer? Most moderns in reading Paul's letter naturally assume that Paul operated then as we operate now in regard to letter writing, only without the benefit of computers or typewriters. This assumption however is really quite false, as in antiquity letter writing, especially when we are talking about letters as long as Paul's, was a very time-consuming and expensive process, especially expensive if one had to hire a scribe or amanuensis to make a fair copy of the letter.

If we compare Paul to the two other most famous letter writers of his era, Seneca and Cicero, we discover immediately that Paul is far more longwinded. The longest Pauline letter contains 7,114 words while the longest letters of Cicero and Seneca contain 2,530 and 4,134 words. Cicero's average number of words in a letter is 295, while Seneca used 995 and Paul 2,495. Scribes ranged in skill from pedestrian to exceptional, and only some had the skill of tachiography (an ancient sort of shorthand). There are some 207 lines in 1 Thessalonians and some 111 in 2 Thessalonians, and it would have taken a normal scribe two and a half hours to take down the first and perhaps an hour and a half for 2 Thessalonians. Making a fair copy of each after that would bring a scribe to about a half day's work for each. Even if we calculate the cost at the lowest known rate of about 25 dinars for 10,000 lines, Romans would have cost $2,275 dollars to copy while 1 and 2 Thessalonians would have cost $484 and $255 dollars respectively. If anything these estimates are low and do not count the cost of supplies or of sending the letter.[11]

It is unlikely that Paul could afford an elite amanuensis, and to judge from Rom 16.22 he used fellow Christians for scribes, whether or not they were professionals. A Sosthenes (1 Cor. 1.1) or Tertius (Rom. 16.1) usually bore the lion's share of the load, and perhaps they offered their services gratis as part of their contribution to the Christian cause. This may explain the aporia and infelicities in some of Paul's letters. Yet still he had to choose persons who fell within the only 10% of the population who could read and write. The Christian movement was often dependent on the more educated to get its messages from place to place.

There is some evidence that Paul's scribes took dictation verbatim and could not always keep up (e.g., anacolutha). A letter like 2 Thessalonians which has its rough patches grammatically and otherwise may be one that Paul did not take the time to have a fair copy made of. He was frequently a man in a hurry.

It does not appear to me likely that 2 Thessalonians was written with 1 Thessalonians in front of the scribe. The small differences in phrases that are strongly similar (e.g. 2 Thess. 3.8 and 1 Thess. 2.9) suggest that the letters were composed close in time

---

11. See E. R. Richards, *Paul and First Century Letter Writing* (Downers Grove: InterVarsity, 2004), pp. 163-70. One should also compare B. Witherington, *The Paul Quest* (Downers Grove: InterVarsity, 1998), pp. 100ff.; H. Gamble, *Books and Readers in the Early Church* (New Haven: Yale University Press, 1995), J. Murphy-O'Connor, *Paul the Letter Writer* (Collegeville: Liturgical, 1995); and E. R. Richards, *The Secretary in the Letters of Paul* (Tübingen: Mohr, 1991). There is also a helpful discussion in *New Docs* 7, pp. 48-57.

but with the first only remembered. It would have been expensive and in some cases time prohibitive as well to make extra copies. These were after all ad hoc letters, and both were composed into specific situations that were in extremis. 1 Thessalonians took more time and shows more care in composition, 2 Thessalonians less so, another good reason why it is not likely that 2 Thessalonians is by a later slavish imitator of Paul.

While certainly, as we have seen from 1 Thess. 2.13, Paul as a prophetic figure believed he spoke (and wrote) the word of God to the Thessalonians,[12] there is no evidence that he thought he was composing and preserving documents to be included in a later canon of Scripture. Whether he kept copies must remain uncertain, though it is possible. What is more likely is that Paul's coworkers like Timothy delivered these letters both physically and orally and were able to convey more private remarks and interpret Paul's public remarks while doing so. There was no postal system except for official imperial business. Letters would be handed over to strangers going to the right place. Perhaps Paul's were given to trusted fellow Christians and especially coworkers, apparently usually the latter.

A feeling for the length of Paul's letters, including 2 Thessalonians, can be gained from the following very substantial, by ancient standards lengthy, and angry missive (*P. Iand.* 6 [1934] 97 [pl. 19]) fired off by one Aurelius Zoilos, a literate household servant, to his younger master (!) Diogenes:

> Aurelius Zoilos to Diogenes. I received your letter on the second and found it . . . when I learned of your stupidity. I am reproached though I serve (you). I have not lost my senses and I am not impudent and I am not a mouse. Give heed to my letter. Understand. therefore that I have spent fourteen years now serving your parents, and I was not impudent and I was not like you or my sister. You ought not to have done this, and gone away for twelve years and committed adultery in the Kynopolite district. Whatever you do, you cannot beat me. For when I was young you begged me to pick you up over and over again. Now, when I have become an older man, you intend to beat me. In this connection, I put up with you, (but) I do not intend to put up with you in the future. And I shall also give witness (of this decision) to my sister Thaesis, if she comes to me with the help of the gods. Year 5, Choiak the 3rd.[13]

Letters such as this one generally do not have the religious and liturgical elements we find in Paul's letters, though occasionally they may include a health wish or a wish prayer. Paul's letters of course stand out for their high degree of religious content, and they also stand out from most predecessors in their use of rhetorical form. Paul's letters, in that respect, are in the upper echelon of letters in their degree of literary quality.

---

12. See pp. 82-83 above.
13. *New Docs* 4, pp. 63-64.

Besides the signature Paul adds a closing anathema in 1 Cor. 16.22, so the issue is not just a signature, but a personal way of concluding the document. In Gal. 6.11-16 much more than a signature is involved, and Rom. 16.23-27 does not mention a signature but does include various concluding greetings, a wish-prayer, and a final benediction. In all this we see Paul the pastor at work, ending on a more personal and personable note and wishing his converts well. He apparently had a special reason to mention his signature in 2 Thessalonians, namely that there was indeed some special concern about forgery in Thessalonike (see 2.2 and cf. 1 Thess. 5.19-20).[14] "In every letter" or "in all letters" may seem grandiose if this were truly only Paul's second letter that he ever wrote to a church. As Lightfoot says,[15] many earlier letters may have disappeared. But, more to the point, if, as we have argued, both Galatians and 1 Thessalonians were written before this letter and no others, we could still account for the form of expression here.[16] In any case the final words in one's own hand is an indirect means of asserting that what is in this letter has the authority of Paul himself and must be taken seriously.[17]

It may not be accidental that in v. 18 Paul offers grace on *all*, unlike 1 Thess. 5.28.[18] Perhaps we may see Paul's pastor's heart here, wishing blessing even on the disorderly in the congregation.[19] Nevertheless, no two benedictions of Paul's are exactly the same.[20]

The epistolary subscripts added by later scribes provide early speculations about the location of the apostle when he wrote. For example, manuscripts A, B, K, P, and various minuscles add that this letter was written from Athens (which is unlikely), and the Coptic and Boharic manuscripts reiterate that it was written by three authors — Paul, Timothy, and Silas.[21] What the former indicate is that it was widely believed that Paul wrote 2 Thessalonians while still in Greece, which is probably correct, though as we have seen Corinth is the more likely spot where this letter originated.

14. See pp. 213-14 above.

15. Lightfoot, *Notes*, p. 136.

16. On which see pp. 9-15 above and the Introduction to B. Witherington, *Grace in Galatia* (Grand Rapids: Eerdmans, 1998).

17. Marshall, *1 and 2 Thessalonians*, p. 232.

18. See B. Rigaux, *Les Épitres aux Thessaloniciens* (Paris: Gabalda, 1956), p. 718.

19. So rightly Lightfoot, *Notes*, p. 136.

20. Malherbe, *The Letters*, p. 463.

21. See Metzger, *TC*, p. 638.

Bridging the Horizons

The numerous prayers in 1 and 2 Thessalonians reflect the deep and profound piety of the apostle to the Gentiles. They also reflect his belief that prayer changes things, or, better said, the God who has chosen to respond to and answer prayer changes things. All this praying reflects Paul's belief that both God and human beings are actors in the human drama and the conduct of both affects the historical outcome of things. Of course it is true that Paul believes that God is not merely one actor in the drama. God is *the* major actor, and by comparison humans have bit parts to play in the drama. Nevertheless, those small parts, such as praying, are not merely important: God has chosen to make them crucial. God has chosen to make human beings and their choices and actions vital to the divine enterprise, even though God could also have chosen to do otherwise. The overall impression one gets from reading the prayer reports in 2 Thessalonians 1–3 is how profoundly and deeply Paul cared about the spiritual wellbeing of his converts and how much he trusted God to preserve and protect the Thessalonians, who were in a difficult situation.

What F. Buechner has said about Jesus' view of prayer applies equally well to our texts. "According to Jesus, by far the most important thing about prayer is to keep at it. The images he uses to explain this are all rather comic to have to explain at all. He says God is like a friend you go to borrow bread from at midnight. The friend tells you in effect to drop dead, but you go on knocking anyway until finally he gives you what you want so he can go back to bed again (Luke 11.5-8). . . . Be importunate, Jesus says — not, one assumes, because you have to beat a path to God's door before he'll open it, but because until you beat the path maybe there's no way of getting to 'your' door."[22] There is something to this and it may explain why Paul in 1 Thessalonians 5 speaks of praying "without ceasing." Prayer opens the one praying to God and makes that person a more viable instrument in God's hand. God is getting through to us when we pray, perhaps even more than we are reaching God, who in any case is not hard of hearing and knows quite well what we need before we speak. God chooses to use our prayers to accomplish much in the lives of others, and there is something of a mystery and a miracle to this whole process.

It is interesting that Paul focuses on prayer and work at the end of his discourse in 2 Thessalonians, because some would see these two things as polar opposites. For example, D. Bonhoeffer once said: "Praying and working are two different things. Prayer should not be hindered by work, but neither should work be hindered by prayer. . . . Without the burden and labour of the day, prayer is not prayer, and without prayer, work is not work." Charles Ringma, in commenting

---

22. F. Buechner, *Listening to Your Life* (San Francisco: HarperSanFrancisco, 1992), p. 213.

on this quotation, adds, "Work should never become so all-consuming that no time is left for prayer. Prayer should not draw us away from the reality of life so that we no longer fulfill our duties and responsibilities. Prayer should not alienate us from the world. Work should not draw us away from God."[23]

There is something profoundly odd about these reflections. Prayer itself is often hard work, or at least a form of labor, not an alternative to it. Contrasting the two is rather like saying talking to the architect and maker of the blueprint is just chitchat in comparison to actually building the building prescribed by the blueprint. Both are necessary to get the building built right. Paul certainly did not see prayer as an alternative to his other ministerial activities. He says in these very letters that it was something he pursued day and night in earnest and urges his audience to pursue it constantly! And he urges this on both the industrious and the idle. Prayer is a form of remembering that there are forces in this world larger than the one praying, which the one praying cannot control, but which God alone can control. In other words, prayer is a form of recognizing one is not the master of one's own fate in so very many ways.

It is difficult to talk about a Christian approach to work in a culture where people are defined by their professions. Doctors are seen as doctors first and persons second, and the same can be said about lawyers, bankers, politicians, ministers, and a host of others. Our western culture reinforces the idea that we are what we do. This is in some ways odd since many in our society despise what they do, and cannot wait to get out of work and on with what they view as "real life" or something that is "fun," with leisure time and holidays (and in the end retirement) viewed as what we are all ultimately working for. In this setting how can Paul's exhortations about idleness, exhortations to be busy without being a busybody, and his apodictic statement that the person who will not work should not eat, be heard and applied?

A word of caution is in order to start with. If it is true Paul is talking about a patron-client situation in his critique of idleness, then our situations are rather different from this. Of course they could perhaps be applied to people who are unnecessarily on the dole, but the "busybody" part of his exhortation refers to acting as a promoter of the patron, which is a whole different matter.

Another difficulty we face is that our culture actually encourages us to sever the link between work and having what we need in life. There are so many ways in which a person can be involved in gambling, or responding to promotions for almost anything imaginable for free — free trips, free cars, free computers, the list is endless. There are certainly ways in our culture to get something for nothing, or at least for very little. And the gambling industry would

---

23. C. Ringma, *Seize the Day with Dietrich Bonhoeffer* (Sutherland: Albatross, 1991), on the page for February 23. The quotation is from Bonhoeffer's *Life Together* (New York: Harper, 1954).

encourage us to think that this is a good thing. "If you win X amount, you won't have to work ever again" says the advertisement. Against this Paul says that one should earn one's necessities through honest labor. To be idle is not a good thing. Indeed, Paul believes that work is one of the things for which human beings were created. If work should not be the sole thing that defines who we are, nevertheless it is one of the things God would have us do to be truly human. This is all the more the case when work is viewed rightly as not merely vocation but as service to God, as a form of ministry.

The prayer of my spiritual forebear John Wesley was "O Lord do not let me live to be idle." I understand this prayer. It was natural for a person who was profoundly convinced of the Puritan dictum that "idle hands are the Devil's playground." While that may be a bit too extreme a view of things, it nonetheless is true that people with too much time on their hands often end up doing very selfish and self-seeking things in their search for a way beyond boredom. Boredom is almost always the attitude of a person who does not have something to do about which they are passionate and to which they have committed their whole selves.

Of course retirement can be a vehicle for doing other forms of work and ministry — more time for prayer, more time to do service projects and the like. But it may be doubted that Paul would in any way encourage us to "save for retirement" or "look forward to when you don't have to do anything for a living." He was a man who certainly believed in dying with his boots on.

Paul is urging a countercultural approach. He is urging work on people for whom clientage has been seen as a perfectly viable cultural option. I suspect he would take a similarly countercultural approach with us. What the Christian should look forward to in the future is either more opportunities to serve God or dying and going to be with the Lord, not some secular vision of having more leisure time or retiring early so one can become fat and lazy or "see the world." Of course there must be balance in one's life. There is a place for rest as well as work, play as well as work, celebration as well as work, and Paul does not say otherwise. But whatever good thing we attempt to do or say we should do with our whole hearts and to the glory of God.

Index of Authors

Aquinas, T., 114n.27
Arnold, B., 114n.26
Ascough, R. S., 38n.119, 39, 39n.124, 43n.138
Aus, R. D., 188, 188n.7, 195n.47, 215n.45

Bammel, E., 93n.140
Barclay, J., 76n.59
Barrett, C. K., 204n.21
Bassler, J. M., 192n.31, 193n.34, 236, 237n.25
Bauckham, R. J., 13n.60, 127, 127n.5, 128, 128n.8, 129, 129n.13
Beale, G. K., 131n.22, 132nn.25, 28, 136n.47, 137n.52, 142n.71, 144n.76, 148n.101, 149n.107, 150, 150n.115, 151n.120, 152n.120, 153n.127, 161n.10, 162n.18, 163n.19, 167, 167nn.11, 12, 168n.15, 170n.29, 174n.12, 176n.7, 190n.18, 195n.50, 198n.65, 201, 201n.12, 202, 202n.14, 213n.28, 214n.38, 215n.42, 216n.49, 220n.68, 221n.77, 224n.101, 226, 226n.111, 233nn.9, 12, 16, 241nn.7, 9, 242nn.13, 15, 251n.20, 256n.13, 258n.3
Bede, 8n.41
Beker, J. C., 89n.119
Best, E., 51nn.17, 20, 72n.39, 74n.48, 75n.53, 77n.65, 79n.76, 91n.128, 92n.133, 94n.142, 104n.11, 111n.10, 113n.20, 114n.27, 117nn.38, 39, 119n.52, 120n.60, 124n.77, 133n.30, 134, 134n.38, 142, 142n.73, 143, 143n.74, 148nn.95, 100, 153nn.126, 130, 161n.11, 162n.13, 166n.9, 176n.4, 188n.8, 189nn.12, 15, 191, 191n.24, 192n.32, 193n.36, 195n.51, 196n.54, 198nn.68, 69, 201n.8, 210n.17, 212n.23, 213n.29, 214nn.36, 40, 216n.49, 218n.60, 220nn.68, 69, 222n.84, 224n.97, 225n.104, 226n.110, 232n.8, 233n.14, 234n.23, 239nn.7, 11, 241n.9, 242n.19, 244, 244n.32, 251n.21, 252n.26, 255n.7, 259n.7
Betz, H. D., xi, 221n.77
Beutler, J., xiv, 10n.45, 108n.4
Beza, T., 114n.27
Bjerklund, C. J., 111n.9
Bonhoeffer, D., 263, 264n.23
Broer, I., 84n.99
Bruce, F. F., 49n.8, 59n.23, 72n.34, 74n.49, 76n.57, 77n.63, 77n.70, 78n.73, 80n.80, 88n.112, 90n.124, 91n.126, 93nn.136, 139, 94n.143, 96n.160, 97n.164, 104n.14, 110n.6, 111n.8, 113nn.18, 22, 117n.40, 118nn.46, 49, 132n.27, 133n.31, 137n.53, 138nn.55, 56, 139, 139n.61, 150n.114, 152n.124, 160n.5, 161n.8, 162n.18, 166n.10, 168n.17, 170n.29, 172, 172nn.3, 4, 173n.9, 176n.8, 189n.16, 190n.20,

266

Index of References